Perception
in
Criminology

Perception in Criminology

RICHARD L. HENSHEL
AND ROBERT A. SILVERMAN
EDITORS

1975
COLUMBIA UNIVERSITY PRESS
NEW YORK AND LONDON

Library of Congress Cataloging in Publication Data

Henshel, Richard L   comp.
    Perception in criminology.

    Includes bibliographies.
    1. Crime and criminals—Addresses, essays, lectures.
I. Silverman, Robert A., 1943–   joint comp.
II. Title.
HV6028.H46   364   74-23621
ISBN 0-231-03760-0
ISBN 0-231-03761-9 pbk.

Contents

Foreword

EDWARD SAGARIN

The concept of perception has a long and complex history in the study of mankind, yet only now is it coming into its own. It has been immortalized in the sociology and social philosophy of thinkers whose works are read, or at least cited, with great frequency: Max Weber, W. I. Thomas, George Herbert Mead, the German phenomenologists and the American pragmatists, the major architects of the sociology of knowledge (particularly Karl Mannheim), commentators on the American racial scene, students of nationalism and of ethnocentrism, the phenomenologist disciples of Alfred Schutz and ethnomethodologists, and the investigators of deviance who are gathered around the viewpoint known as tagging or labeling. Add to this, most recently, and with depth of insight seldom equaled, the microsociology of Erving Goffman.

Nevertheless, a long and illustrious background notwithstanding, the literature that utilizes perception as a central theme is scattered, often meager but, most significantly, highly praised and then conveniently overlooked, deliberately ignored, or simply forgotten. It is hoped that this collection, brought together by Richard Henshel and Robert Silverman, will contribute to correcting the neglect and restoring to its rightful place the concept of perception, not only insofar as criminology is concerned but, in a larger measure, to all aspects of the study of human behavior.

Perception is a word encountered more frequently in psychology than in sociology or its subdisciplines (I like to think—no doubt with the peculiar perception indicative of my own training—of criminology as one such entity). But in psychology it has come to denote primarily the neuro-physiological process rather than the cerebral-cognitive. Thus, psychologists speak of sensory perception, the thresholds of perception, and the illusions and distortions to which the recipient or beholder is subject.

The concern of sociologists has been with the *content* of the views that man holds—views of social actions, interactions, objective situations, or groups, including the views that he holds of himself. To cite an example from the work of one of the editors of this collection (Richard Henshel), it is not particularly useful or meaningful to discuss crime deterrence in terms of the severity, certainty, or celerity of sanctions, as has usually been done in the past; the meaningful and useful study would have to center around the knowledge, beliefs, viewpoints, illusions, and ideas—in short, the percep-tions—that are held by people with respect to these sanctions. The point would seem to be so self-evident as to hardly warrant reiteration (something that is true with some frequency in human behavioral studies), yet it has been overlooked and ignored by people who have spent considerable time and expended energy and money on the most sophisticated studies compar-ing various crime rates in different times and places, or among diverse cohorts, and drawing conclusions about the efficacy or inefficacy of punitive measures without once considering how much the population knew of them.

The problems that must be encountered by a perceptually oriented approach to crime, or to any other aspect of behavior, are complex. One must beware of certain directions whose long-term value, to be charitable, would be doubtful. The editors of this volume take care to explicitly re-nounce one such pitfall: the error of solipsism, the statement that only the perceptions that men hold are real, and that there is no other reality. More than two centuries after the writings of Bishop Berkeley, it hardly seems that one is doing more than beating a dead horse—deceased, buried, forgotten— to try to defend the notion of a real world that actually exists out there. But a careful reading of some of the modern literature suggests that the horse has been exhumed and an effort is being made to resuscitate it. The modern-day solipsists do not deny that an objective world of concrete objects exists, and they may not even deny that abstract phenomena have an existence of their own (as acts, words, love, or hate), but they downgrade these to such a level of unimportance that their existence ceases to be meaningful. All that is im-portant, supposedly, is how people see the world, not how that world really is. Or rather, how that world really "is" cannot be known, or is a meaningless concept, because the world "is" on different levels, all perceptual, as seen by diverse categories of people.

There are many methodological problems and issues in an approach to criminology (or to any other area) with a perceptual emphasis. Some of these are covered by the authors of the articles in this collection, and some by the editors in their introductions. There are in addition aspects to which I would like to direct a call for further attention in the future.

One issue involves the question of what Goffman has called impression management, discussed by Irwin Deutscher under the heading of the clash between what we do and what we say, between the public and the private, the presentation that is made for others to see and what is going on backstage. How much of the perceived perception (that is, the perception perceived by the student of social behavior) is a put-on, a mask deliberately and consciously worn so as to bring about a desired result? Or, more subtly, how much of it is a presentation of self, a projection of an image, on not quite so conscious a level, in which there is confusion within the individual himself as to what he really believes and what he is making believe that he believes. Particularly in the area of crime, whether the accused stands with lowered eyelids and contrite, or defiant and angry, or self-righteous because his morality is (in his opinion) higher than that of his accusers, that offender's perception of the world must be *inferred* from cues, stances, words, all of which may be inextricably interwoven with dissembling and dissimulation.

A second issue involves how much the sociologist really knows, and how much he assumes, about public attitudes, and particularly about prejudice. There are, of course, questionnaires and computers that will tell the scholar something about how people think about various matters, but they are fraught with dangers, and although better than nothing (that is, if they are well structured and capably interpreted), they may lull one into believing that he knows what others believe, when he has very little knowledge. So that it will be said by some sociologists that people think of widows and divorcees as sex-hungry women available for sexual exploitation, of Southerners as bigoted, of homosexuals as effeminate, of blind men and women as helpless, and of blacks as preferring to be on welfare than working (although in this latter instance there is also the image that they—the blacks—want to take away the jobs that "belong" to the whites). Now, it may or may not be so that large numbers of people hold some of these images or perceptions, but sociologists often *assume* that they are held, offer no research to validate such assumptions, and state little about who holds them, how many people, in what categories, and how strongly the beliefs are adhered to.

I come now to a third area for expansion: what are the sources of perceptions and of misperceptions? W. E. B. DuBois, Robert K. Merton, and others working in the area of race relations emphasized situations in which the perceptions were based on a reality that had been created by the beliefs. In other words, to use Merton's term, some perceptions become self-fulfilling prophecies, by being translated into discriminatory practices, lesser opportunities, and, ultimately, lower expectations on the part of those discriminated against. There are other perceptions that may be created by rumor, by selective memory of real events, by a need for belief and justification, by an ideology that has certain goals which such perceptions will help one to reach. It would appear to be a fruitful area for further study to explore the sources of such perceptions.

Finally, in what must be only the briefest summary of the many exciting avenues of investigation stimulated by this collection, much more research on stereotypes is demanded if this concept is to be made socially useful. It is not enough to denounce stereotypes; they must be studied. What if a stereotype turns out to be true—to be typical, if not of everyone within a category, then at least of large numbers? Suppose there is a widely held vision of the homosexual as compulsively promiscuous, or of the child molester as one who will murder in order to silence his victim, or of the drug addict as a person who will steal from his own family? It is one thing, as so many have said in recent years, to combat the stereotype because of the social atmosphere of hostility, the lynch spirit, that it creates. But it is something else again to be true to the canons of science, and study this phenomenon in order to determine the extent (if at all) that the stereotype corresponds with reality; and if it does, whether the correlations are higher than among a population of those not in the deviant category.

It is an excellent collection that the editors have brought together; its significance is that it should stimulate considerable new thinking and good research, not only along the few lines that I have suggested here, but in other directions not dreamed of by those who, like myself, have given this matter too little thought in the past. Now I have already said too much on a subject on which this book has so much to say for itself. May I be forgiven if I conclude with this final word of hope that the book will inspire as much contemplation in other readers as it already has in me.

New York City
July 1974

Preface

Perception in Criminology is designed to integrate and encourage an emerging perceptual perspective in criminological theory and research. As a collection it complements general treatments of the field which have recently appeared, notably Quinney's *The Social Reality of Crime*. Several major works have been published in this framework in the past few years, e.g., Becker's *Outsiders;* Hogarth's *Sentencing as a Human Process;* LaFave's *Arrest: The Decision to Take a Suspect into Custody;* Kalven and Zeisal's *The American Jury.* Numerous articles have appeared using the perceptual perspective to illuminate historical developments and to analyze crime and criminal justice.

While the perceptual perspective is apparently burgeoning, it has thus far suffered from a traditional difficulty of an emerging orientation. Previous collections and indexing systems are not organized around the new focus, and researchers experience considerable difficulties in reviewing earlier efforts, examining scattered materials, and sifting out those of greatest value to their work. With the exception of collections on labeling theory, there has heretofore been no effort to gather together those primary sources relating to perception in criminology, either as an aid to professional research or for classroom use. In the absence of an edited work, those wishing to review the literature would have to do what we have done: devote a considerable amount of time to winnowing the work available in widely scattered (and not always easily available) sources.

Perception in Criminology is an attempt to bring these works together under a single cover. It incorporates labeling material, criminogenic perception, and perception in the administration of justice. We see its advantages as two-fold. Professionally, it should facilitate the research efforts of criminologists who wish to deal with the subjective aspects of their field. Instructionally, it supplements such works as Quinney's for both undergraduate and graduate courses in criminology.

One aspect which especially pleases us is the international cast of our collection. Without making any effort to achieve it, we have in the end selected works from the United States, Canada, and Great Britain. This has the advantage of cross-cultural fertilization, of course, but it also lends support to our contention that there is a growing recognition of the importance of perception in the field of criminology.

In order to provide a coherent focus for the collection and to keep it within reasonable limits of length, it became necessary to impose constraints on the types of material included, in addition to normal criteria of quality. Perhaps our most important constraint was the exclusion of material in which perception did not refer to individual appraisals of some *objective reality,* such as crime rate, average sentence severity, or public hostility toward the police. (The last is representative of "attitudinal facts," which we consider to be theoretically knowable notwithstanding certain questions about the meaning of attitudes.) There are other subjects which are sometimes regarded as "perceptual." We can loosely speak of "perceptions" of the innate heinousness (severity) of offenses (e.g., the Wolfgang-Sellin scale, 1964), the appropriateness of given sanctions (e.g., the Rose and Prell study, 1955), or the worthiness of different penal philosophies (e.g., Tarde, 1912). Such questions are important, but the "perceptions" involved are essentially moral or ethical evaluations. From this anthology we have excluded "perceptions" which have no apparently knowable ("real") referent.[1]

Another way to clarify this is in terms of perceptual error. One of the aims of the collection is to reinforce awareness of the importance of perceptual error in the production of criminality and the actual operation of criminal justice systems. It makes no sense to say that a delinquent is in error because he perceives the world as a jungle, and all persons as suckers or sharpies. Nettler (1961) argues persuasively that these conceptions may be no less valid than their converse. But it does make sense to speak of percep-

---

[1] Of course even for those perceptions with inherently knowable referents (e.g., the objective crime rate), the objective items are not known with complete accuracy.

tual error with respect to probability of capture, inherent criminality of blacks, or the recent growth of crime. It is the potential for misperception of these and other matters, and the consequences of perceptual error, that is the central "theme" of the collection. For this reason we have with regret chosen to exclude such perceptually oriented classics as Sykes and Matza (1957) on techniques of neutralization or Walter Miller's (1958) analysis of the lower class cultural milieu.

This rationale also led directly to a limitation for the material on crim-inogenic (i.e., crime-producing) perception. Strictly, this area would in-clude studies of the *acquisition* of perceptual viewpoints. This has been a traditional interest of criminology; the voluminous literature includes such diverse theories as differential association, culture conflict, and masculine identity crisis. There was little need for a new collection here, and in keep-ing with our theme we decided to concentrate on the actual perceptions themselves (content) and their behavioral consequences.

In terms of internal organization, there was a question of how to in-tegrate labeling theory. Labeling is to some extent a departure from our focus on consequences: obviously it is a cause of criminogenic self-percep-tion. But labeling is also a consequence of earlier, official preconceptions: There is more than one set of perceptions involved. Labeling is relevant to the collection because it can demonstrate perceptual error and its conse-quences, but unless the labeled person has not committed an offense it refers to secondary criminalization (Lemert, 1951), and we therefore placed it in a section separate from primary criminogenic perception.

The book falls into four divisions. First is the theoretical Introduction to the volume and to perception in criminology. Part One deals with crimin-ogenic perception and its behavioral consequences. Part Two examines per-ception in criminal law and justice. Part Three looks at labeling, considered as secondary criminogenic perception. Parts One through Three begin with section introductions which fit their material into the overall schema and provide background or overview for the specific articles. Although a limited amount of cross-referencing is provided by these introductions, the reader is encouraged to consult the index in this regard.

We would like to acknowledge the helpful comments by Herbert Blu-mer, Herbert Gans, Orrin Klapp, Richard Quinney, and R. Jay Turner with respect to the Introduction and other sections. At various times we consulted Edwin Schur, Leslie Wilkins, and Marvin Wolfgang, and we are grateful for their support and encouragement. John Hogarth also deserves our thanks in this regard. Of course we exercised our prerogatives and maintained a scholarly disagreement over certain points. Shirley Fox, Elaine Silverman, Vincent Sacco, Alexandra Adams, Helen Trew, and Mary Jo Wiersma helped greatly in the preparation of the manuscript. Finally, many of the usual difficulties in preparing such a collection were eased by the able assistance of John Moore at Columbia University Press. To all of these we express our thanks; naturally the remaining flaws and shortcomings are our own.

October 1974   R.L.H.
                                                                                     R.A.S.

References

Miller, Walter B. 1958. "Lower-Class Culture as a Generating Milieu of Gang Delinquency," *Journal of Social Issues* 14:5–19.

Nettler, Gwynn. 1961. "Good Men, Bad Men, and the Perception of Reality," *Sociometry* 24:279–94.

Rose, Arnold M. and Arthur E. Brell. 1955. "Does the Punishment Fit the Crime? A Study in Social Valuation," *American Journal of Sociology* 61:247–59.

Sykes, Gresham and David Matza. 1957. "Techniques of Neutralization: A Theory of Delinquency," *American Sociological Review* 22:664–70.

Tarde, Gabriel. 1912. *Penal Philosophy*. Boston: Little, Brown.

*Perception
in
Criminology*

1

Introduction

RICHARD L. HENSHEL
AND ROBERT A. SILVERMAN

There is a tradition in criminology to rely on hard statistics about factual information. Reliance on criminal statistics (official and otherwise) is understandable in terms of the reassurance that comes from quantification and apparent objectivity. Given the volume, and even the quality, of data that is provided by such sources as the Uniform Crime Reports, National Prisoner Statistics, and Juvenile Court Statistics, criminological statistics must be acknowledged as one of the best available approximations of "social indicators" at the same time that its grave weaknesses are acknowledged.[1] As recognition of the failings of official statistics grows, supplemental surveys on such areas as unreported crime fill a sorely needed function. Yet these surveys can only fill part of the gap since there are signs that official statistics are not only inaccurate but, in large measure, *inappropriate* as well.

The appropriateness of officially derived statistics has been attacked more than once on the basis of conceptual inadequacy. It is variously argued that data should be obtained for a social as well as the legal interpretation of crime (Johnson, 1968: 10–16), that official crime statistics are collected for the wrong hierarchical "level" (Biderman, 1970), that most of the data for sociologists come from bureaucracies which produce the material for nonscientific purposes (Cicourel, 1964: 36–37) and that the very collection of

A shorter version of this chapter appeared as "Perception and the Criminal Process," *Canadian Journal of Sociology* 1 (1975). Copyright © 1975 *Canadian Journal of Sociology*. Reprinted with permission.

[1] For a realistically pessimistic survey of the present state of social indicators in general, see Gross (1969). Wolfgang (1963) and Morris and Hawkins (1970) present a discussion of the weaknesses of criminal statistics.

official statistics—e.g., data on the extent of crime—is heavily influenced by perception and by agency ground rules (Cicourel, 1974: 93–94; Becker, 1973: 192–193; Quinney, 1970: 114–115). Supplemental data collection by criminologists and other social scientists can do much to alleviate these difficulties,[2] but a more fundamental problem of conceptualization remains. *The use of criminal statistics is so widespread among social researchers—so familiar and commonplace—that they become insensitive to the ignorance of most other persons about such information.* Criminal statistics as currently employed thus obscure and deemphasize what a growing number of studies have shown to be of fundamental importance: the "social reality" of crime, that is, the manifold disparity of perception with the objective reality of crime, and the influence of their perceptions on what the several actors in the drama of crime actually do.[3] This is not a proscription of quantitative research, for the alternative we will propose can also be quantitative.[4] Rather, it is a rethinking of precisely what should be quantified.

Obviously we have an alternative to suggest. Discussion of this alternative will lead us into considerations about the nature of man and society— even to considerations of reality and knowledge. Some of the questions are either inherently unanswerable or at least unanswerable in the prevailing state of wisdom. We will therefore try to avoid presenting the alternative as a reflection of absolute truth; rather, we regard its acceptance as a *strategy*— as the best available strategy, in fact, for criminology at this time.

Criminology, Rationality, and Meaning

We suggest that a focus upon purposefulness, decision-making, knowledge and ignorance, and perception will be profitable for criminological investiga-

[2] An important literature of victimization and hidden deviance studies has emerged. See as examples Biderman et al. (1967); Short and Nye (1957).

[3] Objective reality, like alternative terms, can unfortunately be interpreted in two ways, only one of which is intended. On the one hand it can be contrasted with *subjective (private) mental states*. Although it is undoubtedly true that the percepts of subjective states never entirely match the objective reality, this is not the contrast which is intended. Throughout we will employ "objective reality" and similar terms to contrast with *false or erroneous interpretations* of the "real world," be they public or private conceptions. See the distinction discussed in Brodbeck (1968: 79).

[4] Those who wish to examine a nonquantitative approach are referred to Douglas (1970a).

tion. This implies not so much a shift in the methods of analysis (although this is often demanded by other advocates of these topics) as a shift in the focal points of whatever methods are used, away from "what *is*" toward "what the relevant actors *think* is."

Some theories operate under a model of the individual in which goal-seeking, purpose, and intent are considered as essential and central aspects of his behavior. Other theories assume that meaning and purpose as aspects of behavior are unimportant and believe that behavior can be accounted for adequately without such conceptions. The latter theorists regard these subjective states as epiphenomena—accompanying behavior but not producing it—and place their confidence in individual or social "forces." One way to describe the contrast is to speak of reasons versus causes, but this may be misleading.[5] Writers adhering to the former approach can be roughly termed voluntarists; those of the latter persuasion can be called mechanists.

One arena in which the debate became highly visible in the 1960s was the investigation of student unrest. On the one hand, some researchers investigated traditional social factors: social class (student radicals tended to come from upper middle-class families), parental political views (their parents also tended to be left of center), number of siblings, age of parents, birth order, and such institutional variables as size of the university, geographical location, and so on. The critics maintained that this was diverting attention from the "real" reasons why a person joined a protest group: he joined because he rationally felt repelled by the Vietnam War (e.g.), because he rationally recognized the corruptness of the national leadership, and so on. In short, he protested because there were *reasons* for doing so. We believe there is a place for behaviorial explanations of both types.

In recent years a detectable shift has taken place within social science away from "mechanism" toward reestablishing an older emphasis on purposiveness, intentionality, and meaningfulness. See Catton (1966) for distinctions. Traditional ways of looking at these concepts have changed to a considerable degree—most phenomenologists no longer search for "essences"; teleology is now explainable without metaphysics via cybernetic principles (Ackoff and Emery, 1972). But the very resurgence of phenomenology, *Verstehen,* and symbolic interactionism, as well as the emergence of new perspectives, bespeaks increasing rejection of purely mechanistic mod-

[5] See Dray (1964: 41–44).

els of man and society.[6] Not sharing this rejection entirely, we feel that explanation in terms of social forces will continue to have an important role. At the same time it has become increasingly clear that the volitional component is no mere epiphenomenon which can be safely disregarded.

This emphasis upon intentionality (in the sense of voluntarism, of the *meaning* of an event or situation to the actors) is in direct contrast to an emphasis on impersonal forces or *factors* that lead to specific behavior— "mechanisms for the robot," according to critics. But we feel that there is a place for both views. As we see it, on the one hand, man's actions are indeed purposive, the direct product of consciousness and choice, and the individual ascribes meaning to a situation by interpreting the information he obtains about it. This is a process unique for each individual, but on the other hand certain common tendencies in how interpretation is done can be found in persons with similar previous experiences, while persons occupying similar social positions will tend to receive similar information out of the total informational matrix. To that extent, it does seem legitimate to speak of "factors" being involved in human behavior, and we must part company with those who feel that acceptance of a voluntaristic component precludes the possibility of social forces (for instance, Blumer, 1969; Duncan, 1968; Matza, 1969). We will wish to retain both, and we think it is possible.

Accompanying the emphasis on intentionality is a resurgence of interest in rationality in explaining human activities. This is certainly not the rationality of the economic calculator, of Bentham's "hedonic calculus." The nineteenth century's rational man bears faint resemblance to the new model of rationality; a fair number of the goals of the new-model rational actor are apparently pleasure-avoiding. It is a new kind of "rationality" which takes into account each person's peculiar beliefs, goals, and values. If a game-player does not maximize his winnings because he does not wish to hurt the other players, that can be rational in the new conception.[7]

These considerations point to the possible importance of *decision-mak-*

---

[6] For illustrations of this resurgence, see Blumer (1969), Matson (1964), and Schutz (1964). In the realm of deviance see especially Matza (1969) and Douglas (1970b).

[7] One admittedly can very easily become enmeshed in tautology at this point as, for example, in the philosophical phenomenologist's use of "intentionality" (see Natanson, 1966: 15). Or as Kenneth Boulding once put it, "decision theory states that everybody does what he thinks is best at the time, which is hard to deny." For illustrative works on the new conceptions of rationality, see Wilson (1970).

ing in areas other than those in which it has traditionally received attention—i.e., political science, management, and studies of formal organizations. Specifically it would appear to be of the greatest importance for the subject-areas of criminology. In fact, it is possible to view the system of criminal justice in its entirety as a system of interlocking decisions—not only decisions by legislators and police executives but those of criminals, judges, juries, the crime press, and all other relevant actors. If indeed a modified "rationality" must be taken into account in explanations of human affairs, then one way to proceed in analyzing the criminal justice system is to concentrate on decision-points.[8] For instance:

1. Decisions by potential law violators
2. Decisions by police executives
3. Decisions by witnesses to report infractions
4. Decisions by police to arrest
5. Decisions by prosecuting attorneys
6. Decisions by defense attorneys
7. Decisions by juries
8. Decisions by judges
9. Decisions by parole boards
10. Decisions by legislators
11. Decisions by media "gate-keepers"

We will shortly present models depicting some major areas of criminological interest in precisely such a fashion. At the present time, studies are not available for many of these decision-points, but it is the strategy which is of prime concern. There appear to be neither practical nor theoretical hindrances which could effectively thwart such investigations.[9]

The emphases just described contrast with the traditional concentration in criminology on the etiology of criminal behavior. Clearly there is an im-

[8] There is a problem of naming the complex of subject-matter dealt with by criminology. Objectionable as it may be to some, "criminal justice system" seems to have a somewhat better fit than other alternatives.

[9] Despite the well-known occasion in which efforts to record jury deliberations were thwarted (Kalven and Zeisel, 1966: vi–vii), the selections by Hogarth and Simon in this collection show what can be done even in the most sensitive areas of criminal justice. See also Arens and Meadow (1956).

portant place for such concerns—in our own scheme as in most others—but there is a growing reaction against exclusive treatment of crime causation while ignoring, for example, the factors which lead to the proscription and criminalization of certain acts in the first place (see Henshel and Henshel, 1973; Matza, 1969; Quinney, 1970). Of course, other foci than decision-making might be chosen, but the nature of crime and correction is peculiarly appropriate for this approach. The formal machinery of criminal justice itself facilitates such an analysis. For example, legal procedure locates precisely the timing, alternatives, and responsible persons for key decisions. Even the decision to commit an illegal action, still often portrayed as the irrational behavior of a "sick" mind, is rendered—forced to be—a major, conscious decision by the very severity of the possible sanctions which the criminal law can impose, in contrast to informal expressions of social disapproval.[10] We are not ready to dismiss entirely the "crimes-of-passion" interpretation, nor (of course) instances of true psychopathology, but we do reject pseudo-scientific interpretations of criminals as essentially irrational, of the world views of deviants as necessarily "sick" or distorted.[11] Throughout the processes of crime and reaction, moral emphasis is continuously placed on the *importance* of the decisions involved—the legislator's power, the jury's influence on the accused's life, the judge's influence, the parole board's power.

In short, the subject areas of crime, justice, and correction seem almost uniquely suited for a concentration on the making of decisions.

The Ignorance of the Actors [12]

To say that the key elements in a criminal justice system are conscious, overt decisions does not mean that such decisions are always, or even usually, "correct." What does "correct" mean in this context? The decisions and actions of the participants can be explained in terms of the values

[10] An excellent discussion of this feature of criminal law is found in Matza (1969: ch. 7). For discussion of the goal-oriented nature of crime, see the approaches in Rottenberg (1973).

[11] See Nettler (1961) for a persuasive argument to this effect.

[12] We use "ignorance" in the following sections to refer to any lack of correspondence between belief and reality, not merely to situations of "no opinion."

the actors hold (or their attitudes toward the objects of their decision) and their construction (definition) of the situation at hand. It is in terms of their definition or construction of the situation that knowledge enters most directly. The actors may simply be unaware of the true state of affairs, and in this case it is entirely proper to speak of "incorrect" decisions: they are inappropriate in terms of the *actor's own values and goals*. Potential criminals may be misinformed about the formal sanctions for a particular act, policemen may be misinformed about the real amount of hostility toward them, defense attorneys incorrect concerning the acting ability of their clients, judges in error about the length of sentences their peers impose, and so on. We may paraphrase the economist Nelson (1966) to the effect that the true description of man is: *rational, but not information-seeking*. Yet, though their knowledge may be inadequate, *people still act—must act*—on the basis of what they think the situation is (Merton, 1936: 898–90).

Why are people in error about the relevant facts? Obviously this is an immense question; to respond to it in detail is well beyond the capacity of this Introduction. Yet it is so important for a perceptual perspective that the *systematic* tendencies which foster ignorance within the criminal justice system deserve a brief review. We can begin by dividing the relevant actors into "experts"—in some capacity within the system—and "laymen." The experts include professional criminals, policemen, criminal lawyers, prosecutors, judges, corrections and probation personnel, and crime reporters. Laymen include victims and witnesses, most delinquents, many criminals, most members of juries, and legislators. The boundary is not drawn so much in terms of actual knowledge as with respect to the actor's *self-image* of his expertise, since this seems to be significant in terms of the dynamics of ignorance. In criminal justice this corresponds to so great an extent with the individual's formal role that the latter is employed as a reasonable approximation.

The Ignorance of Laymen

"Laymen" can be expected to be truly ignorant of most aspects of the criminal justice system, both of its informal subtleties and even of its less complex formal structure. Knowledge of some systems is simply not part of the pragmatically necessary knowledge for the conduct of everyday life (Berger and Luckman, 1967). For most victims, witnesses, delinquents, and jurors, as well as many adult criminals, this applies to the criminal justice system—indeed, jurors are valued precisely because they are the nonexpert "peers" of the person being tried. The formal and informal arrangements of criminal justice can be expected to be very low in such persons' "hierarchy of relevances." For recidivists and professional criminals, the extent of ignorance becomes far more problematic. Their structures of relevance have been altered—in the first instance by personal experience and in the second by the socially given systems of relevance of their peers (Wagner, 1970: 24). Legislators are largely ignorant of the informal aspects of the system but can avail themselves of expert advice in fulfilling their roles. (Yet the type of expert they choose to hear is conditioned by their judgment of who is reliable, trustworthy, and knowledgeable—a decision in itself of the greatest importance.)

In addition to this general component of ignorance there are positive barriers to the acquisition of knowledge about the criminal justice system. Protection of juveniles from publicity has led to the restriction of information about juvenile courts. Protection of the rights of the accused has led to press restrictions on "trial by newspaper"—the free-press–fair-trial clash. Sociologists have long documented the secretiveness of bureaucracies in general; criminal justice organizations are no different except, perhaps, for displaying an excess of zeal for secrecy. And of course when data are provided there are major questions raised about their accuracy.

The *misinformation* available through the mass media, on the other hand, is overwhelming. Fiction about crime and criminal justice is ridden with formula and stereotype, its primary purpose being the satisfaction of the emotional needs of the viewing audience rather than the portrayal of crime in an authentic way. So also with crime news itself, which seldom portrays any but the most sensational and bizarre events.[13] All of which leads to pervasive and impressive ignorance among laymen; an ignorance well documented in one area by the study of the California Assembly Committee on Criminal Procedure, included in this collection.

---

[13] For an overview of the problems of crime reporting, as well as the barriers mentioned above, see Friendly and Goldfarb (1968).

The Ignorance of Experts

However well the expert can surmount some of the problems confronting the layman, some very important mechanisms still operate in systematic fashion to maintain his ignorance—although the expert's ignorance is much more selective. In order to appreciate the expert's ignorance, a few lines should be devoted to the several streams of thought on distortions of reality.

Some specific social dynamics of reality distortion in modern society have by now become well documented. Occupational selection, whereby persons with specific personalities or values are attracted or repelled by particular occupations, plays a major role in distinguishing the orientation toward identical facts by those in the various areas of expertise within criminal justice. The policeman and the social worker are obvious cases in point, but the criminal justice structure is replete with outstanding illustrations of occupational selection. Occupational selection is also based on various educational attainments which further differentiate the members of different areas. And the educational requisites themselves constitute a modality of shared experience which differentiates occupational groups from one another, while at the same time heightening the similarity of views within a group. Evidence from a wide variety of sources confirms that once similar persons are attracted to certain niches, "consensual affirmation" of norms and consensual validation of the attitudes they share intensifies their eccentricity of thought, as do the common experiences which those with highly similar jobs tend to acquire. Such occupational viewpoints are stabilized by group censure for participation in disapproved experiences (direct or vicarious, as in reading disapproved literature), and intrapsychically by the well-documented mechanisms of selective exposure, selective perception, and selective retention.[14] Obstacles to the spread and acceptance of innovations in thought or method are well covered by Rogers (1962).

The expert, in short, comes to share and maintain a particular set of blinders which shut off certain aspects of reality, a problem reinforced in a way by his very competence and arrogance about his expertise (Lewinsohn, 1958: 41). Ultimately, he may develop what Veblen called a "trained inca-

[14] See the literature on these strong tendencies reviewed in Klapper (1969: 19–25, 64–65) and Berelson and Steiner (1964: 529–33).

pacity'' to observe or deal with situations except in the traditional ways in which he is experienced. The criminal justice system is virtually a "text-book case" of such dynamics at work.[15]

Perception and Reality in Criminology

We must now look at the results of decision-making under conditions of partial knowledge. So-called "irrational choices" are often merely poorly informed choices. Our model of man is: rational, but not knowledge-seeking. Under this conception, individual perceptions of reality enjoy a central role, and the major emphasis in criminology should be on what people *think* the situation is rather than upon the actual state of affairs.

Of course error might on many occasions stem from purely idiosyncratic causes: It is obviously possible for persons to simply be uninformed through chance, with no deeper "undercurrent" involved in their situation.[16] But most of the attention that the social sciences have paid to ignorance has, perhaps understandably, been devoted to more systematic tendencies. Psychological phenomenology has emphasized the distortion that comes from the lingering aftereffects of earlier experiences. For symbolic interactionism, man's reality can be distorted by a combination of the presentations and interpretations of his social unit, his "negotiation" with others about the meaning of specific events, and his own selective "filtering" of the interpretations of others. Schutz's phenomenology is a relatively recent synthesis of these perspectives, emphasizing both unique experiences and social urgings. The sociology of knowledge sees man's reality as shaped by common experiences shared by persons in similar positions in the social structure. Finally, historicism sees common unspoken assumptions underlying the articulated thought of particular times and places—a "spirit of the times" and, in more integrated instances, a world view: *Zeitgeist* and *Weltanschauung*.

[15] We must note parenthetically that the same dynamics are at work among the academic criminologist or sociologist, even if we wish it were otherwise. See Henshel and Henshel (1973: ch. 6).

[16] This may be endorsed even by strong advocates of deterministic theories of ignorance since there are obviously some cases in which people believe the opposite of what the theories predict—the wealthy man who is not a social Darwinist, for instance, or the poor man who is.

It should be emphasized that these orientations have a venerable history in sociology. Historicism was already prominent in Hegel, fully developed in Dilthey, while the sociology of knowledge was virtually complete in Marx. These are figures of the nineteenth century. Edmund Husserl, the founder of philosophical phenomenology, did his chief writing in the first quarter of the twentieth century, as did Cooley and Mead, the two principal originators of symbolic interactionism. But the foremost early proponent of the perceptual viewpoint in sociology was W. I. Thomas, a man difficult to place in any particular school. His "definition of the situation" is the earliest clear articulation of the perspective of modern reality constructionism. The "Thomas theorem," as Robert Merton has called it, the idea that "situations defined as real are real in their consequences," is pregnant with intimations of later elaborations on the significance of individual and socially mediated perception. More recently, sociologists of knowledge have experimented with the concept of "image," which seems to have much the same characteristics as Thomas' "definition."

We have chosen perception as our major framework rather than phenomenology, reality construction, or the sociology of knowledge because we endorse a research tradition, principally from social psychology, which on the one hand emphasizes the role of distorted views of reality, but also endorses *quantification* in its investigations and has a principle of *veridicality*—i.e., maintains that there *is* some objective reality other than what is constructed by observers. According to this view, both the "stuff" of objective states ("noumena") and that of subjective states ("phenomena") are "real" in some sense, and often capable of quantification. This is not to imply that adherents of other perspectives never adopt these positions, but the tradition is clearer and more obviously in line with our own viewpoint in the perceptual framework and the emerging framework of attribution theory.[17] Clearly, we have used appropriate ideas from any source.

---

[17] Traditional psychophysics considers as a type of perception the transformation of stimuli (distal and proximal) into sensations. We mention this "eyeball perception" only to eliminate it from further discussion. The meaning of "perception" is a difficult problem, especially when the term is applied to complex selective and combinational processes which some would prefer to call "cognition." When it is applied to complex processes which may even be conscious, some would prefer to call it "inference." While these distinctions should be recognized, it has seemed far simpler to designate all of the above "perception." For working purposes, perception may be considered to be the various ways of becoming aware of (recognizing, giving meaning to) the objects and conditions around us, including complex as well as simple ob-

We thus reject the extreme epistemological position that nothing is knowable because (supposedly) all knowledge is contingent upon experience, historical epoch, or position in the social structure. (See Remmling, 1967, for the philosophical and historical roots of extreme epistemological relativism.) There is a well-known circularity to such pronouncements, but equally importantly we will want to *contrast* objective reality with subjective impression. Indeed there is a certain two-faced character to extreme exponents of reality construction in criminology. On the one hand they sometimes deny the existence of a reality independent of the observer when explaining the labeling process,[18] but when they mention the redneck bigot and his conception of blacks as inherently stupid they will want to say that he is *wrong*. This is understandable but it does not lead to conceptual clarification. Clarity is also sacrificed by such eliptical statements as ''reality construction'' or the ''negotiation of reality.'' What is intended, or at least what the evidence shows, is that people construct, or negotiate, a *picture* of reality. But it has not been demonstrated that underlying reality changes as our conception of it shifts, that reality does not exist independently of cognition, or that because *some* knowledge is contingent upon epoch, social position, or experience, we can never, therefore, speak of perceptual error. Such considerations may seem far afield from the concerns of criminology, but we believe they are pertinent given certain recent tendencies.

Although we are sympathetic to the idea that perceptions of reality influence behavior, and are constructed or negotiated rather than ''given'' by the contents of the situation (and, of course, that this is important to criminology), still we adopt a less extreme view than some who seem to be saying, however indirectly, that there is no reality other than that which is constructed. This is true only under highly specific conditions. If all the participants at a trial suddenly agree that it is not a trial, then truly it is not.[19] But if all participants agree that blacks are less intelligent than whites,

---

jects. Key references in perception include Bruner and Tagiuri (1954); Tagiuri and Petrullo (1958); Ichheiser (1970); Hastorf et al. (1970); Jones et al. (1971); and Kelley (1971).

[18] See an examination of this feature of labeling in Becker (1973: 195–96).

[19] There is, in addition, the interesting case in which the difference between official and private reality is recognized by all, but the official fiction is maintained.
  ''You aren't pleading guilty because of any consideration or promise, are you?''
  ''Oh no, your Honor.''
Yet plea bargaining is openly used. See Scheff (1968).

that the crime rate doubled last month, or that there is no drug addiction in the United States, there is a certain stubbornness about reality in such cases. They may act on their conceptions, and their acts will certainly have consequences, but the objective reality is unmoved. (To be sure, it is sometimes exceedingly difficult to avoid biases and measurement problems in empirical observation, so that our depiction of reality must perforce be tentative and approximate. But this is another issue.) We hold, in other words, that an independent reality exists, even for most social phenomena, and that perceptions do not in most cases change that reality. Perceptions can be (in the older psychological language) more or less "veridical"—that is, free from error or distortion.[20]

Some Illustrative Models of Perception and Criminology

The advantage of perception in the study of criminological topics becomes clear when the processes and decisions can be seen to involve perceptual components. Indeed, in some processes it is apparently the perception of reality which is the main determinant of the outcome, although the objective reality is typically one influence on the perception. The centrality of perception is most graphically illustrated by the use of models of specific criminological processes. In the following pages we present as illustrations three models concerning, respectively, the crime rate (and deterrence), the societal opportunity structure, and labeling.[21]

THE CRIME RATE AND FEEDBACK MECHANISMS

A feedback model of the interaction of objective crime rate with other phenomena (general and special deterrence, collective reaffirmation, and criminal opportunities) sharply points up the significance of perception. In Figures 1.1 to 1.4, objective components are shown unenclosed while perceptual components are encircled. It must be emphasized that the processual patterns shown are largely hypothetical, since little or no research has been performed

[20] For a contrasting view, see Harre and Secord (1972).

[21] Other, less global models are contained in several of the articles reprinted in this collection. See, e.g., Hogarth's "black box" model (chapter 20), or Henshel and Carey's "perfectly informed hedonist" (chapter 3).

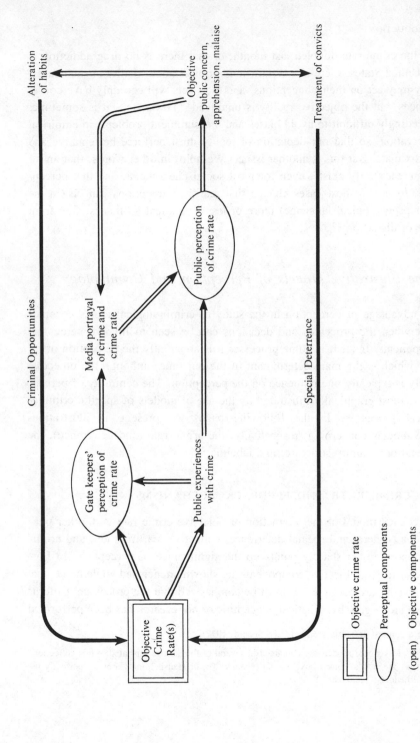

Figure 1.1 Objective Crime Rate, Criminal Opportunities, and Special Deterrence

Criminal Opportunities

Alteration
of habits

Media portrayal
of crime and
crime rate

Gate keepers'
perception of
crime rate

Public perception
of crime rate

Objective
public concern,
apprehension, malaise

Public experiences
with crime

Objective
Crime
Rate(s)

Special Deterrence

Treatment of convicts

Objective crime rate

Perceptual components

(open)   Objective components

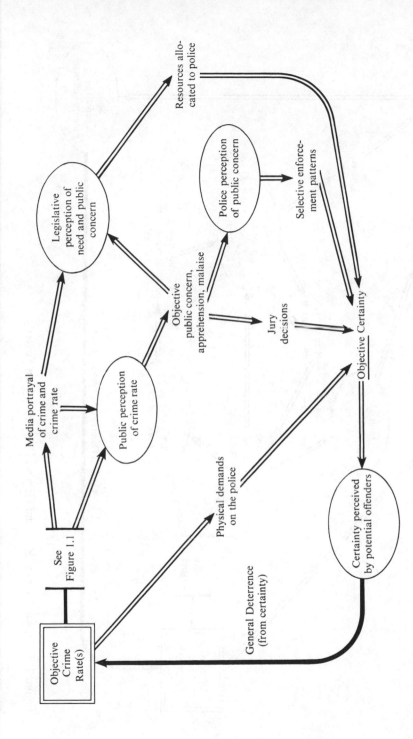

Figure 1.2 Objective Crime Rate and General Deterrence from Certainty

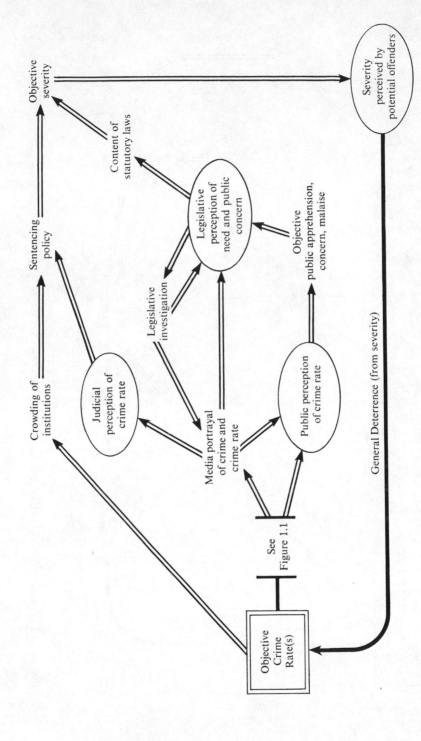

Figure 1.3 Objective Crime Rate and General Deterrence from Severity

on numerous segments, while for others (e.g., severity and general deterrence) the linkage is still in question after much investigation.[22]

A few words should be devoted to defining the less obvious terms in these figures. General deterrence refers to the effects of sanctions on potential offenders, while special deterrence refers to the effects of sanctions on the specific persons who receive them. General deterrence is divided into certainty and severity; swiftness (celerity) is not included here. Collective reaffirmation refers to the Durkheimian concept (extended by Lewis Coser) in which public awareness of punishment for violation of the norms strengthens (reaffirms) the norm. Of course revulsion could also take place if the legal reaction was regarded as unjust or excessive (Kalven and Zeisel, 1966: 306–312). Criminal opportunities refer to facilitation at the scene of criminal acts. Some examples are adoption by manufacturers of improved ignition locks for automobiles or consideration of "defensible space" in the designing of apartments. Jeffery (1971) and Newman (1973) have argued that the most effective way for planners to reduce crime is to concentrate on such opportunities, rather than on deterrence.

This model is by no means intended as a complete representation of the factors which influence objective crime rate. It intentionally omits a number of economic, social, and cultural variables, and even omits certain perceptual factors which influence the crime rate. Those factors that are not themselves influenced in turn by the volume of crime are omitted.[23] The model represents the cybernetic feedback loops which center on the crime rate and, among other consequences, dampen any sudden dramatic increases.[24]

With the possible exception of collective reaffirmation, the effect of all of the loops is to *reduce deviation*, which is to say they tend to reduce departures in either direction from the previous crime rate. As the crime rate falls, for example, people may become more careless, offering greater opportunities for successful crimes. As the crime rate rises, on the other hand, resources allocated to the police may rise, increasing the probability of apprehension. However, there are three countervailing factors within this general framework: crowding of institutions and physical demands on police

[22] For an excellent overview of the status of research on the effectiveness of general deterrence see Bowers (1972) and Zimring and Hawkins (1973).

[23] Thus some of the papers in this collection are not included in the model, for instance the work by Short et al. (chapter 2) on perceived economic opportunities.

[24] We have not shown feedbacks between certainty and severity set forth by Logan (1972).

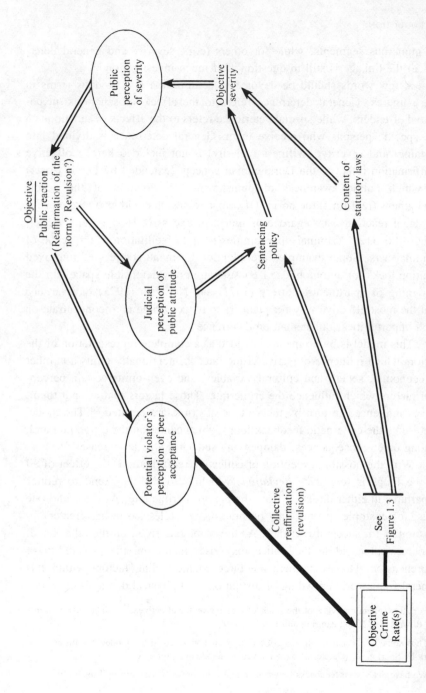

Figure 1.4 Objective Crime Rate and Collective Reaffirmation (or Revulsion)

are inherently *deviation-amplifying*. (For example, as crime rate falls, institutions become less crowded. Judges can impose harsher sentences, which may further reduce the crime rate.) And instead of collective reaffirmation from the punishing of offenders there may be collective revulsion (as, e.g., against severe sanctions for marihuana use), which reaction is also deviation-amplifying.[25] But the central point is that all loops closely integrate objective reality and subjective impression, so that the feedback provided by the loops depends as much on the public's perception of crime-rate changes, on the legislators' perception of public concern, and on the judges' perception of general sentencing practice, as it does on the actualities.

SOCIAL CONTROL AND THE DEVELOPMENT OF DEVIANT SUBCULTURES

A somewhat different model of the problem of control of activities defined as criminal is presented by Wilkins (1965). Although we do him an injustice by omitting his general model and postulates, the central ideas can be seen through one application.

In the United States of America drug addiction is a very serious problem; indeed, large proportions of those imprisoned are incarcerated for drug addiction or peddling. In Great Britain and the Scandinavian countries there is no drug addiction problem. In the United States drug addiction is treated as a most serious crime and convicted offenders are sentenced to very long terms of imprisonment, whereas in Great Britain the drug addict is dealt with as a sick person and treated with sympathy, if not with tolerance. But drug addiction used to be a serious problem in England.

It is possible that some societies, for some reason, find it necessary to treat deviance with extreme intolerance, and others are able to accommodate greater degrees of deviance, and, *as a result of such tolerance, experience less serious deviance*. It seems that it is possible for a society to operate in such a way that its social-sanctions systems become devalued (Wilkins, 1965: 86–87).

Wilkins proposes the following *deviation-amplifying* model to explain this and the growth of other deviant subcultures.

(a) Certain types of information, in relation to certain systems, lead to more acts being defined as deviant. . . . [e.g., testimony before Congress on the "evils" of marihuana.]

(b) The individuals involved in the acts so defined are "cut off" from the values of the parent system by the very process of definition.

[25] For the definitive discussion of deviation-amplifying feedback, see Maruyama (1963).

(c) The defining act provides an information set for the individuals concerned and they begin to perceive themselves as deviant. (Perhaps the main way in which any person gets to know what sort of person he is is through feedback from other persons.)

(d) The action taken by society and the resulting self-perception of the individuals defined as deviant, lead to the isolation and alienation of the specified individuals.

(e) This provides the first part of a deviation-amplifying system. The definition of society leads to the development of the self-perception as "deviant" on the part of the "outliers" (outlaws), and it is hardly to be expected that people who are excluded by a system will continue to regard themselves as part of it.

(f) The deviant groups will tend to develop their own values which may run counter to the values of the parent system, the system which defined them as "outliers."

(g) The increased deviance demonstrated by the deviant groups (resulting from the deviation-amplifying effect of the self-perception, which in turn may have derived from the defining acts of society) results in more forceful action by the conforming groups against the nonconformists.

(h) Thus information about the behaviour of the nonconformists (i.e., as (f) above) received by the conforming groups leads to more acts being defined as deviant, or to more stringent action against the "outliers"; and thus the whole system (a)–(g) can itself continue round and round again in an amplifying circuit (Wilkins, 1965: 91–92).

He then applies this model to the drug problem. But at first it does not work so well.

Many observers from the United States have studied the system of drug addiction and narcotics control in England. Although different observers from America were in England at the same time and discussed with the same people, their views differ regarding what was observed. Some writers have reported that they could find no differences between the British and the United States systems of control, others have found what they believe to be major differences. It would appear that the perception of systems of control differs between observers who are, in fact, observing the same thing and taking similar evidence. Some have claimed that the different systems of control in the two countries could explain the difference in the incidence of addiction, others have claimed that since there are no differences, or none of any significance, the different patterns of addiction cannot be due to any differences in the systems of control (Wilkins, 1965: 93).

Wilkins resolves this impass by noting that the *perception* of the control systems may differ even if the systems themselves are objectively similar.

(a) the perception ("image") of the use of drugs in England differs from that in the United States;

(b) the perception of the addict differs;

(c) the perception of the police differs;

(d) small differences in the control system, or even in the perception of the control system, could generate large differences in the perception of addiction, which could amplify the effects of the official controls;

(e) less action is defined as "crime" in Britain, and as a result, or in addition, fewer people are defined as "criminal," whatever the objective differences may be;

(f) the balance between legitimate and illegitimate means for obtaining drugs in the two countries differs;

(g) the "information set" (or folklore—it does not have to be true!) regarding the official control system and the function of drugs, both culturally and in the sub-cultures of the two countries, differs;

(h) a different perception of a situation will give rise to behaviour which differs, since behaviour tends to be consistent with perception.

If this model is a sound one, it would be possible for the situation in England to change rapidly and radically owing only to minor changes in the balance of factors. Which factors are critical in an unstable (feedback) situation of this kind is not a particularly meaningful question—any change in the situation may change the outcome throughout the whole field. It is possible or even probable, that any attempt to tighten up the British regulations with a view to making a minor problem even less of a problem may be a disturbance of the generating system of perceptions which could produce a more serious problem (Wilkins, 1965: 93–94).[26]

Wilkins' theory of the elaboration of deviant subcultures bears a resemblance to the scheme proposed by Cohen in *Delinquent Boys* (1955), although it is uniquely clear in depicting the importance of perception. It also bears a close resemblance to certain components of labeling theory.

PERCEPTION IN THE SITUATION OF LABELING

Scheff's (1966) sociological theory of mental illness is one of the clearest expositions of labeling theory, and Walter Buckley (1967) has taken the Scheff scheme and provided a flow-chart model of the process. Perception enters this model twice: once in the impressions others have of a deviant individual, and again in potential shifts in his own perception of the situation, and of himself, from the reactions of others.

Since he is availing himself of the Scheff model—quite understandable in view of its clarity—Buckley explicitly discusses labeling in mental illness. But it can easily be transferred to reactions to criminal deviance.

[26] Extracts from Wilkins reprinted by permission of Prentice-Hall and of Tavistock Publications Ltd., London.

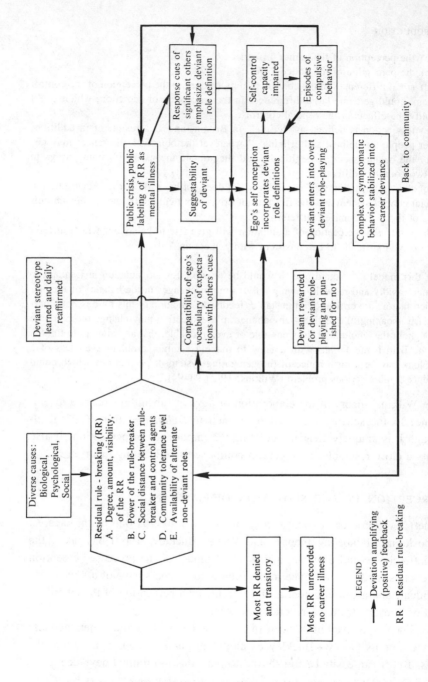

Figure 1.5 Flow Chart: Stabilization of Deviance in a Social System (from Buckley, 1967, page 170)

For diverse causes—biological, psychological, and/or social—most individuals at some time or other engage in *residual rule-breaking* or unusual behavior that is potentially definable by some members of society as abnormal or wrong. (These "diverse causes," of course, call for the plugging in of sociological and psychological theories of strain generation.) Most such residual rule-breaking is *denied,* not defined or reacted to as of consequence, and is thus not amplified; it is transitory and without issue. On the other hand, depending on the status of the individual, the visibility of his residual rule-breaking, community tolerance level, and so on, his behavior and its effects on family or friends may lead to a "public crisis" wherein it comes to be defined and "labeled" as "mental illness." These social responses of others significant to him, in conjunction with his own suggestibility at such a time of stress, and along with the stereotyped behaviors of the mentally disturbed he has learned during the normal socialization process, all contribute to his definition of himself as deviant. (This is very much the same process whereby *any* aspect of one's role and self-conception are socially elaborated, though without the stress and crisis.) Inasmuch as this is unsettling to an already disturbed person, his self-control is further impaired, making further episodes of "unusual" behavior likely. A deviation-amplifying feedback loop is thus set up as suggested in Figure 6-1, [*our Figure 1.5*], reverberating from "ego" and his behavior to significant others, to the public such as psychiatrist, court judge, family physician, or solicitous neighbor, and back to ego's self-conception. Ego's advance into overt deviant role-playing is furthered when the psychiatrist, for example, attempts to fit ego's presumed symptomatic behaviors into traditional clinical categories, and inadvertently rewards ego for the "correct" behavior symptoms and verbal responses, and punishes him for attempting to deny his deviant role. This also constitutes a potential deviation-amplifying source, contributing to the final stabilization of ego into the career deviant role—the neurotic or psychotic (Buckley, 1967: 169, 171).

Before concluding our examination of these models, two important points should be clarified. First, for our own model and—we are certain they would agree—for the models of Wilkins and Buckley, the relations displayed are only approximations, representations which conform to the best information available. Under these approximations the perceptual component stands out prominently; we hazard a prediction that future alterations—however else they may shift the models from their present forms—will not do away with perception as a central element. Second, we regard these models as *illustrations only* of what can be created under the perceptual perspective. For example, we have included no model on perception in the correctional process, although it may be equally applicable there.[27] The dynamics of prisons and other institutions display the same reliance on

[27] For indications of some possibilities here, see Gibbs (1966b: 154–55) or Hazelrigg (1967).

decision-making by administrators, correctional personnel, and inmates, and each must rely heavily on his perception of reality given the secretive and deceitful atmosphere of the total institution. The apparently paradoxical rise in unrest following relaxations of institutional harshness can perhaps best be treated within a perceptual framework. But all that we have tried to establish at this point is the viability of perceptual models, and their utility as a strategy of inquiry in criminology.

Toward a Shift of Emphasis in Criminology

We have noted at several points the existence of older traditions in criminology which emphasize official statistics, the etiology of criminal behavior, and the actuarial prediction of various parole or probation "risks." Again, we do not advocate abandonment of such pursuits, especially since real progress has been made in investigating the causes of some forms of criminal activity.[28] But we do advocate a decided change in emphasis, a shift toward the perceptual dimension.

   Criminological investigations can in principle emphasize the actual situation, the perceived situation, or the decisions reached by the actors. (The latter can be examined through compilations or typologies.) It can then examine various forms of influence, or apparent causality, among these three foci. It can look at the influence of the real situation on the perceived situation, the influence of the real situation on decision-making, the influence of the perceived situation on decision-making, and—since decision-making has consequences—the influence of decisions on the real and perceived situations. Finally, it can remain "within" a given category, either by focusing on the influence of the real situation on another aspect thereof (for instance, the relation between objective certainty of capture and objective crime rate) or by investigating the influence of perceptions on other perceptions (for example, a defendant's perception of the extent of corruption as an influence on his interpetation of a judge's behavior).[29] Historically the interrelations

[28] See, e.g., Hirschi (1969). For an example of a sustained attack on "traditional criminology's" concern with crime causation, see Phillipson (1971).

[29] For examples of correlational analysis between perceptions, see the selection by Short, Rivera, and Tennyson (chapter 2) and Huff and Scott (1973).

among the objective components have received the lion's share of attention.[30]

Of the possibilities mentioned above, we are promoting, of course, the
perceptual components. But it should be clear that one can often best *infer*
perceptions by examining "objective" data. Thus, in advocating a perceptual approach, we are speaking of the theoretical focus of attention, not of
the method actually used in a given case to observe it. The ideal, in fact,
would seem to be a rigorous, systematic, and, wherever possible, quantitative examination of perception in criminology.[31]

There is increasing evidence that such a shift is indeed taking place.
Alongside the emergence in general sociology of ethnomethodology and
Schutzian phenomenology, and the resurgence of symbolic interactionism
and the sociology of knowledge, a perceptual orientation is developing in
criminology.

Studies of the distribution of knowledge in society are belatedly receiving attention.[32] Of course this engages our own interest in the dynamics of
ignorance for decision-making in criminology. And we can see numerous
signs in the field of increasing emphasis on the perceptual dimension. Johnson (1968: 16) is too pessimistic in view of modern developments when he
says that only lip-service is paid to the social interpretation of crime. Indeed,
material with a perceptual orientation has long been available in criminology—some of the studies in the present collection have a respectable age.
But the emphasis that is given this approach is new. Labeling theory must be
cited first, in view of the immense outpouring of research in this domain
over the past few years.[33] But we hope our collection conclusively demon-

[30] Although his conclusions are not entirely congruent with our own, readers may find interesting Blumer's treatment of these issues in social analysis (1969: 132–39).

[31] We have used in this Introduction a form of shorthand in which "objective reality," when it
is to be compared empirically with "perception," is really the scientific approximation of that
reality. In so doing we are only following the conventional practice in sociology (see, e.g., the
articles reprinted here), but in greater detail there are four distinct "levels": (1) "objective
reality"—unknowable but conceivable (e.g., the objective crime rate), (2) scientific approximation of (1) (e.g., a statistical crime rate), (3) lay perception (e.g., laymen's perception of the
crime rate), and (4) scientific approximation of (3) (e.g., a survey analysis of laymen's beliefs
about the crime rate). In sociology we would of course be dealing with (2) and (4). In our
"shorthand" we call (2) "objective reality" and (4) "perceived or constructed reality." We are
indebted to Herbert Blumer for calling these distinctions to our attention.

[32] As an example of pleas for such studies, see Schutz (1963: 314).

[33] In addition to Lemert's (1951) now-classic work, the present-day labeling school has had
numerous early precursors, including studies of discrimination and stereotypy, racial prejudice,

strates how much broader are the implications than even the wide range of problems engaged by reaction theory. Quinney's *Social Reality of Crime* is a landmark in the development of the new emphasis, and indeed Quinney takes note of the shift in criminology (1970: 24). The Douglas collection (1970a) emphasizes nonquantitative methods and covers deviance rather than criminology, but it is a major example of a similar perspective—and it too is by no means confined to labeling. Hogarth (1971) prefaces his book on sentencing with a statement of his own inclination for a "rigorous methodology [applied] to data generated from a phenomenological perspective." He briefly describes an approach indistinguishable from our own, and speculates on the emergence of a "school" of this persuasion in Toronto. Examples could be multiplied.[34] The studies compiled in this collection are a case in point of the shift in emphasis, since most are of comparatively recent publication.

Thus we cannot claim either to have invented the perspective nor to have started the trend toward its use. We are, rather, in the position of elaborating it and celebrating it with the first collection in criminology using perception as its focus of attention. And hopefully by creating the collection and this Introduction we are stimulating its greater development—accelerating it and encouraging it.

Hadley Cantril relates the story of three baseball umpires discussing their profession.

The first umpire said, "Some are balls and some are strikes, and I call them as they are." The second replied, "Some's balls and some's strikes, and I call 'em as I see 'em." The third thought about it and said, "Some's balls and some's strikes, but they ain't nothin' 'till I calls 'em."

If we may use this little tale for our own purposes, the second umpire is correct in assuming that a reality exists independently of his judgment, but in terms of social consequences the third umpire is also correct. Studies in criminology, meanwhile, have too long assumed that actors in the drama of crime are like the *first* umpire, an assumption for which there is virtually no justification.

---

and self-fulfilling perceptions. But the magnitude of the recent surge of effort is virtually without parallel in criminology.

[34] As our selection from Jock Young illustrates, the York group in Britain has emphasized the volitional element within an interactionist framework. A decade ago Turk (1964) emphasized the significance for the development of theoretical criminology of studying what he called "differential perception."

References

Ackoff, Russell and Fred E. Emery. 1972. *On Purposeful Systems*. Chicago: Aldine.

Arens, Richard and Arnold Meadow. 1956. "Psycholinquistics and the Confession Dilemma," *Columbia Law Review* 56:19–46.

Becker, Howard. 1973. "Labeling Theory Reconsidered." In Howard Becker (ed.), *Outsiders* (enlarged ed.). New York: Free Press, ch. 10.

Berelson, Bernard and Gary Steiner. 1964. *Human Behavior: An Inventory of Scientific Findings*. New York: Harcourt.

Berger, Peter L. and Thomas Luckmann. 1967. *The Social Construction of Reality: A Treatise in the Sociology of Knowledge*. Garden City, N.Y.: Anchor.

Biderman, Albert. 1970. "Information, Intelligence, Enlightened Public Policy: Functions and Organization of Societal Feedback," *Policy Sciences* 1:217–30.

Biderman, Albert, Louise Johnson, Jennie McIntyre, and Adrianne Weir. 1967. Report on a Pilot Study in the District of Columbia on Victimization and Attitudes Toward Law Enforcement. Washington, D.C.: U.S. Government Printing Office.

Blumer, Herbert. 1969. *Symbolic Interactionism: Perspective and Method*. Englewood Cliffs, N.J.: Prentice-Hall.

Bowers, William J. 1972. "A Causal Framework for the Analysis of Deterrence." American Society of Criminology Meetings, Caracas.

Brodbeck, May (ed.). 1968. *Readings in the Philosophy of the Social Sciences*. New York: Macmillan.

Bruner, Jerome and Renato Tagiuri. 1954. "The Perception of People." In G. Lindzey (ed.), *Handbook of Social Psychology*. Cambridge, Mass.: Addison-Wesley, Vol. 2, pp. 634–54.

Buckley, Walter, 1967. *Sociology and Modern Systems Theory*. Englewood Cliffs, N.J.: Prentice-Hall.

Catton, William R., Jr. 1966. *From Animistic to Naturalistic Sociology*. New York: McGraw-Hill.

Cicourel, Aaron V. 1964. *Method and Measurement in Sociology*. New York: Free Press.

1974. "Police Practices and Official Records." In Roy Turner (ed.), *Ethnomethodology*. Harmondsworth: Penguin, pp. 85–95.

Cohen, Albert K. 1955. *Delinquent Boys*. New York: Free Press.

Douglas, Jack D. (ed.). 1970a. *Deviance and Respectability: The Social Construction of Moral Meanings*. New York: Basic Books.

1970b. *Observations of Deviance*. New York: Random House.

Dray, William H. 1964. *Philosophy of History*. Englewood Cliffs, N.J.: Prentice-Hall.

Duncan, Hugh. 1968. *Symbols in Society*. New York: Oxford.

Friendly, Alfred and Ronald Goldfarb. 1968. *Crime and Publicity*. New York: Vintage Books.

Gibbs, Jack P. 1966a. "Conceptions of Deviant Behavior: The Old and the New," *Pacific Sociological Review* 9:9–14.

1966b. "Sanctions," *Social Problems* 14 (Fall):147–59.

Gross, Bertram M. (ed.). 1969. *Social Intelligence for America's Future: Explorations in Societal Problems*. Boston: Allyn and Bacon.

Harre, R. and Paul F. Secord. 1972. *The Explanation of Social Behavior*. Totowa, N.J.: Rowman and Littlefield.

Hastorf, Albert H., David J. Schneider, and Judith Polefka. 1970. *Person Perception*. Reading, Mass.: Addison-Wesley.

Hazelrigg, Lawrence E. 1967. "An Examination of the Accuracy and Relevance of Staff Perceptions of the Inmate in the Correctional Institution," *Journal of Criminal Law, Criminology, and Police Science* 58 (June):204–10.

Henshel, Richard L. and Anne-Marie Henshel. 1973. *Perspectives on Social Problems*. Toronto: Longmans.

Hirschi, Travis. 1969. *Causes of Delinquency*. Berkeley: University of California Press.

Hogarth, John. 1971. *Sentencing as a Human Process*. Toronto: University of Toronto Press.

Huff, C. Ronald and Joseph E. Scott. 1973. "Public Attitudes toward Deviance: The Case for Patterned Perspectives." Unpublished paper, the Ohio State University.

Ichheiser, Gustav. 1970. *Appearances and Realities*. San Francisco: Jossey-Bass.

Jeffery, C. Ray. 1971. *Crime Prevention through Environmental Design*. Beverly Hills: Sage.

Johnson, Elmer H. 1968. *Crime, Correction, and Society*. Rev. ed. Homewood, Ill.: Dorsey Press.

Jones, Edward E. et al. (eds.). 1971. *Attribution: Perceiving the Causes of Behavior*. Morristown, N.J.: General Learning Press.

Kalven, Harry, Jr. and Hans Zeisel. 1966. *The American Jury*. Boston: Little, Brown.

Kelley, H. H. 1971. *Attribution in Social Interaction*. New York: General Learning Press.

Klapper, Joseph T. 1969. *The Effects of Mass Communication*. New York: Free Press.

Lemert, Edwin M. 1951. *Social Pathology*. New York: McGraw-Hill.

Lewinsohn, Richard. 1958. *Prophets and Pediction*. London: Secker and Warburg.

Logan, Charles H. 1972. "General Deterrent Effects of Imprisonment," *Social Forces* 51:64–73.

Maruyama, Magoroh. 1963. "The Second Cybernetics: Deviation-Amplifying Mutual Causal Processes," *American Scientist* 51:164–79.

Matson, Floyd W. 1964. *The Broken Image*. New York: Braziller.

Matza, David. 1969. *Becoming Deviant*. Englewood Cliffs, N.J.: Prentice-Hall.

Merton, Robert K. 1936. "The Unanticipated Consequences of Purposive Social Action," *American Sociological Review* 1:894–904.

Morris, Norval and Gordon Hawkins. 1970. *The Honest Politician's Guide to Crime Control*. Chicago: University of Chicago Press.

Natanson, Maurice (ed.). 1966. *Essays in Phenomenology*. The Hague: Martinus Nijhoff.

Nelson, Philip J. 1966. "An Essay in Normative Economics," *Social Research* 33 (Summer):314–31.

Nettler, Gwynn. 1961. "Good Men, Bad Men, and the Perception of Reality," *Sociometry* 24 (3):279–94.

Newman, Oscar. 1973. *Defensible Space: Crime Prevention through Urban Design*. New York: Macmillan.

Phillipson, Michael. 1971. *Sociological Aspects of Crime and Delinquency*. London: Routledge and Kegan Paul.

Quinney, Richard. 1970. *The Social Reality of Crime*. Boston: Little, Brown.

Remmling, Gunter W. 1967. *Road to Suspicion: A Study of Modern Mentality and the Sociology of Knowledge*. New York: Appleton-Century-Crofts.

Rogers, Everett M. 1962. *Diffusion of Innovations*. New York: Free Press.

Rottenberg, Simon (ed.). 1973. *The Economics of Crime and Punishment*. Washington: American Enterprise Institute for Public Policy Research.

Scheff, Thomas J. 1966. *Being Mentally Ill*. Chicago: Aldine.

1968. "Negotiating Reality: A Note on Power in the Assessment of Responsibility," *Social Problems* 16 (Summer):3–17.

Schutz, Alfred. 1963. "Common Sense and Scientific Interpretation of Human Action." In Maurice Natanson (ed.), *Philosophy of the Social Sciences: A Reader*. New York: Random House, pp. 302–46.

1964, 1967. *Collected Papers,* Vols. I and II, ed. A. Brodersen. The Hague: Martinus Nijhoff.

Short, James F., Jr. and F. Ivan Nye. 1957. "Reported Behavior as a Criterion of Deviant Behavior," *Social Problems* 5:207–13.

Sykes, Gresham and David Matza. 1957. "Techniques of Neutralization: A Theory of Delinquency," *American Sociological Review* 22:664–70.

Tagiuri, Renato and Luigi Petrullo (eds.). 1958. *Person Perception and Interpersonal Behavior*. Stanford: Stanford University Press.

Tarde, Gabriel. 1912. *Penal Philosophy*. Boston: Little, Brown.

Turk, Austin T. 1964. "Prospects for Theories of Criminal Behavior," *Journal of Criminal Law, Criminology, and Police Science* 55:454–61.

Wagner, Helmut. 1970. "Introduction." In Alfred Schutz, *On Phenomenology and Social Relations* (Helmut Wagner, arranger). Chicago: University of Chicago Press.

Wilkins, Leslie T. 1965. *Social Deviance: Social Policy, Action, and Research*. Englewood Cliffs, N.J.: Prentice-Hall; London: Tavistock Publications Ltd.

Wilson, Bryan R. (ed.). 1970. *Rationality*. New York: Harper Torchbooks.

Wolfgang, Marvin E. 1963. "Uniform Crime Reports: A Critical Appraisal," *University of Pennsylvania Law Review* 111:708–38.

Zimring, Franklin and Gordon Hawkins. 1973. *Deterrence*. Chicago: University of Chicago Press.

PART ONE:

Criminogenic
Perceptions
and
Behavioral
Outcomes

Criminogenic perception refers to beliefs about the social world which, in company with individual goals, lead to criminal behaviors. In terms of research, the perceptions themselves and the behavioral consequences are equally salient features; as will be seen, the authors in this section tend to emphasize both components. It should be clear to most readers that there are a myriad of perceptions that might be included as precursors of criminal behavior. Nettler (1961) in his excellent piece "Good Men, Bad Men, and the Perception of Reality," indicates that while deviants and "good men" have differing perceptions of the legal process and its components, neither have necessarily cornered the market in terms of accuracy. We despaired at having to omit Nettler but, alas, most of the perceptual comparisons he makes do not involve those aspects of the real world which can be ascertained with reasonable reliability, violating the guidelines set forth in the Preface.

We have chosen to exclude pieces which explain *how* a criminal or delinquent happens to acquire a world view and set of perceptions—for example, Sutherland's (1939) writings on differential association. This would necessitate inclusion of the bulk of that part of criminology dealing with crime causation—excluding only those theories which are based on biological factors or ecological explanations in the broad sense. This literature is covered adequately in other edited and synthesizing works (e.g., Mannheim, 1965; Wolfgang et al., 1962). For reasons emphasized in the Introduction, we intend to focus on criminogenic perception *in contrast to* objective reality. That this is a major self-limitation there can be no doubt. The reader must judge for himself whether the emphases described in the Introduction are worth pursuing further.

The dominant topic in the articles included is deterrence—a result, quite simply, of the limitations we have imposed and the distribution of existing research.[1] With the important exception of articles by Short, Rivera, and Tennyson, and by Walker and Argyle, the result is a series of articles representing a decade of research, with increasing sophistication, on the ways in which peoples' perceptions of legal sanctions relate to their participation or nonparticipation in illicit activity. What a person thinks the criminal law is, what he thinks the probability of capture is, and how severe he believes the punishment for infraction to be are all likely to affect his behavior in terms of criminal participation.[2] As the articles themselves make clear, there are important internal subdivisions for each of these beliefs—for instance, whether the person is referring to the likelihood of capture in general or to the likelihood of *his* capture. Given the general ignorance of the public concerning sanctions, it is clear that it is the perception of the sanction that relates to a decision to participate, not the objective aspects of the sanction *per se*.

[1] For an excellent up-to-date survey of deterrence research and analysis, see Zimring and Hawkins (1973). For a brief overview of the historical development of this research, see Henshel and Carey (chapter 3).

[2] Traditional speculation on deterrence spoke of the effects of certainty, severity, and celerity (speed of application of the sanction). Although learning theory lends a certain credibility to celerity, it is commonly ignored in the literature, and we have followed that practice here. Another distinction—that between general and special deterrence—is set forth in the Introduction.

After the decision to participate has been made, there are of course other perceptions that might be analyzed. There are probably important shifts in perception after perpetration and capture or noncapture. It has been pointed out by Gibbs (1966) and others that while the public may consider the judicial process to be nonpunitive in itself (until sentence is carried out), the defendant may find the entire process punishing.[3] This is of course beyond the scope of this book, but it does offer interesting possibilities for research in perception in penology. The potential for such research is well illustrated by some of the articles that have been included in Part Two of this volume.

The selections in this section should shed some light on the mechanisms by which criminogenic perceptions effect individual behavior. So far we have concentrated on mechanisms and agents of social control. But there is, naturally, another side to criminogenic perception: the beliefs about *gains* from illegal activity. The piece by Short, Rivera, and Tennyson (chapter 2) may be held up as a model of how objective and perceptual data can be integrated. The major thrust of this study is an examination of Cloward and Ohlin's (1960) delinquency and opportunity hypothesis, with lineage traceable to Merton's (1939) anomie theory.[4] Success goals (legitimate and illegitimate) and perception of the best means of obtaining such success goals (legitimate and illegitimate) are examined for various sectors of the population. The authors then compare the perceptions of the opportunities for goal attainment by legal and illegal means with objective crime rates. Differential perception is the principal explanatory variable.

In "Deviance, Deterrence, and Knowledge of Sanctions," Henshel and Carey (chapter 3) point out that deterrence is a perceptual fact—deterrence is essentially "in the mind of the beholder." They set forth the numerous reasons why widespread ignorance about sanctions can be anticipated. They outline the two possible "routes" by which punishment can affect criminal behavior, and they conclude that both involve public knowledge of the sanction. Finally, they outline alternatives to traditional nonperceptual research on deterrence.

We have included the progress report of the California Assembly Committee on Criminal Procedure (chapter 4) despite its occasional lapses of

[3] There is some support for this contention in Cameron's (1964) analysis. From her discussion it appears that the nonprofessional, occasional shoplifter will be very much affected by the entire judicial process. See also the discussion by Waldo and Chiricos (chapter 7).

[4] The research on anomie has been extensively evaluated in a major symposium edited by Clinard (1964).

reasoning. Longitudinal and cross-sectional analysis are sometimes confused, causal relationships are strongly imputed where the analysis does not permit even weak imputation, and in certain cases it is arguable that cause and effect are inverted in the discussion. We reprint a section of this study because it is one of the very few clear demonstrations of the extreme ignorance which prevails concerning the severity of formal sanctions. It even reveals that a systematic bias exists among the perceptions of the ignorant. The careful reader obtains from the article an excellent conception of the gulf between citizens' perceptions of sanctions for crime commission and the actual statutory penalties.[5]

Claster, Jensen, Waldo and Chiricos, and Teevan take up both empirical and theoretical aspects of perception and deterrence. Claster (chapter 5) deals with risk perception, and his findings lend empirical support to the notion that there is a "differential impact of deterrence in terms of differences in personality expressed as perceptions of self *vis-à-vis* the legal structure." He further finds that perceptual distortion on the part of delinquents leads them to feel invulnerable to arrest. (But they feel no corresponding immunity to conviction).

Jensen (chapter 6) investigates the general belief that lawbreakers are caught and punished. His analysis indicates such a belief to be a deterrent and that a shared misunderstanding—a distortion of an objective reality— leads to such a perception.

Waldo and Chiricos (chapter 7) investigate the deterrent powers of perceived severity of sanctions on behavior. They find no relationship between perceived severity and behavior, but they do find evidence supportive of deterrence from perceived certainty of capture. A hypothetical relationship between deterrent efficacy and type of crime (i.e., whether the crimes are *mala in se* or *mala prohibita*) is examined empirically.[6] This study represents a signal advance on several fronts in the empirical study of the perceptual components of deterrence.

Teevan's discussion (chapter 8) is a logical sequel to the other papers. He offers a critical overview of the literature on perception and deterrence and then reports on a study of his own. Teevan's innovative measure of per-

[5] Other less extensive studies showing public ignorance are cited in Henshel and Carey (chapter 3).

[6] For a similar hypothesis based on the distinction between instrumental deviance and expressive deviance, see Chambliss (1969: 368–72).

ceived severity does indicate a positive relationship between perceived severity and deterrence. Further, Teevan advances the notion of a "threshold of salience" for certainty of punishment to explain some of the findings which have heretofore been confusing.

In "Does the Law Effect Moral Judgements?," Walker and Argyle (chapter 9) show how particular perceptions of the law result in various attitudes and public opinions. They also show that some people (a minority to be sure) actually change their moral judgments as the law changes, hence perception that changes in the law have taken place can affect moral judgments. Their overridding finding, however, is that alterations in the criminal law are unlikely to weaken moral attitudes.

In a sense this collection on criminogenic perception is a keynote section. The articles and studies included investigate the general notion of perception and the behavioral consequences that arise from such perceptual errors as a misreading of the probability of capture, or the real sanctions imposed for various law violations. The pieces herein set the tone for the remainder of the anthology.

References

Cameron, Mary Owen. 1964. *The Booster and the Snitch*. New York: Wiley.

Chambliss, William J. 1969. *Crime and the Legal Process*. New York: McGraw-Hill.

Clinard, Marshall B. 1964. *Anomie and Deviant Behavior: A Discussion and Critique*. New York: Free Press.

Cloward, Richard A. and Lloyd E. Ohlin. 1960. *Delinquency and Opportunity*. New York: Free Press.

Gibbs, Jack P. 1966. "Sanctions," *Social Problems* 14 (Fall):147–59.

Mannheim, Hermann. 1965. *Comparative Criminology*. Boston: Houghton Mifflin.

Merton, Robert K. 1939. "Social Structure and Anomie," *American Sociological Review* 3:635–59.

Nettler, Gwynn. 1961. "Good Men, Bad Men, and the Perception of Reality," *Sociometry* 24(3):279–94.

Sutherland, Edwin. 1939. *Principles of Criminology* (3d ed.). New York: Lippincott.

Wolfgang, Marvin E., L. Savitz and N. Johnston. 1962. *The Sociology of Crime and Delinquency*. New York: Wiley.

Zimring, Franklin and Gordon Hawkins. 1973. *Deterrence*. Chicago: University of Chicago Press.

2

Perceived Opportunities,
Gang Membership,
and Delinquency

JAMES F. SHORT JR.,
RAMON RIVERA,
AND RAY A. TENNYSON

Not since the advent of psychoanalysis has a theory had such impact on institutionalized delinquency control as the theory, explicit or implied, in *Delinquency and Opportunity* (Cloward and Ohlin, 1960). Given the impetus of major foundation and federal support, the theory has been extensively adopted as a rationale for action programs in many areas of the country. There is some danger that, like psychoanalysis, "opportunity structure theory" may be rationalized and elaborated so rapidly and extensively as to discourage, if not render impossible, empirical testing, pragmatic validation, or demonstration of worth by any other criterion of "good theory." *Delinquency and Opportunity* has been widely praised for its theoretical integra-

Reprinted with permission of the American Sociological Association from "Perceived Opportunities, Gang Membership, and Delinquency," *ASR* 30 (February 1965) by James F. Short Jr., Ramon Rivera, and Ray A. Tennyson. This research is supported by grants from the Behavior Science Study Section of the National Institute of Mental Health (M-3301 and MH-07158); the Office of Juvenile Delinquency and Youth Development, Welfare Administration, U.S. Department of Health, Education, and Welfare in cooperation with the President's Committee on Juvenile Delinquency and Youth Crime (#62220); the Ford Foundation; and the Research Committee of Washington State University. We are grateful for this support and for the support and encouragement of staff members at the University of Chicago, Washington State University, and the Program for Detached Workers of the YMCA of Metropolitan Chicago, whose wholehearted cooperation makes the entire enterprise such an exciting "opportunity." An earlier version of this paper was read at the annual meetings of the Pacific Sociological Association, 1963.

tion, e.g., as "a logically sound deductive system that is rich in its implications for delinquency causation and control," but the same critic also notes that "examined in terms of its logical, operational, and empirical adequacy, the theory poses a number of questions concerning the accuracy of some of its postulates and theorems" (Schrag, 1962). Our paper will bring data to bear on certain aspects of the opportunity structure paradigm as we operationalized it in a study of delinquent gangs in Chicago.

[Table 2.1] reproduces in paradigm form the principal elements of "opportunity structure theory" concerning *criminal* and *conflict* subcultures. It subdivides the "Innovation" category of Merton's deviance paradigm, referring to acceptance (internalization) of culturally prescribed success goals and rejection (incomplete internalization) of institutional norms or culturally prescribed means, by those for whom legitimate means to success goals are restricted (Merton, 1958, ch. 4). To this the paradigm adds Cloward's four sets of defining conditions for the relative availability of illegitimate means to success goals (Cloward, 1959), and the two hypothesized types of "collective response among delinquents" produced by the preceding conditions.[1]

In our research in Chicago we have attempted to measure variables specified in this paradigm and to investigate their inter-relations. For this purpose we have studied lower-class "delinquent gangs" involved in a "detached worker" program of the YMCA of Metropolitan Chicago, control groups of lower-class nongang boys from the same neighborhoods as the gang boys, and middle-class nongang boys.[2] Elements of the paradigm were operationalized in terms of the *perceptions* reported by the boys studied.[3] In

[1] Cloward and Ohlin (1960: 25–27, 178ff) use a different theoretical rationale to explain "retreatist" subcultures, but our data are not relevant specifically to this aspect of the theory.

[2] Selection and description of study populations and other characteristics of the research program are described in previous publications and in greatest detail in *Group Processes and Gang Delinquency,* (Short and Strodtbeck, 1965). See, also Short et al. (1962); Short (1963).

[3] Cloward and Ohlin (1960) refer to "common perceptions" of opportunities, and Schrag (1962: 168) explains that one of the basic postulates of the theory is that "perceived disadvantage, regardless of the accuracy of the perception, is for lower-class youth the functional equivalent of objectively verified disadvantage in that it has the same effect on overt behavior." This is not to deny the importance of *objective* opportunities, legitimate and illegitimate. The former can be demonstrated to be greater for whites than Negroes, and for middle- than for lower-class persons. It is more difficult to demonstrate gang-nongang differences except in terms of the cumulative *effects*—school performance, relations with the police, etc.—which favor nongang boys. Differences in objective illegitimate opportunities are similarly difficult to demonstrate,

TABLE 2.1. SOCIAL CONTEXT AND MODES OF DELINQUENT BEHAVIOR: A PARADIGM

Structural Features	Type of Subculture	
	Criminal	Conflict
I. *Independent Variable*	(Integrated areas)	(Unintegrated areas)
A. Culturally prescribed success goals	internalized	internalized
B. Availability of legitimate means to success goals	limited; hence intense pressures toward deviant behavior	limited; hence intense pressures toward deviant behavior
II. *Intervening Variables*		
A. Institutional norms	incomplete internalization	incomplete internalization
B. Availability of illegal means to success goals	available	unavailable
1. Relations between adult carriers of conventional and criminal values	accommodative; each participates in value system of other	conflicted; neither group well organized; value systems implicit, and opposed to one another
2. Criminal learning structure	available; offenders at different age levels integrated	unavailable; attenuated relations between offenders at different age levels
3. Criminal opportunity structure	stable sets of criminal roles graded for different ages and levels of competence; continuous income; protection from detection and prosecution	unarticulated opportunity structure; individual rather than organized crime; sporadic income; little protection from detection and prosecution
4. Social control	strong controls originate in *both* legitimate and illegal structures	diminished social control; "weak" relations between adults and adolescents
III. *Dependent Variable*		
A. Expected type of collective response among delinquents	pressures toward deviance originate in limited accessibility to success goals by legitimate means, but are ameliorated by opportunities for access by illegal means. Hence, delinquent behavior is rational, disciplined, and crime-oriented	pressures toward deviance originate in blocked opportunity by *any* institutionalized system of means. Hence, delinquent behavior displays expressive conflict patterns

this paper we direct attention to perceptions of legitimate and illegitimate opportunities by Negro and white lower-class gang and nongang boys and middle-class boys of both races, and to the relations among these perceptions. Detailed discussion of the relation of perceived opportunities and patterns of behavior derived from self-reports and, for gang boys only, from detached-worker ratings, is deferred for later presentation.[4]

Data reported elsewhere establish different levels of aspiration among the boys studied, but they show that regardless of race, class, or gang membership, mean levels of both occupational and educational aspirations considerably exceed fathers' achieved levels of occupation and education.[5] In this sense the independent variable—internalization of culturally prescribed success goals—may be said to have a positive value among all the boys studied. For the first intervening variable in the paradigm, however—internalization of institutional norms—our gang members are less positive than the other boys studied. With "values" data from semantic differential scales, we established the fact that all groups assign equally high value and degree of legitimacy to such "middle-class" images as "someone who works for good grades at school" and "someone who likes to read good books"—again indicating that certain values are common to all groups—but gang boys of both races hold more positive attitudes toward *deviant* images than do the other boys (Gordon et al., 1963). These deviant images represented hypothesized "delinquent subcultures;" e.g., conflict ("someone who is a good fighter with a tough reputation"), criminal ("someone who knows where to sell what he steals" and "someone who has good connections to avoid trouble with the law"), and retreatist ("someone who makes easy money by pimping and other illegal hustles" and "someone who gets his kicks by using drugs"). Middle-class boys generally attribute to these deviant images a lower value and less legitimacy, as we expected.

This paper is concerned with other elements in the paradigm, based on data from one part of an extensive interview schedule administered by spe-

---

though the illegal enterprises are more likely to be present in a lower-class than in a middle-class environment.

[4] Behavior factors based on detached-worker ratings of gang boys are reported in Short et al. (1963). Self-reported behavior factors are presented in Short and Strodtbeck (1965: ch. 7).

[5] See Short, "Gang Delinquency" (1964a); see also Freedman and Rivera (1962). Elliott's (1962) study of "200 delinquent and nondelinquent boys attending two adjoining high schools in a large West Coast city" supports these findings.

cially trained interviewers to more than 500 boys in the six categories (race by class status and gang membership) under study. Respondents were instructed to indicate whether each of a series of statements was true of the "area where your group hangs out." In this way we hoped to measure perceptions of relatively specific legitimate and illegal opportunities. Perceptions of legitimate means to success goals, for example, were sampled by a series of statements concerning the *educational* and *occupational* orientations, abilities, and prospects for "guys in our area." We hoped by the impersonal referent to avoid the personalized ambitions and expectations which were the subject of inquiry in another part of the interview and thus to obtain measures referring to the boys' perceptions of general opportunities for legitimate and illegal achievement in their respective areas.

Aspects of the availability of illegal means to success goals to which attention was directed concerned the relative integration of the carriers of criminal and noncriminal values (in terms of the respectability of persons making money illegally and the orientation of local police toward law violation); adult "connections" and opportunities for learning and abetting criminal activities; the availability of criminal role models; and the probability of successful criminal enterprise in the area. Finally, because Cloward and Ohlin stress the importance of these matters for social control, perceptions of appropriate adult role models and their interest and sincerity concerning the problems of adolescents were also covered. The list of statements is in Table 1, [Ed. note: not displayed in this edited version], together with the percentage of boys in each group answering "true." [6]

In most cases responses to the statements concerning open legitimate opportunities and adult helpfulness form a gradient: gang boys are least likely to answer "true," followed by nongang and then by middle-class boys of each race. For negatively stated legitimate opportunity questions, and for the two negative adult power ("clout") statements, this gradient is reversed.[7] White gang boys generally are more sanguine than Negro gang boys about occupational opportunities and adult "clout," while Negroes tend to be slightly more optimistic concerning education and adult helpful-

[6] In the interview schedule the statements were not labeled according to which "opportunity structures" were being studied, and they were arranged in different order.

[7] Elliott (1962) finds that delinquents consistently perceive lower opportunities for educational and occupational "success" than do nondelinquents. For evidence of other gradients among boys in the present study, see Gordon et al. (1963), and Short and Strodtbeck (1965).

ness. For all these areas, white middle-class boys have the most *open* view of "opportunities."

Conversely, gang boys are more likely to perceive illegitimate opportunities as open than are other boys, and these perceptions are held by more Negro than white boys in each stratum. The latter finding is somewhat surprising, in view of the acknowledged white domination of organized crime in Chicago. Informal observation suggests that vice organized on a large scale does flourish in Negro communities, and that "independent entrepreneurship" in such forms as small (and large) policy wheels, marijuana peddling, street-walking prostitutes, pool sharks, professional burglars and robbers, and the like, is more common in lower-class Negro than in lower-class white communities (Short and Strodtbeck, 1965: ch. 5). In any case, illegitimate opportunities appeared to be open to more Negro than white boys. . . .

Table 2.2 presents mean opportunity structure scores, by race, class, and gang status of respondents. . . .

In addition, it is clear that for *legitimate* opportunities, gang-nongang and middle-class differences *within* racial categories are greater than the Negro-white differences for each of the three gang and class strata. For *illegitimate* opportunities, differences between races are greater than within-race differences.

Perceived Opportunities and an Official Delinquency Rate

In Table 2.3 ranking on each of the summary opportunity scores is compared with the official delinquency rates of the six race-by-class-by-gang-status groups.[8] As far as the *ordering* of the six groups is concerned, perception of *legitimate* opportunities is more strongly associated with delinquency rates than is perception of illegitimate opportunities. This is consistent with the assumption that perceived legitimate opportunities are independent variables, while perceived illegitimate opportunities intervene, after legitimate opportunities have been appraised and found wanting. Legitimate achievement tends to be the universal standard in our culture, highly valued even by

[8] These rates refer to the mean number of offenses known to the police, per boy, in each group. Data are based on Wise (1962).

TABLE 2.2. MEAN OPPORTUNITY STRUCTURE SCORES, BY RACE, CLASS, AND GANG STATUS

	Negro			White		
Aspect of Opportunity Structure [a]	Lower-class gang N = 206 [b]	Lower-class nongang N = 89	Middle class N = 26	Lower-class gang N = 89	Lower-class nongang N = 75	Middle class N = 53
Legitimate educational (0–12)	4.8	5.7	9.0	3.8	6.4	11.2
Legitimate occupational (0–10)	4.2	5.2	6.6	5.4	7.3	9.1
Integration of carriers of criminal and noncriminal values (0–4)	2.1	1.4	1.2	1.5	1.0	0.5
Criminal learning structures (0–6)	4.0	3.6	2.3	3.0	2.2	0.7
Visibility of criminal careers (0–4)	3.4	3.2	3.0	3.0	2.5	1.4
Criminal opportunities (0–10)	4.7	4.0	4.6	4.7	4.3	4.6
Adult *clout* (0–4)	1.5	1.9	3.0	2.0	2.4	3.7
Adult helpfulness (0–4)	3.0	3.7	3.2	2.6	3.2	3.7
Criminal opportunities (0–4)	1.8	1.2	1.8	1.5	1.0	0.9
Summary Scores						
Legitimate educational and occupational opportunities (0–22)	9.0	11.0	15.6	9.3	13.7	20.2
Illegitimate opportunities (0–24)	14.3	12.3	11.0	12.1	10.0	7.2
Illegitimate opportunities less inclusive (0–18)	11.4	9.5	8.2	9.0	6.7	3.5
Adult power and helpfulness (0–8)	4.5	5.6	6.2	4.7	5.6	7.4

[a] Figures in parentheses indicate the possible range for each score.

[b] Ns vary slightly for some scores, due to nonresponse. Scores are based in each case on the number of boys who actually gave meaningful responses.

very deviant individuals (Gordon et al., 1963). Note, however, that *within* racial categories, perception of illegitimate opportunities does order the groups according to official delinquency rates.

Official delinquency rates measure the hypothesized dependent variables only in a very gross sense. The gang-nongang distinction probably measures participation in delinquent subcultural activity, and adding the middle-class–lower-class division permits a test of the theory in terms somewhat broader than it was originally set forth. Here the theory holds up well: gang boys of both races perceive greater restrictions on legitimate opportunities than do nongang boys in the same neighborhoods or middle-class

TABLE 2.3. MEAN OPPORTUNITY STRUCTURE SCORES KNOWN TO THE
POLICE, BY RACE, CLASS, AND GANG STATUS [a]

Legitimate Educational and Occupational Opportunities (0 to 22)	Perception of Illegitimate Opportunities (less inclusive; 0 to 18)	Perception of Adult Power and Helpfulness (0 to 8)	Total Opportunities Score [b] (−18 to 30)	Mean Number of Offenses Known to Police (per boy)
NG (9.0)	NG (11.4)	NG (4.5)	NG (2.1)	NG (3.14)
WG (9.3)	NLC (9.5)	WG (4.7)	WG (5.0)	WG (2.73)
NLC (11.0)	WG (9.0)	NLC (5.6)	NLC (7.1)	NLC (0.47)
WLC (13.7)	NMC (8.2)	WLC (5.6)	WLC (12.6)	WLC (0.31)
NMC (15.6)	WLC (6.7)	NMC (6.2)	NMC (13.6)	NMC (0.06)
WMC (20.2)	WMC (3.5)	WMC (7.4)	WMC (24.1)	WMC (0.02)

[a] NG stands for Negro gang members, NLC for Negro lower-class boys, and so on.

[b] Total Opportunities Score is designed to reflect both legitimate and illegitimate pressures toward delinquency. It is obtained by adding together legitimate educational and occupational opportunities and adult power and helpfulness scores, and from this sum subtracting illegitimate opportunity scores. Hence it should be negatively correlated with delinquency.

boys. Thus, the *negative* pressure toward deviance is greater for gang boys. Within each racial group, gang boys perceive better illegitimate opportunities; hence the greater "pull" toward deviance. While perceived adult power and helpfulness, combined, rank the groups very much as do official delinquency rates, adult power alone turns out, as predicted, to be negatively related to delinquency, while helpfulness, which may be exercised by carriers of criminal as well as noncriminal values, is related inconsistently to delinquency among Negro boys.

Adult power and helpfulness are both hypothesized by Cloward and Ohlin to be negatively related to the emergence and maintenance of conflict subcultures. "The term that the bopper uses most frequently to characterize his relationships with adults is 'weak'. . . . He views himself as isolated and the adult world as indifferent. The commitments of adults are to their own interests and not to his. Their explanations of why he should behave differently are 'weak,' as are their efforts to help him" (Cloward and Ohlin, 1960: 24–25). This description holds up well with respect to "clout." Gang boys score lower than the others and Negro gang boys—by far our most conflict oriented [9]—score lowest of all. But helpfulness scores are compara-

[9] For documentation, see Short et al. (1963). It was in large part because they were involved in gang fighting that most of the Negro gangs received the attention of newspapers, police, and the

tively high for all groups, and they are lowest for the less conflict-oriented white gang boys.[10]

Differences between nongang and gang boys on both scores are sufficient to suggest that these factors are important in selection for gang membership, though their relation to a particular type of delinquent subculture—conflict—is inconsistent with the theory. The previously noted higher illegitimate opportunity scores registered by the Negro boys are also inconsistent, but the greater visibility and availability of petty criminal activities in lower-class Negro communities may account for this. Similarly, the comparatively low Negro middle-class scores on clout and helpfulness are consistent with Frazier's descriptions of the superficial show put on by Negro middle-class "society," which he regards as a somewhat futile attempt to compensate for status insecurities relative to whites (Frazier, 1962).

The hypothesis that perceived adult power is inversely related to gang conflict is essentially a social control argument. But helpfulness, when exercised by illegitimate adults, may be conducive to involvement in a criminal subculture. To investigate this possibility, we examined the relation *between* perceptions of various types of opportunities.

The Relation Between Legitimate and Illegitimate Opportunities

The product-moment correlations between opportunity scores, for all boys and for gang boys only, by race, are in Table 2.4. Legitimate opportunity scores tend to be positively correlated with one another, as are illegitimate opportunity scores, and between legitimate and illegitimate scores correlations are negative. There are exceptions to this general pattern, however; for example, perceptions of legitimate educational and occupational opportunities are significantly correlated for all groups except white gang boys. The

---

Program for Detached Workers with which this research program was associated. Close observation of the gangs over periods ranging from several months to more than three years suggests that nearly all the Negro gangs had at one time been more involved in "conflict subcultures" than had any of the white gangs. Finally, detailed analysis of behavior ratings by detached workers indicates greater conflict involvement by Negro than white gangs.

[10] These findings are consistent with boys' ratings of a series of adult roles in the same interview. See Short et al. (1964).

TABLE 2.4. CORRELATIONS AMONG OPPORTUNITY STRUCTURE SCORES, BY RACE[a]

	Legitimate Educational		Legitimate Occupational		Adult Clout		Adult Helpfulness		Criminal, Noncriminal Integration		Criminal Learning Opportunities		Visibility of Criminal Careers		Criminal Opportunities Elite (less inclusive)		Criminal Opportunities Elite (inclusive)	
	W[b]	N[c]	W	N	W	N	W	N	W	N	W	N	W	N	W	N	W	N
Legitimate educational	1.00		.48	.38	.45	.34	.35	.27	-.36	-.17	-.49	-.22	-.42	-.23	-.27	-.13	-.06	-.03
Legitimate occupational	.13	.34	1.00		.42	.35	.28	.28	-.26	-.32	-.31	-.37	-.26	-.30	-.25	-.23	-.10	-.08
Adult clout	.10	.22	.28	.37	1.00		.29	.29	-.14	-.25	-.13	-.23	-.19	-.23	.04	-.01	.10	.05
Adult helpfulness	.23	.32	.23	.35	.19	.32	1.00		-.23	-.26	-.19	-.15	-.26	-.14	-.27	-.21	-.19	-.13
Criminal, noncriminal integration	-.26	-.19	-.18	-.33	.05	-.23	-.27	-.29	1.00		.49	.51	.37	.32	.46	.32	.20	.14
Criminal learning opportunities	-.26	-.20	-.15	-.31	.16	-.22	-.20	-.19	.59	.52	1.00		.54	.43	.52	.27	.19	-.02
Visibility of criminal careers	-.28	-.27	-.17	-.39	.10	-.22	-.34	-.16	.37	.34	.46	.37	1.00		.38	.21	.00	-.14
Criminal opportunities elite (less inclusive)	-.21	-.18	-.24	-.25	.24	-.04	-.32	-.24	.60	.31	.64	.29	.49	.23	1.00		.73	.70
Criminal opportunities elite (inclusive)	-.03	-.05	-.15	-.07	.19	.01	-.23	-.15	.32	.08	.41	-.03	.16	-.10	.74	.66	1.00	

[a] Italicized coefficients below the diagonal represent gang boys only; coefficients above the diagonal represent all boys, including gang members.

[b] White: $p < .05 = .13$ (all boys) and .21 (gang boys); $p < .01 = .18$ (all boys) and .27 (gang boys).

[c] Negro: $p < .05 = .11$ (all boys) and .14 (gang boys); $p < .01 = .14$ (all boys) and .18 (gang boys).

low correlation in the latter group suggests that perceptions of legitimate educational and occupational opportunities often are not mutually reinforcing.

The relation between adult power and perceived illegitimate opportunities suggests greater "integration" of the carriers of criminal and conventional values in white neighborhoods: the correlations are low but *positive* among white boys, and *negative* among Negroes. For both races, adult helpfulness is negatively correlated with illegitimate opportunities.

Correlations between perceived illegitimate opportunities are higher for white boys, particularly those involving the criminal *elite* measures. Thus, while white boys perceive illegitimate opportunities as less available than do Negro boys, "integration" as we have operationalized it is actually more characteristic of white than Negro gang areas. Negro gang boys perceive illegitimate opportunities as relatively open, but they tend to perceive illegitimate adults as neither powerful nor helpful. White gang boys, however, tend to perceive illegitimate adults as powerful but not very helpful. A similar pattern occurs in data from another section of the interview, in which boys were asked to indicate four characteristics of several adult roles in their local areas. Among Negro gang boys, 38 percent, compared with 53 percent of white gang boys, felt that adults making money illegally have "a lot of clout," while only about one boy in five in both racial groups felt that such adults are "interested in the problem of teen-agers." Lower-class nongang boys consistently rated legitimate adult roles higher than gang boys did on scales reflecting their interest in and degree of contact with teen-agers, their "clout," and the extent to which they are considered "right guys." [11]

In the present analysis, the relations between various opportunity scores reveal no significant or consistent differences that explain behavioral differences between gang and nongang lower-class boys. The most striking differences are between middle-class Negro boys and all other groups in the correlation between adult helpfulness and perceived elite criminal opportunities. This correlation is positive for both elite scores (.34 for the more inclusive measure, .20 for the less inclusive measure) among Negro middle-class boys, but both correlations are negative in all other groups. Adult clout was also correlated positively with the two elite criminal opportunity scores among Negro middle-class boys (.22 and .30), and among white gang members, but negatively in the other groups. Again, reference to Frazier's perceptive analysis is pertinent (Frazier, 1962).

[11] A more detailed report of these data is in Short et al. (1964).

Summary

Legitimate occupational opportunities are perceived as available less often by gang than by nongang boys, and most often by middle-class boys. White boys are more likely than Negro boys to perceive such opportunities as available, in each of the strata examined. With respect to legitimate educational opportunities, the same pattern occurs, except that the racial difference does not occur among gang boys. Race and class-by-gang-status gradients are both present concerning adult clout, but not perceived adult helpfulness, among lower-class boys. These data are consistent with the apparently greater *protest* orientation of white as compared with Negro gang boys (Short et al., 1963; Short and Strodtbeck, 1965: ch. 5). Gradients with racial groups are consistent with inferences from the Cloward and Ohlin theory.

Differences in perceptions of illegitimate opportunities reverse most of those found for legitimate opportunities, as expected. These differences are inconsistent with the greater conflict orientation of Negro gang boys, but when adult clout is correlated with criminal opportunity scores, and other data are introduced, "integration" of criminal opportunities and between criminal and legitimate opportunities is greater for white than for Negro boys. Even for white gang boys, however, the negative correlations between adult helpfulness and criminal opportunity scores, and their small positive correlations with adult clout suggest a low degree of "integration" between the carriers of criminal and conventional values.[12]

The logic of the theory clearly presumes that perceptions of opportunities *precede* involvement in delinquency, while our data reflect perceptions "after the fact." We cannot fully resolve this problem. Evidence concerning the relation of *individual* gang boys' perceptions of opportunities to their behavior as individuals, is relevant, however, and its mention permits brief discussion of the somewhat different causal model that has emerged from the larger study of which this paper is a partial report. Correlations between opportunity scores and theoretically relevant behavior scores for individual gang boys are low. For example, *conflict factor scores,* consisting of a combination of individual and gang fighting (with and without weapons), assault, and carrying concealed weapons, are not systematically related to per-

---

[12] This perhaps explains why we had such difficulty locating criminal gangs. See Short and Strodtbeck (1965: chaps. 1, 9).

ceptions of either legitimate or illegitimate opportunity scores. That is, boys with high scores do not have lower opportunity scores.[13] It seems unlikely, therefore, that data reported in this paper reflect the boys' efforts to rationalize delinquent behavior by "blaming" the lack of opportunity. Although this does not solve the problem of temporal order, it is presumptive evidence against an alternative interpretation based on the assumption of "after-the-fact" (of delinquency or gang membership) influences on perception.

Our argument is not that the latter are unimportant. Other data from our study suggest that social structure influences the development of ethnic, class, life-cycle, and perhaps "delinquent" subcultures with relatively distinctive content. Social structural theories are therefore appropriately applied to the social distribution of many phenomena—to delinquency "rates" rather than to individual episodes or degrees of involvement in delinquency. It is to the question of "rates" or the social distribution of delinquent subcultures, that the Cloward and Ohlin theory is addressed—appropriately. To account for selection into subcultures—into gang membership, for example—from the youngsters available, and for individual behavior within the context of a subculture, requires reference to "levels" of explanation other than social structure.[14] We have found it necessary to invoke personality level variables, as Inkeles (1959) suggested,[15] and *group process* considerations, to explain delinquent behavior *within* our gangs.[16] The give and take of interaction among gang boys, and between gang boys and others; a variety of role relations within the gang and status considerations related to these roles and to opportunities present in situations of the moment—these are prime determinants of what happens in the gang, of who becomes involved in what type of behavior, and with whom.[17] This *level* of explanation "washes out" variations in perceptions of opportunities related to social structure as a major determinant of individuals' behavior in the gang context.

[13] Derivation of the scores is detailed in Short et al. (1963). Full presentation of the data concerning individual opportunity perception and behavior is beyond the scope of this paper.

[14] See David Bordua's (1960, 1961) critique of social structural theories in this regard. See also Short and Strodtbeck (1965); and Short, "Social Structure" (1964b).

[15] From the present study, see Gordon and Short (1965).

[16] See, especially, Short, "Gang Delinquency" (1964b); Short and Strodtbeck (1963; 1964; 1965); and Strodtbeck and Short (1964).

[17] The point is made in more general theoretical terms in Cohen (1966).

References

Bordua, David. 1960. "Sociological Theories and Their Implications for Juvenile Delinquency." In Children's Bureau, *Juvenile Delinquency: Facts and Facets,* No. 2. Washington, D.C.: U.S. Government Printing Office.

1961. "Delinquent Subcultures: Sociological Interpretations of Gang Delinquency," *Annals of the American Academy of Political and Social Science* 338 (November).

Cloward, Richard A. 1959. "Illegitimate Means, Anomie, and Deviant Behavior," *American Sociological Review* 24 (April): 164–76.

Cloward, Richard A. and Lloyd E. Ohlin. 1960. *Delinquency and Opportunity: A Theory of Delinquent Gangs.* New York: Free Press of Glencoe.

Cohen, Albert K. 1966. "The Sociology of the Deviant Act: Anomie Theory and Beyond," *American Sociological Review* 30 (February).

Elliott, Delbert S. 1962. "Delinquency and Perceived Opportunity," *Sociology and Inquiry* 32 (Spring): 216–17.

Frazier, E. Franklin. 1962. *Black Bourgeoisie.* New York: Collier.

Freedman, Jonathan and Ramon Rivera. 1962. "Education, Social Class, and Patterns of Delinquency." Paper read at the annual meetings of the American Sociological Association.

Gordon, Robert A., James F. Short, Jr., Desmond S. Cartwright, and Fred L. Strodtbeck. 1963. "Values and Gang Delinquency: A Study of Street Corner Groups," *American Journal of Sociology* 69 (September): 109–28.

Gordon, Robert A. and James F. Short, Jr. 1968. "Social Level, Social Disability, and Gang Interaction." In James F. Short, Jr. and Fred L. Strodtbeck (eds.), *Group Process and Gang Delinquency.* Chicago: University of Chicago Press.

Inkeles, Alex. 1959. "Personality and Social Structure." In Robert K. Merton, Leonard Broom, and Leonard S. Cottrell, Jr. (eds.), *Sociology Today.* New York: Basic Books.

Merton, Robert K. 1958. *Social Theory and Social Structure.* Rev. ed. New York: Free Press of Glencoe.

Short, James F., Jr. 1963. "Street Corner Groups and Patterns of Delinquency: A Progress Report," *American Catholic Sociological Review* 28 (June): 411–28.

1964a. "Gang Delinquency and Anomie." In Marshall B. Clinard (ed.), *Deviant Behavior and Anomie*. New York: Free Press of Glencoe.

1964b. "Social Structure and Group Process in Explanations of Gang Delinquency." Paper read at the Fifth Social Psychology Symposium, University of Oklahoma.

Short, James F., Jr., Ramon Rivera, and Harvey Marshall. 1964. "Adult-Adolescent Relations and Gang Delinquency: An Empirical Report," *Pacific Sociological Review* (Fall).

Short, James, F., Jr. and Fred L. Strodtbeck. 1963. "The Response of Gang Leaders to Status Threats: An Observation of Group Process and Delinquent Behavior," *American Journal of Sociology* 68 (March): 571–79.

1964. "Why Gangs Fight," *Trans-Action* 1 (September–October): 25–29.

1965. *Group Process and Gang Delinquency*. Chicago, University of Chicago Press.

Short, James F. Jr., Fred L. Strodtbeck, and Desmond Cartwright. 1962. "A Strategy for Utilizing Research Dilemmas: A Case from the Study of Parenthood in a Street Corner Gang," *Sociological Inquiry* 32 (Spring): 185–202.

Short, James F., Jr., Ray A. Tennyson, and Kenneth I. Howard. 1963. "Behavior Dimensions of Gang Delinquency," *American Sociological Review* 28 (June): 411–28.

Schrag, Clarence. 1962. "Delinquency and Opportunity: Analysis of a Theory," *Sociology and Social Research* 46 (January): 167–75.

Strodtbeck, Fred L. and James F. Short, Jr. 1964. "Aleatory Risks v. Short-Run Hedonism in Explanation of Gang Action," *Social Problems* (Fall).

Wise, John M. 1962. "A Comparison of Sources of Data as Indexes of Delinquent Behavior." M.A. thesis, University of Chicago.

3

Deviance, Deterrence,

and Knowledge of Sanctions

RICHARD L. HENSHEL
AND SANDRA H. CAREY

It will be our thesis that empirical investigation of sanctions and deterrence has unfortunately neglected an essential point, so central that its absence calls into question the conclusions of most work that has been done— although for some the data could be reanalyzed. The point referred to is that of public knowledge. People are deterred (if at all) by what they *think* is the certainty of capture, and by what they *think* is the severity of the sanction, not by what the certainty and severity is objectively. It is our purpose to describe this deficiency in research and to explore its theoretical basis.[1] Strangely, many theoretical discussions of deterrence have correctly discerned the problem, yet their insight has rarely, and only very recently, been translated or incorporated into empirical inquiry. Even more strangely, other empirical work in criminology has explicitly demonstrated the shaky basis of most extant deterrence research, yet the two traditions have but rarely come into contact. The fact that this has occurred not only within the same discipline but even within a single "speciality" raises interesting questions of communication which transcend criminology.

To state the problem forthrightly, most empirical research on deterrence

We are indebted to Theodore Chiricos, David Edwards, Walter Firey, Jack Gibbs, and Gordon Waldo for their helpful suggestions. Earlier versions of this paper were presented at the Eastern Sociological Society meetings, Boston, April 1972, and at the Interamerican Congress of the American Society of Criminology, Caracas, November 1972.

[1] It is instructive that many of the earlier lists of "unfinished problems" in the study of deterrence (e.g., Cushing, 1969; Morris and Zimring, 1969; Tittle, 1969a) neglected this central issue of knowledge and perception. More recent lists have begun to include it.

has been done in ways which do not permit the kinds of interpretation which have been made. Even after decades of study, after position statements by an impressive array of experts (Ehrmann, 1962), we still have no valid knowledge respecting the efficacy of capital punishment. (This of course does not reflect upon the arbitrariness of death sentences, nor on the other arguments for abolition which persuaded the Supreme Court.) The same is true *a fortiori* of the more recently studied questions of the deterrent efficacy of other sanctions. Inasmuch as important policy decisions may be based on studies of deterrence, and inasmuch as sociological theory ultimately takes them into account, the conceptual error becomes of more than marginal importance.[2] These are strong statements; naturally they require justification.

The effects of sanctions on deviant conduct has for decades been a central question of sociology. From time to time American social science has manifested extreme skepticism respecting the efficacy of legal punishment upon the pervasiveness of crime, maintaining that deterrent doctrines are outmoded and totally out of place in modern society.[3] Punishment has been seen as a barbaric hangover from primitive beliefs in *lex talionis,* an eye for an eye—for example, Menninger's *The Crime of Punishment* (1968). Occasionally reference was made to the certainty and swiftness of sanctions, rarely during this period to severity as a deterrent factor. More recently, however, and commendably, there has been increased resistance to this facile approach, and serious challenge to the beliefs on which it was based. The theoretical hiatus which results, when, uniquely among forms of social control, the legal sanction alone is denied all efficacy, has been noted. What was, for long, a polemical issue has thus come to be identified as a legitimate topic for empirical examination.

The history of empirical research on deterrence may be viewed as progressing through a number of stages with increasing sophistication—a process which, as the opening paragraph signifies, is by no means terminated. Subsequent to the preinvestigation era was a period of exclusive concentration on the death penalty. Of the half-dozen empirical studies of general deterrence prior to 1960, virtually all pertained to capital punishment.

[2] As an example of the policy component, one of the central tasks of the Law Reform Commission of Canada (a permanent official body) is to evaluate the effects of laws, including the deterrent and rehabilitative consequences of the criminal law.

[3] See summaries of this trend in Ball (1955), Gibbs (1966), and Toby (1964).

These are summarized in Sutherland and Cressey (1970: 330–336). In the past decade this trickle has swollen into a torrent of empirical effort, principally located in journal articles and presented papers. Writers have called attention to the dangers inherent in rejecting so broad a doctrine purely on the lack of proven deterrent differential between capital punishment (when actually applied) and life imprisonment, and have begun to direct their attention to other deterrent situations, e.g., such seemingly simple matters as severity of parking fines.[4] The phase was also marked by increasingly sophisticated measures of severity and certainty, but not by an overwhelming increase in *theoretical* sophistication.

Theoretically, deterrence has a distinctive meaning which has become increasingly significant in the research effort. The importance of considering the penalties actually imposed rather than the legal possibilities has received increasing attention, beginning with Gibbs (1968) and culminating in the careful attention to this consideration in Jayewardene (1972). And although this paper is among the first to examine in detail the importance of ascertaining what people *think* the sanctioning outcomes are, there are certain anticipations going back to Ball (1955) among modern criminologists, and in other ways back to Bentham (1843) and Tarde (1912).

Deterministic Man versus the Perfectly Informed Hedonist: An Unconscious Resurrection

Deterrence studies have taken the form of comparing crime rates (dependent variable) under varying conditions of severity, certainty, and celerity of the legal sanction.[5] Such studies indeed have the advantage of accessible data and a relatively high level of measurement (Cushing, 1969: 207). Their critical weakness is that they ignore the central theoretical conception that deterrence is in the mind of the beholder. Deterrence, when and if it exists, is a

---

[4] See, e.g., Chambliss (1966) and Beutel (1957). The possibility of "thresholds" has also now been raised. It may be observed that the denial of general deterrent efficacy also runs counter to the concept of vicarious reinforcement in theories of learning. The criticisms of earlier arguments and studies are summarized succinctly in Gibbs (1968) and Tittle (1969b).

[5] For a survey of alternative measures of these factors see Kuykendall (1969: ch. 2).

state of mind.[6] If the mind in question holds no cognition relative to the punitive sanction (i.e., it has not been heard of, believed in, or felt applicable), then the *objective existence* of sanctions with specified levels of severity, certainty, and swiftness is of no consequence—deterrence in the particular instance cannot exist for this person, but not because deterrence as a general phenomenon does not exist. By concentrating on the objective properties of the legal sanction, studies have presumed that these objective properties are actually correctly conceptualized by the people, or at least by a sufficient number of them; or, at least, that errors are randomly distributed. These assumptions, as shall be seen, may be very unlikely indeed.

Modern opponents of punishment for long have adopted a deterministic, mechanistic model of man. Man did as he had been "programmed" by his genes, experiences, and/or associations. Punishment was therefore ineffective; and, being of no effect, it was barbarous. In contrast, the more recent empirical approach to deterrence has, implicitly or explicitly, put this assumption to the test. But in so doing it has only contrasted the viability of two *extreme* models of man: the man as mechanism, depicted above, versus the completely free, rational actor. We thus have a robot pitted against "rational man," with no testing of yet a third posture: a conception of man as *goal-seeking but not information-seeking*. Such a man might indeed be swayed by severity of punishment, for example, but only if he "stumbled" on the news, and only if he believed it where it appeared to contradict, e.g., television drama. That this hypothetical man bears a suspicious resemblance to what much sociological literature depicts is a severe indictment of deterrence research, for investigators in deterrence have virtually ignored him.[7] If

---

[6] This is not to say that sanctions necessarily have no effects other than deterrence. Venerable theories have related the application of formal sanctions to the strength of the normative order (what is sometimes called their "general prevention" function). It should be noted that in this chapter we will exclusively be concerned with general deterrence—the influence of sanctions on members of society at large—and not with special deterrence—the influence on individuals actually punished. For excellent treatment of these and other important distinctions, see Morris and Zimring (1969).

[7] As Gibbs notes (1968: 518, 530), we do not yet have an updated restatement of the theory of deterrence, although this situation may at last be changing. See Zimring and Hawkins (1973). Classical doctrines are stated in terms of ideas such as "free will" and "indeterminism," which are grossly out of place in contemporary social science. Given this hiatus, it is no wonder that modern researchers have taken the classical doctrine at face value and thus contrasted only two extreme conceptions of man. Yet deterrence can also be formulated in terms of modern reinforcement theory—a position "uncontaminated" by association with indeterminism.

the earliest criminologists and penologists assumed a calculating, hedonistic man, and if their reformist replacements assumed a preprogrammed, non-calculating man, the new penal positivists, even while rationally contrasting the two above, have taken the perfectly informed man, or at least his cousin the adequately informed man, as the only alternative to mechanism. This is not a consciously chosen position, but one implicit in their entire mode of research.[8] In many respects, the specific models of man chosen for contrast delimit the possible conclusions (Kunkel and Garrick, 1969).

It is certainly possible that the difference in severity between execution and life imprisonment really does not deter people from crimes which may legally result in capital punishment. (Homicide in particular is among the crimes least subject to influence by any known means.) What is essential is that this is not presently known, and indeed is not knowable, simply by comparing capital crime rates across jurisdictions that do or do not have capital punishment, for it may be that potential offenders do not know the law for capital-type crimes in their jurisdiction but would act in accordance with severity if they knew it. Nor is it to be ascertained by comparisons across time, in which either executions have occurred or laws changed, unless it can be shown that the public was aware of such changes. The extent of *public awareness* of sanctioning outcomes has been neglected in studies of the efficacy of capital punishment—although not, as will be seen, by criminologists with other concerns. What if, as seems intuitively likely, the residents of two adjoining states, one of which provided capital punishment, were not aware of the true state of their laws? What if the survey were to reveal that public belief about the existence of the death penalty in a given jurisdiction was virtually independent of whether or not it actually existed therein?[9] Substantial independence of objective reality and public belief,

---

[8] Nelson (1966: 317) points out that a similar problem confronts the traditional economist. He suggests replacing rational economic man with rational but ill-informed man. Every man has truely the best information about his own utilities, but experts have far better information about the usual consequences of acts. "The assumption that an individual always has the maximum information relevant to decisions about his consumption is an exceedingly strong assumption. It is no wonder that non-economists almost universally reject it."

[9] This is not implausible: if the average adult watches hours of television drama each week, if television programs deal with death beyond the point of monotony, and if they invariably associate murder (the typical crime displayed) with the death penalty, how well, indeed, does the citizen know the laws of his locale? As Van den Haag (1969: 146) puts it: "Contrary to what

while definitely not an affirmation of deterrent efficacy, would necessitate a complete reanalysis (where possible) of studies which have failed to consider their implicit assumption of public awareness, and would in addition require new research based on the correct problem of whether the people's *assumptions* about the existence and application of a particular penalty may deter them from the crime it is prescribed for.

The Importance of Public Knowledge

Examining criminal sanctions in general, it must be asked whether in point of fact the public knows the sanctions applicable under the law. To what extent is the objective likelihood of receiving a sentence of given severity for a given act correctly perceived? What of perceptions of the probable certainty and swiftness of these sanctions, or of perceptions of "effective" sentence length—e.g., after parole is included? Evidence from a separate research tradition indicates that the public is in fact terribly ignorant, and typically in error, on such matters. *Nor are the large errors necessarily random in nature.* It is important—vital, in fact—that public ignorance be more than a mere hypothesis, however plausible. For as data emerge which show such ignorance, the burden of proof shifts and it now becomes incumbent upon those deterrence researchers utilizing one of the traditional approaches to demonstrate that, in spite of widespread ignorance, *there remain substantial residual differences in perception* between different times or jurisdictions. Otherwise, a failure to detect a deterrent effect ceases to illustrate inefficacy of the given sanctioning differential itself and becomes merely the outcome to be *expected* where public anticipations are not systematically different.

Perhaps the most important study of public knowledge has been conducted in California by the Assembly Committee on Criminal Procedure (1968) [Ed. note: reprinted in this volume], which is quite convincing in its

---

Professor Sellin et al. seem to presume, I doubt that offenders are aware of the absence or presence of the death penalty state by state or period by period." It would be instructive (if no longer possible) to determine whether a single jurisdiction existed in the United States at the time of Sellin's studies in which the majority of adults did not believe that the death penalty existed in their locale. As we shall see, knowledge about sanctions is indeed low.

demonstration of the public's ignorance—both of existing severity and of recent changes in severity.

A range of 21 percent to 49 percent of the respondents had complete ignorance or were unable to even guess the maximum sentences for these crimes. Furthermore; even among those who made an estimate, the percent of correct responses ranged from 8 to 39 percent. If one combined the number of correct responses into a single index score of accuracy, no one person correctly answered all 11 questions about penalties, while, at the other extreme, 69 percent of the respondents answered 3 or less items correctly (1968: 12–13). [Italics deleted]

It is significant that perceptual errors were not "unbiased"; a general tendency to *underestimate* penalties became clear (1968: 13). In the study's own words (1968: 17), "They [Californians surveyed] were extremely ignorant about penalties for crimes . . . the general public simply *does not know* what the penalties are." Interestingly, while the investigation uncovers ample evidence to require gross reanalysis for most existing deterrence studies, the investigators believe instead that they have demonstrated the general inefficacy of punishment because only convicts apparently know anything at all about the magnitude of the sanctions (1968: 13, 15). But of course they would have demonstrated this only if the surveyed individuals were incapable of learning any more than they knew, which no one wishes to claim. For that matter, many Californians may be deterred by their misconceptions of the law—in Thomas' celebrated phrase, situations defined as real are real in their consequences.

Not only were the Californians surveyed ignorant of the nature of recent changes in criminal law, they were on the whole unaware that alterations of any sort had been made (1968: 13). Similarly, Walker and Argyle (1964) found some 76 percent of an English sample were unaware that the law against attempted suicide had been abolished. A poll in Nebraska, reported in Zimring and Hawkins (1973: 143), found 41 percent of adult males thought that the state's long-standing bad-check law would not apply if restitution was made.[10] Similar findings of public ignorance with respect to certainty of apprehension are briefly reported in Jensen (1969: 200).

Numerous traditions within sociology have explored factors which would predict public ignorance of these matters. Requirements of space prohibit extended treatment, but sociologists have devoted considerable atten-

---

[10] The proportion of public error may be exaggerated somewhat because of low enforcement level.

tion to difficulties in getting correct information—bureaucratic secretiveness, complexity of legal machinery, inadequacies of criminal statistics, protection of information (e.g., in juvenile court), the free-press–fair-trial clash, and selective coverage by the press.[11] The distribution of knowledge in society is often viewed as structured in terms of individual relevances (Berger and Luckmann, 1966: 45). Sanctioning outcomes are not typically part of the pragmatically necessary knowledge of men in modern society, with the possible exception of professional criminals and criminal lawyers. Equally important is the ease of obtaining *erroneous* information via fictional drama. Thus the hours spent by the average television viewer before the screen, as well as the frequency (and breakdown) of various incidents of violence have

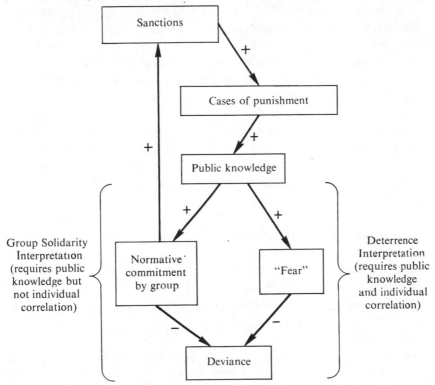

Figure 3.1 Relations of Sanctions and Deviance

[11] On this last factor, it is interesting that at the time of the survey by McCafferty (1954: 36–41), four states *prohibited* publication of any official statement on an execution with details other than that a prisoner had been executed according to law.

been counted on numerous occasions. It is well known that the network system of television produces reliance on "formula plots," of which the murder trial with lurking death penalty has been a stock-in-trade. It is no wonder that public ignorance of sanctioning outcomes is all but ubiquitous under such constraints. What might be a source of wonder is that the above analytical traditions could exist alongside efforts in deterrence research with so little stimulation to the latter.[12]

At this point we must examine precisely why objective sanctioning differences without variations in rates of deviance do not preclude the *possibility* that the sanctioning differential might reduce the proscribed behavior. A complete answer to this question would require a general theory of punishment, but we might begin by demonstrating the central position of public knowledge in the relation between sanctions and deviance. Figure 3.1 depicts the alternative explanations for a negative relation between formal sanctions and deviance. (It should be distinguished from an overall analysis of the inhibitors of deviance. See Blake and Davis, 1964: 477–481, for an attempt at this task.) The two traditional explanations are deterrence and consensual reaffirmation of the norm. Deterrence, stated very crudely, assumes that cases of punishment produce fear of the consequences in would-be offenders, leading to a decline in deviance. The essentially Durkheimian notion of strengthened consensus assumes that cases of punishment primarily serve as reaffirmation of the community norms, but extensions propose that this thereby mobilizes the informal social disapproval which may itself diminish deviance (Coser, 1967; see also Eirkson, 1966: 3–4.) [13] The two conceptions thus provide alternative (nonconflicting) bases for the efficacy of punishment as a reducer of crime. Both can potentially explain the negative relation between sanctioning and deviance, and are the *only* positions which do so.[14] This is significant since *both positions tacitly require public knowledge.* Public knowledge (or ignorance) thus emerges as the

---

[12] It is interesting that classical legal philosophers were frequently cognizant of the importance of public knowledge.

[13] Since knowledge of deviations may tend *per se* to lower normative consensus, it is arguable whether punishment actually heightens normative consensus beyond previous levels or merely restores it to the status quo ante. In spite of the age of Durkheim's interpretation there have been few efforts at verification. Exploratory efforts are presented in Jensen (1969), Walker and Argyle (1964), and Salem and Bowers (1969).

[14] The doctrine of disablement or incapacitation, although typically punishing in consequences, actually reflects a *mistrust* of the efficacy of deterrence as a means to reduce crime.

great, virtually unexamined, intervening variable, irrespective of which candidate interpretation is considered.[15]

Public Knowledge and Deterrence Research

It is clear that most existing studies of deterrence have unconsciously related differences in objective sanctions to corresponding objective crime rates, without sufficient examination of the deterrence concept to recognize the hidden intermediary. Of course, if the *only* objective of a given study is to find out whether, in the particular instances examined, objective sanctioning differences correspond to objective differences in the crime rate, this can indeed by ascertained. Examination of the discourse, however, reveals that most if not all deterrence research is undertaken to contribute more than a mere historical account of a specific relationship: researchers intend for their analysis to become part of a growing set of generalizations relating to the broad questions of deterrence. There is no need to display exegetical skill here; such statements are ubiquitous in the deterrence literature, and we shall refrain from singling out individual authors. Tentative judgments have been passed on the efficacy of general deterrence, on the relative potency of severity and certainty, on their interaction, and on possible boundaries and thresholds.[16]

Unfortunately, it is only where public knowledge is reasonably accurate

[15] This chapter emphasizes deterrence, but most of the comments respecting public knowledge apply as well to collective reaffirmation. Though similar in their dependence upon public knowledge, the two differ in their amenability to *ecological correlation*. Whereas the *same* individual must be knowledgeable and restrained under a deterrence conception, the solidarity approach could accept knowledge and constraint in *different persons*. See Waldo and Chiricos (1972) for a discussion of similar issues.

[16] Some readers have felt that these researchers were really not unaware of this failing of their research but simply were determined to get on with the job with the tools at hand. The literature has been specifically scrutinized for signs of such recognition, but it is simply not encountered in the empirical work on deterrence until circa 1970 or 1971, even among writers who scrupulously enumerated the *other* shortcomings of their research. Even those earlier workers who used a perceptual approach did not analyze the inherent drawbacks of the "objective" method. Historically, the senior writer, presenting a guest seminar on these drawbacks at Florida State University in the spring of 1971, was surprised to find that Theodore Chiricos and Gordon Waldo were independently developing the same idea.

(and errors more or less randomly distributed) that the efficacy of objective sanctioning differences can be correctly appraised by the standard, traditional research procedure (Chiricos and Waldo, 1970: 215). The possibly confounding effect of widespread ignorance is still not generally appreciated, and public awareness has not therefore been ascertained in most existing studies of deterrence. In view of the fact that separate and distinct studies of public awareness of sanctioning outcomes find it to be discouragingly low, the validity of the reported findings with respect to deterrent efficacy is open to serious challenge.

Recognition of the importance of the public awareness dimension has slowly moved forward in recent years, over a decade after the emergence of empirical studies. The factor is acknowledged but not explored in the work of the Assembly Committee (1968), Chiricos and Waldo (1970: 215), Morris and Zimring (1969: 145), Van den Haag (1969: 146), and Wilkins (1969: 17–18, 160–161). Hints are found in Tittle (1969b: 422), Crowther (1969: 153), and Gibbs (1968: 530). With the exception of the classic paper by Ball (1955), virtually all recognition within modern criminology is quite recent. Most recently, Zimring and Hawkins (1973) treat the matter theoretically, and Waldo and Chiricos (1972) treat it empirically.

But none of these creative efforts is as "tough" on earlier research as seems to be necessary. In a spirit of cohesiveness, some even pay homage to the conclusions of their predecessors. Homage to the empirical emphasis which these pioneers displayed is well deserved, but acquiescence to their conclusions is inappropriate. Logic would seem to require the position that most earlier deterrence research must either be reanalyzed (where this is still possible), interpreted far more narrowly than its originators intended, or, reluctantly, in some cases disregarded. The analysts' implicit models of man have been too long and too seriously ignored.

Reassessment and Future Investigations

Two issues now confront the analyst. First, how must existing studies be evaluated? Second, how should future studies of deterrence proceed? With respect to evaluations of existing studies, quite obviously we do not intend in the limited space available to weigh previous work on all theoretical and methodological criteria. It is the status of existing studies in the light of our specific conceptual analysis—in terms both of logical status and from the standpoint of policy implications—which must be considered. It might be implied from comments to this point that all findings not providing data on the state of relevant public knowledge are, of necessity, unsound. But studies of deterrence have been of sufficient variety that a blanket appraisal of this nature seems wholly unwise. In particular, results which do manifest a strong relationship between a sanctioning quality and crime rate may be employable. In a sense this appears to stack the cards in favor of deterrence, but its rationale is based on the apparent tendency of studies which neglect public ignorance to *underestimate* any deterrent effect. Admittedly such an approach has its risks, for we do not know what the inhabitants were actually thinking. But the hypothetical knowledge-states which would lead to erroneously *strong* relationships appear to be unlikely.

We may consider, for example, a hypothetical pair of states, A and B, chosen for research because they differ in objective sanctioning severity. Let us assume state A typically imposes 20 years for an offense and B imposes 10. This difference could be (1) *magnified* in the public consciousness (e.g., inhabitants of A tend to guess 25 years for their own state and those in B guess 5 for theirs); (2) the sanctions conceptualized could differ by about the *true amount;* (3) the objective difference could be *minimized* in the public consciousness (e.g., those in A tend to guess 16 years for it; those in B guess 14 for it); (4) the public could falsely conceive of their respective sanctions as *equivalent* (say, 15 and 15); and (5) they might even *reverse* in their conception the severity difference, so that those in state A guess 10 years and those in state B, 20. Of the possibilities, only a mistaken magnification of the real differences (1) could lead to an erroneously strong deterrent relationship.

It is highly significant that for the severity difference between life imprisonment and execution there is *no* possibility of public ignorance increasing the apparent deterrent effect. Since the society imposes no more severe sanction than death, we in effect put a ceiling on erroneous magnification of sanction difference without a similar restriction on erroneous minimization. Thus the most intensively studied sanctioning difference is also possibly the most vulnerable to the effects of public ignorance.

It is necessary at this point to differentiate the logical status of a finding—or its status for theory construction—from its policy or programmatic status.[17] One hope of deterrence research has traditionally been to influence sanctioning policy through research. This possibility is by no means precluded for the alternative research procedures to be discussed, but with respect to extant investigations it appears largely out of the question. Although the logical status of certain findings may remain acceptable, inasmuch as the state of public knowledge is unknown a finding cannot be used as the basis for policy decisions.[18]

It is clear that new directions must be found in deterrence research. Figure 3.2 is a combined schema which is useful at this point. Across its top are found the elements of the causal chain which seem to be the basis for expectations of deterrent efficacy. (The term "seem to be" is used judiciously, for these elements are typically unstated in contemporary analysis.) Directly below these elements are found the assumptions and measurements of the traditional approach to deterrence research. Presented in this fashion its untenable chain of assumptions is vividly illustrated. The schema also depicts alternative approaches which do not assume excellent public knowledge.

We are left with a number of options for research into the problems of general deterrence. One alternative, diagrammed in Figure 3.2, is most suitable for less severe offenses in which self-reporting of participation under conditions of anonymity may be reasonably trustworthy. In the study by Jensen (1969), for instance, respondents in a sample survey were asked for their impressions of a particular sanctioning outcome (certainty of apprehension) for a number of offenses, and later to anonymously report whether they have ever done these prohibited acts.[19] Similar research, in which both certainty and severity impressions are elicited, is reported by Waldo and Chiricos

[17] We assume here that criminal justice policy based on research would take one of the following forms: (1) sanctions would be tightened should this appear to increase deterrence, but (2) if deterrence is not adversely affected, sanctions would be relaxed. There are, naturally, limits to the realism of these assumptions.

[18] This reasoning follows from the possibility that instances of real deterrence can be produced with inaccurate as well as accurate public perceptions of sanctioning outcomes. Although a statistical relationship might still be establishable and of theoretical significance, the "optimum" policy decision would be impossible to obtain in the absence of data on public knowledge. Of course, data inputs for such decisions are obtainable—e.g., the more severe penalty *as practiced* does not reduce crime below the less severe level. But without knowing the state of public knowledge the *policy meaning* of any such relationship is uninterpretable.

[19] Of course the question arises here of whether respondents held the same perception of sanctioning outcomes at the time of commission. Systematic bias seems unlikely here. Jensen limited reporting to acts committed within the year.

(1972). Minor offenses are the only instances in which such an approach seems feasible.[20] Advantages of this approach, where applicable, stem from its avoidance of untenable assumptions about public knowledge of the sanctions, on the one hand, and avoidance of the pitfalls of ecological correlations on the other.

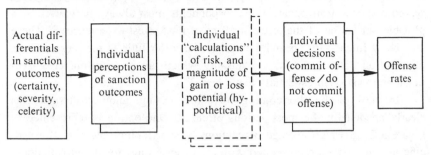

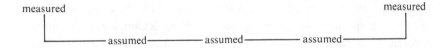

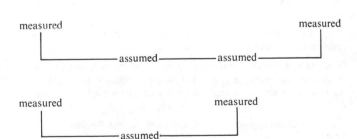

Figure 3.2 Assumptions and Measurements under Traditional and Alternative Approaches to Deterrence Research

[20] The difficulties and biases encountered in self-reporting are well known. See especially Rosenthal and Rosnow (1969) on "evaluation apprehension."

A variation of this alternative has been demonstrated by Claster (1967), also with respect to perception of certainty. In this approach, perceptions of institutionalized offenders were contrasted with those from a noninstitutionalized population. Unfortunately it is difficult if not impossible to isolate for the confined group the perceptions held *before apprehension*. Any observed response from incarcerated respondents must always be viewed as a possible derivation of the arrest itself or of post-arrest experiences.[21] These may be of interest for special deterrence, but offer little to the present focus of attention. The questions of causality which always confront cross-sectional analysis seem especially acute here.[22]

In view of the shortcomings of self-reporting, another alternative is clearly needed for the most serious offenses. One option is represented in Figure 3.2, in which average perceptions of sanctioning outcomes (for specific jurisdictions) are correlated with the offense rates for the jurisdictions. Here, the perceived sanctions are averaged over each jurisdiction, while offense rates for the jurisdiction are obtained from official statistics or, preferably, victimization surveys.[23] This procedure eliminates unwarranted assumptions on the state of public knowledge, and, additionally, reduces reliance on the honesty of respondents. It poses new dilemmas of its own, however, respecting the sampling base and the legitimacy of its form of ecological correlation.

While neglecting public ignorance risks underestimating the correlation between perceived sanctions and behavior, the alternative as described risks overestimating the "individual" correlations.[24] In a sense, then, for studies

[21] Again it is instructive to note that convicts constituted the only social category displaying considerable knowledge of sanctioning outcomes in the California study.

[22] In addition, confined offenders are by no means a random selection of apprehended offenders, themselves probably a biased sample of offenders in general. What effects these potential biases may have is uncertain, but it is clear that perceptions of deterred and nondeterred individuals are not contrasted in any uniform way.

[23] For the advantages of the latter approach, see the President's Commission (1967: 17–19, 22–24).

[24] See Robinson (1950) and especially Menzel (1950). None of the resolutions so far proposed match the present situation, in which one quantitative variable lacks within-area standard deviation (Goodman, 1959, especially 620–23). O. D. Duncan has also done considerable work on the problem from the standpoint of statistical geography. But as far as we can tell, the above difficulty remains.

of very serious offenses we are confronted with a choice of opposing biases. But, under another construction, *previous* research also runs afoul of the "ecological fallacy." [25]

We risk, however, becoming involved with statistical procedures at the expense of the underlying interpretation. To apply Robinson's central insight on ecological correlation to a typical deterrence situation, if we find that, by jurisdictions, as average perceived severity rises the crime rate falls, it must be acknowledged that this does not necessarily imply that those *individuals* who believed severe sanctions exist are committing fewer crimes. But it would indisputably remain a finding of major importance, and irrespective of whether an individual or ecological interpretation were applied we would still celebrate a significant empirical breakthrough. Wherever direct interpretation is impossible in social research, it becomes the analytic task to select among competing explanations through indirect means, by extrapolation or analogy.[26] While the present analysis renders deterrence investigations for major offenses more difficult, research by no means becomes prohibitive or uninterpretable. Certainly its theoretical and practical significance remain impressive.[27]

Discussion

The conclusions reached in the preceding pages have serious consequences. In conjunction with data revealing pervasive public ignorance, they throw serious doubt upon much previous effort and necessitate modified replica-

---

[25] While such research might have concerned itself solely with the jurisdictions themselves (e.g., whether having severe sanctions in an area reduces crime), in fact the researchers depict the deterrent hypothesis as one of individual choices by rational "hedonists." If, therefore, their data supported deterrence they could only offer for theoretical explanation an individualistic interpretation. Thus they too would in effect be ascribing both knowledge and behavioral restraint to the same individuals, on the basis of ecological data.

[26] See, e.g., the excellent example of Pettigrew and Spier (1962) with ecological data. It might also be possible to apply the consensual interpretation displayed in Figure 3.1, which does not require individual correlation. This, however, has rarely been employed. It is equally plausible for either traditional or alternative approaches.

[27] It should be noted that the same basic approaches are amenable to comparisons across time as well as to the cross-sectional analysis we have surveyed (Fig. 3.2).

tion. The difficulties involved in accomplishing meaningful research on the important questions of deterrence are exacerbated. This chapter will have accomplished one central purpose if it eliminates future efforts with inadequate theoretical foundations and stimulates the study of perceptions of the criminal sanction and the prevention of criminal acts.

References

Assembly Committee on Criminal Procedure (State of California). 1968. "Part One—Survey of Knowledge of Criminal Penalties." *Deterrent Effects of Criminal Sanctions* (Progress Report, May):9–20.

Ball, John C. 1955. "The Deterrence Concept in Criminology and Law," *Journal of Criminal Law, Criminology, and Police Science* 46 (September–October):347–54.

Bentham, Jeremy. 1843. "Principles of Penal Law." *Works,* Vol. 1. Edinburgh: Tait.

Berger, Peter L. and Thomas Luckmann. 1966. *The Social Construction of Reality*. Garden City, N.Y.: Doubleday.

Beutel, Frederick K. 1957. *Some Potentialities of Experimental Jurisprudence as a New Branch of Social Science*. Lincoln: University of Nebraska Press.

Blake, Judith and Kingsley Davis. 1964. "Norms, Values, and Sanctions." In Robert E. L. Faris (ed.), *Handbook of Modern Sociology*. Chicago: Rand McNally.

Chambliss, William J. 1966. "The Deterrent Influence of Punishment," *Crime and Delinquency* 12 (January):70–75.

Chiricos, Theodore G. and Gordon P. Waldo. 1970. "Punishment and Crime: An Examination of Some Empirical Evidence," *Social Problems* 18 (Fall):200–17.

Claster, Daniel S. 1967. "Comparison of Risk Perception between Delinquents and Nondelinquents," *Journal of Criminal Law, Criminology, and Police Science* 58 (March):80–86.

Coser, Lewis A. 1967. *Continuities in the Study of Social Conflict*. New York: Free Press.

Crowther, Carol. 1969. "Crime, Penalties, and Legislatures," *The Annals* 381 (January):147–58.

Cushing, Robert G. 1969. "The Relative Impact of Changing Urban Characteristics, Adequacy of Law Enforcement Resources, and Punishment on the Incidence and Nature of Major Crime," *Proceedings,* Annual Convention, Southwestern Sociological Association, pp. 205–9.

Ehrmann, Sara R. 1962. "For Whom the Chair Waits," *Federal Probation* 26 (March):14–25.

Erikson, Kai T. 1966. *Wayward Puritans*. New York: Wiley.

Gibbs, Jack. 1966. "Sanctions," *Social Problems* 14 (Fall):147–59.

1968. "Crime, Punishment, and Deterrence," *Southwestern Social Science Quarterly* 48 (March):515–30.

Goodman, Leo A. 1959. "Some Alternatives to Ecological Correlation," *American Journal of Sociology* 64 (May):610–25.

Jayewardene, C. H. S. 1972. "Homicide and Punishment. A Study in Deterrence." Paper presented to the Canadian Sociology and Anthropology Association, Montreal (May).

Jensen, Gary F. 1969. " 'Crime Doesn't Pay': Correlates of a Shared Misunderstanding," *Social Problems* 17 (Fall):189–201.

Kunkel, John H. and Michael A. Garrick. 1969. "Models of Man in Sociological Analysis," *Social Science Quarterly* 50 (June):136–52.

Kuykendall, Helen K. 1969. "The Deterrent Efficacy of Punishment." Unpublished Masters thesis, University of Texas.

McCafferty, James A. 1954. "Capital Punishment in the United States: 1930 to 1952." Unpublished Masters thesis, Ohio State University.

Menninger, Karl. 1968. *The Crime of Punishment*. New York: Viking Press.

Menzel, Herbert. 1950. "Comment on Robinson's 'Ecological Correlations and the Behavior of Individuals,' " *American Sociological Review* 15 (October):674.

Morris, Norval and Frank Zimring. 1969. "Deterrence and Corrections," *Annals of the American Academy of Political and Social Science* 381 (January):137–46.

Nelson, Philip J. 1966. "An Essay in Normative Economics," *Social Research* 33 (Summer):314–31.

Pettigrew, Thomas F. and Rosalind Barclay Spier. 1962. "The Ecological Structure of Negro Homicide," *American Journal of Sociology* 67 (May):621–29.

President's Commission on Law Enforcement and Administration of Justice. 1967. Task Force Report: Crime and its Impact—An Assessment. Washington, D.C.: U.S. Government Printing Office.

Robinson, W. S. 1950. "Ecological Correlations and the Behavior of Individuals," *American Sociological Review* 15 (June):351–57.

Rosenthal, Robert and Ralph L. Rosnow (eds.). 1969. *Artifact in Behavioral Research*. New York: Academic Press.

Salem, Richard G. and William J. Bowers. 1969. "The Deterrent Effects of Formal Sanctions." Paper presented to the American Sociological Association meetings, San Francisco (September).

Sutherland, Edwin H. and Donald R. Cressey. 1970. *Criminology*, 8th ed., Philadelphia: Lippincott.

Tarde, Gabriel. 1912. *Penal Philosophy*. Boston: Little, Brown.

Tittle, Charles R. 1969a. "Crime and Deterrence." Paper presented to the American Sociological Association meetings, San Francisco (September).

1969b. "Crime Rates and Legal Sanctions," *Social Problems* 16 (Spring):409–23.

Toby, Jackson. 1964. "Is Punishment Necessary?" *Journal of Criminal Law, Criminology, and Police Science* 55 (September):332–33.

Van den Haag, Ernest. 1969. "On Deterrence and the Death Penalty," *Journal of Criminal Law, Criminology, and Police Science* 60 (June):141–47.

Waldo, Gordon P. and Theodore Chiricos. 1972. "Perceived Penal Sanction and Self-Reported Criminality: A Neglected Approach to Deterrence Research," *Social Problems* 20 (Spring):522–40.

Walker, Nigel and Michael Argyle. 1964. "Does the Law Affect Moral Judgments?" *British Journal of Criminology* 4 (October):570–81.

Wilkins, Leslie T. 1969. *Evaluation of Penal Measures*. New York: Random House.

Zimring, Franklin and Gordon Hawkins. 1973. *Deterrence*. Chicago: University of Chicago Press.

4

Public Knowledge
of Criminal Penalties

ASSEMBLY COMMITTEE
ON CRIMINAL PROCEDURE
(CALIFORNIA)

Scope of This Study

In an attempt to investigate public knowledge regarding criminal penalties in California, with the use of social survey methods, we asked a number of citizens to answer the following questions:

1. How knowledgeable are the people in California about penalties for various crimes?
2. What is the public's perception of the "crime problem" and what do they think should be done to lessen the crime rate?
3. What is the relationship between knowledge of penalties and criminal behavior?

All of these questions may be viewed differently by different social and ethnic groups in our communities. We, therefore, also were concerned about the effect of race, age, educational, and occupational categories upon responses to such questions.

Reprinted with permission of the Assembly Office of Research, California Legislature from *Deterrent Effects of Criminal Sanctions*. Part I: "Public Knowledge of Criminal Sanctions." Progress Report of the Assembly Committee on Criminal Procedure, California Legislature.

Methodology

In order to examine these questions, a questionnaire was designed and administered to various groups and subgroups in California.

The questionnaire was designed to tap the respondents' knowledge of penalties for specific crimes, knowledge of the cost of incarcerating criminals, and knowledge of the recent changes in criminal penalties. Questions were also posed regarding attitudes about how serious respondents felt the crime problem to be, and what they felt would help ease the crime rate. Hypothetical situations were presented to elicit ideas about what would deter the respondents from potential criminal activity. Data on the respondents' age, education, occupation, and race was obtained. Additional comments made on the questionnaire by the respondents were coded. These comments which reflected their attitudes toward criminals fell into the following categories: (1) punitive, (2) somewhat punitive, (3) rehabilitative or ameliorative, (4) admission of ignorance, or (5) miscellaneous or mundane comment.

Prior to the final study, a pilot study was conducted to test the questionnaire. A group of male registered voters, chosen at random, along with a group of prisoners, California Youth Authority wards, and classes of boys from high- and low-delinquency area high schools participated in this pilot study. As a result of the pilot, the revised questionnaire was developed for this survey.

This representative sample includes 3,348 male registered voters selected at random from Alameda, Contra Costa, San Francisco, Los Angeles, Kern, and San Bernardino Counties. (Since most crime occurs in large urban areas, we selected four urban counties and two rural, suburban counties for this study.) An equal number of Democrats and Republicans were selected from lists of registered male voters. Questionnaires were then administered, largely by mail, to these subjects. A letter from the Chairman of the Criminal Procedure Committee accompanied the questionnaire which requested the cooperation of each subject.

The questionnaire was also administered to two adult subsamples: 115 male inmates of the Deuel Vocational Institute and 54 students at the University of the Pacific.

As most crimes in California are committed by males between the ages of 15 and 29, 96 boys from a low-delinquency high school in San Francisco,

165 inmates of the CYA Preston School of Industry, and 98 students at a high-delinquency San Francisco high school were selected for a subgroup.

A total of 3,348 questionnaires were administered to these variously selected groups. The total number of usable questionnaires returned was 1,567 or nearly one-half of the total number administered. This rate of return for a survey is relatively high, since only one mail-out was used. Had a careful followup or additional time been available, the return rate could have been increased. However, we feel this group is representative of the most vocal and articulate of Californians, and represent the opinion-leaders. Information in this report is based on these 1,567 completed forms.

How Representative Was This Sample?

The special subgroups selected for study were representative young men who live in high- and low-delinquency areas. The mailed survey sample, when evaluated for possible bias, was found to be largely representative of the urban adult California population as reflected by comparison with the distribution of the sample with U.S. census figures and projections. As shown in Table 4.1, the age, ethnic, and occupational distribution compared closely, while the sample group were better educated than the general California population.

The education of the sampled group as measured by years of completed formal schooling revealed that the sample contained an overrepresentation of the college-educated group. Presumably these college-educated citizens who are overrepresented in this sample are representative of those persons most likely to participate in surveys, most likely to be community leaders, most likely to be influential, and most likely to symbolize the opinions and attitudes of the younger, more active, and better educated citizenry in California. Since population trends indicate that this group will be ever-growing in the future, perhaps the responses from this sample point to attitude trends of the future.

TABLE 4.1. AGE, EDUCATION AND RACE OF RESPONDENTS IN SAMPLE COMPARED WITH U.S. CENSUS STATISTICS FOR SELECTED CALIFORNIA COUNTIES ($N = 1024$)

Age	Sample (percent)	U.S. Census (percent)
20–29	28	23.9
30–39	18	18.7
40–49	17	20.6
50–59	17	15.9
60+	15	20
Under 21, no response	6	

(No statistically significant difference between two groups on age.)

Education	Sample	U.S. Census
Elementary	8	28
High school	44	48
Some college	23	14
College graduate	24	10

(General population has more college educated persons than would be expected from census projections. Thus responses reflect attitudes of best-educated group in California.)

Race (In Urban Areas)	General Population Sample	U.S. Census
White	69	76
Nonwhite	31	24

(No statistical difference by race between two groups.)

Major Findings

The major findings from the survey relates to the four central questions investigated.

Each of these central questions raise other questions, some of which were analyzed, others of which, remain for further study.

1. *How knowledgeable are the people in California about penalties for various crimes?* Eleven questions were asked about penalties for various crimes.

TABLE 4.2. AVERAGE NUMBER OF CORRECT ANSWERS REGARDING PENALTIES FOR CRIMES AND PERCENT OF POSSIBLE ANSWERS FOR ALL GROUPS TESTED ($N = 1567$)

	Mean Number Correct Responses	Percent of Total Items Correct	N
General population	M = 2.6	24	1,024
College men	M = 3.2	29	54
Low-delinquent high school boys	M = 3.0	27	96
High-delinquent high school boys	M = 3.0	27	113
Youth authority	M = 3.4	31	165
Adult corrections	M = 6.3	57	115
			1,567

Among the general public there was considerable variation in the extent of knowledge about sentences for selected felonies. First of all, a range of 21 to 49 percent of the respondents had complete ignorance or were unable to ever guess the maximum sentences for these crimes. Futhermore, even among those who made an estimate, the correct responses ranged from 8 to 39 percent. If one combined the number of correct responses into a single index score of accuracy, *no one person correctly answered all 11 questions about penalties,* while, at the other extreme, *69 percent of the respondents answered 3 or less items correctly.* This finding is evidence that there is profound lack of information concerning criminal penalties. This finding is less true for the delinquent or institutionalized groups since first-hand experience would presumably expose such groups to information about penalties. But, while criminal groups knew more about penalties than did the general population, such knowledge had seemingly not deterred them from criminal acts.

The general population had the least amount of knowledge about criminal penalties, while those who had engaged in crime had the greatest knowledge of penalties. It appears that knowledge of penalties comes *after* the crime—that is, penalties cannot act as deterrents since these are unknown until after a person has committed a crime or become a prisoner. Since approximately one-third of all persons who are imprisoned once, continue to engage in crime after their release, it would appear that even when they have knowledge about penalties, it does not act as a strong deterrent to their continuation of criminal activity.

Knowledge of criminal penalties varied among the population tested according to certain crimes, as shown in Table 4.3.

As can be seen, the general population had the most knowledge about penalties for assault with a deadly weapon and borrowing a car; among college men, the penalty for borrowing a car was best known; among low-delinquency high school boys, the car borrowing penalty was also the best known one; among the high delinquency high school boys, the penalty for cashing a check from a closed account was best known; among boys now in a Youth Authority institution, the best known penalty was for borrowing a car; while convicts were most knowledgeable about penalties for first degree robbery. Between these groups, the differences in amount of correct knowledge about criminal penalties was marked, as can be seen by comparing the general population's knowledge against the Deuel Vocational Institution inmates percent of correct answers. Criminals have the greatest knowledge about penalties, yet seemingly have been deterred the least from crime.

Did respondents under- or overestimate penalties? Among the general

TABLE 4.3. PERCENT OF CORRECT RESPONSES REGARDING PENALTIES FOR SPECIFIC CRIMES BY CALIFORNIA CITIZENS, HIGH SCHOOL, COLLEGE, AND INSTITUTIONAL POPULATION

Knowledge of Penalties	General Population	Low-Delinquency College	Low-Delinquency High school	High Delinquency, High School	Institutional Youth authority	Institutional Adult corrections
(4) Assault with deadly weapon	35	26	24	33	30	59
(5) Second-degree burglary	15	22	26	26	16	63
(6) First-degree robbery	8	11	11	10	21	85
(7) Forcible rape	24	30	14	22	36	52
(8) Taking a car and leaving it	35	44	35	31	40	65
(9) Check from closed account	17	20	27	42	33	50

TABLE 4.4. GENERAL POPULATION RESPONSES INDICATING UNDER-, CORRECT, OVER-, OR NO ESTIMATE OF SEVERITY OF SENTENCES FOR SIX CRIMES ($N = 1,024$)

	Under-estimate (percent)	Correct Answer (percent)	Over-estimate (percent)	No Estimate (percent)	Total (percent)
Assault with deadly weapon	—	35	40	25	100
Second-degree burglary	52	15	5	28	100
First-degree robbery	65	8	1	26	100
Rape	35	24	20	21	100
Joy-riding	28	35	15	22	100
Check on closed account	59	17	—	24	100

population, the tendency *was to underestimate* the penalties, as can be seen in Table 4.4, which examines the knowledge of penalties for six crimes.

As can be seen, over one-half of the population underestimated the penalties for second-degree burglary, first-degree robbery, and writing a check on a closed account. Could this finding indicate that the actual maximum penalties now levied for those crimes are viewed by the public as being excessive?

The finding that over one-fourth of all the respondents could not *even* guess what the penalty for these crimes were, indicates the great lack of knowledge about criminal penalties in the community.

Several crimes were reviewed by the Legislature in the 1967 session and penalties increased. In general, this action reflected an attempt on the part of the Legislature to respond to growing public concern over the rise of "crime in the streets." All of the crimes for which the penalties were raised involved great bodily injury to the victim—the crimes which have created the greatest fear in the minds of the public. These crimes were rape, robbery, and burglary where great bodily injury was involved. The minimum for all these crimes was increased to 15 years imprisonment.

The penalties for these crimes as well as two additional crimes were included in the questionnaire. Driving under the influence of alcohol, and possession of marijuana were added to the three crimes with increased penalties. Both of these offenses are currently of public concern, as both have received much attention from the public media. The last Legislature had not increased penalties for these crimes.

These five items received greater percentages of "don't know" responses than other questions about criminal penalties. Nearly 50 percent of the population answered that they did not know if the Legislature had acted or not on the crimes involving great bodily injury. For the other two crimes, about a third of the population could not answer the questions.

When answers were given, people were more likely to respond that the *Legislature* had not acted at all. Very few were able to give correct answers. While the Legislature had supposedly responded to public appeal and increased the penalties for crimes of violence to victims, this was not known by the public. Table 4.5 shows the percent of correct responses made to these five questions.

The public was as likely to say they did not know as to guess one of the answers to questions involving crimes of a personal nature—driving under the influence of alcohol or possession of marijuana. Where an incorrect answer was given, it was most likely to be that these *penalties* had been *decreased*. (The Legislature did not decrease any penalties.)

Thus, people were in general unaware that the Legislature had taken any action at all when in fact the Legislature had increased the minimum penalties for crimes involving bodily injury to the victim. The public was inclined to answer "don't know" as often as to give a correct response on

TABLE 4.5. PERCENT OF CORRECT ANSWERS ON RECENTLY INCREASED PENALTIES FOR CRIMES BY GENERAL PUBLIC, HIGH- AND LOW-DELINQUENCY GROUPS, AND INSTITUTIONAL POPULATIONS

Knowledge of Increased Penalties	General Population	College	Low-Delinquency High School	High Delinquency High School	Institutional	
					Youth authority	Adult corrections
Rape	16	17	30	27	24	43
Drunk driving	39	46	48	34	26	37
Robbery with bodily injury	20	20	23	33	30	76
Burglary with bodily injury	16	15	25	29	21	57
Possession of marijuana	36	65	38	16	25	47

questions concerning drunk driving and possession of marijuana. (The only major exception occurred among college students who were correct in 65 percent of cases on the question about marijuana.)

When the public did answer these items, they tended to underestimate the amount of the penalty, as is shown in Table 4.6.

When there seems to be a public outcry against crimes, this finding may indicate that a legislative body should pause and reflect that most people in the general public will *not* know of their action of increasing legal penalties. Further, the public thinks that *penalties for most crimes are actually less than they really are!*

TABLE 4.6 GENERAL PUBLIC'S ESTIMATE OF SEVERITY OF PENALTY FOR FIVE CRIMES (*N* = 1,024)

	Under-estimate (percent)	Correct Answer (percent)	Over-estimate (percent)	Can't Guess (percent)	Total (percent)
Rape with bodily injury	22	16	13	49	100
Driving under influence of alcohol	21	39	4	36	100
Robbery and bodily injury	28	20	6	46	100
Burglary and bodily injury	30	16	5	49	100
Possession of marijuana	16	36	10	38	100

We asked the respondents their concern about the crime rate. Over one-half of the respondents indicated that the present crime rate is so great that it constitutes a public problem. Another one-fourth indicated that the crime rate is higher than it should be. Hence, among the population responding to the survey, nearly three-fourths indicated concern about California's rising crime rate.

2. *What is the public's perception of the "crime problem" and what do they think should be done about it?*

What do people feel will help to lessen the rising crime rate in California? A question asked about various alternatives.

As can be seen in Table 4.7 responses to the question varied.

One-fourth of the respondents felt that stiffer sentences and longer imprisonments would be the greatest help in lessening the current crime rate. Who are these people, and how knowledgeable are they about the dimensions of the problem?

Respondents from the general population averaged a correct score of 2.8 responses out of a possible 11 responses regarding the penalties for various crimes. However, people who felt that stiffer sentences and longer period of imprisonment should be applied correctly answered questions about criminal penalties in only 18 percent of the cases, i.e., to answer correctly an average of 2 questions out of the total of 11. Thus those respondents who felt stiffer penalties were needed, were even *less* knowledgeable about present penalties than was true for the general population. For this group, the lack of knowledge about existing penalties was not a consideration in suggesting increased penalties as a solution to the crime problem.

TABLE 4.7.   RESPONSES TO "WHAT DO YOU THINK WOULD HELP MOST TO LESSEN THE CURRENT CRIME RATE?"

	N	Percent
Better opportunities for poor people	246	24
More law enforcement officers	109	11
Social and psychiatric help for offenders	81	8
Stiffer sentences and longer imprisonment	250	24
Increased scientific study of the causes of crime, etc.	291	28
No response	47	5
Total	1,024	100

In general, the older, retired and less-well-educated groups were more primitive in their general attitude about crime as compared with the younger, better-educated, or employed respondents. Conversely, the better-educated group suggested more scientific study about the causes of crime or better opportunities for jobs and education. In general, there were two groups of respondents. One group wanted short-term answers for the present crime situations, i.e., more law enforcement officers and stiffer sentences. The other group felt attention should be paid, with a long-range view, to the indirect causes of crime, such as poverty, poor education, lack of opportunities, etc. For example, the better educated the respondent, the more likely he was to see the need for more scientific study regarding the causes of crime. Persons from the lower socioeconomic groups, such as laborers or semiskilled workers, were more likely to suggest better opportunities for the poor as a remedy for the rising crime rate in California.

Forty percent of the respondents added comments on their forms. Of those who commented, 18 percent felt that judges were too lenient, that police should have more power, and in general, indicated a sense of irritation of the present administration of justice. An additional one-third were mildly punitive in their attitude toward the courts and police power. Only a few respondents commented about penalties *per se*. Most comments calling for stricter law enforcement pointed at the courts and its administration of the present laws. Twenty percent of those who wrote comments expressed concern about individual rights, or the guarantees of protection from excessive legal harassment. It was also of interest to note that one-fourth of those who commented noted their ignorance of the penalties and expressed some amazement at how little they knew about such laws. Many also commented favorably upon the work of the Criminal Procedure Committee.

Since some respondents suggested longer imprisonment, how much did the public know about the cost of prison? The average cost per year for caring for a prisoner in California is $2,560. The respondents were asked to estimate this cost, and the results are shown in Table 4.8.

Only one-fourth of the people knew the actual cost of keeping a prisoner for each year, while another one-third couldn't even guess. It is of interest to note that the respondents who are presently in an institution tended to underestimate the actual cost of their care while one-third of the general public overestimated the cost of caring for a prisoner.

3. What is the relationship between knowledge of penalties and criminal behavior?

As was shown in Table 4.2, persons who have already engaged in crime have the most knowledge about penalties. This seems paradoxical,

TABLE 4.8. ESTIMATE OF COST OF PRISON AMONG GENERAL POPULATION AND OTHER SUBGROUPS

	Don't Know (percent)	Under- estimate $1,500 (percent)	Correct $2,560 (percent)	Over- estimate $3,100 (percent)	Total (percent)
General population	36	9	23	32	100
College men	26	4	24	46	100
Low-delinquency high school	42	18	26	15	100
High-delinquency high school	47	18	22	13	100
Youth authority	32	24	24	20	100
Adult corrections	23	30	30	17	100

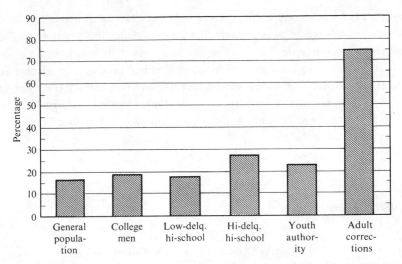

Figure 4.1 Comparison between Groups on Percentage of Correct Responses to Penalty Questions

i.e. that if knowledge of penalties is an essential ingredient for deterrence, then how is it that criminals have the most knowledge and are seemingly the least deterred?

Two-thirds of the institutionalized persons also indicated that the crime rate is too high and constitutes a public problem, similar to the responses of the general population. But they differed as to what they thought should be done to remedy this high crime rate.

What do criminals think would lower the crime rate? As can be seen in Table 4.7, both institutionalized groups felt that better opportunities for poor people (32 percent), social and psychiatric help for offenders (23 percent), and increased study of causes of crime (26 percent) would help in lessening the crime rate.

In Figure 4.1, the influence of criminal activity upon knowledge about penalties is shown. As can be seen, as the group's identity as a deviant one increases, so does the amount of correct knowledge about criminal penalties. To put it another way, those who knew the least about criminal penalties were the least likely to engage in crime.

Of course, *this does not mean that knowledge of criminal penalties causes crime.* It may simply mean that a penal institution is a fine training grounds for learning law and criminology. But it also seems to indicate that penalties become of interest to a person only *after* he engages in criminal behavior. Knowledge of penalties does not seem to deter, but it may be important for "copping a plea" or making the best "deal" in court.

It can be conjectured that the cause of criminal behavior lies elsewhere, and the understanding of the motivation for criminal actions does not involve a balance sheet of penalty vs. gain. Rather, people engage in crime and learn of the penalties, not as deterrents, but only as factors of a criminal career faced *after the* fact. . . .

Appendix

CALIFORNIA ASSEMBLY COMMITTEE ON CRIMINAL PROCEDURE SURVEY REGARDING THE PUBLIC'S KNOWLEDGE OF CRIME IN CALIFORNIA

For items 1 through 9, check the space next to the answer which best describes your knowledge or feeling about the question.

Please Check Only One Space

1. Do you feel the crime rate in California is
   1. _____ about what one would expect.
   2. _____ lower than one might expect.
   3. _____ higher than one might expect.
   4. _____ so high as to be a major public problem.

2. What do you think would help most to lessen the current crime rate? (Check only *1* space)
   1. _____ better opportunities for poor people.
   2. _____ more law enforcement officers.
   3. _____ social and psychiatric help for offenders.
   4. _____ stiffer sentences and longer imprisonment.
   5. _____ increased scientific study of the causes of crime.
   6. _____ other, please specify _____

3. How much does it cost taxpayers to keep a person in prison for one year?
   1. _____ $1,550.
   X2. _____ $2,500.
   3. _____ $3,100.
   4. _____ don't know, can't guess.

4. What is the maximum penalty, the *most* a person could get, if he was convicted of assault with a deadly weapon?
   X1.____ 10 years.
   2.____ 15 years.
   3.____ 30 years.
   4.____ life imprisonment.
   5.____ death penalty.
   6.____ don't know, can't guess.

5. What is the maximum penalty, the *most* a person could get, if he was convicted of 2nd degree burglary?
   1.____ 10 years.
   X2.____ 15 years.
   3.____ 30 years.
   4.____ life imprisonment.
   5.____ death penalty.
   6.____ don't know, can't guess.

6. What is the maximum penalty, the *most* a person could get, if he was convicted of 1st degree robbery?
   1.____ 10 years.
   2.____ 15 years.
   3.____ 30 years.
   X4.____ life imprisonment.
   5.____ death penalty.
   6.____ don't know, can't guess.

7. What is the maximum penalty, the *most* a person could get, if he was convicted of forcible rape?
   1.____ 10 years.
   2.____ 15 years.
   3.____ 30 years.
   X4.____ life imprisonment.
   5.____ death penalty.
   6.____ don't know, can't guess.

8. If a person takes a car which does not belong to him, uses it for a few days and leaves it parked, unharmed and unchanged, what is the maximum penalty, the *most* he can get, if he is caught and convicted?
   1.____ 1 year.
   X2.____ 5 years.
   3.____ 10 years.
   4.____ 30 years.
   5.____ don't know, can't guess.

9. If a person uses a leftover check from a closed account to purchase a $75 radio, what is the maximum penalty he could get if he was caught?
   1. ____ He would be required to make the check good as he is just overdrawn.
   2. ____ Up to one year in jail because he didn't intend to cover the check.
X3. ____ He would go to prison for up to 14 years because that is forgery.
   4. ____ don't know, can't guess.

For questions 10 through 14, check the space which describes what the Legislature did last year in regard to the minimum penalty (the *least* a person could get) for the crime listed.

10. Rape with great bodily injury to the victim.
   1. ____ minimum decreased to one year.
   2. ____ no change made in the minimum.
X3. ____ minimum increased to 15 years.
   4. ____ minimum increased to 25 years.
   5. ____ don't know, can't guess.

11. Driving under the influence of alcohol.
   1. ____ minimum decreased to one year.
X2. ____ no change made in the minimum.
   3. ____ minimum increased to 15 years.
   4. ____ minimum increased to 25 years.
   5. ____ don't know, can't guess.

12. Robbery with bodily injury to the victim.
   1. ____ minimum decreased to one year.
   2. ____ no change made in the minimum.
X3. ____ minimum increased to 15 years.
   4. ____ minimum increased to 25 years.
   5. ____ don't know, can't guess.

13. Burglary with bodily injury to the victim.
   1. ____ minimum decreased to one year.
   2. ____ no change made in the minimum.
X3. ____ minimum increased to 15 years.
   4. ____ minimum increased to 25 years.
   5. ____ don't know, can't guess.

14. Possession of marijuana.
   1. ____ minimum decreased to one yeear.
X2. ____ no change made in the minimum.
   3. ____ minimum increased to 15 years.
   4. ____ minimum increased to 25 years.
   5. ____ don't know, can't guess.

15. If you were convicted of a serious crime, such as forging your employer's signature to a $1,000 check or stealing a color TV, what would *bother* you the most? (Check only 1 space).

    1. ____ It would not make any difference because my record is bad anyway.

    2. ____ I would feel stupid because I got caught.

    3. ____ I would go to prison.

    4. ____ I would lose my job, possessions, etc.

    5. ____ My family would turn against me.

    6. ____ My reputation would be ruined.

    7. ____ I would feel ashamed and guilty.

16. If you had suffered such a run of bad luck that you needed money *badly*, and found that you were in a position to accept a bribe or a fix without much fear of getting caught, what, if anything, would *stop* you? (Check the one which would be most likely to *stop* you.)

    1. ____ If I needed money badly enough, I would take the bribe.

    2. ____ If I thought I could get away with it, I might accept the bribe.

    3. ____ I would be afraid to trust the person who would offer a bribe.

    4. ____ Knowing I might be arrested.

    5. ____ I would be afraid of my family's disapproval.

    6. ____ I would feel guilty even if no one found out about it.

    7. ____ I cannot imagine myself having to make such a decision, therefore I can't evaluate my decision.

17. Has a serious crime ever been committed against you? (i.e. have you ever been robbed, assaulted, had your car stolen, house burglarized, etc.?)

    1. ____ no.

    2. ____ yes. If so, what crime? _____

18. Have you ever known anyone besides yourself who was a victim of a serious crime? (If you have known more than one, check the space that describes the most recent victim.)

    1. ____ no, I do not know anyone who was ever a victim.

    2. ____ yes, a member of my immediate family.

    3. ____ yes, some other relative.

    4. ____ yes, a friend or neighbor.

19. Please indicate your age.

    1. ____ under 20.

    2. ____ 20–29.

    3. ____ 30–39.

    4. ____ 40–49.

    5. ____ 50–59.

    6. ____ 60 or over.

20. What is the highest level of school you finished?
    1. ____ grade school or less.
    2. ____ some high school.
    3. ____ high school graduate.
    4. ____ trade school or special training (barber or beauty school, business school, union training, etc.).
    5. ____ some college.
    6. ____ college graduate or above.

21. What is your (father's *) present occupation?
    1. ____ professional, executive.
    2. ____ business manager, officer in armed forces, performer, teacher, civil service.
    3. ____ clerical, sales, personal service (barber, beautician, etc.).
    4. ____ skilled labor, craft, farmer, armed service enlisted.
    5. ____ semiskilled, unskilled, domestic.
    6. ____ student.
    7. ____ unemployed at present.
    8. ____ retired, incapacitated, institutionalized.
    9. ____ other, please specify _____

22. Please indicate your race.
    1. ____ White.
    2. ____ Black.
    3. ____ Oriental.
    4. ____ Mexican-American.
    5. ____ Other, please specify _____

X—Correct answers.
* For youth questionnaire only.

5

Perception of Certainty: A Comparison of Delinquents and Nondelinquents

DANIEL CLASTER

The classical school of criminology asserts that criminal behavior can be deterred by fear of punishment (Beccaria, 1819). The positivist school does not reject this concept of deterrence, but it rejects the classical assumption that deterrence is equally applicable to all persons. By emphasizing differences in crime proneness (Vold, 1958), positivism views deterrence in terms of factors that make some persons less susceptible to threatened sanctions than others (Ball, 1955).

The present study was undertaken to determine whether different susceptibilities to sanctions can be explained by differences in perceiving the risk of arrest and conviction for criminal behavior. A questionnaire was constructed to measure risk perception. Using official statistics as a baseline,[1] delinquents and nondelinquents are first compared as to how they perceive

Reprinted with permission of the *Journal of Criminal Law, Criminology, and Police Science* from "Comparison of Risk Perception between Delinquents and Nondelinquents, *Journal of Criminal Law, Criminology, and Police Science* 58 (1967) by Daniel Claster. Copyright © 1967 Northwestern University School of Law. The author wishes to express his gratitude to Dr. A. Lee Coleman, Director, Social Research Service, University of Kentucky, for support of the study, to Messrs. Owen Clifford, Ben Freeman, Lyle Lauber, Samuel Noe, and Gerald Rossell for making subjects available, and especially to Miss Lois Cassell for pretesting the questionnaire.

[1] The Federal Bureau of Investigation's Annual Uniform Crime Reports present comparable data of this sort from law enforcement agencies throughout the United States.

arrest and conviction rates for various crimes. Second, their perceptions of the risk to themselves of arrest and conviction for three hypothetical offenses are compared.

Three major hypotheses are tested: (1) delinquents perceive law enforcement, measured by percentage of crimes cleared by arrest and conviction in the United States, to be less effective than do nondelinquents; (2) delinquents see themselves as more likely to violate the law in hypothetical situations than do nondelinquents; and (3) delinquents perceive their chances of apprehension and conviction for these hypothetical offenses to be less than nondelinquents perceive their own chances. Hypothesis (1) reflects the position that delinquents view the external world differently from nondelinquents, (2), that delinquents perceive themselves differently from nondelinquents, and (3), that delinquents differ in how they perceive themselves in relation to the larger social environment.

The first hypothesis is an example of the sociological approach to criminality (Glaser, 1958). That view explains criminality as part of a larger cultural pattern, characteristic of persons who have been socialized in groups which support antisocial values. Members of these groups begin early to learn about police inefficiency and corruption, unfair court practices, etc. They are exposed to adults who make a living, frequently a good living, by crime. Among them, the idea does not exist of law as a desirable institution, assented to by society's members to protect themselves. On the contrary, they see it as an obstacle to desired goals and are attuned to the weaknesses of the legal structure. If this view of delinquent subcultures is correct, that they are characterized by considerable skepticism of the general efficiency of law-enforcement, then this skepticism should lead members of these groups to make lower judgments of arrest and conviction rates for the United States than others not so acculturated, as predicted by the hypothesis.

Hypothesis (2) is addressed to the conceptualization of delinquency as a psychological impulse disorder (McCord and McCord, 1956). It is based on two assumptions: first, that offenders are less capable of controlling the impulse to act out in an antisocial fashion, and second, that this tendency is in some way accessible to conscious awareness. Previous studies encourage us to pursue this hypothesis. Reckless, Dinitz, and Murray (1956) found nondelinquents higher on the social responsibility scale of the California Personality Inventory than delinquents, which is indicative of greater "social control" according to Gough, who developed the scale. Another study, using

Cattell's Junior Personality Questionnaire, showed delinquents high on impulsivity (surgency scale) (Kelly and Veldman, 1964). Our hypothesis differs from the findings of these studies in that it operationalizes impulsivity situationally, by describing hypothetical circumstances in which an individual might commit a criminal offense through loss of control, while the studies cited measure impulsivity as a more general personality characteristic.

The third hypothesis expresses what Redl and Wineman (1957) call the "delusion of exceptionalistic exemption from the laws of cause and effect." They describe how delinquents develop a peculiar notion involving both self-perception and perception of law-enforcement: that they themselves are immune from the legally prescribed consequences of their misdeeds. For such individuals, visible enforcement against others and even against themselves when they have previously been caught is said to have no deterrency effect. Describing this defect in reality testing, Schmideberg (1960) notes:

One of the most striking things about offenders is that they do not believe that they will ever be caught or brought to justice. Even after going to jail, many believe that they will never be caught again. They have a magical belief in their own cleverness, luck, or whatever they call it—often in obvious contrast to the facts. One patient expressed to me, as an explanation for committing his offenses, his "sense of gloating" that he got away. I said, somewhat amazed, "But you did not get away, you got arrested several times." In his mind he had managed to deny the fact of the arrests and dwelt only on the occasions when he had escaped.

This phenomenon derives from the impulsivity attributed to delinquents in the second hypothesis, but the third hypothesis goes further and holds that impulsivity is not confronted squarely; to do so would be too painful because it would evoke the fear of apprehension and punishment. This view posits that delinquents deny their lack of control by perceiving themselves to be beyond the reach of the law. Insofar as it characterizes delinquency in terms relating personality to perception of the social environment, it may be called a social-psychological hypothesis.

Method

A questionnaire was constructed to measure the perceptions hypothesized among delinquents and nondelinquents. It consists of three parts. In the first part there are six items. Each item consists of a definition of one class of criminal offense, an example of that offense, and a question requiring respondents to check one of four percentage figures, at 10-percent intervals, which they believe correctly represents the "cleared by arrest" rates for that crime. The first item is: "Murder—killing a person on purpose. For instance: a man plans to kill his wife. He buys a gun, takes it home, and shoots her. What percent of murders end up with someone being arrested for the crime? 62, 72, 82, 92." Similar items are included for the crimes of negligent manslaughter, aggravated assault, robbery, burglary, and auto theft.

The second part of the questionnaire contains six items that ask respondents to give the percentage of persons arrested for the crimes mentioned in the first part who are convicted.

In both these parts, one of the alternatives is based on official statistics for the year 1960 (U.S. F.B.I., 1961). Alternatives are presented in ascending order in each item. The position of the correct alternative is varied for the twelve items in the first two parts of the questionnaire, so that it comes first in three cases, second in three cases, etc.

The third part of the questionnaire consists of three hypothetical situations in which a criminal act results from the absence of customary control. The first situation is one of anger giving way to murder; the second, burglary resulting from financial necessity; and the third, careless driving leading to vehicular homicide. For each situation there are three questions, sections *a*, *b*, and *c*. In section *a* the respondent is asked whether he thinks he definitely could, probably could, probably could not, or definitely could not commit the acts in the situations described. Only if he definitely could, or probably could, is he to answer sections *b* and *c* for that situation. Section *b* asks him to judge whether his chances of evading arrest, if he did commit such an act, would be greater, less than, or equal to 50 percent, and section *c* asks what he perceives his chances of conviction if arrested to be, given the same forced-choice alternatives as in section *b*.

The delinquents to whom questionnaires were administered consisted of all the inmates in the sixth grade and above at the training school for juvenile offenders of one of the East South Central states. Nondelinquent responses were obtained from all the eighth and ninth grade boys who were assigned to study halls at a given hour, at a lower to lower-middle-class school in a large city in that state.[2] Only questionnaires from white male respondents were used in the analysis reported here. Training school respondents with I.Q. scores less than 80 were also excluded.

The 42 delinquents remaining range in age from 13 years, 7 months to 18 years, 9 months, with a median of 15 years, 10 months. Their median I.Q. measured by the Wechsler Intelligence Scale for Children (W.I.S.C.) is 95, with a range from 80 to 117.

The 65 boys in the nondelinquent group range in age between 13 years, 1 month and 16 years, 1 month; the median is 14 years, 2 months. Their I.Q. scores are based on the California Test of Mental Maturity, and extend from 90 to 133 with a median of 109.

Questionnaires were administered to both training school and junior high school students in class groups during school hours. The stated purpose of the questionnaire was "to find out people's ideas of how laws work in the United States." Respondents were assured of confidentiality by being told the investigator would not reveal their answers to anyone at their schools. An incentive was offered—a two-dollar prize—for the person in each school who had the most correct answers on items 1 through 12, those questions for which there are "correct" answers.

The items in the first part, percent of reported crimes cleared by arrest, and items in the second part, percent of arrested persons who were convicted, were scored in this same way. A correctly estimated item received a score of 0. If the correct percent was overestimated by 10 points the item was scored $+1$, by 20 points, $+2$, by 30 points, $+3$, and corresponding minus scores were given for underestimation.

The six items in each part were combined in two ways for each respondent. One consisted of simply counting the number of correct responses he gave. The other consisted of adding the overestimation and underestimation scores to arrive at a net plus or minus score, reflecting tendency to overestimate or underestimate. Thus the first six items yielded a score for number of correct estimates and a score for over, or under, estimation of the cleared

[2] Unfortunately, it was not possible to ascertain whether any of the public school boys had been convicted of delinquency, but we assume that the incarcerated subjects were more delinquent than those at liberty. If questionnaires of convicted delinquents could have been purged from the public school group, the probable effect would have been to increase the magnitude of difference found.

by arrest rates for the crimes included. In like manner the second six items yielded a score for correctness and an overestimation or underestimation score for conviction rates.

In the third part of the questionnaire, the *a* sections of items 13, 14, and 15, asking whether respondents thought they might commit the criminal acts in the situations given, were scored on a four-point scale, "definitely could" equal to three points and "definitely could not" equal to zero points. These scores were then summed across the three situations to reflect self-perceived absence of control. Sections *b* and *c* were similarly scored on a three-point scale, high scores reflecting perception of relative likelihood of arrest and conviction, respectively. Because sections *b* and *c* were to be answered only if the response to section *a* of the corresponding situation was "definitely could" or "probably could," individuals' summated scores for sections *b* and *c* were sometimes based on one response, sometimes on two, and sometimes on three. In order to give each individual equal weight in comparing groups, the summated *b* and *c* scores were divided by the number of responses appropriate for him.[3]

Results

Results of the analysis of the first two parts of the questionnaire are given in Table 5.1. None of the differences between means for delinquents and nondelinquents reached the criterion of significance at the .05 level. The direction of the difference which did appear for estimates of the cleared by arrest rate was opposite to that hypothesized: mean judgment of delinquents was an overestimate of 0.38 points, while that of nondelinquents was an underestimate of 0.26 points. In judgment of conviction rate there was virtually no difference between delinquents and nondelinquents; both groups overestimated by a little more than 4 points.

No hypothesis as to accuracy of judgments has been advanced. It was felt that the selective experiences of delinquents and nondelinquents would lead each group to systematic distortion, but there was no reason to think the

[3] If respondents did not acknowledge that they probably could commit any of the acts there would be no responses in sections *b* and *c*. Of course, such respondents were omitted in the analysis of these sections.

TABLE 5.1. COMPARISON OF DELINQUENTS AND NONDELINQUENTS ON OVERESTIMATION AND CORRECTNESS OF U.S. ARREST AND CONVICTION RATES FOR SIX CRIMES

	Delinquents (N = 42)	Nondelinquents (N = 65)	t	Level of Significance
Mean overestimation of arrest rates	0.38	−0.26 [a]	1.20	p < .20 [b]
Mean overestimation of conviction rates	4.05	4.09	0.08	p > .90 [b]
Mean number of correct arrest rate estimates	2.31	2.06	1.10	p < .40 [c]
Mean number of correct conviction rate estimates	1.67	1.48	0.97	p < .40 [c]

[a] Minus score indicates mean underestimation.
[b] One-tailed test.
[c] Two-tailed test.

degree of distortion would be greater for one group than the other. Nevertheless, the data were analyzed to see if there is such a difference. It turns out that the mean number of correct estimates by delinquents is slightly greater than that for nondelinquents, both in arrest rate and conviction rate estimates, but the probability is two in five that these differences are due to chance, so that the hypothesis of no difference cannot be rejected with confidence.

Tables 5.2 and 5.3, however, which deal with self-perceptions, indicate more striking differences between delinquents and nondelinquents. In Table 5.2 the delinquent group is higher, with a mean score of 4.75, than nondelinquents, whose mean is 3.57, in the extent to which they think themselves prone to commit crimes by failing to exercise self control in situations where

TABLE 5.2. COMPARISON OF DELINQUENTS AND NONDELINQUENTS ON PERCEPTION OF LIKELIHOOD THAT THEY COULD COMMIT THREE HYPOTHETICAL CRIMES

	Delinquents (N = 42)	Nondelinquents (N = 64)	z	Level of Significance [a]
Self-perceived likelihood of committing crimes	4.75	3.57	2.72	p = .003

[a] One-tailed test.

TABLE 5.3. COMPARISON OF DELINQUENTS AND NONDELINQUENTS ON
PERCEPTION OF OWN LIKELIHOOD OF ARREST AND CONVICTION IF THEY
COMMITTED HYPOTHETICAL CRIMES

	Delinquents (N = 40)	Nondelinquents (N = 42)	z	Level of Significance [a]
Self-perceived likelihood of being arrested	1.18	1.54	2.73	p = .003
Self-perceived likelihood of being convicted	1.29	1.39	1.13	p = .13

[a] One-tailed test.

such controls are normally expected to operate. This difference, analyzed by
the Mann Whitney U test, turns out to be highly significant; there are only
three chances in a thousand that it is due to sampling error.

Table 5.3 is based on only those boys who admitted that they might
commit one or more of the offenses in the three situations described; thus
two of the original 42 training school boys and 23 of the 65 junior high
school respondents previously used were omitted from the analysis of sections b and c of questions 13, 14, and 15. Comparing those who remained in
these groups, the hypothesis that delinquents perceive themselves to be more
immune from arrest than nondelinquents was strongly confirmed. Nondelinquents' score for self-perceived likelihood of being arrested is 1.54, while
that for delinquents is 1.18, a difference significant at the .003 level of
confidence.

Self-perceptions as to probability of conviction if arrested for these offenses differ in the same direction as probability of arrest between the
groups, but the difference does not reach an acceptable level of significance.
The nondelinquents estimated the likelihood for themselves of conviction if
arrested with an average score of 1.39 points, and the delinquents' average
score was 1.29. The difference between them might have a one-eighth probability resulting from chance, though, so that it cannot be taken as a real difference.

As noted above, there were differences between training school and
public school boys on two attributes, age and I.Q., in addition to the main
independent variable, current incarceration for delinquency. Thus it was
necessary to examine the relationship between these antecedent variables

and the scores on which delinquents differed from nondelinquents, to determine whether the delinquent-nondelinquent differences are artifacts of the group differences in age and I.Q. For this purpose, both training school and public school boys were divided into subgroups of those above and below the group median in age. Those below the median were then compared with those above, within each group, on the scores for which significant delinquent-nondelinquent differences were found. The results indicated no significant differences between older and younger boys in questionnaire responses. Similar comparisons of higher-I.Q. with lower-I.Q. boys likewise revealed no differences. Thus the possibility that delinquent-nondelinquent differences in questionnaire scores are explainable by age and I.Q. differences between the groups is not supported.

Discussion

Taking our findings as a whole, they support an explanation of the differential impact of deterrence in terms of differences in personality expressed as perceptions of self *vis-à-vis* the legal structure. The delinquent group's greater self-perceived propensity to engage in violations, confirming hypothesis (2), and greater belief in ability to evade arrest, confirming the first part of hypothesis (3), provides quantitative evidence for the "magical immunity" mechanism posited in psychoanalytic ego psychology. Moreover, it suggests a more careful examination of the greater "impulsivity" attributed to delinquents. Frequently, the concept of "impulsivity" carries with it the connotation that some force overwhelms the individual's attempts to restrain himself—for example, the legal notion of "irresistible impulse" implies that some effort is made to resist. However, the indication in this study that the presumed effect of sanctions is significantly less applicable to delinquents suggests that the exercise of restraint is repressed, and appears in consciousness as distorted self-perception.

At what point does this distorted perception come about? The delinquents had committed their delinquent acts and been incarcerated before expressing their perceptions for this study, so that perceptual distortion cannot be taken to have preceded delinquency. To demonstrate perception as causal, it would be necessary to administer the questionnaire to nondelin-

quents and to predict delinquency from it. Yet the present findings are striking just because the perception of immunity was shown among boys who
were caught and incarcerated, many of them repeatedly, for delinquent offenses.

The mechanism of perceptual distortion leads delinquents to perceive
themselves invulnerable to arrest, but there is not a correspondingly significant difference in perceived immunity from conviction. Why does the mechanism operate selectively? Perhaps the very fact that the first part of the
hypothesis was confirmed explains the failure to confirm the second part: if a
magical belief in immunity from arrest serves to neutralize fear of punishment, a simultaneous belief in immunity from conviction is unnecessary. An
alternative explanation is that the delinquent may be able to develop a rationale to support the delusion of arrest immunity on the basis of abilities he
thinks he has in the area of crime commission and evasion of arresting
authorities, but the process of trial conviction, in which the principal actors
are lawyers, judges, etc., may be too remote to support such a rationale.

Failure to confirm the first hypothesis supports the view, recently advanced by Matza (1964), that the discrepancy between delinquents' and
nondelinquents' relations to larger social processes has been heretofore
greatly exaggerated. Inkeles (1959) has argued cogently for interpreting the
interplay between social structure and behavior by means of mediating psychological processes, and the Gluecks' (1950) approach to delinquency provides an example of such interpretation. As a whole, our findings lend support to interpretations at this level.

The present investigation bears on two areas of inquiry not usually concerned with criminology. One of these, the study of decision-making under
conditions of risk,[4] has received much recent research attention. McClelland
(1958) and Atkinson et al. (1960) have shown that a particular pattern of
risk preference is characteristic of persons oriented toward achievement
through socially acceptable channels. If the delinquent is also seen as motivated to achieve, but differs from the middle-class achiever in the criteria
of success (Cohen, 1955), he too may turn out to have the middle-class
achiever's pattern of risk preference. Future research might explore the rela-

---

[4] This approach has been applied to formal legal decisions on the part of judges, jurors, and enforcement officers. See examples in Schubert (1963), Strodtbeck (1962), and LaFave (1965).
A study in progress by Kaplan (1965) applies decision theory to the criminal process.

tion between perception as measured in this study, risk preference, and achievement motivation among delinquents.

A second area concerns the relation between fear of punishment and the sense of morality. As child psychology explains it, normal development consists of "internalizing" prohibitions, so that the fear of external punishment becomes a moral standard, which then produces conformity in the absence of situational sanctions (Kohlberg, 1963). Part of the "ethical risk" hypothesis which was confirmed by Rettig and Rawson (1963) holds that unethical behavior depends on expectancy of censure. Aronfreed (1961) has shown that middle-class children are more likely to give self-critical responses to stories of transgression, while working-class children focus more on external responsibility. Sears, Maccoby, and Levin (1957) have studied some of the socialization practices which are likely to lead to such "internalization," and Redl and Wineman (1952) describe a program for helping children develop internal controls. But these methods do not bear directly on the task of a psychotherapist concerned with how to correct deficiencies in internal control for persons whose characters have reached a relatively stable equilibrium. Schmideberg (1960: 334) sees the aims of psychotherapy with offenders as threefold: to sensitize them to social pressure, to develop a normal attitude toward punishment, and to teach them to foresee consequences and be motivated rationally by such foresight. The present study supports this focus by confirming the location of offenders' problems as a distortion of self-perception in relation to the real world.

References

Atkinson, J. W., J. R. Bastian, R. W. Earl, and G. H. Litwin. 1960. "The Achievement Motive, Goal Setting, and Probability Preferences," *Journal of Abnormal and Social Psychology* 60:27.

Aronfreed, J. 1961. "The Nature, Variety, and Social Patterning of Moral Response to Transgression," *Journal of Abnormal and Social Psychology* 63:223.

Ball, John C. 1955. "The Deterrence Concept in Criminology and Law," *Journal of Criminal Law, Criminology, and Police Science* 46:347.

Becarria, C. 1819. *An Essay on Crimes and Punishments*. p. 31.

Cohen, Albert K. 1955. *Delinquent Boys*. Glencoe, Ill.: Free Press. p. 27.

Glaser, Daniel. 1958. "The Sociological Approach to Crime and Correction," *Law and Contemporary Problems* 23:683.

Glueck, S. and E. Glueck. 1950. *Unraveling Juvenile Delinquency*. New York: Oxford University Press. p. 278.

Inkeles, Alex. 1959. "Personality and Social Structure." In Robert K. Merton, Leonard Broom, and Leonard S. Cottrell (eds.), *Sociology Today*. New York: Basic Books. p. 249.

Kaplan, S. J. 1965. In J. H. Skolnick, "The Sociology of Law in America: Overview and Trends," *Social Problems: Supplement on Law and Society* 13:36.

Kelly, F. J. and D. J. Veldman. 1964. "Delinquency and School Behavior as a Function of Impulsivity and Nondominant Values," *Journal of Abnormal and Social Psychology* 69:190.

Kohlburg, L. 1963. "Moral Development and Identification." In National Society for the Study of Education, *Child Psychology*. 62nd year book. University of Chicago Press. p. 277.

LaFave, W. R. 1965. *Arrest: The Decision to Take a Suspect Into Custody*. Boston: Little, Brown.

Matza, David. 1964. *Delinquency and Drift*. New York: Wiley. p. 62.

McClelland, David C. 1958. "Risk-Taking in Children with High and Low Need for Achievement." In J. W. Atkinson (ed.), *Motives in Fantasy, Action, and Society*. New York: Van Nostrand. p. 306.

McCord, W. M. and J. McCord. 1956. *Psychopathy and Delinquency*. New York: Grune. p. 8.

Reckless, Walter, Simon Dinitz, and Ellen Murray. 1956. "Self Concept as an Insulator Against Delinquency," *American Sociological Review* 21:744.

Redl, Fritz and David Wineman. 1952. *Controls from Within*. Glencoe, Ill.: Free Press.

1957. *The Aggressive Child*. Glencoe, Ill.: Free Press. p. 163.

Rettig, S. and H. E. Rawson. 1963. "The Risk Hypothesis in Predictive

Judgments of Unethical Behavior," *Journal of Abnormal and Social Psychology* 66:243.

Schmideberg, Melitta. 1960. "The Offender's Attitude Toward Punishment," *Journal of Criminal Law, Criminology, and Police Science* 51:332.

Schubert, G. A. 1963. *Judicial Decision Making*. New York: Macmillan.

Sears, R. R., E. E. Maccoby, and H. Levin. 1957. *Patterns of Child Rearing*. Cambridge, Mass.: Harvard University Press. p. 362.

Strodtbeck, Fred L. 1962. "Social Process, the Law, and Jury Functioning." In W. M. Evan (ed.), *Law and Sociology,* New York: Free Press. p. 152.

U.S. Federal Bureau of Investigation. 1961. *Uniform Crime Reports* 13:15.

Vold, G. B. 1958. *Theoretical Criminology*. New York: Oxford University Press.

6

Perception of "Payoff" and Criminal Activity

GARY F. JENSEN

Evidence on law enforcement suggests that a firm belief that most people who break the law are caught and punished is something of a naive misunderstanding of the real situation.[1] A great many crimes are never reported to the police and, even when reported, the chances of apprehension and punishment are slim in most instances. This is especially true for the most common offenses. However, even if based on a misreading of the objective situation,[2] the *belief* that "you can't get away with it" has long been held by the general public, "law-and-order" politicians and social scientists alike to deter potential offenders. But does such a belief accomplish this end? If it is learned that the belief is incorrect, is one then more likely to commit offenses?

Reprinted with permission of the Society for the Study of Social Problems from "Crime Doesn't Pay: Correlates of a Shared Misunderstanding," *Social Problems* 17 (Fall 1969) by Gary F. Jensen. The data upon which this study is based were collected under the direction of Alan B. Wilson. The author gratefully acknowledges Travis Hirschi and Ronald L. Akers for their help in revising the paper.

[1] For a recent summary of official and survey data on reported and unreported crime as well as on risks of apprehension for reported crimes, see the report of The President's Commission on Law Enforcement and Administration of Justice (1968: 87–106, 556–564). There have been a number of studies reporting specifically on the extent of undetected delinquent behaviour. For example, see Short and Nye (1958: 207–213) and Gold (1966: 27–46).

[2] While official data suggest that the chances of apprehension are slim, it may be that the belief that "you can't get away with it" applies more to the probabilities of apprehension for repeated offenses than for any single offense. However, the central concern of this study is the effects of variation in this belief, irrespective of its accuracy in relation to "reality."

Those sociologists who have paid some attention to the impact of "misunderstandings" or "misapprehensions" on rule-breaking would seem to answer both questions in the affirmative. For example, Garfinkel (1964: 225–250) assigned students the task of breaking the single price norm surrounding consumer purchases by "bargaining" with clerks over the price of various items. The students were surprised to learn that their anticipations of negative outcomes of violating this norm were in error and many eventually began to enjoy breaking the rule. However, the shared misunderstanding that violations of this rule would be met with hostile reaction seems to have served initially to ensure conformity. Similarly, Becker's (1963: 64–72) analysis of the development of a stable pattern of marihuana use suggests that an initial overestimate or misperception of the actual risk of detention and apprehension can have a deterrent effect; once marihuana use has been accomplished safely, the individual redefines the situation and fear of apprehension no longer prevents purchase and use. Yet another theorist, Matza (1964: 186–188), argues that "drifters"—those who have neutralized their ties to the conventional moral order—may be unable to overcome the apprehensiveness component in infraction. Before the "will to crime" can be activated, this apprehensiveness must be discounted or neutralized. This is done through subcultural beliefs which deprecate the potency of law-enforcement officials and define the situation as one in which the chances of capture are slight. Matza isolates such beliefs regarding apprehension and punishment as one factor which can deter those already in a state of drift.

However, such discussions of the problem remain only suggestive, for there has been little systematic research dealing directly with causes and effects of beliefs regarding apprehension and punishment. Only two empirical investigations have focused specifically on the relationship between perception of risk and rule breaking. Claster (1967: 80–86) hypothesized that delinquents perceive law enforcement to be less effective than do nondelinquents and that they perceive less chance of apprehension and conviction for a set of hypothetical offenses as well. Comparing the responses of institutionalized delinquents to questionnaire items with the responses of nondelinquents, he found no significant differences in their perceptions of the general efficacy of the law-enforcement system except as it applied to the probability that *they themselves* would be apprehended. However, Claster was comparing an institutionalized delinquent population with a control group of nondelinquents on the basis of their estimates of the probabilities of apprehension for a specific set of offenses. An investigation utilizing a self-report measure of delinquency and a very general measure of perception of apprehension and punishment may reach different conclusions.

Rettig and Rawson (1963: 243–248) examined the hypothesis that unethical behavior varies as a function of perceived risk. Students were asked to predict whether or not a student would steal money under a variety of conditions. They found that the reinforcement value of the money gained (financial need) and the expectancy that the money would fulfill the need are as strongly related to the prediction of unethical behavior as expectancy of apprehension. Severity of consequences was the most important source of variation with elements of risk and gain separate, but significant, sources of variation as well.

The studies summarized above focus on the consequences of a belief in the efficacy of enforcement for rule-breaking behavior. This belief may also have an impact on one's attitudes toward agents of control and the legal order itself. It can be posited that those who see deviation from legal norms as likely to lead to apprehension have more respect for the police. Moreover, following Durkheim's (1933: 96–103) view that those who break the law must be caught and punished to repair the wounds to the "collective conscience," there should be a connection between attachment to legal norms and a belief that lawbreakers are caught and punished. This is the essence of Merton's (1957: 180) claim that "a mounting frequency of deviant but 'successful' behavior tends to lessen and, as an extreme potentiality, to eliminate the legitimacy of the institutional norms for others in the system." Thus, beliefs regarding apprehension and punishment are central in creating "a strain toward anomie."

In sum, it has been argued that beliefs concerning apprehension and punishment for rule-breaking affect not only behavior but respect for the law and its agents as well. These general arguments will be examined here through an investigation of the relationships between the belief that lawbreakers are caught and punished and delinquent behavior, respect for the law, and respect for the police. Moreover, the effects of age on this belief will be examined. If this is one of the myths of childhood—a misunderstanding fostered by conventional society—then with increased age one's childhood beliefs should become more "realistic."

Study Design

These relationships will be examined by means of questionnaire data and official records collected by the Survey Research Center (University of California at Berkeley) in 1965.[3] While the original sample consisted of both black and white, male and female adolescents in grades seven through twelve, the present analysis is limited to 1,588 white boys. Thus, variations cannot be attributed to differences by sex or race.[4]

The measure of self-reported delinquency is a score based on the respondent's answers to a series of six questions concerning offenses of varying degrees of seriousness. Only acts committed within a year previous to the administration of the questionnaire are included in the score. The respondents are categorized as having committed (1) no delinquent acts, (2) one act, or (3) two or more acts. The measure of official delinquency used in the analysis is based on police records and is categorized similarly.

Respect for the police is measured by responses to the statement "I have a lot of respect for the Richmond police." The response categories provided ranged from strongly agree to strongly disagree. Respect for the law is measured by responses to the item "It's alright to get around the law if you can get away with it." Grade in school is used as a measure of age.

The belief item was measured by responses to the following statement: "People who break the law are almost always caught and punished." As such it is a general measure, unanchored to any set of specific offenses. It is an overall estimate based on whatever types of legal violations the respondent had in mind. Some violations are no doubt perceived as less "risky" than others and this may have implications for the deterrence of specific acts but this study is limited to the data available. Only one's *overall, general perception or belief* regarding apprehension and punishment can be exam-

[3] Details concerning the collection of data are reported elsewhere by Hirschi (1968: 38–74).

[4] While it was not possible to do an analysis on all four race-sex categories, the distribution of responses to the belief item are virtually identical for the four categories. In his analysis of delinquency, with these same data, Hirschi (1968) found little relationship between race and self-reported delinquency. While race and sex are controlled by exclusion, no attempt will be made to control for social class. There is no relationship between measures of social class and the belief item and, as with race, there is virtually no relationship between self-reported delinquency and social class.

ined with the data at hand. Moreover, no distinction can be made between perceptions of the apprehensive process and the sanctioning process since the questionnaire item asked for their belief regarding the chances of being caught *and* punished.

Findings

AGE

The findings presented in Table 6.1 support the view that the belief that persons who break the law are almost always caught and punished represents a certain naiveté which decreases with age. Seventy percent of the seventh-grade students as compared to between 47 and 50 percent of the eleventh- and twelfth-graders agree with the belief statement. Since the age range encompassed by the sample is somewhat limited, students enrolled in a sophomore-level course on deviant behavior were asked the same questions. *None of these college students agreed that people who break the law are almost always caught and punished.* While no firm conclusion can be drawn regarding the relation between this belief and age beyond the twelfth grade, it is apparent that the beliefs of college students about the probabilities of apprehension and punishment differ markedly from high school juniors and seniors. At any rate, there are differences in belief among the various age

TABLE 6.1.   BELIEF IN APPREHENSION AND PUNISHMENT BY GRADE

Grade		7th	8th	9th	10th	11th	12th	College Sample
		(%)	(%)	(%)	(%)	(%)	(%)	(%)
	SA [a]	20	24	16	15	10	9	0
	A	50	42	45	40	37	41	0
Belief	U	11	14	15	15	17	12	3
	D	14	16	18	23	26	30	44
	SD	6	4	5	7	9	7	53
	N=	275	251	303	275	277	217	32

Gamma = − .18.

[a] Letters refer to the five response categories.

categories, and the college data give some crude indication that the attenuation of this belief continues into adulthood.[5]

These data can be interpreted as suggesting that those responsible for socializing the young are often fostering a belief or perception of the world which they themselves do not hold. They are often, consciously or unconsciously, fostering a misunderstanding that will be shared by a great proportion of the younger generation.

RESPECT FOR THE POLICE AND THE LAW

The data in Table 6.2 show marked differences in respect for the police among categories of respondents differing in their belief regarding apprehension and punishment. Thirty-seven percent of those who strongly disagree with the belief item are relatively certain they respect the police as compared to 72 percent at the other extreme. Two arguments of spuriousness have been eliminated by controlling for grade and delinquency. While the zero-order gamma is .26, the net-partials when controlling for grade, self-reported, and official delinquency are .25, .22, and .25 respectively.[6]

TABLE 6.2. RESPECT FOR POLICE BY BELIEF IN APPREHENSION AND PUNISHMENT

Belief		Strongly Agree	Agree	Undecided	Disagree	Strongly Disagree
		(%)	(%)	(%)	(%)	(%)
	SA	42	18	17	16	19
Respect for police	A	30	46	41	33	18
	U	18	25	31	29	28
	D	5	6	5	14	8
	SD	5	5	6	8	28
	$N^a=$	244	654	216	316	97

Gamma = .26.
[a] These marginals will vary by a few cases from table to table due to nonresponses to some items.

[5] It is probably the case that conceptions of the law and lawbreaking behavior vary with age, and the relation may reflect such differing conceptions as well.

[6] Gamma coefficients and percentage distributions are used to assess the relationships. Gamma is a measure of association with a "proportional-reduction-in-error" interpretation (Costner,

TABLE 6.3.   OK TO BREAK THE LAW BY BELIEF IN APPREHENSION AND PUNISHMENT

Belief		Strongly Agree	Agree	Undecided	Disagree	Strongly Disagree
		(%)	(%)	(%)	(%)	(%)
	SA	6	2	4	3	15
OK to break law	A	4	7	8	10	12
	U	10	17	24	20	13
	D	30	42	39	40	28
	SD	50	32	25	27	32
	N =	245	651	216	318	98

Gamma = − .19.

This belief is more strongly related to attitudes towards the police than towards "the law." As summarized in Table 6.3, there is a relationship between the belief that people who break the law are caught and punished and attachment to, or respect for, the law. Those who believe this are more likely to feel that the law is morally binding. Again, grade, self-reported delinquency, and official delinquency were controlled by subdivision and net partial gamma coefficients computed. The net partials were − .16, − .17, and − .20, respectively. Thus, while the relationship is weak it cannot be accounted for by a common connection with age or the two measures of delinquency.

In sum, it appears that respect for the law as such is a general value orientation whose validity is not as readily influenced by beliefs or perceptions

1965: 341–352) appropriate to an ordinal level of measurement and, thus, is appropriate to this investigation. Net partial gamma coefficients (Davis, 1967: 189–193) were computed to summarize the relationship between two variables while holding a third variable constant by subdivision. As with average within-class correlation coefficients, net partial gamma is a weighted average and can "hide" conditional and contingent relationships. Controlling for the measures of delinquency, there appears to be little variation in the magnitude of the relationships when respect for the police is the dependent variable (partials range from .20 to .27). The relationship between the law and the belief item is consistently weak, with some variation in the gamma coefficients within subcategories. Among nondelinquents on the self-reported measure the gamma coefficient is − .19 and − .10 among delinquents. The comparable coefficients when controlling for the official measure are −.20 and −.08. Thus, while the net partial gamma coefficients suggest that the relationships persist when controlling for these measures, there is some variation within subdivisions. An attempt is made later in the paper to explain some of the most marked variation in gamma coefficients within grade categories.

of the realities of enforcement as are attitudes towards those enforcing the law. The view that perceived, unpunished deviance has demoralizing consequences is given some support but it should be noted that even among those believing that people can get away with violating the law the majority accept the law as morally binding. These relations persist when age, self-reported delinquency, and official delinquency are individually controlled. Since we cannot say what violations respondents had in mind when they responded to the belief item it is well to keep Packer's (1968: 288–289) caution in mind when interpreting the findings. As he suggests, perceptions of lax enforcement of some laws may not undermine respect for "the law" in general. It may be that this perception or belief, while not having much effect on orientations towards law in general, is more strongly related to respect for the laws that the respondent was thinking of when considering the belief item.

DELINQUENT BEHAVIOR

Tables 6.4 and 6.5 show that this belief is related to both self-reported and official delinquency. At one extreme the respondents are nearly four times more likely to report two or more delinquent acts. The finding that the belief item is not as strongly related to official delinquency as it is to self-reported delinquency suggests that processing by the law-enforcement system may lead to revisions in one's overall perception of the impunity of legal violation. Thus, it was hypothesized that self-reported delinquents who had been caught for some offense would differ in their perception from self-reported delinquents with no official record. However, there is virtually no difference

TABLE 6.4. SELF-REPORTED DELINQUENCY BY BELIEF IN APPREHENSION
AND PUNISHMENT

Belief		Strongly Agree	Agree	Undecided	Disagree	Strongly Disagree
		(%)	(%)	(%)	(%)	(%)
Delinquent acts	0	64	61	56	48	35
	1	25	23	24	26	26
	2+	10	17	21	26	39
	N =	248	651	214	318	98

Gamma = .22.

TABLE 6.5.   OFFICIAL DELINQUENCY BY BELIEF IN APPREHENSION AND PUNISHMENT

Belief		Strongly Agree	Agree	Undecided	Disagree	Strongly Disagree
		(%)	(%)	(%)	(%)	(%)
Official delinquent acts	0	85	82	83	76	71
	1	9	10	8	15	14
	2+	6	8	9	9	15
	N =	248	661	217	323	99

Gamma = .15.

between the two groups. Of those reporting one offense who had no official record, 58 percent agree with the belief statement as compared to 54 percent of those who report one act and do have an official record.

Another explanation for the difference between the relationship involving self-reported delinquency and the one involving official delinquency might be that, while this belief has a deterrent effect, those who commit an offense and believe that most people are caught and punished *are* more likely to be caught and punished. The data, however, do not support this argument. Of those who believe and have committed one self-reported act, 19 percent have an official record as compared to 18 percent of those who do not agree and report one offense.

A third possibility is that the difference may rest with the seriousness of the offense. If we can assume that official delinquents have committed more serious offenses than most self-reported delinquents, then it may be the case that the belief item differentiates less serious offenses better than the relatively more serious. To examine this possibility, four self-reported items were examined individually (including all offenses, not just those committed within a year of the questionnaire). Table 6.6 shows that the belief item is more strongly related to the less serious theft offenses than to the more serious offenses. While it differentiates for the theft of something worth more than fifty dollars, the relationship is not as strong as for the theft of less valuable items. Thus, the difference between the relation with self-reports as opposed to official measures may reflect the weaker relation of this variable to the commission of more serious offenses. It is possible that it was these less serious legal violations that respondents had in mind when responding to the belief item.

TABLE 6.6 PERCENT COMMITTING ONE OR MORE THEFTS OF VARYING
DEGREES OF SERIOUSNESS BY BELIEF IN APPREHENSION AND PUNISHMENT [a]

Belief		Strongly Agree	Agree	Undecided	Disagree	Strongly Disagree
	$2	41%	51%	54%	58%	77%
		(247)	(642)	(213)	(316)	(97)
	$2–$50	11	16	20	25	36
		(246)	(650)	(214)	(316)	(97)
Theft						
	$50+	5	5	7	8	19
		(247)	(649)	(213)	(319)	(98)
	Auto	7	8	12	17	19
		(247)	(656)	(213)	(319)	(98)

[a] Numbers in parentheses refer to the base from which the percentage was calculated.

At any rate, the belief is related to delinquency as measured by self-reports and official records. It may be that those most likely to break the law are those who believe that people can break the law with impunity but it may also be the case that variation in this belief reflects involvement in delinquency. As Garfinkel and Becker seem to suggest, one's definition of the situation is altered when the rule in question is violated and it is discovered that one can get away with breaking it. In contrast, Matza implies that the belief dealt with in this study can precede delinquency. If it is interpreted as another "definition favorable to the violation of the law," then Sutherland and Cressey (1966: 77–100) as well seem to argue that it precedes delinquent behavior. It may also be the case that there is a feedback relationship between experience and this belief—supporting both arguments. Variation in the apprehensiveness component may precede involvement in delinquent behavior with the belief capable of modification as a result of behavior and its contingencies as well. However, this study did find that those who admit to at least one delinquent act and also have an official record do not differ on the belief item from those who have not been caught. Thus, the correlation obtained should be a stimulus for further investigation.

DRIFT, BELIEF, AND DELINQUENT BEHAVIOR

While this study has examined the general argument that there is a negative association between the belief that lawbreakers are caught and punished and delinquency, Matza specifically argues that such beliefs have a deterrent im-

TABLE 6.7. PERCENT REPORTING TWO OR MORE DELINQUENT ACTS BY
BELIEF IN APPREHENSION AND PUNISHMENT WITHIN VARIOUS SUBGROUPS [a]

Belief		SA	A	U	D-SD
	High	6%	7%	10%	13%
		(70)	(162)	(51)	(85)
Closeness of father-son relation	2	9	13	19	14
		(46)	(139)	(36)	(71)
	3	11	23	18	25
		(46)	(110)	(34)	(76)
	Low	18	23	29	44
		(50)	(148)	(59)	(119)
	High	7	12	17	23
		(150)	(392)	(132)	(279)
Educational aspirations	Medium	16	24	26	38
		(43)	(127)	(31)	(77)
	Low	21	24	31	47
		(44)	(101)	(32)	(47)
	High	6	6	17	16
		(123)	(205)	(54)	(115)
Attachment to the law	Medium	8	15	15	24
		(74)	(270)	(84)	(150)
	Low	27	32	31	50
		(48)	(167)	(75)	(145)

[a] Numbers in parentheses refer to the base from which the percentage was calculated.

pact among "drifters." For purposes of this study "drifters" will be defined
as those with relatively few ties to the conventional system. Several indices
will be used: relations with one's father, educational aspirations, and attachment to the law. Table 6.7 supports his arguments in that the belief item differentiates among juveniles who are not tied into the conventional system.

While Matza's discussion focuses on the deterrent impact of such a
belief among drifters, he makes no specific claims regarding its impact
among those attached to conventional society. One might argue that the perception of general risk would have the most effect on boys with a lot to lose
as measured by attachments and commitments. It is more costly for them to
be apprehended since they are involved in social relations that would more
likely be affected and have commitments that might be endangered. The
drifters have less to lose in terms of these variables and the "costs" of
apprehension should not be as great. The data, however, do not support this

argument and, if percentage differences are considered, the belief seems to have a slightly greater effect among drifters. At any rate, while boys with few ties to conventional society have been found to be prone to delinquency, these findings suggest that variation in the belief that law-breakers are caught and punished is an independent source of variation and a possible line of attack in dealing with drifters (and nondrifters as well). In sum, the empirical results of this study are compatible with Matza's arguments regarding drift and delinquency.

SPECIFICATION BY GRADE LEVEL

It was mentioned earlier that the sample is limited to high school and junior high school students and, thus, excludes dropouts. However, by examining some of the relationships among seventh- and eighth-graders we can assess the arguments on a population more representative of the total adolescent population of the same age and sex. Table 6.8 summarizes the partial gamma coefficients for some of the relationships within the grade sub-groups. The relationships are actually stronger among the seventh- and eighth-graders than in the sample as a whole.[7]

TABLE 6.8.   CORRELATES OR BELIEF IN APPREHENSION AND PUNISHMENT WITHIN GRADE CATEGORIES [a]

	Grade	7th	8th	9th	10th	11th	12th
	Respect police	0.28	0.30	0.31	0.21	0.22	0.15
Belief by:	OK to break law	−0.31	−0.19	−0.19	−0.13	0.03	0.00
	Self-reported delinquency	−0.40	−0.31	−0.17	−0.19	−0.12	−0.07

[a] The gamma coefficients were generated on tables with total number of cases ranging between 214 and 299.

[7] Several factors suggest that this interaction is not likely to be due to chance or to characteristics of the gamma measure itself: (1) The coefficients in Table 6.8 were generated from cross-classifications involving between 214 and 299 respondents. (2) While gamma coefficients can vary due to differences in marginal distributions, the above differences in the magnitude of the relationships persist when the variables are dichotomized and percentage differences within sub-categories compared. (3) W^2 (Goodman 1965: 291) was computed to assess the significance of the difference in magnitude of the relationship between the law item and the belief item among seventh-graders as compared to twelfth-graders. It was statistically significant at the .01 level. (Both variables were dichotomized and Yule's Q computed to carry out the test.) (4) Finally,

TABLE 6.9.   BELIEF IN APPREHENSION AND PUNISHMENT BY GRADE LEVEL
WITHIN RESPECT FOR THE LAW SUBCATEGORIES

Subcategory:				Low Respect			
	Grade	7th	8th	9th	10th	11th	12th
	High	59%	73%	66%	67%	68%	68%
Belief	Low	41%	27%	34%	33%	32%	32%
	N=	56	59	94	92	82	62
Subcategory:				Medium Respect			
	Grade	7th	8th	9th	10th	11th	12th
	High	90%	80%	78%	72%	63%	60%
Belief	Low	10%	20%	22%	28%	37%	40%
	N=	89	90	116	96	92	100
Subcategory:				High Respect			
	Grade	7th	8th	9th	10th	11th	12th
	High	84%	83%	82%	72%	58%	62%
Belief	Low	16%	17%	18%	28%	42%	38%
	N=	127	101	86	83	48	55

In fact, there is no relationship between the belief item and attachment to the law among eleventh and twelfth graders. It may be that variation in the belief that "crime doesn't pay" is an important determinant of respect for the law among "impressionable," younger adolescents but that in higher grade levels revision in this belief has little effect on basic value orientations. It is commonly assumed that the young are more impressionable, that what they are exposed to in the mass media, for example, can have a greater effect on their "moral fiber." It may be that those who believe that crime does not pay, and thus, are attached to the law when they are young remain attached to the law as they get older even though their perceptions of risk are revised. Those who believe that people can get away with breaking the law are likely to be unattached to the law and to remain unattached. Since their belief is closer to the objective reality of the situation, it may be less likely to change as well. In sum, with increasing age, beliefs regarding apprehension and punishment of those attached to the law may come to parallel those of the unattached while the latter group's beliefs remain relatively constant. The outcome may then be reflected in the interaction noted in Table 6.8.

the explanation for this interaction led to a prediction which was supported by the data and which is reported below. The compatibility of the data with the prediction suggests that the interaction was meaningful.

This argument requires longitudinal analysis for a proper assessment but Table 6.9 suggests that it is at least tenable. When the unattached at each grade level are compared, there is some slight erratic variation in the belief item but for those attached to the law the percent who feel that people get away with breaking the law increases with grade in school from 16 percent in the seventh grade to about 40 percent in the eleventh and twelfth grades. For the latter grade levels the perceptions of the attached move closer to those of the unattached than was the case in the lower grade levels. In fact, by the eleventh and twelfth grades more of the attached than of the unattached believe that people can break the law with impunity.

While the argument outlined above goes beyond the sophistication of the data, this analysis is compatible with notions of "internalization" and is compatible with the data. In sum, it can be argued that one's perception of the world when young affects the "internalization" of basic attitudes towards the law but that the revision in belief that occurs with age does little to change basic value orientations.[8] An adequate assessment of these claims awaits further analysis.

Summary and Implications

This study has attempted to deal with some hypothesized connections between perceptions of the apprehensive process and various attitude and behavior patterns. While one's general perception of the reality of the situation may reflect a misunderstanding, shared by many others, it has been argued by both layman and professional alike to play some role in crime prevention and in the development of attitudes towards the law and those charged with enforcing the law. These claims have been given some measure of empirical support as have the more specific claims involved in Matza's theory of delinquency and drift. The notion that the belief is a misunderstanding fostered by nonbelievers has also gained some support.[9]

[8] A parallel argument might account for the interaction involving self-reported delinquency. It may be that beliefs regarding apprehension and punishment more readily change than the "life style" and normative orientations reflected in patterns of deviant and conforming behavior. It may be that while with increasing age beliefs of nondelinquents come to more closely parallel those of delinquents, this change does little to change basic normative behavior patterns.

[9] While little has been said about possible antecedents of the belief, several possible sources of variation in the belief were examined. As noted earlier, race, sex, and social class do not dif-

The implications of the findings for social policy may seem quite clear-cut to some. Through stricter law enforcement one can change the perception of risk and deter potential offenders, affect respect for the police and possibly even affect respect for the law in general. However, in addition to questions of causality that always confront cross-sectional survey analysis, other cautions are required when reaching such conclusions. As Claster's study seems to suggest, adolescents may not differ in their perception of the probabilities of apprehension and yet still feel that *they themselves* can break the law with impunity. Moreover, the great variation in beliefs regarding the possibility of apprehension and punishment illustrates the tenuous connection between the "objective" situation and definitions of the situation. A change in the realities of enforcement may have little effect on actual beliefs or perceptions of these realities.[10] Even if the risks of apprehension and punishment were increased there is no guarantee that there would not be another "shared misunderstanding" of the situation.

Defining deterrence as "the preventive effect which actual or threatened punishment of offenders has upon potential offenders," Ball (1955: 347–354) summarized the state of research in the area as of 1955 as methodologically inadequate and doctrinaire, centering more around exhortation than the collection of evidence. The situation since that time has remained essentially unchanged and beliefs regarding apprehension and punishment have been largely ignored in delinquency research. The present analysis has dealt empirically with some of the important issues in this much neglected area and it is hoped that it will stimulate further inquiry and new lines of thought.

---

ferentiate respondents on the belief item. There is however, a positive relationship between belief that lawbreakers are caught and punished and measures of attachment to conventional role models, supervision by the father, academic orientation, and achievement motivation. Delinquent associations were found to be negatively related. In sum, those tied to the conventional system are more likely to believe that people who break the law are caught and punished, while ties to unconventional role models have the opposite effect.

[10] The same college students who were asked to respond to the belief item were asked to give their estimates of the proportion of various types of offenses cleared by arrest. The estimates for each offense ranged from 10 to between 80 and 100 percent. For most offenses the estimates were fairly evenly distributed over this range. This seems to suggest that there is no guarantee that a change in the objective situation will have any effect on the beliefs of respondents regarding the situation.

References

Ball, John C. 1955. "The Deterrence Concept in Criminology and Law," *Journal of Criminology and Police Science* 46 (September–October):347–354.

Becker, Howard S. 1963. *Outsiders*. New York: Free Press.

Claster, Daniel S. 1967. "Comparisons of Risk Perception between Delinquents and Nondelinquents," *Journal of Criminal Law, Criminology, and Police Science* 58 (March):80–86.

Costner, Herbert L. 1965. "Criteria for Measures of Association," *American Sociological Review* 30 (June):341–353.

Davis, James A. 1967. "A Partial Coefficient for Goodman and Kruskal's Gamma," *Journal of the American Statistical Association* 53 (March):189–193.

Durkheim, Emile. 1933. *The Division of Labor in Society*. Glencoe, Ill.: Free Press.

Garfinkel, Harold. 1964. "The Routine Grounds of Everyday Activities," *Social Problems* II (Winter):225–250.

Gold, Martin. 1966. "Undetected Delinquent Behavior," *Journal of Research in Crime and Delinquency* 3 (January):27–46.

Goodman, Leo A. 1965. "On the Multivariate Analysis of Three Dichotomous Variables," *American Journal of Sociology* 71 (November):290–301.

Hirschi, Travis. 1968. "Infraction as Action." Ph.D. dissertation. University of California, Berkeley.

Matza, David. 1964. *Delinquency and Drift*. New York: Wiley.

Merton, Robert K. 1957. *Social Theory and Social Structure*. London: Free Press of Glencoe.

Packer, Herbert L. 1968. *The Limits of Criminal Sanction*. Stanford: Stanford University Press.

President's Commission on Law Enforcement and Administration of Justice. 1968. *The Challenge of Crime in a Free Society*. New York: Avon.

Rettig, Solomon and Harvey E. Rawson. 1963. "The Risk Hypothesis in Predictive Judgments of Unethical Behavior," *Journal of Abnormal and Social Psychology* 66 (March):243–248.

Short, James F., Jr. and F. Ivan Nye. 1958. "Extent of Unrecorded Delinquency, Tentative Conclusions," *Journal of Criminal Law, Criminology and Police Science* 49 (November–December):296–302.

Sutherland, Edwin H. and Donald R. Cressey. 1966. *Principles of Criminology*. New York: Lippincott.

7

Perceived Penal Sanction
and Self-Reported Criminality

GORDON P. WALDO
AND THEODORE G. CHIRICOS

The entire system of American criminal justice—from the debate of legislators to the maximum custody prison—is based, in part, on the assumption that punishment of criminal offenders will deter future criminality. Despite its antiquity,[1] this assumption has received little more than speculative attention from legal philosophers, jurists, politicians, and the general public.[2] Only recently have social scientists put this assumption to empirical test, and to date, the evidence appears somewhat contradictory and inconclusive.

The earlier studies by Schuessler and Savitz questioned the deterrent effectiveness of *capital* punishment. Their research showed little difference in homicide rates when (1) comparable abolitionist and retentionist states were examined (Schuessler, 1952) and (2) when rates were compared before and after well-publicized executions (Savitz, 1958). Sellin (1967: 124) later

Reprinted with permission of the Society for the Study of Social Problems from "Perceived Penal Sanction and Self-Reported Criminality: A Neglected Approach to Deterrence Research," *Social Problems* 19 (Spring 1971) by Gordon P. Waldo and Theodore G. Chiricos. This research was supported, in part, by Ford Foundation grant number 67-586. The authors would like to express their appreciation to John Cardascia and Robert Camacho for their assistance in this project.

[1] Among the earliest to crystallize this issue was Jeremy Bentham, whose "Principles of Penal Law" was published in 1843.

[2] Even among social scientists, most of the input on this issue has been theoretical or moralistic in nature (Mead, 1918; Wood, 1938; Ball, 1955; Polier, 1956; Barnes and Teeters, 1959; Toby, 1964; Jeffery, 1965; Bittner and Platt, 1966; Zimring and Hawkins, 1968) and as noted by Chambliss (1966: 70), ". . . the question of deterrence has frequently turned into a debate over the morality of capital punishment."

showed that rates of homicide were relatively unaffected by the temporary abolition and eventual reinstatement of capital punishment in eleven states. He concluded that

. . . there is no evidence that the abolition of the death penalty generally causes an increase in criminal homicides or that its reintroduction is followed by a decline. The explanation of changes in homicide rates must be sought elsewhere.

The study of crime rates for clues to questions about deterrence was extended by Gibbs (1968) to alternative measures of the severity and certainty of punishment,[3] and by Tittle (1969) to alternative criminal offenses.[4] The former (Gibbs, 1968: 523–527) found inverse relationships between rates of homicide and the severity ($phi = -.25$) and certainty ($phi = -.48$) of punishment. This contradiction of earlier deterrence findings was reinforced by Tittle's (1969: 409) study of seven criminal offenses, which revealed:

Strong and consistent negative associations . . . between certainty of punishment and crime rates, while a negative association is observed between severity of punishment and crime rates only for homicide.

However, Tittle's findings were called into question by Chiricos and Waldo (1970) who extended a similar mode of analysis to additional points in time and to measures of change in the levels of certainty, severity, and criminality.[5] Their data showed little consistent support for the assumption

[3] Severity of punishment was operationally defined by Gibbs as "the median number of months served on a homicide sentence by all persons in prison on December 31, 1960. This measurement was taken for each state in the United States, as was his index of the certainty of imprisonment:

$$\frac{\text{No. of State Prison Admissions for Homicide in 1960}}{\text{Mean No. of Homicides Known to Police for 1959–1960}}$$

[4] Tittle examined the following offenses: homicide, assault; sex offenses; robbery; larceny; burglary and auto theft. His principal measure of severity was provided by the "mean length of time served for felony prisoners released from state prisons in 1960." Certainty of punishment for the several felonies was given by the following ratio:

$$\frac{\text{No. of State Prison Admissions for "X" Offense in 1960 and 1963}}{\text{No. of "X" Crimes Known to the Police in 1959 and 1962}}$$

[5] Certainty of punishment was calculated for three time periods, 1950, 1960, and 1963. The general format for certainty measures is given by the 1950 index:

$$\frac{\text{1950 Admissions to Prison for "X" Offense}}{\text{Mean of "X" Crimes Known to the Police in 1949 and 1950}}$$

Severity of punishment for 1960 and 1964 were given by the "median length of sentence served by state prisoners released in 1960 and 1964," respectively.

that rates of crime are inversely related to the certainty and severity of punishment, and several methodological issues were raised which cast doubt upon the appropriateness of findings derived from this approach to deterrence research.[6]

The studies cited represent the major thrust of sociological research in the area of criminal deterrence and each has operationalized the dependent variable—criminality—by some use of available, aggregate *rates* of crime. For several reasons, not the least of which is the inconsistency of conclusions among the studies, such an approach to questions of deterrence may never prove definitive. A major problem is the sensitivity of official crime rates to changes in the reporting of crime to the police and the recording of crime by the police. These difficulties are compounded by the fact that variation in the *official* level of crime may reflect variation in the age distribution of the population or in the concentration of that population in urban areas.[7]

In addition, official statistics limit the researcher to seven "crime index" offenses, inasmuch as "crimes known to the police" are unavailable for additional specific crimes.[8] If one wished to examine deterrence for other types of criminality—such as victimless crime or white collar crime—official statistics would be of little use. Indeed, the need for deterrence research to distinguish among types of crimes is underscored by Andenaes' (1966: 957) distinction between crimes that are *mala per se* and those that are *mala quia prohibita:*

In the case of *mala per se,* the law supports the moral codes of society. If the threats of legal punishment were removed, moral feelings and the fear of public judgment

---

[6] In brief, this criticism suggests that Tittle's "strong and consistent" inverse relationships between certainty of punishment and crime rates may be the product of correlated bias existing in his measures of certainty and criminality. That is, the numerator of Tittle's criminality index is almost identical to the denominator of his certainty index. Thus, any computed relationship between such variables would have to be inverse. Implementing successive samples of random digits in the terms of the certainty and criminality measures, it was found that Tittle's actual relationships were no greater than could be found using random data.

[7] See, for example, *Crime and Its Impact: An Assessment* (President's Commission, 1967: 24–28), which summarizes the effects of these and other sociological factors upon the official rates of crime. For a discussion of problems in the underreporting of crimes to the police, see the victimization survey conducted by the National Opinion Research Center (President's Commission, 1967: 17–19). The impact of irregularities in the reporting of crime by the police is discussed in the same volume (President's Commission, 1967: 22–24).

[8] One may consult any recent issue of Uniform Crime Reports, published annually by the Federal Bureau of Investigation, Washington, D.C., to confirm this limitation.

would remain as powerful crime prevention forces, at least for a limited period. In the case of *mala quia prohibita,* the law stands alone; conformity is essentially a matter of effective legal sanctions.

A further limitation of the aggregate data approach is the researcher's inability to discern those social-psychological processes by which the presumed effects of punishment are realized.[9] For example, when correlating crime rates with the severity of statutory provisions for punishment, one knows nothing of how the penalties are perceived by potential offenders—if, indeed, they are perceived at all. Clearly, the deterrent effectiveness of punishment presumes that potential offenders *know* or *think* they know what the penalties are. Further, it must be assumed that offenders and nonoffenders *act* on the basis of their knowledge. However, these assumptions received critical attention in a recent California survey (Assembly Committee on Criminal Procedure, 1968: 13–14):

While the Legislature has supposedly responded to public appeal and increased the penalties for crimes of violence to victims, this was not known by the public . . . people were in general unaware that the Legislature had taken any action at all when in fact the Legislature had increased the minimum penalties . . . When the public did answer these items, they tended to underestimate the amount of the penalty. . . .

Even assuming awareness of penal sanctions it remains impossible, using aggregate data (with states or other political categories as the unit of analysis), for the researcher to determine whether individual offenders are actually deterred by the threat of formal punishment or by the social embarrassment of detection. The functional relationship between formal and informal sanctions is well summarized by Andenaes (1966: 961):

If the criminal can be sure that there will be no police action, he can generally rest assured that there will be no social reprobation. The legal machinery, therefore, is in itself the most effective means of mobilizing that kind of social control which emanates from community condemnation.

Finally, the approach to deterrence research through aggregate data precludes an examination of situational differences that could affect an individual's response to threats of punishment. For example, one cannot ask whether some people are deterred from some crimes in certain situations by a particular set of deterrents, or whether different persons in different situa-

[9] See the discussion by Zimring (1971: 56–61) concerning "Public Knowledge as a Threshold Requirement" in the study of deterrence.

tions may be differentially affected by threats of penal sanction. Further, the possibility that the *same* individual would respond to different deterrents for different crimes in different situations must be ignored when dealing with these data.[10]

In short, while official aggregate data have been useful in the study of deterrence, alternative modes of analysis must be tried if some of the remaining deterrence questions are to be answered. The research reported here provides one alternative approach to several deterrence questions that have not, as yet, been answered by traditional (i.e., based upon official aggregate statistics) deterrence research. In all, six related questions are being considered.

1. Is the admitted frequency of a specific criminal offense lowest for those who perceive the most severe penalties for that offense?

From deterrence theory, one would expect those perceiving the harshest penalties for a specific offense to be the least likely to engage in that offense. However, the empirical evidence that does exist (Schuessler, 1952; Sellin, 1967; Gibbs, 1968; Tittle, 1969; Chiricos and Waldo, 1970) neither deals with the issue of perceptions, nor does it confirm deterrence theory. In short, prior research has shown that *official* rates of crime are generally insensitive to variations in penal severity. It remains to be seen whether self-reported crime is responsive to *perceptions* of severe punishment.

2. Is the admitted frequency of a specific criminal offense lowest among those who perceive the greatest likelihood of someone like themselves receiving the maximum penalty if convicted for that offense?

Harsh statutory penalties would seem to have little deterrent effectiveness if potential offenders perceive little chance that the courts will invoke them. Such a situation may, in fact, currently exist with regard to marijuana offenses. Grupp and Lucas (1969) have documented a widely held suspision that court dispositions of marijuana cases have become less severe over time. Their study in California during the period from 1960 to 1967 indicates that while arrests for marijuana offenses have increased by 525 percent in those eight years, the percentage of convictions that resulted in a *prison sentence* dropped from 27 percent in 1960 to 11 percent in 1967. At

[10] Zimring's (1971: 33–96) entire discussion of the many factors related to the success or failure of deterrence threats, is supportive of this point.

the same time, the use of probation increased to the point that 46 percent of those convicted in 1967 were placed on probation, as opposed to 24 percent in 1960 (Grupp and Lucas, 1969: 5–8).

3. Is the admitted frequency of a specific criminal offense lowest for those who perceive the greatest likelihood that law-violators will be caught by the police?

While the deterrence hypothesis would anticipate such an inverse relationship, existing empirical evidence is somewhat contradictory. With regard to a belief that "people who break the law are almost always caught and punished," Jensen (1969: 194–196) found the greatest support from self-reported *nondelinquents*,[11] and the slightest support from youths reporting two or more delinquencies. On the other hand, Claster (1967: 83–84) showed that "training school" delinquents had a pronounced tendency to *overestimate* arrest rates for the general public,[12] whereas "nondelinquents" had an almost equivalent tendency to *underestimate* those rates. Clearly, if one considers the perceptions of law-enforcement efficiency to precede delinquent activity, then Jensen's data support classical deterrence expectations, while Claster's does not.[13]

4. Is the admitted frequency of a specific criminal offense lowest for those who have had the greatest contact with others who have been arrested or convicted for that offense?

It is assumed that persons who have had the greatest contact with others who have been punished for a specific crime, will have the most proximate knowledge of the consequences of the criminal justice system. On that ac-

---

[11] Jensen's (1969) "nondelinquents" are those who admit to no delinquent activities.

[12] It must be remembered, when comparing Claster's (1967) "delinquent" with Jensen's (1967), that the former "delinquents" are those who had been admitted to training school— whereas Jensen used self-reporting techniques.

[13] In actuality, however, one could argue that the experiences of the two samples of "delinquents" may have resulted in their perceptions of law enforcement. That is, training school "delinquents" might easily be expected to overestimate arrest probabilities—simply because they have experienced the formal sanctions of the police. On the other hand, self-reported "delinquents", because they have not received such formal sanction, could be just as likely to underestimate police efficiency. Should this be the case, then the logical time-order of deterrence relationships does not obtain.

count, they should be more readily deterred from that crime than others having less contact with the "clients" of criminal justice. At an earlier time, public penitence was demanded from offenders and public executions were significant community events. Today, the process of formal community response and the affixing of criminal labels is still intended to be a public ritual with at least two objectives: (1) the exemplary transfer of the offender from the status of "law-abiding citizen," to the "temporary" role of criminal, and (2) the definition of acceptable behavioral boundaries for the remainder of the community.[14]

5. Is the admitted frequency of a specific criminal offense lowest for those who perceive the greatest likelihood of arrest for someone like themselves committing that offense?

While the prior questions deal with arrests of "others," this question considers perceptions of law enforcement for a specific offense and for "someone like" the respondent. For example, in accord with deterrence theory, the lowest frequency of admitted marijuana use was expected for those who perceive the greatest likelihood of someone like themselves being arrested *if* they used marijuana. This expectation receives some support from another aspect of Claster's (1967: 83–84) work with training school delinquents. Even though his "official" delinquents overestimated the chances of arrest for the general public, they perceived significantly lower probabilities of being arrested *themselves* for a hypothetical offense, than did a sample of "nondelinquents." Curiously, these "delinquents" who had been officially responded to by society were still willing to believe in their relative immunity from legal sanction. From a deterrence perspective, one could argue that this type of perception helps facilitate delinquency, rather than deter it.

6. Are the foregoing deterrence relationships any stronger for crimes that are *mala prohibita* (e.g., marijuana use) than they are for crimes that are *mala in se* (e.g., larceny)?

This question recognizes the need for deterrence research to consider fundamental differences in *types* of crimes that may or may not be deterred by legal threats. Most empirical studies of deterrence have limited them-

[14] Excellent discussions of these consequences of labelling are provided by Erikson (1962) and Garfinkel (1956).

selves either to homicide or to F.B.I. "crime index" offenses,[15] all of which are *mala in se*. The legal sanctions against these crimes have massive support in the mores, and on that account, may be relatively unnecessary for deterrence.

On the other hand, many criminal activities such as gambling, marijuana use, underage drinking, etc., are widely practiced and condoned among large segments of our society—despite the legal proscriptions. In the case of these crimes, which are *mala prohibita,* the mores may be sufficiently ambivalent to cause the law to "stand alone" as a deterrent (Andenaes, 1966: 957). These distinctions have prompted Zimring (1971: 44–45) to hypothesize that:

. . . where a threatened behavior is considered to be a serious breach of society's moral code [i.e., larceny] the major explanation for the higher rate of compliant behavior is the strongly socialized citizen's sense of right and wrong, rather than his special sensitivity to the negative aspects of threatened consequences. Where a threatened behavior is considered a less drastic breach of the moral code [i.e., marijuana use], a special sensitivity to the negative aspects of threatened consequences may play a noteworthy part in explaining the difference between these two groups.

In short, this hypothesis suggests that "the effectiveness of deterrence varies in inverse proportion to the moral seriousness of the crime" (Morris, 1951: 13). For the purposes of this study, we are assuming that stealing is a crime of greater moral seriousness than possession of marijuana. This assumption is supported by the fact that 98.2 percent of the study population *disagreed* with the statement that "stealing *shouldn't* be a crime," whereas only 25 percent disagreed with a similar assertion for marijuana possession. Thus, if Andenaes, Zimring, and Morris are correct, deterrence relationships should be stronger for marijuana offenses than they are for theft crimes.[16]

[15] Exceptions to this concentration on crimes that are *mala in se* are, of course, provided by Chambliss' (1966) work with parking violations and Schwartz and Orleans' (1967) work with income tax evasion—both of which may be considered *mala prohibita*.

[16] An alternative perspective on "types of crime" and deterrence is offered by Chambliss (1969: 368–370) who hypothesized that instrumental actions (i.e., theft) are subject to greater control through formal sanctions than expressive actions (i.e., marijuana use), inasmuch as the latter are engaged in as a part of a broader style of life to which the individual may be committed. Applying this perspective, we might expect deterrence relationships to be stronger for larceny offenses than for marijuana offenses.

Research Method

An approach to the foregoing questions is sought through data collected in 321 interviews of undergraduates at The Florida State University.[17] The completed interviews represent 82.3 percent of an original sample of 390 students. From the latter group, which represents a 3-percent random sample of the undergraduate population (stratified by school year), 44 were out of town on internships, or had dropped from school sometime after the registrar's lists were completed. An additional 25 interviews could not be completed after initial contact was made. Of these, only seven involved refusals on the part of potential respondents. Given the size of the sample and the low rate of incompleted interviews, it is felt that a representative sample of the undergraduate population was obtained.

The interviews were carried out between January and May, 1970, by five undergraduate research assistants who had participated in the construction, pre-testing, and revision of the interview schedule. Respondents were assigned to the five interviewers in a random manner.

A short, self-reported crime inventory was included in the interview schedule. Comprising the inventory were questions relating to several dimensions of criminal activity: (1) how often has it been done; (2) at what age was it first done; (3) with how many other people was it first done; (4) how often has it been done in the past year; (5) with how many other people is it normally done? Several of these questions were used to distinguish self-reported users of marijuana from those who claim to have "never used," while similar distinctions were made between those who admit to stealing and those who have "never stolen." [18]

---

[17] The limitations of a student sample are readily acknowledged; however, the researchers were not expecting to settle the issue of deterrence for all time. Quite the contrary, for they would argue that different kinds of people in different kinds of situations are deterred from different kinds of crimes for entirely different reasons. This sample deals with a segment of our population that may be overrepresented on one of the crime we are studying—marijuana use, and, perhaps, underrepresented on the second crime—theft. We simply want to know whether the perceptions of this particular sample are related to the performance of two specific criminal activities.

[18] Several possible methods of delimiting "levels" of admitted theft were attempted. A simple distinction between those admitting to grand larceny and those admitting to petit larceny was

Perception of the severity of penalties for theft and marijuana offenses was indicated by responses to the following questions: What would you say is the maximum prison penalty in Florida for someone who: a) takes or steals something worth less than $100? b) illegally possesses marijuana— first offense?

For purposes of contingency analysis, respondents were grouped into three categories for each of the crimes: (1) those *overestimating* the penalty; (2) those with *accurate* perceptions of the penalty; and (3) those *underestimating* the penalty.

Perceptions of the certainty of punishment were obtained from responses to several questions. Respondents were asked to estimate the percentage of people committing crimes who are caught by the police. This general question was followed by estimates pertaining to specific offenses and to persons "like the respondent." In this latter instance, students were asked how likely the police were to catch "someone like yourself" if you used marijuana or stole something worth less than $100. The responses were given in a Likert-type format ranging from "very likely" to "very unlikely." A third set of questions—also in Likert format—asked the respondent how likely it was for "someone like yourself" to receive the maximum prison sentence if you were convicted for one of the several offenses under consideration. Finally, contact with previously punished offenders was determined by asking the respondent how many individuals he knew personally who had been arrested and/or convicted for theft and marijuana offenses.

Findings

The relationships between self-reported criminal behavior and perceptions of the penal structure are analyzed in contingency tables with gamma computed to indicate the strength of association. The data in Table 7.4 are not appropriate for the 2 × 3 format used in other tables, and a Q-value rather than gamma is reported.

---

not feasible because only seven students admitted to the more serious offense. Simple frequency of petit larceny was rejected, inasmuch as most of the frequent larcenies were committed at an early age—and it was felt that larcenies committed in the past year would probably be more significant.

Deterrence theory suggests that use of marijuana and admitted larceny should be most frequent among those who underestimate the penalties, and least frequent among those who overestimate the penalties for each offense. An inspection of Tables 7.1A and 7.1B reveals that the present data do not confirm this expectation. While marijuana use is least frequent among those who overestimate the penalties, it is *most* frequent among those whose perceptions of the law are the *most accurate*. Further, admitted use of marijuana is less common for those *underestimating* the penalties than for those whose estimates are accurate. At the same time, deterrence logic is contradicted by the fact that admitted theft (Table 7.1B) is as prevalent among respondents who overestimate penalties for petty larceny as it is among those who underestimate. In addition, the most frequent theft activity is found among those who accurately perceive the penalty for petty larceny. The low gamma values reinforce the conclusion that admitted criminality ap-

TABLE 7.1A. ADMITTED MARIJUANA USE BY PERCEIVED SEVERITY OF FLORIDA PENALTY FOR FIRST MARIJUANA POSSESSION [a]

Perceived Penalty	Percent Having Used Marijuana	Percent Never Using Marijuana	Total	(N)
Overestimated	27.0	73.0	100.0	(74)
Accurately estimated	37.3	62.7	100.0	(102)
Underestimated	33.6	66.4	100.0	(137)

Gamma = − .07

TABLE 7.1B. ADMITTED STEALING BY PERCEIVED SEVERITY OF FLORIDA PENALTY FOR PETTY LARCENCY [a]

Perceived Penalty	Percent Having Stolen	Percent Never Stealing	Total	(N)
Overestimated	54.9	45.1	100.0	(142)
Accurately estimated	61.7	38.3	100.0	(115)
Underestimated	54.8	45.2	100.0	(62)

Gamma = − .04

[a] Data for these items are obtained from responses to the question, "Could you estimate the maximum prison penalty in Florida for illegal possession of marijuana—first offense?" "What would you say the maximum prison penalty in Florida is for someone who takes or steals something worth *less* than $100?"

pears unrelated to perceptions of the severity of punishment. This interpretation applies to theft, which is *mala in se,* as well as to marijuana use, which is *mala prohibita.*

It is interesting to note that a larger proportion of the respondents underestimated penalties for marijuana possession (43.7 percent) than for petty larceny (19.3 percent). This greater tendency to underestimate marijuana penalties should, according to deterrence theory, eventuate in a greater frequency of marijuana as opposed to theft offenses. However, the opposite is true. Whereas a total of 33.3 percent of the respondents admit to some experience with marijuana, 58.6 percent have stolen something in their life. Thus, something other than a perception of severe penalties appears to be operating in the presumed deterrence of these students from marijuana and theft crimes.

The actual level of punishment available for any crime may be irrelevant as a deterrent if citizens understand or believe that courts are unwilling to impose harsh penalties. The strength of this belief was elicited for both offenses, with the expectation that criminal behavior would be more frequent among those who believe that the courts would spare them the maximum allowable penalty. This expectation is borne out for marijuana offenders, but not for theft offenders.

Tables 7.2A and 7.2B give the frequency of marijuana use and admitted theft for groups of respondents with varying perceptions of the court's leniency. Among those respondents who are most optimistic about avoiding the maximum penalty upon conviction, marijuana use is more than twice as common (43.4 percent) as it is among those who consider the maximum penalty "likely" (19 percent). A moderately strong gamma value $(-.41)$ suggests that this optimism may be closely associated with the admitted use of marijuana. While admitted theft is more common among those who think the maximum penalty is "unlikely" than it is among those who consider it "likely," it is *most* common among those who see the maximum penalty as a 50/50 probability. However, the percentage differences among the several groups are sufficiently small to generate a very small gamma value $(-.02)$ and a conclusion that the perceived likelihood of severe court disposition is apparently unrelated to admitted theft activity. The discrepancy between deterrence relationships involving marijuana and theft behavior is consistent with the expectation raised by Zimring (1971), who hypothesized stronger

TABLE 7.2A. ADMITTED MARIJUANA USE BY PERCEIVED LIKELIHOOD OF RECEIVING MAXIMUM PENALTY UPON CONVICTION FOR MARIJUANA POSSESSION [a]

Perceived Likelihood of Maximum Penalty	Percent Having Used Marijuana	Percent Never Using Marijuana	Total	(N)
Likely	19.0	81.0	100.0	(79)
50/50	26.5	73.5	100.0	(83)
Unlikely	43.4	56.6	100.0	(159)

Gamma = − .41
$p < .001$

TABLE 7.2B. ADMITTED THEFT BY PERCEIVED LIKELIHOOD OF RECEIVING MAXIMUM PENALTY UPON CONVICTION FOR PETTY LARCENY [a]

Perceived Likelihood of Maximum Penalty	Percent Having Stolen	Percent Never Stealing	Total	(N)
Likely	44.4	55.6	100.0	(18)
50/50	63.1	36.9	100.0	(65)
Unlikely	56.7	43.3	100.0	(238)

Gamma = − .02

[a] Data for these items are obtained from responses to the questions, "If you were convicted of possession of marijuana, how likely would you be to get the maximum Florida penalty?" "If you were convicted of stealing something worth *less* than $100, how likely would you be to get the maximum Florida penalty?"

deterrence relationships for crimes that are *mala prohibita* (marijuana use) than for crimes that are *mala in se* (larceny).

As suggested by Jensen's (1969) findings cited earlier, a deterrent to crime may be provided by the perception that law-violators in general are caught by the police. This approach, dealing with certainty of punishment at the *general* level, assumes that punishment of "others" will deter "ego's" criminal behavior. Tables 7.3A and 7.3B show the frequency of admitted criminality for respondents with varying perceptions of the probability that law-violators will be caught by the police.

As expected from deterrence theory, the lowest frequency of marijuana use (25.0 percent) and larceny (51.0 percent) is found among those who perceive the greatest likelihood (50 percent +) that law-violators will be appre-

TABLE 7.3A.   ADMITTED MARIJUANA USE BY PERCEIVED PROBABILITY OF
ARREST FOR LAW VIOLATORS [a]

Percent of Law Violators Arrested by Police	Percent Having Used Marijuana	Percent Never Using Marijuana	Total	(N)
50 +	25.0	75.0	100.0	(104)
21–49	30.6	69.4	100.0	(108)
0–20	43.5	56.5	100.0	(108)

Gamma = − .28
p < .01

TABLE 7.3B.   ADMITTED THEFT BY BELIEF IN THE PROBABILITY OF AR-
REST FOR LAW VIOLATORS [a]

Percent of Law Violators Arrested by Police	Percent Having Stolen	Percent Never Stealing	Total	(N)
50 +	51.0	49.0	100.0	(104)
21–49	60.2	39.8	100.0	(108)
0–20	61.1	38.9	100.0	(108)

Gamma = − .14

[a] Data for these items are obtained from responses to the question, "What percentage of
the people who commit crimes do you think ever get caught by the police?"

hended by the police. Conversely, those perceiving little chance (0 to 20
percent) for such apprehension are much more likely to have used marijuana
(43.5 percent) or to have stolen something (61.1 percent). Given the middle-
class character of the student sample,[19] it is not surprising that potential *arrest* should, by itself, loom so important as a deterrent to crime. For "respectable" criminals, an arrest—with its attendant publicity—may be as
socially and personally consequential as any subsequent court action. This
point was considered by Cameron (1964), who noted that formal legal action
was frequently not taken in the cases of apprehended middle-class shoplifters. Both police and storekeepers apparently felt that the situation of arrest, even without publicity, was a sufficient deterrent to future pilfering. In
the case of our student sample, *arrest* for a drug offense carries a particularly harsh consequence. A recent and well-publicized Florida statute

[19] The median income of the respondents' fathers was $10,000, and 55 percent of the fathers
had at least some college training.

requires the summary suspension of any student arrested for drug offenses.[20] Since reinstatement must await court disposition and since trial delays are excessive, and a loss of student status could result (for males) in a change of military draft status, an arrest for marijuana possession could have drastic consequences for the accused student. Thus, arrest may carry as strong a sanction as a subsequent conviction—which frequently results in probation for first offenders.

For the punishment of "other" to have an impact upon one's own behavior, that punishment must, of course, be known. Thus, proponents of *general* deterrence would argue that knowledge of society's punishment of others will deter one from similar criminal endeavor. Presumably, then, the *less* contact one has had with punished "others" the *more likely* is he to commit the punished act. Tables 7.4A and 7.4B summarize data pertaining to respondent contacts with others who had been arrested or convicted for marijuana possession and petit larceny.[21]

Contrary to general deterrence expectations, use of marijuana is more than twice as great among respondents who had knowledge of someone arrested for possession (47.2 percent) than among those without such knowledge (21.8 percent). A computed Q-value (.53) that is statistically significant but in the "wrong" direction for the deterrence hypothesis, further indicates that general deterrence appears *not* to be working among marijuana offenders. Of course, we cannot tell from these data whether one's knowledge of another's arrest for marijuana possession preceded or followed his use of marijuana. However, one-half of the self-reported users of marijuana admit to having used it at least six times in the previous year. Thus, it is probable that for many of the marijuana users at least some criminal activity was preceded by knowledge of an arrested "other."

In this regard, it is interesting to note that 104 of the 105 admitted marijuana users indicate that their crime was initially committed *in the company* of at least one other person and 48 of those using for the first time were

[20] Legislation passed in 1969 called for automatic suspension of any student arrested for a drug offense. Subsequent legislation passed in 1970, and effective on October 1 of that year, gives university officials the authority to suspend such a student if they so desire.

[21] The question of how many "others" one knew who had been arrested or convicted of selling marijuana was deliberately not asked, so as to avoid the appearance of seeking information that was too sensitive. Too few students knew "others" who had been arrested or convicted of grand larceny to warrant the inclusion of this crime.

TABLE 7.4A. ADMITTED MARIJUANA USE BY KNOWLEDGE OF OTHERS
ARRESTED FOR MARIJUANA POSSESSION [a]

Number Known	Percent Having Used Marijuana	Percent Never Using Marijuana	Total	(N)
1 or more	47.2	52.8	100.0	(142)
None	21.8	78.2	100.0	(179)

$Q = .53$
$p < .001$

TABLE 7.4B. ADMITTED THEFT BY KNOWLEDGE OF OTHERS ARRESTED
FOR PETTY LARCENY [a]

Number Known	Percent Having Stolen	Percent Never Stealing	Total	(N)
1 or more	66.7	33.3	100.0	(105)
None	52.8	47.2	100.0	(214)

$Q = .28$
$p < .01$

[a] Data for these items are obtained from responses to the questions, "Altogether, how many people that you know personally, have been arrested for illegal possession of marijuana?" "How many people that you know personally have ever been arrested for stealing something of little value (worth less than $100)?"

with three or more persons. Indeed, the social character of this offense makes it more likely that one will have contact with similar offenders—some of whom may have been arrested and/or convicted.[22] At the same time, a subculture of drug use probably countermands the deterrent effect of knowing punished offenders, by providing "definitions favorable to violation" of marijuana laws, as well as the opportunity and techniques for doing so.[23]

Knowledge of arrested offenders, while generally not as extensive for

[22] Among the earliest to describe the social character of marijuana use, and the processes of socialization into marijuana subcultures, was Becker (1963: 41–58).

[23] For a discussion of the importance of "definitions favorable to violation of law," in the genesis of crime, see Sutherland and Cressey (1970: chap. 4). Cloward and Ohlin (1960) offer a cogent analysis of differential access to "illegitimate opportunity."

theft as for marijuana use, also appears positively related to admitted theft activity. As seen in Table 7.4B, those respondents who know of at least one other person arrested for petty larceny, are more likely to have committed some larceny themselves (66.7 percent) than those who have no such knowledge (52.8 percent). Again, something other than general deterrence appears to be working inasmuch as the computed Q-value is statistically significant in the "wrong" direction. The fact that the positive relationship between knowledge of apprehended others and criminality is stronger for marijuana use than for theft, may be partially explained by the fact that larceny is not as "social" an offense as marijuana use. Approximately 42 percent of those admitting to some theft activity (77/184) indicate that their first petty larceny was committed alone. Thus, it may be somewhat more difficult for petty thieves to meet others who have been arrested for that offense.

The deterrent effectiveness of arrest is brought into sharper focus when perceptions of its likelihood for *specific* offenses, and for *oneself,* are considered. Tables 7.5A and 7.5B show the relative frequency of admitted criminality for respondents with varying perceptions of the likelihood that *they* would be arrested for the specific offenses of stealing or marijuana use. The data, though varying somewhat by crime, provide what appears to be consistent support for deterrence theory.

As expected, the use of marijuana and belief in the likelihood of arrest for marijuana possession, were inversely related (gamma = −.84, $p < .001$). In fact, *none* of the respondents believing that their use of marijuana would *likely* lead to an arrest, have ever used marijuana! By contrast, 38.9 percent of those believing that such an arrest is *unlikely,* admit to some use of marijuana. The large gamma value may be slightly misleading, however, since it is greatly enhanced by the one zero cell in the table. While intraoffense comparisons suggest that perceptions of arrest potential may be serving as a deterrent, the fact is that hardly anyone, user or nonuser, sees that potential as very great. Indeed, 75 percent of the nonusers and almost all of the users think there is *less* than a 50/50 chance of being arrested for marijuana possession. Thus, it is not entirely clear just how strong a deterrent is offered by the threat of arrest for marijuana possession.

Also as expected, those who think their chances of arrest for petty larceny are lowest, are the most likely to have committed a theft (62.4 percent). Those who believe they are likely to be arrested should they ever steal

TABLE 7.5A. ADMITTED MARIJUANA USE BY PERCEIVED LIKELIHOOD OF ARREST FOR MARIJUANA POSSESSION [a]

Perceived Likelihood of Arrest	Percent Having Used Marijuana	Percent Never Using Marijuana	Total	(N)
Likely	0.0	100.0	100.0	(28)
50/50	10.7	89.3	100.0	(28)
Unlikely	38.9	61.1	100.0	(265)

Gamma = − .84
p < .001

TABLE 7.5B. ADMITTED THEFT BY PERCEIVED LIKELIHOOD OF ARREST FOR PETTY LARCENY [a]

Perceived Likelihood of Arrest	Percent Having Stolen	Percent Never Stealing	Total	(N)
Likely	40.6	59.4	100.0	(32)
50/50	48.5	51.5	100.0	(68)
Unlikely	62.4	37.6	100.0	(221)

Gamma = − .31
p < .01

[a] Data for these items are obtained from responses to the questions, "If someone like yourself used marijuana occasionally in Tallahassee, how likely are the police to catch him (her)?" "If someone like yourself stole something worth *less* than $100 in Tallahassee, how likely are the police to catch him (her)?"

something, admit to such theft much less frequently (40.6 percent). Although statistically significant ($p < .01$) the gamma value for petty larceny ($− .31$) is appreciably smaller than the corresponding value for marijuana use. This difference in strength of relationship when marijuana and theft data are compared, offers further support for Andenaes' (1966) and Zimring's (1971) contention that for crimes that are *mala prohibita* (marijuana use), the law may stand alone as a deterrent. Because laws have the support of the mores in the case of theft (*mala in se*), the relationship between deterrence and perceptions of the law may be more difficult to establish. For theft, deterrence may, indeed, be more the consequence of internalized morality than internalized legality.

Summary and Discussion

In an effort to answer questions that have not been resolved by prior research, this paper has used a different approach to the empirical study of deterrence theory. Whereas most of the earlier studies were concerned with rates of crime for large geographic units, the present study used the admitted criminality of a specific sample of individuals as the dependent variable. It was expected that deterrence—if it existed—would likely vary with the perceptions of punishment held by potential and actual self-reported criminals, as well as with the types of crime presumably being deterred.

Interviews with 321 university students were used to determine relationships between admitted marijuana use and theft, and perceptions of the severity and certainty of punishment. From deterrence theory it was expected that admitted criminality would be *least frequent* among those who (1) perceive the most severe penalties for larceny and marijuana use, (2) perceive the greatest chances of receiving the maximum penalties for those offenses upon conviction, (3) perceive the greatest probability that law-violators will be arrested, (4) have the greatest familiarity with others who have been arrested for larceny or marijuana possession, and (5) perceive the greatest probability of their own arrest in the event that they stole something or used marijuana.

The data for marijuana use and theft indicate that *no relationship* exists between perceptions of severe punishment and admitted criminality. This finding runs counter to deterrence theory, but is in accord with several earlier studies of deterrence (Schuessler, 1952; Sellin, 1967; Gibbs, 1968; Tittle, 1969; Chiricos and Waldo, 1970). While these and the earlier findings cannot be held conclusive, they strongly question the assertion that crime may be deterred by increasing penalties.

If the viability of severe punishment as a deterrent to crime has been seriously questioned by empirical findings, the same cannot be said for certain punishment. The latter dimension of deterrence has emerged from recent empirical tests with a considerable amount of credibility (Chambliss, 1966; Gibbs, 1968; Tittle, 1969; Jensen, 1969). In the present study, perceived certainty of punishment appears to be related to admitted criminality. However, the strength of this relationship varies by crime and by the index of certainty employed. For each of the certainty indices, marijuana use seems more related than admitted theft activity to perceptions of the certainty of punishment.

Although the present data provide only moderate support for this aspect of deterrence theory, the strongest support is found in the perception that one's own criminality is likely to result in an arrest (Tables 7.5A and 7.5B). The next greatest support appears to come from the perception that one's own criminality is likely to eventuate in the maximum allowable penalty for a specific crime (Table 7.2A). Both of these situations have a common focus on the individual and *his* chances of arrest and punishment for a *specific* crime. Thus, perceptions of the certainty of punishment appear most viable as a deterrent when they involve the potential criminal's estimate of his *own chances* for arrest and harsh penalties for a particular crime—independent of the chances for any "generalized other."

This latter point receives support from two sources. First, the weakest deterrent among the several certainty dimensions is the perception that law-breakers *in general* are likely to be arrested or convicted. Only for marijuana use (Table 7.3A) is the relationship between admitted criminality and this perception of punishment in general, statistically significant ($p < .01$). Second, personal knowledge of the punishment of "others" for marijuana use or theft is apparently ineffective in deterring these offenses. On the contrary, use of marijuana and admitted theft are *most likely* for those who know someone else who has been arested for these offenses. Thus, little support is found for a basic premise of deterrence theory; i.e., the punishment of alter, if known to ego, will serve as a general deterrent, keeping ego from involvement in that criminal activity.

As noted above, marijuana use appears more likely than theft to be deterred by perceptions of the certainty of punishment. Such a finding is consistent with Andenaes' (1966) distinction between crimes that are *mala prohibita* and crimes that are *mala in se,* and with Zimring's (1971) hypothesis cited earlier. That is, one might expect the law to "stand alone" in the deterrence of marijuana use (*mala prohibita*) inasmuch as the law has little support in the mores of the university student subculture. In this regard, it is recalled that only 25 percent of the respondents disagreed with the assertion that "possession of marijuana should be legalized for adults," while 78.5 percent of all respondents agree that the "penalties for possession of marijuana are too harsh." Thus, it seems reasonable to conclude that the norms prevalent in student groups are not likely to deter marijuana use. Whatever deterrence is to occur must be the product of some other force, such as the law.

For the crime of theft, the law has a great deal of support in the mores. Because of this, it may be difficult to separate the deterrent effect of the *law* from other aspects of deterrence.[24] Again, 68 percent of the respondents *disagreed* with an assertion that "the penalties for stealing are too harsh" (even though most perceived the penalty to be *greater* than it actually is), and 98.2 percent *disagreed* with the statement that "stealing shouldn't be a crime." It is not, then, surprising to note that perceived certainty of punishment has little discernible deterrent impact upon the crime of theft. For most who are deterred, pressures from alternative sources—such as moral values that have long been internalized—are likely sufficient to inhibit the proscribed theft activity.

The important point to note is that the law, and more specifically, perceptions of the certainty of punishment, cannot be assumed to deter *all* criminal activities in the same way. The deterrence equation may be more or less complex, depending upon the type of crime and the degree of congruence between formal and informal reactions to that crime. Thus, an understanding of deterrence further presumes an understanding of the kinds of persons involved,[25] and the way in which their values reflect upon the illegal activity. Should these values be inconsistent with the formal dictates of law, then the latter will "stand alone" as a deterrent. How strongly the law stands as a deterrent may further depend upon how serious the conflict between the mores and the law.

Just how strong the marijuana law stands as a deterrent within the par-

---

[24] The possibility that the threat of law will be less a deterrent for crimes that are strongly abhorred in the mores of the people, has been suggested, as well, by Zimring (1971: 44–45) and by Morris (1951: 13).

[25] When considering the variation in deterrence effectiveness for different "kinds of persons," it is interesting to note that "casual users" of marijuana are frequently the most likely to minimize the threat of legal reprisal (data analyzed, but not presented in this paper). It is entirely possible that this response represents an overreaction to the sudden awareness that one can commit the crime without immediate response from the criminal justice system. That is, confidence of immunity may not lead to the use of marijuana, as much as it follows the experience of nonapprehension. "Regular users," who may participate more fully in a subculture of drug use, are much more likely to know others who have been arrested for possession of marijuana. It may well be this knowledge which gives the "regular user" a less optimistic outlook on the chances of apprehension, than that espoused by the "casual user."

ticular group studied is questionable—despite the fact that deterrence relationships *appeared* to be strongest for marijuana offenses. As noted above,
more than three-fourths of the students sampled feel that marijuana laws are
too harsh. In addition, all respondents were asked the following question:

If the penalties for the use of marijuana were reduced, would you consider using
it, or using it more often?

Of the 215 students who claimed to have never used marijuana, only 26 percent affirmed that they would consider using the drug if the laws were made
less harsh. For the remainder, it may not be unreasonable to assume that
their perception of the law was *not* the principal reason for their nonuse of
marijuana. The impact of extralegal factors may be even stronger for theft
offenses than for marijuana use. Ninety-one percent of those who claim to
have never stolen, assert that they would *not* consider stealing if the laws
governing theft were reduced. This further confirms the possibility that the
law itself is not deterring these activities to a significant degree.

It is difficult to foresee what would happen to the situation of deterrence if, in fact, laws were changed or eliminated. To some extent, the informal norms and mores of the people are prompted and supported by the
formal laws [26]—even though it may appear that the mores themselves are
what deter or stimulate criminality. Should, for example, the laws against
theft be eliminated, would the moral repulsion against stealing persist? At
the same time, would the mores of the general public come to accept marijuana if the laws forbidding it were erased? [27] Answers to these and related

[26] This point is supported in the findings of Schwartz and Orleans (1967) who note that: "the
results of the study . . . suggest that the threat of sanction can deter people from violating the
law, perhaps in important part by inducing a moralistic attitude towards compliance."

[27] The Florida Legislature has recently (May 1971) reduced to a misdemeanor the penalty for
possessing a small amount (less than five grams, or about four "joints") of marijuana. The official rationale for this change is that the prosecutors were unwilling to prosecute and the courts
were unwilling to convict under the existing law which provided a maximum of five years in
prison. Clearly, the shift in penal sanction reflects a prior shift in community mores regarding
the use of marijuana. As long as marijuana use was largely confined to black-slum communities, there was apparently little pressure upon the police to enforce marijuana laws. However, as
the popularity of marijuana spread to respectable, white, middle-class colleges and high
schools, the initial expectations was that stronger enforcement of the law only served to crowd
police stations with sons and daughters of judges, business leaders, and law-makers. Indeed, it
was not until the mores of white, middle-class and prosperous youth showed themselves to be
persistent and growing in their acceptance of marijuana that the legislators were motivated to
act. It will be interesting to observe whether this change in law, brought by a change in the

questions are beyond the scope of this paper. However, the results of this study may justify the conclusion that the effects of law in deterring crime are probably not as great, and certainly less uniform than many have heretofore assumed.

References

Andenaes, Johannes. 1966. "The General Preventive Effects of Punishment," *University of Pennsylvania Law Review* 114 (May):949–983.

Assembly Committee on Criminal Procedure. 1968. *Deterrent Effects of Criminal Sanctions*. Assembly of the State of California (May).

Ball, John C. 1955. "The Deterrence Concept in Criminology and Law," *Journal of Criminal Law, Criminology and Police Science* 46 (September–October):347–354.

Barnes, Harry E. and Negley K. Teeters. 1959. *New Horizons in Criminology*. Englewood Cliffs, N.J.: Prentice-Hall.

Becker, Howard. 1963. *Outsiders: Studies in the Sociology of Deviance*. New York: Free Press.

Bentham, Jeremy. 1843. "Principles of Penal Law." In John Bowring (ed.), *The Works of Jeremy Bentham*. Edinburgh: W. Tait.

Bittner, Egon and Anthony Platt. 1966. "The Meaning of Punishment," *Issues in Criminology* 2 (Spring):77 99.

Cameron, Mary. 1964. *The Booster and The Snitch: Department Store Shoplifting*. New York: Free Press.

Chambliss, William J. 1966. "The Deterrent Influence of Punishment," *Crime and Delinquency* 12 (January):70–75.

1969. *Crime and The Legal Process*. New York: McGraw-Hill.

Chiricos, Theodore G. and Gordon P. Waldo. 1970. "Punishment and Crime: An Examination of Empirical Evidence," *Social Problems* 18 (Fall):200–217.

---

mores of youth, will precipitate a wider acceptance of marijuana within the adult or youth communities of Florida.

Claster, Daniel. 1967. "Comparisons of Risk Perception between Delinquents and Nondelinquents," *Journal of Criminal Law, Criminology and Police Science* 58 (March):80–86.

Cloward, Richard and Lloyd Ohlin. 1960. *Delinquency and Opportunity.* New York: Free Press.

Erikson, Kai T. 1962. "Notes on the Sociology of Deviance," *Social Problems* 9 (Spring):307–314.

Federal Bureau of Investigation. 1969. *Crime in the United States: Uniform Crime Reports—1968.* Washington, D.C.: U.S. Government Printing Office, pp. 66–75.

Garfinkel, Harold. 1956. "Conditions of Successful Degradation Ceremonies," *American Journal of Sociology* 61 (March):420–424.

Gibbs, Jack P. 1966. "Sanctions," *Social Problems* 14 (Fall):147–159.

1968. "Crime, Punishment, and Deterrence," *Southwestern Social Science Quarterly* 48 (March):515–530.

Grupp, Stanley and Warren Lucas. 1969. "The 'Marijuana Muddle' as Reflected in California Arrest Statistics and Dispositions." Unpublished revision of a paper read at 1969 Annual Meeting of the American Sociological Association, September 4, San Francisco, California.

Jeffery, C. Ray. 1965. "Criminal Behavior and Learning Theory," *Journal of Criminal Law, Criminology and Police Science* 56 (September):294–300.

Jensen, Gary F. 1969. "Crime Doesn't Pay': Correlates of a Shared Misunderstanding," *Social Problems* 17 (Fall):189–201.

Mead, George H. 1918. "The Psychology of Punitive Justice," *American Journal of Sociology* 23 (March):577–602.

Morris, Norval. 1951. *The Habitual Criminal.* Cambridge: Harvard University Press.

President's Commission on Law Enforcement and Administration of Justice. 1967. *Task Force Report: Crime and Its Impact—An Assessment.* Washington, D.C.: U.S. Government Printing Office.

Polier, Justine W. 1956. "The Woodshed Is No Answer," *Federal Probation* 20 (September):3–6.

Savitz, Leonard D. 1958. "A Study in Capital Punishment," *Journal of Criminal Law, Criminology and Police Science* 49 (November–December):338–341.

Schuessler, Karl. 1952. "The Deterrent Influence of the Death Penalty," *The Annals* 284 (November):54–62.

Schwartz, Richard D. and Sonya Orleans. 1967. "On Legal Sanctions," *The University of Chicago Law Review* 34:274–300.

Sellin, Thorsten. 1967. "Homicides in Retentionist and Abolitionist States." In Thorsten Sellin (ed.), *Capital Punishment*. New York: Harper and Row, pp. 135–138.

Sutherland, Edwin and Donald R. Cressey. 1970. *Criminology* (8th ed.). Philadelphia: Lippincott.

Tittle, Charles R. 1969. "Crime Rates and Legal Sanctions," *Social Problems* 16 (Spring):409–423.

Toby, Jackson. 1964. "Is Punishment Necessary?" *Journal of Criminal Law, Criminology and Police Science* 55 (September):332–337.

Wood, Ledger. 1938. "Responsibility and Punishment," *Journal of Criminal Law, Criminology and Police Science* 28 (January–February):630–640.

Zimring, Frank. 1971. *Perspectives on Deterrence*. Washington, D.C.: National Institute of Mental Health.

Zimring, Frank and Gordon Hawkins. 1968. "Deterrence and Marginal Groups," *Journal of Research in Crime and Delinquency* 5 (July):100–114.

8

Perceptions of Punishment:
Current Research

JAMES J. TEEVAN JR.

Until recently, most studies of the deterrent effects of threatened punishment either ignored the individual's perceptions of the certainty and severity of that punishment or paid lip service to these subjective measures as an ideal but one for which the necessary data were unavailable. Objective measures of deterrence—for example, percentage of criminals convicted (certainty) and median sentence served (severity), both expressed as a ratio to aggregate crime rates—thus were used to test the deterrence hypothesis (see, for example, Gibbs, 1968; Logan, 1972; Tittle, 1969). Such studies were based on the sometimes unstated assumption that the potential criminal is aware of the actual certainty and severity of punishment and acts with that knowledge.

That the individual's perceptions of punishment variables are of crucial importance has been stated by Henshel and Carey (1971; reprinted in this volume, chapter 3). They argue that between actual sanctions and offense rates there is an actor who first perceives or fails to perceive sanctions; second, calculates risks involved; third, makes a decision to commit or not to commit an offense. For punishment to be an effective deterrent *it must exist for that actor*. If the individual "holds no cognition relative to the punitive sanction (i.e., it has not been heard of, believed in, or felt applicable), then the *objective existence* of sanctions with specified levels of severity, certainty, swiftness is of no consequence. . . ." (Henshel and Carey, 1971: 5).

Claster and Jensen

Using a similar perspective, Claster (1967) and Jensen (1969) made empirical tests of a deterrence hypothesis which states that perceptions of increasing certainty and severity of punishment should deter deviance (this volume, chapters 5 and 6). To summarize, briefly, Claster found that (1) although incarcerated delinquents do not underestimate certainty for punishment *for others* more than do nondelinquents, (2) they do, more than nondelinquents, perceive that it is unlikely in a hypothetical situation that *they themselves* would be caught for committing certain offenses. Claster interprets the first finding as evidence against and the second finding as evidence for the deterrence hypotheses. I would argue, however, that Claster's first finding may be irrelevent to the deterrence hypothesis. If the delinquents perceive for themselves a lower certainty of punishment, then their perceptions concerning the certainty of punishment for anonymous others may not be salient for them. Their actions are determined by their perceptions of the risks *to themselves and not by their perceptions of the risks to others*. In this case the calculations of the two risks are not positively related.

Jensen attempted to improve Claster's study by using both self-reported delinquents and a general measure of deterrence rather than Claster's institutionalized sample and deterrence for specific offenses. His study is an advance because of his wider sample, but perhaps a step backward because of his deterrence measure. In effect he is trying to relate a general certainty of punishment to specific offense rates. It could be argued that the potential criminal thinks of the certainty of punishment *for the specific crime he is planning* and not the certainty of punishment for all crimes. This lack of comparability, however, should reduce any deterrent effects. Thus Jensen's findings supporting the deterrence hypothesis may be even more important than he realized. Briefly, he found that as perceptions of certainty of punishment decrease, both self-reported and officially recorded delinquency increase.

Waldo and Chiricos

Both studies thus gave some support to the deterrence hypothesis and, more importantly, they did so using different populations and different measures of deterrence. However, neither study examined perceived severity of punishment. In order to examine the effects of perceived severity of punishment, and to reexamine perceived certainty of punishment within a different context, Waldo and Chiricos (1972) collected data from college students on their perceptions of (1) maximum prison sentences both for possession of marijuana and theft under $100 (severity), (2) the likelihood that someone like them would be caught by the police for those offenses (personal certainty), (3) the probability of *anyone* being caught by the police for those offenses (general certainty), (4) their knowledge of someone who had been apprehended by the police for those offenses, and (5) personal marijuana use and theft.

Waldo and Chiricos found evidence both for and against the deterrence hypothesis. Unlike Claster, they found that individuals who perceive a higher certainty of punishment even *for anonymous others* (general certainty) are slightly less likely to smoke marijuana and to engage in theft than those who perceive a lower certainty. These data support the deterrence hypothesis, and this support is even stronger using the personal certainty measure of perceived likelihood that "someone like them would be arrested." Most individuals, however, feel that it is unlikely that someone like them would be caught. Again, I would argue that the more important measure of certainty is what the individual perceives to be *his* probability of punishment as measured by the personal certainty questions. That general deterrence in this instance is also negatively related to crime may be a function of a positive relationship between personal deterrence and general deterrence—that is, an individual who perceives it is likely that someone like him would be punished may also perceive it likely that anonymous others also would be punished.

On the other hand, the knowledge of a friend being caught is positively related to self-reported deviance. This finding *could* be interpreted as evidence against the deterrence hypothesis in that individuals who know personally of friends who were apprehended for theft and marijuana use were more likely to commit these crimes than were individuals who had no friends apprehended. The unstated assumption is that those individuals who report no friends apprehended know that their friends had committed the crimes, yet went unapprehended. Such individuals, aware of a low certainty of punishment, thus should have been the more criminal. No data were presented to evaluate this important link in the causal chain. It is quite possible that those who report no friends apprehended do so because they know of no friends who had committed any of those specific crimes. Thus apprehension was irrelevant. Waldo and Chiricos explain this possible lack of support for the deterrence hypothesis by arguing that marijuana use is a social act and thus most users would know of someone who was caught. They do not explain why the deterrence hypothesis is unsupported for theft, which presumably may be not as social.

When they examined severity of punishment, Waldo and Chiricos found self-reported marijuana use and theft unrelated to perceptions of severity of punishment. Those respondents who perceive a higher severity of punishment do not report significantly fewer offenses than those who perceive a lesser severity. Finally, type of deviance was examined in their study. They reasoned that if perceptions of punishment do deter, then the amount of deterrence should be greater for a crime that is *mala prohibita* (marijuana use) than for a crime that is *mala in se* (theft). Offenses wrong in themselves (*mala in se*) should be avoided first because they are wrong in themselves and only second because of fear of punishment. Offenses wrong because they are prohibited (*mala prohibita*), however, should be avoided less because they are wrong in themselves and more because of fear of punishment. Waldo and Chiricos found limited support for this hypothesis.

Teevan

Thus three separate studies had shown that a higher perceived certainty of punishment was associated with a lower deviance rate. Why, then, was severity not important? It was to answer this and other questions that Teevan (1973) collected data from a sample of Canadian university students for marijuana use and shoplifting to ascertain (1) perceived certainty of punishment both for friends and for all Canadians, (2) perceived severity of punishment for friends and for all Canadians, (3) the individual's feelings about going to prison, and (4) personal marijuana use and shoplifting incidences.

Respondents were not asked for their perceptions of the certainty and severity of punishment for themselves or "someone like them" because of a possible contamination effect of their past deviant behavior on these perceptions. If they had been deviant previously, then their punishment or lack of punishment for that deviance would bias their perceptions of punishment. Those caught and punished might perceive a higher certainty of punishment, while those not caught might then perceive a lower certainty. Since more respondents had been deviant and unpunished than deviant and punished, the result would have been to increase the relationship between perceived low certainty and high deviance. This conclusion would have been unwarranted since the perception of punishment could have come after and not before the deviant behavior. However, since few had experienced any severity of punishment, it was felt safe to measure perceived personal severity of punishment.

Instead of personal certainty, respondents were asked for their perceptions of the certainty and severity of punishment for all Canadians. Admittedly these perceptions may deter less than perceptions of personal punishment, but to overcome the above limitations these questions were substituted. Moreover, if the perceptions of punishment for others is negatively related to deviance, then one can infer cautiously that there may be a similar and perhaps greater deterrent effect for perceived personal certainty and severity of punishment.

The hypotheses for the study were the usual deterrence hypotheses with the following modifications: (1) The relationship between severity of punishment and offenses should be found only for those respondents who perceive a level of certainty high enough to make severity salient. Thus Teevan raised the point that severity may appear to be unimportant because the certainty was so low as to make it irrelevant. If a higher certainty were perceived, then severity may be important. (2) The relationship between a friend being caught and deviance should be positive. Since one is likely to interact with similar others, then deviants are more likely than nondeviants to know of someone who has been apprehended. In effect, then, the knowledge of a friend being caught is not a valid measure of deterrence. It is not that nondeviants would not be deterred by a friends' arrest but that none of their friends committed the crimes for which to be arrested. For the deviant, it is not that he did not become more cautious after a friends' apprehension but that in his circle one is likely to know of others who have been arrested. (3)

Again, as with Waldo and Chiricos, there should be a greater deterrent effect on *mala prohibita* than for *mala in se* crimes.

Analysis of the data revealed again that there is a weak negative relationship between perception of certainty of punishment and self-reported deviance. As stated previously, the deterrence measure used was one of general deterrence for all Canadians and not personal deterrence for the individual. Were that latter variable measured, a stronger relationship might have been found. Concerning severity of punishment, the deterrence hypothesis was unsupported since those individuals who perceive a more severe punishment for other Canadians are not less deviant than those who perceive a less severe punishment. However, as predicted, when controlling for certainty—that is, examining only those repondents who perceive a higher certainty—perceived increases in severity for others is associated with lower rates of crime. It should be noted again, as with Waldo and Chiricos, that very few respondents perceive a high certainty of punishment.

Using a different measure of severity, a personal measure which requested the respondents' opinions about going to prison, the deterrence hypothesis was supported even when controlling for certainty. Expected personal hardship deters more than does potential severity for all Canadians. Again, the individual's perceptions about his own punishment are crucial in deterring or failing to deter him from deviance.

As predicted, there is a positive relationship between a friend's being caught and the individual's deviance. Thus it appears that deviants more than nondeviants are likely to know someone who has been caught and punished. As explained previously, this finding should be considered as evidence against the deterrence hypothesis.

The relationship between deterrence variables and deviance showed mixed results for the *mala prohibita/mala in se* distinction. The *mala prohibita* offense was not always deterred more by perceived certainty and severity of punishment than the *mala in se* offense. The most probable explanation is that in both the Teevan and Waldo-Chiricos studies the sociologists are making the distinction. The respondents were not asked *how they perceived the offenses*. Some may have perceived shoplifting to be *mala prohibita*—''it hurts no one'' and ''stores should be ripped off.'' Some may have defined marijuana use as *mala in se*. Using the respondents' definitions, *mala in se* offenses may be less affected by threats of punishment than *mala prohibita* offenses. Further research can help explore this dimension.

Finally, Teevan tried to use deterrence as an intervening variable between selected independent variables and marijuana use. He questioned that if boys use marijuana more than do girls and upper-class respondents more than lower-class, is it perception of punishment which deters girls and lower-class respondents from similarly using marijuana? The data reveal this not to be the case. It is not fear of punishment which deters girls and lower-class respondents from marijuana use. Controlling both for perceived level of certainty and severity of punishment, marijuana users are still over-represented among boys and upper-class respondents. Other variables are needed to explain these gender and social class variations.

Summary and Future Research

For all four studies reported, there appears to be a marginal deterrent effect from perceived increases in certainty of punishment. This finding is rendered more important because of the different populations used, the different measures of certainty, and the different offenses. The relationships are not very strong, however. One possible explanation for this weakness may rest in the limit and/or range of perceptions of certainty. The maximum perceived certainty of punishment for some offenses may be so low as to be below a threshold of salience for many individuals. If the perception of certainty of punishment varied between 25 and 95 percent, then an increase in certainty might be associated with lower deviance rates. In Teevan's study, for example, the perceived certainty of being caught for marijuana varies from 0 to 25 percent. Thus the difference between the higher and the lower certainty may be perceived as unimportant. The range may be too narrow and/or the maximum may be too low for increased certainty to have an effect in reducing deviant behavior. Severity of punishment appears to be an important deterrent only if certainty is above this threshold of salience.

Future research should (1) further investigate the threshold of salience problem, (2) more closely examine the relation between certainty and severity (it may be curvilinear—that is, severity may be irrelevant with low certainty because it is so unlikely, then relevant with moderate certainty, and then irrelevant again with high certainty since, at that level, even moderate punishment would deter), (3) help clarify the issues of causality (each of the four studies used cross-sectional data collected at one point in time; thus it could have been that engaging in deviance and not getting caught caused one to perceive low certainty and severity of punishment, rather than perceptions of low certainty and severity causing increased deviance: what is needed is a panel study in which present perceptions of sanctions are related to future behavior), (4) incorporate other variables into the deterrence model—for example, to explain why some individuals perceive a higher probability and severity of punishment than do others (alternatively deterrence variables could be added to a model containing those other variables which sociologists believe to be related to deviance), and (5) attempt to relate the perception studies of deterrence to the growing literature on objective studies of deterrence. Work is presently underway to answer some of these questions.

References

Bentham, Jeremy. 1843. "Principles of Penal Law." In John Bowring (ed.), *The Works of Jeremy Bentham*. Edinburgh: W. Tait.

Chambliss, William J. 1966. "The Deterrent Influence of Punishment," *Crime and Delinquency* 12 (January):70–75.

Chiricos, Theodore and Gordon Waldo. 1970. "Punishment and Crime: An Examination of Some Empirical Evidence," *Social Problems* 18 (Fall):200–217.

Claster, Daniel. 1967. "Comparison of Risk Perception between Delinquents and Nondelinquents," *Journal of Criminal Law, Criminology, and Police Science* 58 (March):80–86.

Gibbs, Jack P. 1968. "Crime, Punishment, and Deterrence," *Southwestern Social Science Quarterly* 49 (March):515–530.

Henshel, Richard and Sandra Carey. 1971. "Deviance, Deterrence, and Knowledge of Sanctions." Paper presented at the Annual Meeting of the Eastern Sociological Society, Boston, Mass.

Jensen, Gary. 1969. "Crime Doesn't Pay: Correlates of a Shared Misunderstanding," *Social Problems* 17 (Fall):189–201.

Logan, Charles H. 1972. "General Deterrent Effects of Imprisonment," *Social Forces* 51 (September):64–73.

Teevan, James J., Jr. 1972. "Deterrent Effects of Punishment: The Canadian Case." In Craig L. Boydell, Carl F. Grindstaff, and Paul C. Whitehead (eds.), *Deviant Behaviour and Societal Reaction in Canada*. Toronto: Holt, Rinehart, and Winston.

1973. "Deterrent Effects of Punishment: Subjective Measures Continued." Paper presented at the Annual Meeting of the Society for the Study of Social Problems, New York.

Teevan, James J., Jr. and Paul C. Whitehead. 1972. "Deterrent Effects of Punishment: Toward Subjective Measures." Paper presented at Eastern Sociological Meetings, Boston, Mass.

Tittle, Charles R. 1969. "Crime Rates and Legal Sanctions," *Social Problems* 16 (Spring):409–422.

Waldo, Gordon and Theodore Chiricos. 1972. "Perceived Penal Sanctions and Self-Reported Criminality: A Neglected Approach to Deterrence Research," *Social Problems* 19 (Spring):522–540.

Zimring, Franklin E. 1971. *Perspectives on Deterrence*. Washington, D.C.: U.S. Government Printing Office.

9

Does the Law Affect Moral Judgments?

NIGEL WALKER
AND MICHAEL ARGYLE

In the course of debates about the propriety of using the criminal law to discourage certain types of conduct, an argument is often used which may be
called "the declaratory argument" (Walker, 1964). It asserts that, whether a
legal prohibition operates as a deterrent or not, to repeal it would give the
impression that the conduct in question is no longer regarded by society as
morally wrong. This argument was used by opponents of the Wolfenden
Committee's (1957) recommendation that homosexual behaviour between
consenting adults in private should no longer be a criminal offence (it can be
found, for example, in the memorandum of dissent by Mr. Adair, one of the
members of the Committee). It can be believed, quite consistently, by people who do not think that the legal prohibition can be enforced, or should be
enforced, and it must therefore be taken very seriously. Moreover, it is by
no means implausible. Experiments by social psychologists have shown that
people's judgments on such matters as moral issues, aesthetic preferences,
and religious questions are influenced by what they are told is the majority
view—either of those present or of groups to which they belong (Dashiell,
1935). Similarly it is found that political opinions are influenced by what is
believed to be the predominant public opinion—the so-called "band-waggon
effect" (Lazarsfeld, Berelson, and Gaudet, 1948). It is quite conceivable

Reprinted with permission of the *British Journal of Criminology* from "Does the Law Affect
Moral Judgments?" *British Journal of Criminology* 4 (1963–1964) by Nigel Walker and Michael Argyle.

that one of the functions of the criminal law (even though it performs it unintentionally) is to inform members of a society of at least some of the moral attitudes of that society, and so to influence their own moral attitudes.

The "declaratory theory" seems capable of being tested empirically, at least to the extent of discovering whether people's moral judgments are affected by their knowledge or belief as to the state of the law.

A Field-Survey of Attitudes to Suicide

The Suicide Act of 1961, which provided that attempted suicide should no longer be a criminal offence, created a situation in which one sort of test could be applied to the declaratory hypothesis, since at any given date some people would, while others would not, know of the change in the law. In the summer of 1962, therefore, about a year after the Act received the Royal Assent, interviewers were recruited from two undergraduate societies and, after briefing, carried out 403 interviews with men and women in different parts of the country. The interview questionnaire included questions on other forms of conduct (euthanasia, litter-dropping, abortion, homosexual acts between males and between females). Male interviewers interviewed only males, females only females. The interviews took place in July, August, and September, 1962. No attempt was made at a strict sampling procedure, although interviewers were asked to interview roughly equal numbers of people in nine categories (professional and white collar aged under 30, aged 30 to 35, aged over 50; skilled manual workers in the same age groups; unskilled manual workers in the same age groups); and the resulting distributions of age groups and occupational groups were not unsatisfactory. Since the object of the survey was simply to see whether there was an association between certain beliefs, these imperfections matter less than they would do in a survey designed to take a plebiscite of public opinion. The use of undergraduates as interviewers is sometimes criticised by people who do not realise that many interviewers employed by market research organisations come from the same age group; if anything, undergraduate volunteers are likely to be more intelligent and responsible.

Among the questions in the survey were the following, in the order shown:

10. "Do you regard attempted suicide as
      morally wrong?
      not morally wrong?
      not morally wrong if . . .
          (*here any special circumstances offered by the respondent were noted*)
11. "Should it be treated as a crime? . . .
          (*if the answer was "Yes," the respondent was asked how it should be dealt with*)
12. "Is it against the law now?"

Sixteen percent of those interviewed knew that the law had been changed; 9 percent were unsure; the remainder believed that attempted suicide was still criminal. If the change in the law had affected the moral judgments of those who knew of the change, there should have been a lower percentage of those who definitely regarded attempted suicide as morally wrong. Since moral judgments on this subject probably vary according to sex and religious denomination, male and female members of the Church of England were tabulated separately (Table 9.1).[1] There is no tendency for either men or women who knew of the change in the law to take a less strict moral view; indeed there is a slight, but statistically insignificant, tendency in the opposite direction. In other words, the figures fail to provide any support for the declaratory theory.

TABLE 9.1.   ATTITUDES TOWARD ATTEMPTED SUICIDE AND KNOWLEDGE OF THE LAW

Church of England members who	believed it to be morally wrong		did not or were unsure		Number
	men (%)	women (%)	men (%)	women (%)	
Believed it to be criminal	62	52	38	48	84 men 64 women
Knew that it was not, or were unsure	74	54	26	46	23 men 24 women

[1] No other single denomination was represented in sufficient number to justify separate tabulation by sex and denomination.

An Experimental Test of the Hypothesis

There are obvious limitations, however, to this sort of evidence. In particular, it relates only to attempts at suicide, which is not an act that most people seriously consider the possibility of committing themselves. Since no other crime (excluding offences under emergency legislation and analogous measures) has been removed from the statute book in the last hundred years, the prospect of a similar opportunity to test the declaratory hypothesis by a field survey about other types of conduct is remote. We therefore devised a test of a different kind, which was applied, with successive refinements, to 308 subjects:

[test] 1. A class of Oxford undergraduates attending a lecture on an aspect of German literature (this class was selected because it was unlikely to include undergraduates who were sophisticated in law, moral philosophy, or the techniques of social psychology) ($N = 65$);
[test] 2. A class of young adult women from a secretarial course at a nearby technical college ($N = 34$); and a class of young adult males taking engineering classes at the same college ($N = 45$);
[test] 3. A group of Young Conservatives in a neighbouring county (chosen because of the possibility that young adults of this political persuasion would be especially influenced by the law) ($N = 36$);
[test] 4. A class of first-year Oxford undergraduates attending a lecture on an aspect of German literature (chosen for the same reason as (1)) ($N = 128$).

Method

Each group of subjects was invited to take part in a survey of views on questions of law and morality by completing an anonymous questionnaire. The questionnaires described a number of actions of different sorts, which the subjects were asked to rate on a six-point scale,[2] ranging from "as wrong as possible" to "very right." The questionnaire told the subjects whether the

[2] In tests 1 to 4 a four-point scale was used, and the more sensitive six-point scale was adopted simply in case the negative results were due to the insensitivity of the shorter scale.

action in question was a criminal offence or not. Thus the first question explained the law on abortion, and then asked subjects to record their judgments on a doctor who performed an abortion "because the baby is likely to be deformed," "because the baby would be illegitimate," and so on.

The next questions dealt similarly with unintentional litter-dropping, negligent injury, public drunkenness, prostitution, and the use of obscene language in public.[3] But whereas the law on abortion was correctly summarised in all the questionnaires, the law on these types of behaviour was differently stated in different questionnaires. In tests 1 to 3 half the questionnaires described each type of behaviour as being a criminal offence, while the other half described it as not being an offence. If the declaratory theory were true, the version of the question which described the conduct as an offence should elicit more censorious moral judgments from the respondents. The two types of questionnaire were distributed randomly throughout each sample, and were indistinguishable in appearance. Respondents were asked not to discuss the questions with each other until they had completed the questionnaire, and did in fact comply with this request.

Two precautions were taken against the possibility that even randomly selected subdivisions of the experimental groups might contain an undue percentage of more censorious subjects. [First,] Replies to question 1 (which dealt with abortion and was worded in exactly the same terms in all questionnaires) were used to ensure that the subgroups were matched in "censoriousness," by discarding individual questionnaires until the distribution of each group's ratings on the scale was similar. This method was devised as a better alternative to matching by means of variables known to be associated with moral judgments (such as religion). [Second,] In wording the other questions, care was taken to ensure that the versions which described the actions as illegal were not confined to one type of questionnaire. Thus, for example, questionnaires which described litter-dropping as criminal described negligent injury as not criminal, and vice versa.

Another sort of precaution had also to be taken. A substantial minority of people believe that it morally wrong to disobey a prohibition which is embodied in the law, irrespective of the morality of the prohibited action itself.

[3] Obviously, the types of conduct selected had to be such that it could be credibly stated either that they were or that they were not offences. This excluded frequently discussed conduct such as homosexuality or euthanasia, about which most young adults are too knowledgeable to be deceived as to the state of the law.

Since the hypothesis which was being tested was that a person's moral judgments on conduct could be affected by his beliefs about the state of the criminal law even if he did not hold that the law automatically governed the morality of the conduct, it was necessary to identify and exclude those who did hold this view, and question 7 was designed to do so:

7. (a) Is heavy smoking morally wrong?   Yes/No/Uncertain [4]
   (b) If Parliament passed a law making heavy
       smoking a criminal offence, would you
       then regard it as morally wrong?   Yes/No/Uncertain [4]

Those who replied "No" to the first question and "Yes" to the second were excluded.

Table 9.2 shows that while very few respondents considered heavy smoking morally wrong, small but by no means negligible minorities would alter their attitude if Parliament legislated to make it criminal. No conclu-

TABLE 9.2.   THE MORALITY OF HEAVY SMOKING

Sample [a]	(a) No. of Replies	(b) No. Saying "No" or "Uncertain" to Qn. 7a	(c) No. Giving Different Reply to Qn. 7b [b]	(d) Column (c) as Percent of Column (b)
males				
Undergraduates (tests 1 and 4)	157	133	26	19.5
Technical college men (test 2)	45	41	1	2.4
females				
Undergraduates (tests 1 and 4)	36	30	3	10.0
Technical college women (test 2)	34	28	2	7.1

[a] Group 3 was given a questionnaire which asked each respondent to give his own example of "some sort of action which does not seem morally wrong to you"; but this proved too difficult for some of them.

[b] I.e., altering their attitude from "No" to "Uncertain" or "Yes," or from "Uncertain" to "Yes."

[4] In test 2, at the technical college, respondents were given only a choice between "Yes" and "No."

sions could be based on the differences in percentages in column (c), since the technical college students were given only a "Yes/No" choice in their replies, while the undergraduates were given a "Yes/No/Uncertain" choice. Comparison with personal data (questions 8 *et seq.*) showed no consistent differences between those who altered their attitudes and those who did not.

As will be shown, tests 1 to 3 failed to produce unmistakeable differences of the predicted sort between the morality judgments of the two groups, and two further refinements were therefore introduced in test 4. Questions 2 to 6 were now stated in three forms. As before, one version described the action as not an offence, while another described it as an offence; but now a third version not only described it as an offence but also described a fictitious case in which an offender had been fined for committing it. This device was introduced in order to see whether a more dramatic way of presenting the action as illegal would succeed where a mere statement of the law had failed. Morton (1962) has suggested that a function of the process of trial and punishment is to emphasise the disapproval of society in so dramatic a way that other members of society will be made aware of it.

The other innovation in test 4 was designed to meet the possible criticism that the entire experiment rested on a false assumption—namely, the assumption that moral attitudes are so easily altered that a technique of this kind could produce measurable differences. Question 6 was therefore designed to confirm whether respondents' moral judgments could be measurably altered by telling them that a large majority of their peers had taken this view or that. In one version the question simply asked: "If a man uses obscene language in a public place, without annoying anybody, as a question not of law but of *morality* is his conduct wrong?" In the other versions, however, it was either stated that while his conduct was *not an offence,* "in a recent sample of undergraduates 82 percent said that his conduct was wrong," or that it *was* an offence but that 82 percent of a recent sample of undergraduates had said that it was *not* wrong.

The results were analysed by dividing the six-point morality scale at the mid-point, and combining the separately matched groups of male and female undergraduates (Table 9.3). The differences between the distributions of the replies ($p < .01$) justifies the assumption that measurable differences in moral judgments can be produced by varying the information given. What is more,

TABLE 9.3.   LAW VERSUS MAJORITY OPINION

	Respondents Who Judged Obscene Language in Public	
Respondents Who Were Told:	Wrong, very wrong, or as wrong as possible	Slightly wrong, not wrong, or very right
That it was not criminal but that most undergraduates regarded it as wrong	24	7
That it was criminal but that most undergraduates did not regard it as wrong	13	21

it provides a certain amount of confirmation that, for young adults at least, what they believe to be the opinion of their peers is a stronger influence than the supposed state of the law.

The remaining questions were simply designed to yield information about the respondent's sex, religion, politics, age, and father's occupation. (Male and female respondents were separated before being matched and tabulated; those whose ages were outside the normal range for the sample were disregarded.) After the completed questionnaires had been collected, respondents were told that they had been deliberately misled, and the true state of the law was explained. . . .

Results of the Experimental Test

With these precautions, the replies were analysed to see whether the distribution of moral judgments on the five issues (litter-dropping, negligent injury, public drunkenness, prostitution, and obscene language) appeared to be affected by the information given to respondents about the state of the law. Since the questions on some of the issues were subdivided, altogether 46 comparisons were made (using the chi-squared test of significance). As Table 9.4 shows, none of the comparisons revealed a difference in distribution that could be accepted as significant, even at the .05 level; and in most cases insignificant differences in the direction predicted by the declaratory hypothesis were counterbalanced by insignificant differences in the opposite

TABLE 9.4. DIFFERENCES IN MORAL JUDGMENTS BETWEEN MATCHED SAMPLES GIVEN DIFFERENT INFORMATION ABOUT THE LAW

	No. of Comparisons Made	No. of Significant [a] Differences in Expected Direction	No. of Non-significant [a] Differences in Expected Direction	No. of Significant [a] Differences in Reverse Direction	No. of Non-significant [a] Differences in Reverse Direction
Dropping litter	10	0	3	0	1
Negligent injury	12	0	3	0	0
Drunkenness	5	0	1	0	1
Prostitution	18	0	7	0	5
Obscene language	1	0	1	0	0
Totals	46	0	15	0	7

[a] I.e., at .05 level of significance.

direction revealed by another of the comparisons. (The nearest approach to confirmation occurs in the case of negligent injury, when the three comparisons which reveal differences are all in the expected direction, but in no case is p less than .15.)

A comparison was also made in test 4 between the moral judgments of respondents who were simply told that the conduct in question was an offence and those who were also told of fictitious cases in which fines had been imposed for the offence. Among the four types of conduct involved (litter-dropping, negligent injury, public drunkenness, and prostitution) there was only one (public drunkenness) for which comparison showed a significant difference ($p < .05$) and this was in the opposite direction to that predicted by the declaratory theory. There was some further evidence of this "boomerang" effect among the comparisons summarised in Table 9.4; the clearest example was the attitudes of the males to prostitution, since in five out of eleven comparisons the information that soliciting by a prostitute is criminal seemed to produce a *less* censorious moral judgment.

The occurrence of such differences in the unexpected direction is interesting, since it draws attention to the possibility that in the case of some types of conduct the use of the criminal law may provoke an antagonistic reaction in people of certain types or viewpoints (for example, young males of above-average intelligence and education). If so, this might well be expressed by a moral judgment which is in effect a protest against the use of the law.

Summary

Two methods of testing the "declaratory theory" of the function of the criminal law produced the following results:

1. A survey of moral attitudes towards a type of act which had recently ceased to be criminal (attempted suicide) showed no significant difference between those who knew of the change in the law and those who did not.

2. It was found possible to devise a "laboratory" situation in which measurable alterations in the moral judgments of young adults in the direction of the "majority view" were induced by telling them the results of a fictitious survey of their peers.

3. There were minorities who believed that legislation which made heavy smoking an offence would make it morally wrong.

4. These apart, however, no significant differences of the kind predicted by the declaratory theory appeared to occur between those who were told that a given type of conduct was a criminal offence and those who were told that it was not.

5. On the other hand, in some cases there appeared to be a slight tendency for those who were told that certain forms of conduct were criminal offences to react by taking a less censorious moral view of it.

6. Nor were significant differences of the predicted kind produced by adding fictitious descriptions of cases in which the "offender" had been fined. Indeed, in the case of public drunkenness this may even have been responsible for a slight shift towards greater moral tolerance in the case of male undergraduates.

These results cast considerable doubt on the "declaratory" argument that alterations of the criminal law are likely to weaken moral attitudes. It is true that they are concerned only with the possibility of short-term effects; and supporters of the declaratory theory could argue that the creation or abolition of offences has long-term effects on attitudes—in other words that the legislation of one generation is the morality of the next. But in the face of the apparent absence of short-term effects the onus of proof seems to lie very definitely on those who believe in long-term effects.

References

Dashiell, J. F. 1935. "Experimental Studies of the Influence of Social Situations on the Behavior of Individual Human Adults." In C. Murchison (ed.), *Handbook of Social Psychology*. Worcester, Mass.: Clark University Press.

Home Office. 1957. *Report of the Committee on Homosexual Offences and Prostitution*. London: H.M.S.O. Cmnd. 247. (Wolfenden Committee.)

Lazarsfeld, P. F., B. Berelson, and H. Gaudet. 1948. *The People's Choice*. New York: Columbia University Press.

Morton, G. D. 1962. *The Function of the Criminal Law in 1962*. Toronto: Canadian Broadcasting Corporation Publications.

Walker, N. D. 1964. "Morality and the Criminal Law," *The Howard Journal* 11:209.

PART TWO

*Perception
in Criminal Law
and Justice*

The content of Part Two is considerably different from that of Parts One or Three since it unavoidably covers a greater amount of territory in criminology—territory which, moreover, has received scant attention from a perceptual point of view. The selections in this section take the reader through the criminal justice process (the social control components of criminology's domain) from a perceptual vantage point. It proceeds along the "flow" of the criminal justice process, touching on the role of perception in the activities of the public,[1] legislatures, police, juries, the judiciary, and finally in

[1] Some would argue that the criminal justice process starts with the police, but in practice the process is often initiated by the public in complainant and witness roles. Public conceptions of crime are important in determining whether and in what way members will act, hence the public is included as part of the first stage of the process.

parole decision-making. There are, of course, gaps in the collection representing corresponding gaps in research about specific areas. (See the discussion in the Introduction to this volume.) The conceptualization of the criminal justice system presented by these selections is not the traditional one.
The point of view is well presented by Quinney in his statement concerning
the perspective emerging in criminological writing:

> Until fairly recent times studies and writings in criminology were shaped almost
> entirely by the criminologist's interest in "the criminal." In the last few years, how-
> ever, those who study crime have realized that crime is relative to different legal sys-
> tems, that an absolute conception of crime—outside of legal definitions—had to be
> replaced by a relativistic (that is, legalistic) conception. Many criminologists have
> therefore turned to studying how criminal definitions are constructed and applied in a
> society.
>   Two schools of thought have developed. Some argue that crime is properly studied
> by examining the offender and his behavior. Others are convinced that the criminal
> law is the correct object: how it is formulated, enforced, and administered. The two
> need not become deadlocked in polemics. The long overdue interest in criminal defi-
> nitions happily corrects the absurdities brought about by studying the offender alone;
> the two approaches actually complement one another. A synthesis of the criminal be-
> havior and criminal definition approaches can provide a new theoretical framework
> for the study of crime. (Quinney, 1970: 3–4)

The legal and social interpretations of crime do stand in competition
with each other but they are not completely incompatible (Johnson, 1968:
12–13). Our stance in making these selections has obviously been to emphasize the social interpretation, which we feel provides a certain theoretical
unity to acts classified as criminal.

Beyond our discussion of the labeling of individuals in Part Three,
there has been a burgeoning interest in the mechanisms by which *acts* become labeled as deviant.[2] Blumer's thesis that "social problems are fundamentally products of a process of *collective definition* instead of existing
independently as a set of objective social arrangements with an intrinsic
make-up" (1971: 298 [emphasis added]) is considered extensively by Henshel and Henshel (1973). In such treatments social problems are seen as at
least partially arising from the perceptions of those involved in defining
them—moral entrepreneurs, victims, intellectuals, and media "gatekeep-
ers." The perceptions are instrumental in defining specific social conditions
as problematic, in emphasizing some conditions and ignoring others, and in

---

[2] There has also been some interest in how acts became *delabeled*. Acts such as divorce and
abortion are currently being examined in these terms.

pointing to certain preferred "solutions" that fit in with the perception of the nature of the problem itself.

The section opens with three examinations of the public's conceptions of crime. Quinney's selection (chapter 10), from *The Social Reality of Crime* (1970), indicates that the construction and diffusion of criminal definitions proceeds simultaneously among individuals and groups. Among the most important agents of such diffusion are the mass media, but conceptions of crime derived from mass communications are mediated by interpersonal networks, with both attitudinal and behavioral consequences.

Jennie McIntyre continues the discussion of public conceptions in "Public Attitudes Toward Crime and Law Enforcement" (chapter 11). Her discussion focuses on the source of perceptions concerning crime trends, and she finds that most knowledge of such events comes vicariously.[3] She finds little relationship between personal victimization and attitudes toward crime. On the other hand, people change their life styles to be consistent with what they believe about crime trends rather than what the objective reality would mandate.

Our final piece on public conceptions is Ralph Turner's "The Public Perception of Protest" (chapter 12). This abridged version of his article indicates some of the conditions under which one group may define situations as disturbances while others view the same situation as social protest. Turner departs from the model we introduced in the Introduction when he denies the existence of an objective reality. But as he also indicates, the controversy over such positions is an enduring one. We respect his point of view, and especially admire his excellent analysis of the perception of social protests/disturbances.

Articles by Lindesmith and Sutherland introduce readers to the role of perception in legislative decision-making.[4] Lindesmith (chapter 13) discusses the role of perception in the creation of the Marihuana Tax Act of 1937, the act that essentially made the use of marihuana illegal in the United States,[5] portraying the campaign of one "moral entrepreneur." It was a publicity campaign rather than objective fact that created sufficient agita-

[3] Readers interested in this topic might also refer to Friendly and Goldfarb (1968).

[4] For other insightful analyses of this topic, see Becker (1963), Platt (1969), Rothman (1971), and Shrieke (1936).

[5] For additional treatment of perception in drug legislation, see "The Marihuana Tax Act," in Becker (1963: 135–146). An item-by-item treatment of beliefs about marihuana is found in ch. 2 of Eldridge (1967).

tion to insure easy passage for the Act. In the case of marihuana legislation we are burdened with the results of these misperceptions even today. It seems clear that many of the incorrect beliefs presently held about drug use can be linked to publicity campaigns of the 1930s.[6]

In "The Diffusion of Sexual Psychopath Laws," Sutherland indicates the sources of public perceptions about sex crimes (chapter 14). He shows how pressure groups can develop, and legislation be instituted on the basis of misperceptions of the situation. At this point, perception in criminology intersects with the sociology of law and the study of lobbies and pressure groups in political science.

John Clark and Wayne LaFave provide pieces on police decision-making. Police discretion is one area that has received a respectable amount of attention. John Clark's empirical work, "Isolation of the Police" (chapter 15), shows that the public and police perception of public standards may not correspond, and that this discrepancy can result in police behavior that departs from the public "consensus." In essence, the perceptions of the police role by officers and the public often differ, and Clark attempts to trace some of the antecedents of this condition in the British and American situations.[7]

In "Police Overperception of Ghetto Hostility," Crawford focuses on one aspect of police isolation (chapter 16). He finds that police perceive the hostility of ghetto residents toward them to be more pronounced than that hostility is in fact. He indicates that such "overperception" of hostility may have negative behavioral consequences in triggering conflicts between police and urban ghetto residents. Such findings, if supported in subsequent research, may have important implications for future police recruitment. Further, sociologists would learn much about police by attempting to go beyond Crawford and examining *why* police perceive that hostility in such a manner.

Wayne LaFave, in "Police Perception and Selective Enforcement," investigates perceptual criteria (other than stereotypy) for police discretion (chapter 17). If police believe that the likelihood of conviction for particular kinds of cases is low then they will not arrest but rather dispose of those cases without invoking the mechanisms of the formal criminal justice sys-

[6] For a discussion of the influence of politics and power on the growth of Canadian narcotics legislation, see Cook (1969).

[7] See also aspects of Young (1971), reprinted in Part Three of this volume.

tem. Additionally, they often act on the basis of what they perceive the standards of the community to be, rather than on grounds set down in the criminal law.[8] In sum, it is perception that controls many police activities.[9] The notion of a law enforcement agency that simply follows rules and enforces all laws is obviously incorrect, and its replacement must take into account the role of perception in police decision-making.

Literature on the functioning of juries is relatively sparse, and we are fortunate that at least one major research has been carried out on perception in jury deliberations. Rita Simon's piece, "Jurors' Assessment of Criminal Responsibility," is part of a set of studies she has performed on decision-making by jurors (chapter 18).[10] It indicates the sources of jurors' perceptions of the "facts of the case" and how they then interpret the law in insanity hearings.[11]

Two pieces by John Hogarth on decision-making processes among magistrates follow the contribution by Simon. Hogarth's fascinating research fits the perceptual model very nicely. In "Perception of Cases and Judicial Sentencing Behaviour," he discusses magistrates' perceptions of cases as those perceptions relate to sentencing behavior (chapter 19). In a penetrating analysis, he finds that once magistrates see cases in the same way, their sentencing behavior is very similar *but* that different magistrates perceive the same cases differently. Hence perception is a controlling factor in sentencing behavior.

In his second piece, "Magistrates' World Views and Sentencing Behaviour," Hogarth indicates that there is a great deal of consistency be-

[8] Readers interested in further discussion of police discretion would find the remainder of LaFave's (1965) book of interest. See also Pilliavin and Briar (1964) and McDougall (1971). Perception and police discretion also operate at the level of the police dispatcher, in terms of decisions on whether to respond to calls to the police (Shearing, 1972).

[9] See McDougall (1971) for a discussion of perception in other aspects of policing.

[10] See Rita James Simon (1967). For a bibliography on the available literature on jury decisions, see Adler (1973). For jury appraisals of the reliability of witnesses, see Davidson (1954).

[11] In another study which used simulated jury trials, Landy and Aronson (1969) systematically varied the prestige characteristics of both the offender and victim, while keeping the story of the incident unchanged. For instance a case involving an auto accident in which an individual was killed had a woman coming home from church as the offender in one trial while in another the offender was a prostitute returning from a contact. The verdicts in these cases varied directly with the prestige of the offender.

For a discussion of how knowledge about potential jurors may influence the outcome of trials, see Schulman et al., 1973.

The work of H. H. Kelley and others in attribution theory should be especially relevant here.

tween a magistrate's general perceptions of the world and his behavior on
the bench (chapter 20). He suggests that one might explain as much or more
about sentencing by knowing certain facts about the judge as by knowing a
great deal about the facts of a case. In this selection Hogarth discusses and
dissects the so-called "black box" model of sentencing and offers a new
model in which perception plays a prominent role.[12]

The final selection is by Joseph Rogers and Norman Hayner: "Perception, Optimism, and Accuracy in Correctional Decision-Making" (chapter
21). The authors examine the perceptions about offenders' characteristics
held by parole board members and other criminal justice decision-makers,
contrasting the predictions by these persons of probable parole success with
the actual experience. Accuracy of perception is then related to occupational
characteristics of the respondents.

It is significant that the variation in age among the articles presented
here is greater than among those in the other sections. Although there is
some very recent material, many of the selections date from the 1950s. In
contrast, none of the articles in Part One were written before 1965, while in
Part Three only Tannenbaum's work predates 1960. Some of the earlier
selections are classics for their kind, and it is our belief that some of the
newer pieces as well are destined to become "landmarks" for emerging foci
of criminological inquiry. Material in this section can be thought of as
representing the first stage in the development of a literature with the perceptual perspective. Selections included represent a slow accumulation of material, with very little self-consciousness on the part of the researchers. The
other parts of this book are intriguingly different in that respect—each represents a research domain that systematically elaborates the perceptual frame
of reference. The articles presented here encompass a broad spectrum of
time and theoretical and methodological sophistication. We hope that greater
familiarity with the contents of this section will stimulate an expansion of
perceptually oriented investigation in the domains represented.

The development of attribution theory in social psychology has special
relevance to this section's topics. We need to know *how* people decide
whether the actions of others are criminal, protesting, or insane, and
whether an offender has reformed. Attribution theory may eventually show
us this.

---

[12] For another work on the sentencing process, see Green (1961). See Bullock (1962) for the
classical study of sentencing bias. Hogarth's book (1971) contains an excellent bibliography on
sentencing research.

References

Adler, Freda. 1973. "Socioeconomic Factors Influencing Jury Verdicts," *New York Review of Law and Social Change* 3 (1) (Winter):1–10.

Becker, Howard. 1963. *Outsiders: Studies in the Sociology of Deviance.* Glencoe, Ill.: Free Press.

Blumer, Herbert. 1971. "Social Problems as Collective Behavior," *Social Problems* 18:298–306.

Bullock, Henry A. 1961. "Significance of the Racial Factor in the Length of Prison Sentences," *Journal of Criminal Law, Criminology, and Police Science* 52:411–17.

Cook, Shirley J. 1969. "Canadian Narcotics Legislation 1908–1923: A Conflict Model Interpretation," *Canadian Review of Sociology and Anthropology* 6 (1):36–46.

Davidson, Henry A. 1954. "Appraisal of Witnesses," *American Journal of Psychiatry* 110:481–86.

Eldridge, William B. 1967. *Narcotics and the Law.* 2d ed. Chicago: University of Chicago Press.

Friendly, Alfred and Ronald Goldfarb. 1968. *Crime and Publicity.* New York: Vintage Books.

Green, Edward. 1961. *Judicial Attitudes in Sentencing.* London: Macmillan.

Henshel, Richard L. and Anne-Marie Henshel. 1973. *Perspectives on Social Problems.* Toronto: Longmans.

Hogarth, John. 1971. *Sentencing as a Human Process.* Toronto: University of Toronto Press.

Johnson, Elmer H. 1968. *Crime, Correction, and Society.* Rev. ed. Homewood, Ill.: Dorsey.

LaFave, Wayne R. 1965. *Arrest: The Decision to Take a Suspect into Custody.* Boston: Little, Brown.

Landy, David and Eliot Aronson. 1969. "The Influence of the Character of the Criminal and His Victims on Decisions of Simulated Jurors," *Journal of Experimental and Social Psychology* 5 (April):141–52.

McDougall, Allan K. 1971. "Policy Issues and Research Problems in the Development of Metropolitan Police Services." Paper presented to the Sixth Annual Conference of Directors of Criminological Research in the United States and Canada, Montreal (October).

Pilliavin, Irving and Scott Briar. 1964. "Police Encounters with Juveniles," *American Journal of Sociology* 70:206–14.

Platt, Anthony. 1969. *The Child Savers: The Invention of Delinquency*. Chicago: University of Chicago Press.

Quinney, Richard. 1970. *The Social Reality of Crime*. Boston: Little, Brown.

Rothman, David J. 1971. *The Discovery of the Asylum*. Boston: Little, Brown.

Schrieke, B. 1936. *Alien Americans*. New York: Viking.

Schulman, Jay, Phillip Shaver, Robert Coleman, Barbara Emrich, and Richard Christie. 1973. "Recipe for a Jury," *Psychology Today* (May):37–44, 77–84.

Shearing, Clifford D. 1972. "Dial-A-Cop: A Study of Police Mobilization." Paper presented to the American Society of Criminology, Inter-American Congress, Caracas.

Simon, Rita James. 1967. *The Jury and the Defense of Insanity*. Boston: Little, Brown.

Young, Jock. 1971. "The Police as Amplifiers of Deviancy, Negotiators of Reality and Translators of Fantasy." In S. Cohen (ed.), *Images of Deviance*. Harmondsworth: Penguin.

10

Public Conceptions of Crime

RICHARD QUINNEY

We human beings construct our own reality. And with the help of others, we create a social world. The construction of this world is related to the knowledge we develop, the ideas to which we are exposed, and the manner in which we select and interpret information to fit the world we are shaping. We behave, then, in reference to our conceptions of reality.

Included in man's social reality are conceptions about crime. Wherever the concept of crime exists, images are communicated in society about the meaning of crime, the nature of the criminal, and the relationship of crime to the social order. *Criminal conceptions* are thus constructed and diffused throughout society by various means of communication. For purposes of analysis, conceptions of crime can be discussed according to (1) social reaction to crime, (2) the diffusion of criminal conceptions, (3) social types in the world of crime, (4) public attitudes toward crime, and (5) public attitudes toward the control of crime. All these issues in the construction of criminal conceptions affect the development of criminal definitions and behavior patterns in a society.

Social Reaction to Crime

The reaction of the public to crime is both a product of the social reality of crime and a source in the construction of conceptions of crime. On the one

Reprinted by permission of Little, Brown and Company Inc., from chapter nine of *The Social Reality of Crime* by Richard Quinney. Copyright © 1970, Little, Brown and Company, Inc.

hand, social reactions to crime are a consequence of the reality the public has constructed in regard to crime. Persons react in specific ways to the occurrence of criminally defined activity, to the enforcement and administration of the law, and to the treatment of the offender. Without a social reality of crime, there would be no reaction to crime. But, on the other hand, the reactions that are elicited in response to crime are at the same time shaping the social reality of crime. As persons react to crime, they develop patterns for the responses of the future. . . .

From the perspective of the individual, responses to crime are influenced by *knowledge* about crime and *perceptions* about the meaning of crime. The attitudes of persons toward such matters as criminal behavior, law enforcement, and the handling of offenders are affected by the kinds and amounts of knowledge they have about these matters. Persons differ greatly in their knowledge about the existence and substance of laws in the society (Segerstedt, 1949; Beutel, 1957). Reaction to all that is associated with crime initially rests upon knowledge about crime. Likewise, perception of the crime phenomenon underlies any social reaction to crime. How a person perceives crime provides a framework for his own understanding of an subsequent reaction to crime.

Attitudes to crime and criminals then, vary, not so much in terms of the intrinsic nature of the criminal act, but in terms of the likelihood of the act being an established part of the observer's own social world. Crime is in the last analysis what the other person does. What I do, if it is against the law, is susceptible to redefinition through rationalization. Even if the observer is unlikely to commit the particular crime in question, his attitude to it will be conditioned by a degree of modification which may result in either a lenient tolerance or a punitive rejection, depending upon how far the crime threatens the observer, or the group to which they all belong. (Morris, 1966)

Perception precedes a response of any kind. . . .

Diffusion of Criminal Conceptions

Once a society has a generalized criminal mythology, conceptions of crime are diffused throughout the population. The *diffusion* of criminal conceptions simultaneously involves the *construction* of conceptions of crime among individuals and groups. This mutual process is accomplished in a number of ways. All the means which facilitate construction of conceptions, however, are mediated by the social context of diffusion and by the interpersonal relations associated with the adoption of criminal conceptions.

Among the most important agents in the diffusion of criminal conceptions are the media of mass communication. Crime coverage in the newspapers, television, and movies affect a person's estimate of the frequency of crime as well as the interpretations that he attaches to crime. Research has shown that a special reality is presented in the newspapers in respect to crime. In one study, it was found that the amount of crime news in each of four Colorado newspapers varied independently of the amount of crime in the state as reflected by crime statistics (Davis, 1952). Persons were then asked, in a public opinion poll, to estimate the amount of crime in the state. The results indicated that public opinion about crime tended to reflect trends in the amount of crime news rather than the actual crime rates. Coverage of crime in the newspapers created a conceptual reality that was meaningful to the public in spite of any other social reality of crime.

Moreover, the mass media provide varying and often divergent portrayals of crime. Perusal of different newspapers in the same city on the same day is enough to illustrate that one's construction of a conception of crime depends upon which newspaper he happens to read. One of the most striking examples is a comparison of two newspapers in New York City that have considerably different orientations to news presentation: the *New York Daily News* and the *New York Times*. In a content analysis of the two newspapers, it was found that over three months the *Daily News* presented nearly twice as many items about juvenile delinquency as did the *Times* (Bachmuth et al., 1960). In front-page coverage, the *Daily News* carried four stories for each one displayed in the *Times*. Furthermore, there were differences between the two papers in the emotionality with which the news items were presented. Differences were seen, especially, in the terminology and phraseology of the headlines of the two papers. Typical of the *Daily News* headlines were: "Cops Nab Two In Cat-Mouse Roof Top Chase," "Stolen Kiss Traps Robber of Girl In Hall," "Hunt Two Boy Bullies Who Killed Lad," "Thugs Finger A Fingerman," and "Beer Gets Guv's Girl Canned From College." The headlines from the *Times,* in comparison, were mild and unemotional: "Museum Theft Laid To Delinquents," "Third Slain In Youth Violence," "Youth Crime Rise Is Held Magnified," and "Three Fires Set In Bronx School."

Thus public conceptions of crime and delinquency are constructed and diffused on the basis of "news" presentations. Specific conceptions are shaped by what is considered to be news about the subject of crime. Since the press is one of the chief dispensers of information about crime, conceptions of crime and delinquency are influenced by the newspaper coverage to which one is exposed. . . .

The style and content of much of the media represent a continual preoccupations with crime. For the many persons who find this sort of coverage to their liking, the real world is a selective one, a crime-centered one. Not only is attention focused on crime, but the more sensational and adventuresome aspects of crime are portrayed. The routine nature of the major portion of crime is also neglected. Coverage of crime in the mass media, therefore, is not only selective but is a distortion of the everyday world of crime. But such is the stuff from which reality worlds are constructed for much of the population.

The effect of the coverage of crime in the mass media has been a topic for considerable speculation and research.[1] Many educators, social observers, and parents have worried about the possible effects of the depiction of crime and violence in the media. It is not my purpose here, however, to survey and evaluate the many arguments and findings. I have no doubt of the selective nature of the coverage of crime in the mass media. Likewise, I am convinced that crime as presented in the media affects the recipient's attitudes and behavior. I am also certain that in some cases persons are "tried" by the press before their cases are decided in a court of law (Friendly and Goldfarb, 1968). But, first, the relationship that I perceive between exposure to media and the attitudes and behaviors of persons is on a more general level. That is, public conceptions of crime are created in part by the images of crime in the mass media. And, second, the realtionship must be viewed along with the mediating forces of social context and interpersonal relations.

Recent research on mass communications has confirmed that the possible effects of the mass media are mediated by interpersonal networks of communication and by such contextual matters as integration in social groups and membership in various kinds of groups (Katz, 1957; Riley and Riley, 1959; Rogers, 1962). Personal contacts in a social context influence one's interpretation of the content of the mass media. Moreover, mass communication, in working through mediators, reinforces existing conceptions. The social nature of exposure to mass media, therefore, influences the nature and impact of the portrayal of crime in mass communication.

[1] Much of the research is reviewed in Klapper (1960: 135–65).

The implication of the above idea is that exposure to such images affects individuals differently according to their past experiences and their present associations. In particular, it appears that persons who are involved in patterns of criminally defined activity are more likely to be influenced by crime portrayals than persons not so involved (Blumer and Hauser, 1933). On an even more subtle level, however, the effect of exposure to crime in the mass media may not be significant until a personal problem or a particular social condition presents itself. Exposure in the past may thus furnish a future alternative for action.

Certainly we can convincingly argue that mass communications are socially mediated. Nevertheless, there would be nothing to mediate if a particular image did not exist in the mass media in the first place. Mass communications *do* make a difference. My argument, reinterpreting the thesis of the effects of mass media, is that a specific kind of crime coverage in the media provides the source for building criminal conceptions. A conception of crime is presented in the mass media. That conception, diffused throughout the society, becomes the basis for the public's view of reality. Not only is a symbolic environment created within the society, but personal actions take their reference from that environment. Indeed, the construction of a conceptual reality is also the creation of a social reality of actions and events.

Social Types in the World of Crime

All the nuances of crime cannot be vividly communicated. In communication, images must be simplified, sharpened, and reduced to their essentials. Thus, in order to facilitate the diffusion of conceptions of crime, *stereotypes* of crime and criminals are created. Offenders, accordingly, are grouped by the public into such categories as the thief, the burglar, the robber, the sex offender, and the murderer. Categories such as these furnish the boundaries for the public's view of crime.

On the basis of stereotypes, then, persons construct their conceptual realities of crime. The criminal becomes a *social type*.[2] As a social type, "the criminal" can be understood by the observer as one who possesses attributes that are believed to be characteristic of a class of people. The crimi-

[2] The concept of social type is from Klapp (1962: 1–24).

nal, as socially typed, is a construct that incorporates a description of what such persons are like, why they act as they do, and how they should act in the future. All that is associated with crime has the possibility of being categorized by the public. Such is the basis of human understanding.

Some systematic evidence exists on the public stereotyping of criminals. In a series of pilot studies the extent and nature of stereotyped images of deviants were investigated (Simmons, 1965). The researcher found, first, public stereotypes for such deviant categories as homosexuals, drug addicts, prostitutes, murderers, and juvenile delinquents. It was then determined that persons also tend to consistently portray each type of deviant in a particular way. Homosexuals were likely to be described as being sexually abnormal, perverted, mentally ill, and maladjusted, whereas marijuana smokers were characterized as persons looking for kicks, escapists, insecure, lacking self-control, and frustrated. It was concluded that "discernible stereotypes of at least several kinds of deviants do exist in our society and that there is a fair amount of agreement on the content of these stereotypes" (Simmons, 1965: 229). Hence, imputed deviance, including deviance which may also be criminally defined, is publicly stereotyped. These stereotypes of human behavior are structured and patterned in society.

On a more general level, the category of "criminal" tends to incorporate its own stereotyped set of characteristics. According to public conception, the criminal is a social type. The principal model for the type is the *villian,* one who is feared, hated, and ridiculed. The criminal is generally the "bad guy" in popular conception. Criminals are the enemies of law and order (desperadoes, rebels, flouters, rogues, troublemakers), villainous strangers (intruders, suspicious isolates, monsters), disloyal and underhanded types (renegades, traitors, deceivers, sneak-attackers, chiselers, shirkers, corrupters), or are among the miscellaneous social undesirables (vagrants, derelicts, convicts, outcasts) (Klapp, 1962: 50–67). Such villains are with us in popular conception, nominally as criminals. The public concept of crime is used to cover a multitude of sins.

But the criminal as a social type incorporates other than the image of villain. He may also be cast in the role of *hero.* Noted outlaws are an example:

Billy the Kid did not make a good villain because he was blonde, blue-eyed, well built, and rather handsome; women fell for him. He was brave and a square shooter. Such discrepancies in the character of a bad man made him resemble others (Robin

Hood, Don Juan, François Villon, Pancho Villa), who perhaps should have been villains but were not. (Klapp, 1962: 50)

Paradoxically (perhaps), the villainous criminal can also be a popular favorite of heroic proportions.

A major reason for the ambiguity between villainous and heroic criminal conceptions is that the roles of villain and hero support similar value themes. Both types depend upon aggressiveness, cleverness, and the ability to "outdo" others in some way.

Not only in fiction but in real life confusion between good guys and bad guys occurs. Since Edwin H. Sutherland's epochal studies, Americans have gotten rather used to the idea that a whitecollar criminal looks very like an honest businessman. Expense account chiseling, kickbacks, payoffs, tax evasion, even a little fraud or larceny, may be all in a day's work. If the old distinction between honesty and dishonesty has become blurred, no less has the quaint notion that "crime does not pay" (if you want to get a laugh from an audience, just smile when you say this). When the Brinks Express robbers were caught a few years back, a housewife remarked, "I was kind of sad. It seemed a shame, when they had only a few days to go before the statute of limitations would have let them keep all that money." A strange kind of casing is occurring today—good guys do not have to live up to codes, bad guys do not have to be caught and punished (especially if they look enough like good guys); it may be that the distinction is ceasing to be important.[3]

.   .   .   .

Perhaps some criminals capture the modern imagination as *antiheroes*. As antihero, the criminal represents the attempt to make it outside the system. Inevitable failure gives charisma to his noble attempt. . . .

Criminals are not only social types that fill the public world of crime. Also included are the social types that are associated with criminals. Policemen, lawyers, and detectives have become socially typed through the various forms of communication. The detective, in particular, has been the object of a great deal of characterizing in the mystery novel. . . .

The crime-fighting heroes of today display virtues for another age. These characters are more likely to be found in suspense and science fiction stories than in detective stories (Hibbert, 1966: 302–314). The "private eye," such as Dashiell Hammett's Sam Spade or Raymond Chandler's Philip Marlowe, is a tough guy, cynical, hard-boiled, and hard drinking, who is at war with criminals in his *own* way, often outside the law. Mickey Spil-

[3] Klapp (1962: 145–46); also see Hare (1963).

lane's Mike Hammer killed numerous innocent people in his pursuits against crime. . . .

Images such as these have been presented to a wide audience by television and the movies as well as by fictional literature. Detective heroes have been portrayed in leading roles as being "smarter than the cops, craftier than the crooks, too quick to be caught and domesticated by the classiest doll." [4] And we have been presented with the shadowy figure of Perry Mason, a lawyer who behaves like a private detective in preparing his cases. The list need not be extended. It is enough to say that the world of crime is readily before us for the taking.

I am not necessarily being critical of the ways in which the characters of the world of crime are presented. The portrayals by criminologists probably have not been any more convincing. I *do,* however, argue that the world of fiction is also the world of reality. Fiction is fact when it is believed and taken as the object of action. When criminals and their counterparts are characterized in a particular way, they are already becoming social types which find their fulfillment in society. Social reality begins in the imagination. . . .

Consequences of Criminal Conceptions

So it is that conceptions of crime are constructed and diffused throughout the segments of society. And the conceptions are important because of their consequences. But since they vary from one segment to another, they have different effects on the total society. . . .

Any conception of crime has its own set of consequences. Each conception provides a perspective as to what is regarded as crime, how crime should be controlled, how criminals should be punished and treated, and how the population is to conduct itself in an environment of crime and criminals. All these issues are resolved in actions. As thoughts become deeds, a social reality is constructed.

[4] Quoted in Hibbert (1966: 311); also see De Fleur (1964).

References

Bachmuth, Rita, S. M. Miller, and Linda Rosen. 1960. "Juvenile Delinquency in the Daily Press," *Alpha Kappa Delta* 30 (Spring):47–51.

Beutel, Frederick. 1957. *Some Potentialities of Experimental Jurisprudence as a New Branch of Social Science*. Lincoln: University of Nebraska Press.

Blumer, Herbert and Philip Hauser. 1933. *Movies, Delinquency, and Crime*. New York: Macmillan.

Davis, F. J. 1952. "Crime News in Colorado Newspapers," *American Journal of Sociology* 57 (January), 325–30.

De Fleur, Melvin L. 1964. "Occupational Roles as Portrayed on Television," *Public Opinion Quarterly* 28 (Spring), 57–74.

Friendly, Alfred and Ronald L. Goldfarb. 1968. *Crime and Publicity: The Impact of News on the Administration of Justice*. New York: Vintage.

Hare, Nathan. 1963. "The Ambivalent Public and Crime," *Crime and Delinquency* 9 (April), 145–51.

Hibbert, Christopher. 1966. *The Roots of Evil: A Social History of Crime and Punishment*. Harmondsworth: Penguin.

Katz, Elihu. 1957. "The Two-Step Flow of Communication: An Up-to-Date Report of an Hypothesis," *Public Opinion Quarterly* 21 (Spring), 61–78.

Klapp, Orrin E. 1962. *Heroes, Villains, and Fools*. Englewood Cliffs, N.J.: Prentice-Hall.

Klapper, Joseph T. 1960. *The Effects of Mass Communication*. New York: Free Press of Glencoe.

Morris, Terence. 1966. "The Social Toleration of Crime." In Hugh J. Klare (ed.), *Changing Concepts of Crime and Its Treatment*, Oxford: Permagon, pp. 33–34.

Riley, John W., Jr. and Mathilda White Riley. 1959. "Mass Communication and the Social System." In Robert K. Merton, Leonard Broom, and Leonard S. Cottrell (eds.), *Sociology Today*, New York: Basic Books, pp. 537–78.

Rogers, Everett M. 1962. *Diffusion of Innovations*. New York: Free Press of Glencoe, pp. 57–75, 208–53.

Segerstedt, Torgny T. 1949. "A Research into the General Sense of Justice," *Theoria* 15:323–38.

Simmons, J. L. 1965. "Public Stereotypes of Deviants," *Social Problems* 13 (Fall):223–32.

11

Public Attitudes
Toward Crime
and Law Enforcement

JENNIE MCINTRYE

Public concern about crime is neither new nor surprising. An interest which was once manifested in attendance at the public punishment of offenders is now expressed in reaction to the news media's reports of crime and criminals in the local community, the nation, and farther afield.[1] Especially since the growth of the mass news media, there have been, from time to time, surges of public alarm concerning current crime waves. A legal scholar who recently reviewed the literature of the last fifty years noted that in each and every decade, there were prominent articles about the need for strong measures to meet the then-current crisis in crime (Kamisar, 1965). From time to time, there were commissions appointed or committees formed to investigate what was seen as intolerable increases in crime. It may be that there has always been a crime crisis.

Reprinted with permission of the American Academy of Political and Social Science from "Public Attitudes towards Crime and Law Enforcement," *The Annals* 374 (November 1967) by Jennie McIntyre. Copyright © 1967 The American Academy of Political and Social Science. In addition to sources cited herein, the writer has drawn upon the following: unpublished consultant papers prepared by Albert D. Biderman for the National Crime Commission, a search of its archives by the Roper Public Opinion Center, and assistance of Albert H. Cantril in searching recent attitude surveys.

[1] For discussions of shifting interpretations of crime as well as the functions of public interest, see Radzinowicz (1966) and Erikson (1962).

Sometimes these crime waves have been synthetic, manufactured by journalists. Lincoln Steffens (1931: 285–291), for example, describes his own creation of a crime wave, accomplished by giving headline treatment to the ordinary occurrences of the day. The intensity of the current concern regarding crime may be due in part, not to fabrication, but rather to the excellence of news coverage.

An entire nation reads of the fearful mass killing of eight nurses in Chicago and the apparently senseless shooting of thirteen passers-by on a Texas campus by a person not known to them. The unpredictable nature of such violence becomes the more fearful and immediate as citizens across the land view the scene and hear the tales of witnesses on television news programs. The public's perception of the incidence of crime as well as the intensity of its reaction may be influenced by the fact that it receives reports of violent crime drawn from a larger pool of crime-incident reports than ever before.

A nationally oriented communications media tends to draw attention to crime as a national problem. Other conditions, too, encourage the perception of a national crime wave rather than the local phenomenon portrayed by Steffens. The crimes which draw the most attention are urban occurrences. While the primarily rural population of an earlier day could view crime as a characteristic of remote and not quite moral cities, the primarily urban population of today perceives urban crime as more directly threatening. In spite of perennial concern, there is some reason to believe that public concern about crime as a national problem is at an unprecedented level.

An understanding of the attitudes of the public regarding crime, the level of concern, the manner in which this concern affects the lives of people, the beliefs regarding the causes of crime, and the appropriate methods of coping with the problem is for some purposes of as much consequence as an understanding of the nature and extent of crime itself. For the public attitudes on these issues to some extent determine the feasibility of alternative methods of crime prevention and law enforcement. The National Crime Commission in 1966 undertook to assess these attitudes through an analysis of national public opinion polls and surveys conducted for the Commission. . . .

Heightened Concern about Crime

The national public opinion polls in recent years provide some evidence of the heightened concern about crime.[2] Until recently, crime was given only peripheral attention by national pollsters. When completely open-ended questions were asked by a Gallup poll about the problems facing the nation, international problems invariably topped the lists; until recently, crime was not mentioned by enough persons to appear on the list of top problems. In 1966 when the National Opinion Research Center (NORC) conducted a national survey for the Crime Commission, interviewers asked citizens to pick from a list of six major domestic problems the one to which they had been paying the most attention recently (Ennis, 1967). Crime was the second most frequently selected from this list; only race relations was picked by more persons. (Lower-income nonwhites placed more emphasis on education than crime.)

When local community problems are considered, juvenile delinquency takes on added significance. In 1963 Gallup asked a sample of adults to select the top problem facing their community from a list of 39. Juvenile delinquency was picked by more persons than almost any other problem; only local real estate taxes were named more frequently. The third most frequently named, the need for more recreational areas, was probably related to the concern with juvenile delinquency.

Whether more concerned about adult or juvenile crime, most people think that the crime situation in their own community is getting worse, and while substantial numbers think the situation is staying about the same, hardly anyone sees improvement. A Gallup survey, in April 1965, showed that this pessimistic perception of the problem prevailed among men and women, well educated and less well educated, and among all age, regional, income, and city-size groupings. When citizens in Washington, D.C., were interviewed by the Bureau of Social Science Research (BSSR) the next year, 75 percent thought that crime had been getting worse in that city during the past year; 16 percent thought that it was about the same (Biderman et al., 1967).

[2] Surveys by George Gallup, Director, American Institute of Public Opinion, Princeton, New Jersey, will be referred to as Gallup polls. Those by Louis Harris, public opinion analyst, will be cited as Harris surveys.

Sources of Attitudes

For the large majority of people, attitudes about crime and crime trends apparently are derived largely from vicarious sources. Whether we judge volume from crimes known to the police or from the far more generous estimates from public surveys conducted for the Crime Commission, its incidence is not so great as to make personal victimization the major determinant of people's perceptions of the crime problem. This is manifestly true of crimes of violence, which, although relatively rare, are the focus of most people's fears. The experience of being robbed or assaulted might well have a most profound effect on the attitudes and habits of a victim, but such experiences are infrequent.

Even taking into consideration the more common, less serious offenses, most people are not victimized sufficiently often for these experiences to make a major impact on their lives. Neither are those offenses which do occur sufficiently important in people's lives to be remembered vividly for any length of time. These are among the conclusions derived from the intensive methodological work undertaken by the BSSR for the Commission, described by Biderman [in *The Annals* 374 (Nov. 1967)]. It was necessary to devise and refine special interviewing techniques in order to facilitate recall of incidents of victimization, particularly those that had happened more than a short time prior to the interview. When people were asked about the worst thing that had happened to them that could be called a crime, few remembered anything that had not happened recently.

The seriousness of the incidents recounted to interviewers further suggests that the experiences of victimization are not remembered for any length of time by most people. If persons being interviewed remembered all criminal victimizations, they could be expected to recount numerous trivial incidents, the minor offenses, such as vandalism and bicycle theft, which occur most frequently. Such was not the case, and the seriousness of the incidents reported to interviewers was much the same as that of those reported to police. It appears that many minor incidents are simply brushed aside and forgotten. Even the more serious offenses, such as burglary, usually involved relatively small monetary loss. Inferentially, then, most incidents of victimization do not appear to constitute very important events in a person's life experience.

If the experience of victimization is not a major event in the lives of most people, it is understandable that this experience does not determine their attitudes regarding crime. The surveys conducted for the commission found little statistical relationship between the experience of victimization and attitudes toward most aspects of the crime problem. The BSSR applied an index of exposure to crime, which included victimization of self, victimization of friends, and having personally witnessed any offense (Biderman et al., 1967: 126). Scores on this index did not correlate with responses to a variety of questions on attitudes toward crime and toward law enforcement. Nor was crime exposure related to anxiety about crime. Victims were neither more nor less likely to believe that crime was increasing or to express a sense of uneasiness about their personal safety. The one exception appeared in the case of the Negro male. Negro men who have been the victim of even one criminal incident were more apprehensive about their safety (Biderman et al., 1967: 127).

The NORC study similarly found little relationship between the experience of victimization and concern about crime (Ennis, 1967). Those who had been victims did worry about the possibility of burglary and robbery somewhat more frequently than did the nonvictims. The differences between men and women were greater than that between victims and nonvictims, however; so that women who had not been victimized more often worried than men who had. Victims and nonvictims were equally likely to have taken strong household security measures, however: 57 percent of victims and 58 percent of nonvictims had high scores on an index of precautionary behavior which included locking doors during the daytime and keeping a watchdog or weapons for protection.

Anxiety about crime was not a simple function of living in areas where crimes are frequent occurrences. The BSSR study in Washington, D.C., found that the average level of concern with crime in a predominantly Negro precinct that had one of the highest rates of crime in the city, according to police data, was lower than it was in another Negro precinct that had a lower crime rate (Biderman et al., 1967: 125).

Perhaps the most direct evidence that people form their attitudes about crime on the basis of something other than experience can be found in their own statements. After respondents in Washington were asked for their estimate of an increase or decrease in crime in the city, they were asked where they had obtained their information on this subject. A preponderant majority said that they got their information either from the news media or from what they heard people say.

But if the actual experience of victimization is not a major determinant of attitudes about crime, there is another sense in which vulnerability does influence fear. In the survey in Washington, D.C., the BSSR constructed an index of anxiety about crime (Biderman et al., 1967: 121). This index reflected a general concern for personal safety as well as the belief that crime is increasing. It found that Negro women had the highest average score, followed by Negro men, white women, and white men. The greater concern of Negroes is consistent with the risks of victimization suggested by police statistics. An analysis of police records in Chicago, for example, indicates that Negroes are far more likely to be the victims of a serious offense against the person than are white persons (Reiss, 1967). The greater anxiety of women than men is not consistent with what is known of the victimization risks, however, and one would have to look for alternative explanations. Anxiety scores were lower at the higher income levels for both Negroes and whites.

Crime Worse Elsewhere

If most people do not base their attitudes on personal experience, neither do they rely on their understanding of the experiences of others in their immediate environs. While most people questioned thought that the situation is terrible and getting worse all the time, they nevertheless believed that they are relatively safe near their own homes. In the NORC study for the Commission, 60 percent of those questioned compared their own neighborhood favorably to other parts of the community in which they lived, with regard to the likelihood that their home would be broken into, while only 14 percent thought that their area presented a greater hazard (Ennis, 1967: Table 47, p. 76). This is true even in areas which are considered crime-ridden by the police—areas which might terrify many suburban dwellers. In the BSSR survey in Washington precincts with average to high crime rates, only one out of five respondents thought that the chances of being beaten were greater in his neighborhood than in other parts of the city (Biderman et al., 1967: 121). Almost half of the national sample interviewed by NORC said that there was no place in their own city (or suburb or county) where they would not feel safe. Two-thirds of the respondents said that they feel safe walking alone when it is dark if they are in their own neighborhood (Ennis, 1967).

Central Role of Fear for the Person

When citizens in Washington were asked what steps they had taken to protect themselves from crime, they spontaneously spoke of avoiding danger on the streets (Biderman et al., 1967: 128–130). They said that they stayed home at night or used taxis, or they avoided talking to strangers. Others spoke of measures to protect themselves and their property at home; they kept firearms or watchdogs or put stronger locks on the doors and windows. In the districts surveyed in Boston and Chicago by the University of Michigan, five out of every eight said that they had changed their habits in one or more of these ways because of the fear of crime (Reiss, 1967: Vol. I, Sec. II, p. 103). No one mentioned efforts to avoid loss through fraud or overly sharp loan practices or any kind of swindle. It was clear that the crimes which they feared were crimes which might endanger their personal safety, especially attack by a stranger.

The national survey by NORC suggests the same conclusion. While two-thirds of those interviewed feel safe walking in their neighborhoods, one-third do not. Over 80 percent lock their doors at night, and 25 percent lock them during the daytime when family members are at home. Twenty-eight percent said their dogs were primarily watchdogs, and 37 percent, that firearms in the home were kept at least partly for protection (Ennis, 1967: Table 44, p. 74).

Possibly indicative of the concern of the public is the reaction of citizens to a question posed in the NORC survey: "If you were walking down the street alone around here in the evening and heard footsteps coming from behind, and turned to see a stranger rapidly approaching, what would you do?" A large majority interpreted the situation as dangerous. One-fourth of the respondents said they would "do nothing, just keep right on walking," but the most frequent reply was "Run as fast as I could or call for help" (Ennis, 1967). This fear of personal victimization is becoming more intense. In recent years, Harris surveys have found that, each year, 50 percent of their respondents have said that they are more worried about their personal safety on the streets than they were in the previous year.

Although many persons felt relatively safe in their own neighborhoods, they were not thereby indifferent or unconcerned about personal safety for themselves or their families. Respondents in Washington, D.C., were asked whether they had thought more about the neighborhood or the house when they had selected their current residence. The largest number said that the neighborhood was most important, and nearly as many said that neighborhood and house were of equal importance (Biderman et al., 1967: 119). Although some respondents selected a location because of its convenience or aesthetic qualities, 56 percent had placed greatest emphasis on the safety or moral characteristics of the neighborhood. Having selected a location which, within the alternatives available, seemed safe, most felt relatively secure. Nonetheless, 24 percent of the respondents in Washington felt that there was so much trouble in the area that they would like to move. In the areas studied in Boston and Chicago, 20 percent thought that they would like to move because of crime; 30 percent wanted to move out of the higher-crime-rate district in Boston (Reiss, 1967: 31).

Significance of the Fear of Crime

The crimes which the public fears most, crimes of violence, are those which occur least frequently. People are much more tolerant of crimes against property. The average citizen probably suffers the greatest economic loss as a result of crimes against businesses and public institutions which pass on their losses in the form of increased prices and taxes. Nevertheless, most shoplifters are never arrested, and employees suspected of dishonesty are either warned or dismissed (Black and Reiss, 1967).

Furthermore, violence and the threat of violence do not present as great a hazard as do other risks in an industrial society. The number of accidental injuries calling for medical attention or restricted activity of one day or more (National Safety Council, 1966) is far greater than the 1.8 offenses per 1,000 Americans involving violence or threat of violence (U.S. FBI, 1965: 30). Inadequate medical care is another example of risk which does not provoke the same horror as violence. A recent study found the quality, num-

bers, and distribution of ambulances and other emergency service
deficient, and estimated that as many as 20,000 persons die each
result of inadequate emergency medical care.[3]

Death or injury as a result of violence, however, has a different significance than death by accident or improper care, a significance consistent with
the repugnance with which Americans view violence. Recent studies have
shown that there is a widespread consensus on the relative seriousness of
different types of crimes (Sellin and Wolfgang, 1964: 289). Offenses involving physical assaults against the person are the most feared, and the greatest
concern is expressed about those in which a weapon is used.

The precautions which people take to protect themselves indicate that
underlying the fear of crime is a profound fear of strangers. They are afraid
that some unknown person will accost them on the street or break into their
homes and take their property or attack them personally. Again, the fears are
not consistent with the objective risks. Not only are the risks of injury by violence slight relative to the risks of injury or death from other causes, but
the risk of serious attack by strangers is about half as great as it is from persons well known to the victim.[4] Injuries in the case of assault are not only
more common but more serious when the victim and offender know each
other well. This hazard does not even stop at the self, for suicide is twice as
common as homicide.

This fear of strangers is impoverishing the lives of many Americans.
People stay behind the locked doors of their homes rather than walk in the
street at night. Poor people take taxis because they are afraid to walk or use
public transportation. Sociable people are afraid to talk to those they do not
know. Society is suffering from what the economists would label opportunity costs. When people stay home, they are not enjoying the pleasurable
and cultural opportunities in their communities; they are not visiting their
friends as frequently as they might. The general level of sociability is diminished. Some are restricting their earning opportunities, as when they ignore
job openings in some neighborhoods. Hospital administrators in large cities
report difficulty in staffing for night duty. Administrators and officials interviewed by the University of Michigan survey team report that Parent-
Teacher Association meetings at night are poorly attended, that library use is

[3] Data obtained by interview from American College of Surgeons, Washington, D.C., 1966.

[4] For a review of findings on the relationship between victim and offender, see U.S. President's
Commission, 1967: 14–15.

decreasing and recreational facilities remain unused, because of stories of robberies and purse-snatchings (Cutler and Reiss, 1967).

As social interaction is reduced and fear of crime becomes fear of the stranger, the social order is further damaged. Not only are there fewer persons on the streets and in public places than there might be, but persons who are afraid may show a lack of concern for each other. The logical consequences of this reduced sociability, mutual fear, and distrust can be seen in the reported incidents of bystanders indifferent to cries for help.

Reliance on Law Enforcement

The surveys regarding beliefs about the causes of crime indicate a pronounced concern with the morals of the country and the moral training of the country's youth. Few persons blamed social conditions or law enforcement. When Gallup asked the causes of crime, most persons who were interviewed gave answers which could be categorized as poor parental guidance or inadequate home life and supervision of teenagers. "Breakdown of moral standards" was also frequently mentioned. Persons interviewed by Harris blamed disturbed and restless teenagers most frequently. Unemployment, racial problems, broken homes, and low moral standards were next in importance.

When Harris asked why people become criminal rather than for an explanation of the crime rate, then the emphasis on moral training became explicit. Sixty-eight percent of the persons interviewed believed that upbringing or bad environment were the main causes. Many of the other causes named, such as broken homes or wrong companions, could also indicate a concern with the moral training and discipline of youth. Few persons suggested innate defects, and even fewer blamed police failure in any of these polls.

Although a majority saw crime as the consequence of a moral breakdown, most tended to believe that stricter law enforcement was the way to cope with the current crime problem. The BSSR survey in Washington, D.C., asked citizens what they thought was the most important thing that could be done to cut down crime in their city (Biderman et al., 1967: 134). Responses were classified as to whether a repressive measure, a measure of social amelioration, or one of moral inculcation was being advocated. Sixty percent recommended repressive measures such as more police, police dogs, stiffer sentences, or "cracking down on teenagers." Forty percent believed that the solution lay in social amelioration or moral inculcation. These included such measures as more jobs, recreation and youth programs, better housing, improved police-community relations, better child-training, religious training and revival, community leadership, or simply inculcating discipline. Only 3½ percent would rely solely on moral measures.

Another indication that many people believe repressive measures, rather than amelioration of social conditions or moral training of youth, to be the more effective means of cutting down crime lies in attitudes about court actions. The BSSR study in Washington, D.C., asked whether the sentences given by courts in that city were generally too lenient or too harsh. Most respondents, including Negroes, thought that the courts were too lenient. A Gallup survey in 1965 also found that a majority of persons interviewed believed that the courts do not deal harshly enough with criminals; only 2 percent said "too harshly."

Reliance on strict policing and law enforcement is somewhat tempered and not altogether repressive, however. When NORC asked whether the main concern of the police should be with preventing crimes or with catching criminals, over 60 percent placed the emphasis on prevention (Ennis, 1967: 59). Gallup asked respondents how they would deal with a hypothetical youth caught stealing an automobile. The most frequent responses were to give him another chance, be lenient.

When the fate of an actual person is to be decided, the demand for stern treatment of the lawbreaker is further relaxed. The clearest illustration of this in studies undertaken for the Commission can be seen in the survey of employers carried out by the University of Michigan in Boston, Chicago, and Washington, D.C. (Black and Reiss, 1967). Only 19 percent of the employers who reported larcenies, fraud, forgery, embezzlement, or misuse of company property by employees said that they had called the police. The most frequent way of handling the offenders was discharge, but in other instances a transfer or demand for restitution sufficed.

More police, more stringent policing, less leniency by the courts—this is how a substantial segment of the population would undertake to reduce crime—except when they are confronted with the necessity of deciding the fate of a particular individual. A smaller proportion of the public believed that social changes could reduce the amount of crime; only a very few suggested improving the moral fiber of the country—although a majority believed that inadequate moral training was responsible for an increase in crime.

Citizen Responsibility for Crime Reduction

Persons who believe that poor upbringing and moral training of youth are a major cause of crime might be willing to assume some responsibility for improved discipline. A Gallup survey which asked adults whether they would be willing to devote one evening a month to working with juvenile delinquents or trying to solve juvenile delinquency problems did, indeed, uncover a considerable potential responsibility. Sixty percent said that they would be willing to spend an evening each month in such activities. On the other hand, citizens in one precinct in Washington were asked whether they had ever "gotten together with other people around here, or has any group or organization you belong to met and discussed the problem of crime or taken some sort of action to combat crime?" Only 12 percent answered affirmatively. Neither did most persons believe that they could do anything about the crime in their own neighborhoods. Just over 17 percent thought that they could do anything.

When administrators and officials of public and quasipublic organizations were asked about the most effective remedies for crime, they suggested the amelioration of social conditions far more frequently than did members of the general public (Cutler and Reiss, 1967). They also recommended improvement of the moral fiber of the population and better training of youth much more often than the general public. Perhaps because of their broader view of crime reduction, they were also able to see more ways in which they might help to reduce crime. A number thought that they might cooperate with the police in ways calculated to make law enforcement easier. A number thought that they might cooperate in neighborhood and community programs, particularly by donating money for youth and recreation groups. The greatest number of suggestions involved what might be termed an extension of the organization's services. Electric-company executives considered more and brighter street lights; park officials, more recreational activities; and school administrators, more youth programs and adult education. Others believed that they might further community goals through integration of work crews and support of community-relations programs. Although most persons have not become involved in any activity intended to prevent or reduce crime, there does exist the potential for citizen involvement when responsible persons are convinced of its value.

Ambivalence Toward Law Enforcement

There is a convergence of attitudes and preferences expressed by large numbers of the citizens interviewed which would tend to predispose them to a preference for strong police agencies, unhampered in their efforts to apprehend and convict criminals. A large majority believes that the crime situation is terrible and getting worse. Accounts of crime rates arouse fears of crimes of violence; the quest for safety becomes an important factor in the ordering of personal lives. Their beliefs regarding the causes of crime notwithstanding, a majority would rely on more strict law enforcement and stern treatment of offenders to lower the crime rate. Few seriously considered any personal efforts to reduce crime, even in their own neighborhoods, either by themselves or in concert with other citizens.

It is not surprising, then, to find considerable willingness to permit whatever practices the police consider important. A majority of those interviewed in Washington, D.C., 73 percent, agreed that the police ought to have leeway to act tough when they have to (Biderman et al., 1967: 146). More than half (56 percent) agreed that there should be more use of police dogs, while fewer than one-third disagreed. Few respondents consistently endorsed either restricting or enlarging police powers, however. Many who take a permissive attitude on one issue refuse to do so on another; more than half of those who oppose the greater use of police dogs are in favor of police freedom to act tough. Neither was there a strong relationship between attitudes toward these issues and more general attitudes toward the police. Respondents were characterized as more or less favorable toward policemen, according to their responses to a six-item scale. Nearly half (47 percent) of those who did not favor police toughness or more police dogs nevertheless indicated strong respect and sympathy for policemen.

A similar ambivalence was observed in the results of the national survey conducted by NORC (Ennis, 1967). Forty-five percent favored civilian review boards (35 percent opposed them; 20 percent were uncertain or indifferent); 52 percent believed that the police should have more power; 42 percent, that police should risk arresting an innocent person rather than risk missing a criminal; and 65 percent favored the ruling that police may not question a suspect without his lawyer being present or the suspect's consent to be questioned without counsel. Most persons were in favor of enlarging police powers on some issues and restricting it on others; only 25 percent were consistently for or against permitting greater powers to the police.

The surveys conducted for the Commission found a strong concern for the civil rights of the individual, including the person who is a suspect or offender, in spite of a wish for strict law enforcement. This is particularly apparent when the issue of rights is explicit. In the districts studied in Boston, Chicago, and Washington, D.C., citizens were asked whether they thought that "too much attention is being paid to the rights of people who get into trouble with the police" (Biderman et al., 1967: 149; Reiss, 1967: 82). In each of the three cities, fewer than half (38 percent) agreed. As was true concerning the issue of police practices, this concern for the individual was not derogatory of the police. In Washington, D.C., more than half of those who took a rights position on this question also expressed strong sympathy and respect for the police.

In addition to a tradition of concern for individual rights, a belief that the police discriminate in the way that they treat various groups may account for some of the ambivalence regarding law enforcement. In Washington, D.C., the BSSR study found that 60 percent of the Negro men, 49 percent of the Negro women, and 27 percent of the white citizens thought that Negroes get worse treatment than other people (Biderman et al., 1967: 144). Among the comments of these respondents were that the police pick on Negroes more, that they are rude to Negroes, use brutality and physical force, or else ignore Negroes more than other people. Others expressed the belief that affluent citizens get better treatment than the poor. In Washington, D.C., half of the persons interviewed agreed that people who have money for lawyers do not have to worry about the police. In Boston and Chicago, there was a tendency for citizens in the predominantly white districts to point out rich and respectable citizens as recipients of more favorable treatment, while citizens in the predominantly nonwhite districts pointed to the less favorable treatment of Negroes by police (Reiss, 1967: 43–47).

When another issue was posed in economic rather than racial terms, there was again a strong indication of concern with rights of the individual. Almost three-quarters of the persons questioned by the NORC study approved the Supreme Court decision that the State must provide a lawyer to suspects who want one but cannot afford to pay the lawyer's fee (Ennis, 1967: Table 40, p. 70). Not only does a strong majority approve the decision, but no income, sex, or racial group opposes it.

Nonreporting of Crimes to the Police

Americans who believe that crime control is strictly a matter for the police and the courts nevertheless frequently fail to take the one action that they as citizens must take if the police and courts are to intervene in any particular situation. Although the surveys undertaken for the Commission represent a more intensive effort to measure the magnitude of nonreported crime than any in the past, students of crime have long recognized the phenomenon of *le chiffre noir* and speculated on the reasons for its existence. In the current studies, persons who were interviewed were asked not only whether they had reported any given incident to the police but also their reasons for not doing so when they had not (Biderman et al., 1967: Tables 3.23, 3.24, pp. 154–155; Ennis, 1967: Table 24, p. 44). The victim's reluctance to get involved was one of the most frequently cited reasons for not calling the police. Sometimes he did not want to take the time to call the police and present evidence, often fearing that this might necessitate spending time in court and away from work.

Some who had witnessed incidents which they thought were crimes denied any responsibility in the matter. An illustration of this sentiment is a comment sometimes made to interviewers: "I am not my brother's keeper." Others said that they did not think that the victim would want the police to be notified or indicated a concern for the offender. The NORC study found that for all classes of offenses except serious crimes against the person, the police were less likely to be notified if the offender were personally known to the victim than if he were a stranger.

The fear of reprisal or other unfortunate consequences sometimes deterred victims or witnesses from notifying the police of an incident. Some feared personal harm might come from the offender or his friends; others, that they themselves would become the subject of police inquiry or action. Other consequences which the victim might wish to avoid include cancellation of insurance or an increase in rates.

The most frequently cited reason for not calling the police was a resigned belief that any efforts would be useless. The victim simply accepted his losses as irrevocable. This was particularly true in the cases of malicious mischief and vandalism, where it often seemed that there were no clues. The damage could not be undone, nor could the police be expected to apprehend and punish the offender.

Often the victim believed that his evidence was insufficient to convince either the police or the courts that a crime had indeed been committed. This was the reason given by nearly half of the employers who said they had not reported cases of employee dishonesty to the police (Black and Reiss, 1967). Given the belief in the ineffectiveness of a call to police, they preferred the more simple and direct method of discharging or otherwise punishing the employee. (Ironically, these same employers often relied on police records for the purpose of screening prospective employees.)

It has been noted that persons interviewed during the national study were far more likely to fail to notify the police if the offender were a relative or person well known to the victim than a stranger. The employer not only knows but is in a special relationship to the employee whom he suspects of dishonesty. In a similar manner, a businessman who cashes a check for a customer has assumed some measure of responsibility for his relationship with this customer. It may be, then, that an undefined sense of responsibility for his own victimization sometimes deters the individual from calling the police. The employers and businessmen who were interviewed had refrained from calling the police more frequently in instances of employee dishonesty and bad checks than shoplifting. Lacking any special relationship with the shoplifter, the businessman could more readily report his offense.

Other persons did not notify the police because of their own uncertainty of what ought to be done. Sometimes they were not sure of what was taking place at the time, or they did not know whether it was a crime or what was the proper procedure for reporting the incident. For these persons, more knowledge of what constitutes reason for calling the police and how to do so would probably increase the rate of reporting. In those cities in which the police department is actively enlisting the aid of the public, dissemination of this information has been effective. Efforts to increase the rate of crime-reporting by citizens would have to take into account also the reluctance of most to get involved, to take responsibility for reporting, and to be willing to spend time testifying.

Summary and Conclusions

Analysis of the findings of the public opinion polls and the surveys conducted for the Commission indicates a widespread concern about crime, both as a national problem and as a problem in assuring personal safety. Persons who were interviewed expressed a belief that crime is increasing. They tend to equate crime with crimes of violence and to fear most violence at the hands of strangers in unfamiliar surroundings. Crimes against the person are far less common than those against property, and an unknown person is the least likely assailant.

Because of their fear of strangers many people restrict their activities. They forgo opportunities for pleasure or cultural enrichment, and they become less sociable, more suspicious. The level of interaction and mutual trust in the society is reduced; public places may become less safe than they otherwise might be. The crime rate is blamed on a breakdown in morals, and especially on inadequate training and discipline of young people. As a threat to the moral and social order, it becomes fearful even to persons who live in relatively safe circumstances and have no personal experience with crime.

Although attributing an increase in crime to lowered moral standards, most persons would depend on the police and courts for stern treatment of offenders in order to diminish the level of crime. Not as many, but nonetheless a substantial proportion, would recommend increased employment opportunities and other improved social conditions to combat crime. Along with the reliance on law-enforcement officials, there was willingness to permit the police considerable latitude in their efforts to apprehend and convict criminals. This apparent harshness toward offenders was immediately mitigated when the issue of the rights of the individual was posed. Some of this concern is related to the belief that there is discrimination against economic and racial groups. Finally, the recommendation for stern treatment of wrong-doers is further tempered when the fate of an individual offender is considered.

References

Biderman, Albert D., Louise A. Johnson, Jennie McIntyre, and Adrienne W. Weir. 1967. Report and Pilot Study in the District of Columbia on Victimization and Attitudes toward Law Enforcement. President's Commission on Law Enforcement and Administration of Justice. Field Survey I. Washington, D.C.: Government Printing Office.

Black, Donald J. and Albert J. Reiss, Jr. 1967. "Problems and Practices for Protection against Crime among Businesses and Organizations." In Albert J. Reiss, Jr. (ed.), *Studies in Crime and Law Enforcement in Metropolitan Areas*. President's Commission on Law Enforcement and Administration of Justice. Field Survey III. Washington D.C.: Government Printing Office.

Cutler, Stephen and Albert J. Reiss, Jr. 1967. "Crimes against Public and Quasi-Public Organizations in Boston, Chicago, and Washington, D.C." In Albert J. Reiss, Jr. (ed.), *Studies in Crime and Law Enforcement in Metropolitan Areas*. President's Commission on Law Enforcement and Administration of Justice. Field Survey III. Washington, D.C.: U.S. Government Printing Office.

Ennis, Philip. 1967. *Criminal Victimization in the United States*. A Report of a National Survey. President's Commission on Law Enforcement and Administration of Justice. Field Survey II. Washington, D.C.: U.S. Government Printing Office.

Erikson, Kai T. 1962. "Notes on the Sociology of Deviance," *Social Problems* 9 (Spring): 307–14.

Kamisar, Yale. 1965. "When the Cops Were Not 'Handcuffed,' " *New York Times Magazine*, November 7.

National Safety Council. 1966. "Accident Facts." Chicago National Safety Council, p. 2.

Radzinowicz, Leon. 1967. *Ideology and Crime*. New York: Columbia University Press.

Reiss, Albert J., Jr. 1967. "Probability of Victimization for Major Crimes Against the Person by Race and Sex, Status of Victims and Offenders." In Albert J. Reiss, Jr., *Studies in Crime and Law Enforcement in Major Metropolitan Areas*. President's Commission on Law Enforcement and Administration of Justice. Field Survey III. Washington, D.C.: Government Printing Office.

Sellin, Thorsten and Marvin E. Wolfgang. 1964. *The Measurement of Delinquency*. New York: Wiley.

Steffens, Lincoln. 1931. *The Autobiography of Lincoln Steffens*. New York: Harcourt, Brace.

U.S. Federal Bureau of Investigation. 1965. *Crime in the United States: Uniform Crime Reports*. Washington, D.C.: U.S. Government Printing Office.

U.S. President's Commission on Law Enforcement and Administration of Justice. 1967. *Task Force Report: Crime and Its Impact—An Assessment*. Washington, D.C.: U.S. Government Printing Office.

12

The Public Perception
of Protest

RALPH H. TURNER

The year 1965 marked a dramatic turning point in American reactions to racial disorder. Starting with Watts, dominant community sentiment and the verdicts of politically sensitive commissions have identified mass violence by blacks primarily as acts of social protest. In spite of its well advertized failings, the McCone Commission (Governor's Commission on the Los Angeles Riots, 1965) devoted most of its attention to reporting the justified complaints of Negroes and proposing their amelioration. The Kerner Report (National Advisory Commission on Civil Disorders, 1968) went further in predicating recommendations for action on the assumption that disorders must be understood as acts of social protest, and not merely as crime, antisocial violence, or revolutionary threats to law and order. A few earlier bodies had seen minority protest as a component in racial disorders (Silver, 1968), but in most cases these commissions were far removed from the political process. Even when whites had perpetrated most of the violence, public officials before 1965 typically vented their most intense anger against Negroes, Negro leaders, and their white allies (Lee and Humphreys, 1943; Rudwick, 1964). If comparable data were available from earlier racial disturbances, it is unlikely they would match Morris and Jeffries' (1967: 5)

Reprinted with permission of the American Sociological Association from "The Public Perception of Protest," *ASR* 34 (December 1969) by Ralph H. Turner. Prepared as Presidential Address, 64th Annual Meetings of the American Sociological Association, September 3, 1969. The author is grateful for the searching critiques of an earlier version of the paper by Herbert Blumer, John Horton, Lewis Killian, Leo Kuper, Kurt Lang, Melvin Seeman, Neil Smelser, and Samuel Surace.

finding that 54 percent in a sample of white Los Angeles residents viewed the disturbance as Negro protest.

The aim of this paper is to suggest several theoretical vantage points from which to predict when a public will and will not view a major disturbance as an act of social protest. Historically, labor strife has sometimes been understood as protest and sometimes not. Apparently the protest meaning in the activities of Caesar Chavez and his farm laborers is discounted by most Americans today. A gang *rumble* is seldom viewed as protest, even when Puerto Ricans and other minorities are prominently involved. Three-fourths of an unspecified sample of Los Angeles residents in May 1969, are reported to have seen disorders in secondary schools as the work of agitators and not as social protest (*Los Angeles Times,* May 19, 1969), even though Mexican-Americans and blacks have played the leading roles. Events of early 1969 hint at a rising movement to redefine all racial and youthful disturbances in other terms than social protest. Hence, it is of both current and continuing sociological interest to advance our understanding of these variable public definitions, in broad terms that might apply to all kinds of disturbances, and eventually to other cultures and eras.

THE MEANING OF PROTEST

Protest has been defined as "an expression or declaration of objection, disapproval, or dissent, often in opposition to something a person is powerless to prevent or avoid" (*Random House Dictionary,* 1967). An act of protest includes the following elements: the action expresses a grievance, a conviction of wrong or injustice; the protestors are unable to correct the condition directly by their own efforts; the action is intended to draw attention to the grievances; the action is further meant to provoke ameliorative steps by some target group; and the protestors depend upon some combination of sympathy and fear to move the target group in their behalf. Protest ranges from relatively persuasive to relatively coercive combinations (Bayley, 1962), but always includes both. Many forms of protest involve no violence or disruption, but these will not concern us further in this paper.

The term protest is sometimes applied to trivial and chronic challenges that are more indicative of a reaction style than of deep grievance. For instance, we speak of a child who protests every command from parent or teacher in the hope of gaining occasional small concessions. It is in this

sense that the protestations by some groups in society are popularly discounted because "they just protest everything." But the subject of this analysis is *social protest,* by which we mean protest that is serious in the feeling
of grievance that moves it and in the intent to provoke ameliorative action.

When violence and disorder are identified as social protest, they constitute a mode of communication more than a form of direct action. Looting is
not primarily a means of acquiring property, as it is normally viewed in di-
saster situations (Dynes and Quarantelli, 1968); breaking store windows and
burning buildings is not merely a perverted form of amusement or immoral
vengeance like the usual vandalism and arson; threats of violence and injury
to persons are not simply criminal actions. All are expressions of outrage
against injustice of sufficient magnitude and duration to render the resort to
such exceptional means of communication understandable to the observer.

In identifying the principal alternatives to protest we must first differentiate crime and deviance on the one hand and rebellion and revolution on the
other. The latter may or may not express a generally understandable grievance, but they constitute direct action rather than communication and their
aim is to destroy the authority of the existing system either totally or so far
as the rebellious group is concerned. Thus protest and rebellion are distinguished according to their ultimate goal and according to whether the disruptions are meant as communication or direct action. Deviance and crime are
actions identified chiefly according to their nonconforming, illegal, or harmful character. Deviance and crime are seen principally in individual terms,
and while there may be "social" causes that require attention, the harmful
or nonconforming features of the behavior are the primary concern. The distinctions are not absolute. Extortion, "power plays," and similar ideas fall
between crime and protest. Nor can the line between protest and rebellion be
drawn precisely. Attributing disorders to agitators is another common variation, in which either criminal or rebellious meaning is ascribed to the agitators, but any criminal, protest, or rebellious meaning is blunted for the mass
of participants.

In deciding that individuals view a disturbance as social protest, it is
helpful but not conclusive to note whether they apply the term protest.
Defining a disturbance as protest does not preclude disapproving the violence or disorder by which the protest is expressed, nor does it preclude advocating immediate measures to control and suppress the disturbance. Thus
Marvin Olsen's (1968) study of the legitimacy that individuals assign to

various types of protest activities is related to the present question, but makes a somewhat different distinction. The principal indicators of a protest definition are concerned with identifying the grievances as the most adequate way of accounting for the disturbance and the belief that the main treatment indicated is to ameliorate the unjust conditions. Fogelson (1968: 37–38) offers an exceptionally explicit statement of this mode of interpreting racial disorder:

. . . the riots of the 1960s are articulate protests against genuine grievances in the Negro ghettos. The riots are protests because they are attempts to call the attention of white society to the Negroes' widespread dissatisfaction with racial subordination and segregation in urban America. The riots are also articulate because they are restrained, selective, and, perhaps even more important, directed at the sources of the Negroes' most immediate and profound grievances.

DEFINITIONS BY PUBLICS

We assume that individuals and groups of individuals assign simplifying meanings to events, and then adjust their perceptions of detail to these comprehensive interpretations. Lemert's (1951) pioneering examination of deviance as a label applied by society's agents serves as a valuable prototype for the analysis of responses to public disturbances. We scrupulously avoid assuming that there are objectifiable phenomena that must be classified as deviance, as protest, or as rebellion. We further assume that participant motivations are complex and diverse, so that a given disturbance is not simply protest, or not protest, according to participant motives. Just as Negroes and whites used different labels for the Watts disturbance (Tomlinson and Sears, 1967), we also assume that publics will often interpret the events quite differently from the participants.

This concern with public definitions contrasts—but is not incompatible—with studies in which protest is defined and examined as an objective phenomenon. For example, Lipsky's (1968) careful statement of the prospects and limitations in the use of protest as a political tool deals with an objectively identified set of tactics rather than a subjective category. Irving Horowitz and Martin Liebowitz (1968: 285) argue that "The line between the social deviant and the political marginal is fading." The political marginal engages in social protest, in our sense, and the authors are pointing out that much of what sociologists heretofore understood as deviance is now taking on the character of social protest, either as objectively defined or according to the motives of the subject individuals.

The question of labelling disturbances has been examined by other investigators from somewhat different points of view. Lang and Lang (1968) have observed that the label "riot" is used to identify quite different kinds of events that are similar only in the kind of official response they evoke. Grimshaw (1968) pointed out the different labels attached to recent disturbances according to whether they are seen as racial clashes, class conflict, or civil disturbances in which the theme of intergroup conflict is deemphasized.

The nature of the public definition undoubtedly has consequences for the course and recurrence of the disturbance, and for short- and long-term suppression or facilitation of reform. One of the most important consequences is probably that a protest definition spurs efforts to make legitimate and nonviolent methods for promoting reform more available than they had been previously, while other definitions are followed by even more restricted access to legitimate means for promoting change (Turner and Killian, 1957: 327–329). Persons to whom the Joseph McCarthy movement was a massive protest against threats to our national integrity were unwilling to oppose the Senator actively even when they acknowledged that his methods were improper. Following the recent student disruption of a Regents meeting at UCLA, a faculty member who perceived the activity as protest against academic injustice advised the Academic Senate to listen more to what the students were saying and less to the tone of voice in which they said it. But the important tasks of specifying and verifying the consequences of protest definition fall beyond the limits of this paper. Any judgment that protest definition is "good" or "bad" must depend upon the findings of such investigation and on such other considerations as one's evaluation of the cause and one's preferred strategy for change.

The rest of this paper will be devoted to suggesting five theoretical vantage points from which it is possible to formulate hypotheses regarding the conditions under which one group of people will define as disturbances and some other group as social protest. First, publics test events for *credibility* in relation to folk-conceptions of social protest and justice. Second, disturbances communicate some combination of *appeal and threat,* and the balance is important in determining whether the disturbances are regarded as social protest. Third, disturbances instigate conflict with a target group, who may define them as social protest in the course of attempted *conciliation* to avoid full scale conflict. Fourth, defining disturbances as protest is an invitation from a third party for the troublemaking group to form a *coalition*. And fifth, acting as if the disturbances were social protest can be a step by public officials in establishing a *bargaining* relationship.

The paper offers theoretical proposals and not tested findings. The proposals are not a complete catalogue of causes for protest interpretation; notably omitted are such variables as understanding, empathy, and kindness. The proposals generally assume that there is no well-established tradition of disruptive or violent protest (Silver, 1968), that the society is not sharply polarized, and that the disturbances emanate from a clearly subordinated segment of the society.

Credibility and Communication

If a disturbance is to be viewed as social protest, it must somehow look and sound like social protest to the people witnessing it. If they see that the events are widely at variance from their conception of social protest, they are unlikely to identify the disturbance as social protest in spite of any intergroup process in which they are involved. On the other hand, if events are clearly seen to correspond precisely with people's idea of social protest, intergroup processes will have to operate with exceptional force to bring about a different definition. It is within the limits imposed by these two extreme conditions that the intergroup process variables may assume paramount importance. Hence it is appropriate to begin our analysis by examining these limiting considerations.

Our first two theoretical perspectives concern this preliminary question, whether the events will be recognizable as social protest or not. First, there are the viewer's preconceptions about protest that render believable the claim that what he sees is protest. We look to the predispositions of individuals and groups to ascertain what characteristics a disturbance must exhibit if it is to be *credible* as protest. Second, the ability of the observer to attend to one or another of the melange of potential messages communicated to him will be affected by the specific nature of the disturbance. For example, the balance between *appeal and threat* messages seems especially crucial for whether observers see the disturbance as social protest.

CREDIBILITY: THE FOLK CONCEPT

The main outlines of a *folk concept* (Turner, 1957) of social protest appear to be identifiable in contemporary American culture. The folk concept is only partially explicit, and is best identified by examining the arguments people make for viewing events and treating trouble-makers in one way or another. Letters to newspapers and editorial and feature columns supply abundant material in which to conduct such a search. More explicit statements are to be found in essays that present reasoned arguments for viewing disturbances as protest (Boskin, 1968). The folk concept supplies the criteria against which people judge whether what they see looks like social protest or not. Often the process works in reverse: people who are predisposed to interpret a disturbance as protest, or as criminal rioting, perceive events selectively so as to correspond with the respective folk concept. But in so far as there is any testing of the events to see whether they look like protest, crime, or rebellion, the folk concepts are the key. The folk concept will not necessarily correspond with what sociologists would find in a study of objectively defined protest behavior. . . .

Since violence and disruption immediately call virtue into question, there must be offsetting indications of goodness in the group's past or current behavior. The group in question must be customarily law-abiding and must have used acceptable means and exercised restraint on other occasions. Nonviolent movements that precede violent disruptions help to establish the credibility of protest. Widespread support and sympathy for the objectives of protest coupled with the group's principled rejection of the violent means employed by a few of their members help to establish the deserving nature of the group without undermining the pervasive character of their grievances.

To be credible as protest, the disturbance itself must be seen either as a spontaneous, unplanned, and naive outburst, or as an openly organized protest of more limited nature that got tragically out of hand. Any evidence of covert planning, conspiracy, or seriously intended threats of violence before the event would weaken the credibility of the protest interpretation. On the other hand, naive expressions of rage, released under the stimulus of rumor and crowd excitement, are consistent with a folk-image of protest. In this connection the protest interpretation is supported by demonstrating that what triggered the disturbances was some incident or act of provocation, and that a succession of recent provocations had prepared the ground for an eruption.

To be credible as protest, indications of the use of riots for self-aggrandisement, the settlement of private feuds, or enjoyment of violence and destruction must be subordinated to naive anger and desperation. Looting for personal gain and the attitude that rioting is "having a ball" are two features of the racial disturbances since 1965 that have repeatedly detracted from the image of social protest. In a widely read article typical of many such statements, Eric Sevareid (1967) challenged the protest definition by describing the carnival atmosphere at certain stages in many of the disturbances. . . .

CREDIBILITY: THE ADMISSION OF INJUSTICE

Interpretations of disruptive activity as protest invoke conceptions of justice and injustice. Homans (1961) and Blau (1964a, 1964b) are among those who interpret the sense of injustice as a feeling of inadequate reciprocation in social exchange. Runciman (1966), applying Merton and Kitt's (1950) conception of relative deprivation, proposes that the selection of reference groups determines whether there is a sense of injustice with respect to the rewards of position. But these theories do not answer the question: when is it possible and probable that one group will see another group's position as unjust to the point of accepting violence and disruption as the natural expression of that injustice?

If we assume that each group tends to employ its own situation as the point of reference in assessing another group's claims of injustice, we are led to the conclusion that groups who are clearly *advantaged* by comparison with the "protestors" can find the claim of injustice more credible than groups less advantaged. Crucial here is the assumption that objective and detached comparison between the situations of the troublemakers and the target groups is less powerful in shaping the assessment of injustice than the observing group's position *vis-à-vis* the troublemakers. Consequently, the great middle segment of American population finds it easier to identify black ghetto disturbances as social protest than to interpret college student demonstrations in the same sense. Similarly, black student demonstrations are less amenable to interpretation as protest than ghetto demonstrations.

According to this view, groups who see themselves as even more disadvantaged than the protestors are least likely to grant their claim. Viewed from below, disturbances are most easily comprehended as power plays or as deviance. Groups who see their situation as about the same as that of the protestors likewise do not find it easy to accord the protest interpretation. Leaders in such groups commonly attempt to weld alliances based on mutual appreciation, and these sometimes work as political devices. But they are hindered rather than helped by the spontaneous reaction to disruptive activity by a group whose position is apparently no worse than that of the group passing judgment. Olsen's (1968) finding that persons who score high on measures of political incapability and political disability are least willing to adjudge direct action to correct grievances as legitimate may also be consistent with this reasoning. . . .

When judgments by different socioeconomic strata are compared, the middle strata find it more difficult to credit massive deviance and crime and less difficult to acknowledge protest because of their commitment to society as a system of values. The lower strata have more day-to-day experience of crime and the rejection of societal values, and are forced to anchor their security to a less consensual image of society. Hence they do not find massive crime so difficult to believe. If these assumptions about credibility are correct, and if we have characterized the strata accurately, investigators should find middle class populations readier to make protest interpretations than working class groups.

Appeal and Threat Messages

It is a reasonable assumption that most observers could, under appropriate circumstances, see both an *appeal* and a *threat* in a violent disturbance. If this combination of messages is present, reading the disturbance as protest means that the appeal component is more salient to the observer than the threat component. For we can safely assume that when the preoccupation with threat to self and to those objects identified with self is foremost, appeals are no longer heard. Threat so often monopolizes attention to the exclusion of appeals, and acknowledging justice in the appeals weakens the foundation for defensive efforts required to meet the threat. Thus we are led to the proposition that disruptions are interpreted as protest only when the experience of threat is not excessive.

The foregoing observation however is incomplete. Somehow the appeal message must command attention, and resistence to acknowledging the protest message must be overcome. The *credibility* requirements we have just outlined are so restrictive that a positive incentive is required to overlook some of the criteria. An appeal by itself is normally a weak attention-getter; threat is much stronger in this respect. A combination of threat and appeal serves to gain attention and to create the sense of urgency necessary to overcome the resistence to acknowledging protest. When threat is insufficient, the events can be disregarded or written off as deviance, to be contained by the established systems of social control. An optimal combination of threat and appeal is necessary for the probability of seeing disturbance as protest. When the threat component falls below the optimal range, the most likely interpretation is deviance; above the optimal range, preoccupation with threat makes rebellion the probable interpretation.

This approach suggests several hypotheses relating interpretation as protest to the nature and bounds of the disorder and to the position of various population segments reacting to the disorders. Certainly the threat posed by disorders during the last half decade has been sufficient to gain attention and force examination of the message. At the same time, threat has been limited by the localization of disorders in the ghettos and by the minimization of direct personal confrontation between whites and blacks. Without replicable measurements of the magnitude of threat and appeal components, predictions regarding specific situations can only be formed intuitively. Intuition suggests that either pitched battles leading to death and injury of any substantial number of whites, or spread of the disorders outside of the boundaries of black neighborhoods and especially into white residence areas, would substantially reduce the likelihood of disorders being interpreted as a form of protest and would seriously divert attention away from black grievances.

Differential perception of threat by population segments is affected by a combination of personal involvement and proximity to the events and of ability to perceive the limits and patterns of disorder realistically. On this basis it is easiest for groups who live a safe distance from black neighborhoods and who have no stake in ghetto businesses to turn their attention toward the appeal component of the disturbance message. But we must also take note of the principle suggested by Diggory's (1956) findings regarding a rabid fox scare in Pennsylvania. While fear was greater among persons near to the rumored center of rabid fox sightings, the tendency to exaggerate the extent of the menace was less. Persons closest to the events were able to form a more realistic picture. Similarly, whites closest to the disturbances may be better able to discount inflated reports of violence against the persons of whites, and to see a pattern in the properties attacked and protected. Thus persons close enough to fear any spread of disorders but not close enough to correct exaggerated reports from personal experience may find it most difficult to see the activities as protest. . . .

Except for understanding protest interpretation as a means to protect the observer from seeing a serious lack of consensus in society, we have thus far treated protest interpretation as a passive matter. But the observation that some of the most unsympathetic interpretations abound among groups far removed from the disorders is difficult to understand with the principles outlined. It is true that small town and rural dwellers often feel somewhat deprived relative to large city dwellers, and therefore may have difficulty seeing justice in the complaints even of ghetto dwellers. They also lack the incentive of the large city dwellers to avoid acknowledging widespread crime by interpreting disturbances as protest. But perhaps the protest interpretation is part of a more active stance, brought about by involvement in a relationship with the troublemaking group. Crime and rebellion are in an important sense easier interpretations to make since they can be inferred from the most conspicuous and superficial aspects of behavior, without a search for the motives and grievances behind the violence and disruption. Our remaining three approaches rest on this assumption.

Conciliation of Conflict

A more complex basis for predicting the assignment of meaning to disorders is supplied by viewing the protestors and the interpreters as engaged in a real or potential process of conflict. The aggressive initiative of the moment lies with the protestors. Interpreting the disturbances as protest can then usefully be seen as a *gesture of conciliation,* an action to forestall the incipient conflict or to reduce or conclude the conflict without victory or surrender. . . .

Third Party Point of View

From both the appeal-threat and conflict-conciliation approaches comes the hint that a *third party* may under some circumstances find it easier to interpret disturbance as protest than does the group against whom the disturbance is directed. For the target group, the merit of conciliation rather than accepting the challenge of conflict declines as the prospective costs of conciliation increase. Furthermore, whenever group membership is a salient aspect of personal identity, it is difficult to accept group fault without offsetting the admission by assessing equal or greater fault to the protestors. But a third party is not so directly threatened and does not pay most of the costs of conciliation and, consequently, is able to sustain a protest view of the disturbances after such an interpretation ceases to be tenable for the target group.

To account for third party protest interpretation, we must first ask why the third party should be sufficiently concerned about a conflict, in which they are bystanders, to acknowledge grievances and take a sympathetic stand. The question implies the answer: that protest interpretations by third parties are only likely to occur when there is some threat of third party involvement in the conflict or a strong basis for identification with one of the two parties. American people seldom concerned themselves sufficiently to make *any* interpretation of student riots abroad until student disorders become an immediate concern at home. Labor-management strife in the United States today attracts sufficient attention only when it threatens the supply of goods and services to the community.

Third party protest interpretations indicate either the defense of neutrality against the threat of partisan involvement in conflict or the active acceptance of partisanship on the side of the protestors. The bystander who is endangered by conflict is not inclined toward a sympathetic interpretation of either side, but rather toward wishing "a plague on both your houses!" Only when identities or interests pull him in one direction or the other can the threat of involvement press him to see the disturbance as protest. . . .

It is interesting that several principles converge to predict the overwhelming tendency for college and university faculties to view campus disruptions as social protest. First, the credibility-injustice principle is invoked by the faculty position of superordination to the students. Through constant contact and intimate familiarity with the circumstances of student life, faculty members readily understand the grievances of students by comparison with their own more favorable position. Second, the earlier student disorders were directed almost wholly against college administrations rather than faculty, making the latter a third party. Structurally, the faculty position makes them subject to strong pressures toward partisan involvement but makes partisanship on either side costly. Organizationally, the faculty belong to the same side as the administration but their contacts with students are more frequent and more crucial to the success of their teaching and research activities on the day to day basis. As third parties, faculty members sought neutrality by interpreting student disturbances as protest. Third, by virtue of the residue of resentments from their own relationships with administrators, some faculty members were inclined to proffer a coalition to the students. On the basis that the higher status partner in a coalition ultimately gains more if the coalition lasts, this could be an effective tactic in strengthening the faculty position *vis-à-vis* administration. However, all of these principles operate differently when students take faculty as the target for their disruptions. Threat soon becomes more salient than appeal; neutrality is no longer attainable; and the only available coalition for faculty is with the administration. . . .

Official Actions

We have spoken of the predisposition by various groups to identify disturbances under varying circumstances as social protest. But we have neglected thus far to assign enough importance to the actions of officials and formal leaders who must react conspicuously. On the basis of well established principles in the study of public opinion, opinion leadership and keynoting by officials should be a substantial determinant of public definitions (Katz and Lazarsfeld, 1955).

The problem of officials in the face of disturbance differs from the problem of others as action differs from attitude. The adoption of an attitude by itself has no consequences, and for most people its public enunciation has very little effect. But official action has consequences with respect to effectiveness, reactions provoked, and public commitments made. Hence, the public definition exhibited by officials is only a simple application of their private views when two conditions are met: the community definitions are overwhelmingly homogeneous; and officials have the resources to be certain their efforts are effective. When Federal Bureau of Investigation officials set out in the 1930s to eradicate gangster leaders, these conditions prevailed, and there was no need to explore the possibility that gangsterism was a protest against ethnic discrimination, cultural assimilation, and poverty. But when these conditions do not prevail, treating disturbances as protest can serve as a hedging tactic. It permits a restrained handling that does not create the expectation of immediate suppression of disturbances, without forestalling a shift toward a harder line after community sentiment and official capability have been tested. Official protest interpretation can serve as an effective hedge only in societies and communities where humanitarian values are strong relative to toughness values, so that failure of official action in the service of humanitarianism is excusable. But since this is true in many parts of American society, and because of the volatility of protest groups and the undependability of community support, official acknowledgment that disturbances are a form of protest has become progressively more common during the span of the last five years. This observation applies to almost all kinds of disturbances, and goes considerably beyond Etzioni's (1969) parallel observation that demonstrations have come increasingly to be accepted as a legitimate tactic of political persuasion.

The effect of these official responses is initially to keynote and legitimate the protest interpretation by various community segments. When these responses coincide with substantial prestigious community definitions of the events, the effect is further to establish a situational norm identifying the proper or publicly acceptable interpretation. Views that the disturbances are simply crime on a larger scale demanding strengthened law enforcement, or that they are sinister rebellions to be handled as internal wars, tend to be suppressed, even though many individuals and groups incline toward such views. The result is an unstable situation in which temporarily the socially sanctioned view sees disturbance as protest, while dissident views subsist as an audible rumbling in the background. . . .

Conclusion

A speculative analysis of this sort should be completed by bringing together all of the predictions and indicating where the sets of assumptions are redundant, where they are contradictory, and where they are complementary. But neither the theories nor the variables can be designated precisely enough at the present time to support this type of summation. Three observations will underline the main thrust of the approach we have employed.

First, the analysis exemplifies the assumption that meanings are attached to events as an aspect of intergroup process. The meaning attributed to a public disturbance expresses in large part the current and anticipated interaction between the various relevant groups. Meanings change both currently and retrospectively as the process unfolds and as intergroup relationships change.

Second, there are important shades of differences in protest interpretations that correspond with the specific types of intergroup process in which the interpreters are involved. Three kinds of relationship have been reviewed. One group may become *partisans* in conflict with the troublemakers, either because they belong to a group that can usefully make common cause against the target group while maintaining an advantageous position in a coalition with the troublemakers, or because of disaffection from their own group so that they ally with its enemies. Concern of the former with the protestors' grievances is constantly tinged with a comparison of benefits that each group gains from the coalition. For the latter, orientation toward conflict is the salient bond, and discomfiture of the target group easily becomes a more important aim than ameliorating the condition of the troublemakers.

A second group may see themselves as prime target for attack or as neutrals in danger of being drawn into conflict with the troublemakers, and thus respond with an offer of conciliation. Conciliation involves a generous interpretation of the troublemakers' activities, acknowledging their grievances, admitting fault, and identifying their activity as social protest. Grievances must be identified if conciliation is to proceed. But the salient condition easily becomes protection of the target group, and the protest interpretation is highly vulnerable in the event that conciliation is not reciprocated.

A third group, consisting of public officials and spokesmen, engages in bargaining by offering some amelioration in return for guarantees against further violence and disorder. But the impersonal and calculating nature of bargaining, especially as it recurs and is routinized, works against seeing the trouble as social protest. The disturbance soon becomes a move in a competitive game, to be met by minimal and calculated concessions. And as the masters of urban political machines have long understood, "buying off" protest leaders, directly, tends to be a less costly and more immediately effective tactic of bargaining than offering programs for amelioration of underlying grievances.

Our third and final observation is that interpreting public disorders as social protest is an unstable and precarious condition. It requires an optimally balanced set of conditions, and is difficult to maintain over an extended period of time. Insofar as such interpretations are favorable to social reform, it appears that they must be capitalized quickly, while conditions are favorable, through programs that can be implemented on a continuing basis by a more routinized and impersonal bargaining. Perhaps a residue of understanding that can be favorable to future reforms may remain in spite of community redefinition. Perhaps, also, reformers should not overestimate what can be gained by disorderly protest in relation to the many other means for effecting change.

References

Bayley, David H. 1962. "The Pedagogy of Democracy: Coercive Public Protest in India," *American Political Science Review* 56 (September): 663–72.

Blau, Peter. 1964a. "Justice in Social Exchange." *Sociological Inquiry* 34 (Spring):193–206.

1964b. *Exchange and Power in Social Life*. New York: Wiley.

Blumer, Herbert. 1939. "Collective Behavior." In Robert E. Park (ed.), *An Outline of the Principles of Sociology*. New York: Barnes and Noble, pp. 221–80.

Boskin, Joseph. 1968. "Violence in the Ghettoes: A Consensus of Attitudes," *New Mexico Quarterly* 37 (Winter):317–34.

Diggory, James C. 1956. "Some Consequences of Proximity to a Disease Threat," *Sociometry,* 19 (March):47–53.

Dynes, Russell and Enrico L. Quarantelli. 1968. "What Looting in Civil Disturbances Really Means," *Trans-action* 5 (May):9–14.

Etzioni, Amitai. 1969. "Demonstrations Becoming a Legitimate Mode of Expression," *Los Angeles Times* (May 18): Sec. F, p. 2.

Fogelson, Robert M. 1968. "Violence as Protest." In Robert H. Connery (ed.), *Urban Riots: Violence and Social Change.* New York: Academy of Political Science, pp. 25–41.

Governor's Commission on the Los Angeles Riots. 1965. *Violence in the City—An End or a Beginning?* Los Angeles.

Grimshaw, Allen D. 1968. "Three Views of Urban Violence: Civil Disturbance, Racial Revolt, Class Assault." In Louis H. Masotti and Don R. Bowen (eds.), *Riots and Rebellion.* Beverly Hills, Calif.: Sage Publications, pp. 103–19.

Homans, George. 1961. *Social Behavior: Its Elementary Forms.* New York: Harcourt, Brace, and World.

Horowitz, Irving L. and Martin Liebowitz. 1968. "Social Deviance and Political Marginality: Toward a Redefinition of the Relation Between Sociology and Politics," *Social Problems* 15 (Winter):280–96.

Katz, Elihu and Paul Lazarsfeld. 1955. *Personal Influence.* Glencoe, Ill.: Free Press.

Kelley, Harold H. 1967. "Attribution Theory in Social Psychology." In *Nebraska Symposium on Motivation,* pp. 192–238.

Lang, Kurt and Gladys E. Lang. 1968. "Racial Disturbances as Collective Protest." In Louis H. Masotti and Don R. Bowen (eds.), *Riots and Rebellion.* Beverly Hills, Calif.: Sage Publications, pp. 121–30.

Lee, Alfred McClung and Norman D. Humphrey. 1943. *Race Riot.* New York: Dryden Press.

Lemert, Edwin. 1951. *Social Pathology.* New York: McGraw-Hill.

Lipsky, Michael. 1968. "Protest as a Political Resource," *American Political Science Review* 62 (December):1144–58.

Merton, Robert K. 1948. "The Self-Fulfilling Prophecy," *Antioch Review* 8 (Summer):193–210.

Merton, Robert K. and Alice S. Kitt. 1950. "Contributions to the Theory of Reference Group Behavior." In Merton and Paul F. Lazarsfeld (eds.), *Studies in the Scope and Method of "The American Soldier."* Glencoe, Ill.: Free Press, pp. 40–105.

Morris, Richard T. and Vincent Jeffries. 1967. *Los Angeles Riot Study: The White Reaction Study.* Los Angeles: U.C.L.A. Institute of Government and Public Affairs.

National Advisory Commission on Civil Disorders. 1968. Report on the National Advisory Commission on Civil Disorders (The Kerner Report). Washington, D.C.: U.S. Government Printing Office.

Olsen, Marvin E. 1968. "Perceived Legitimacy of Social Protest Actions," *Social Problems* 15 (Winter):297–310.

Random House. 1967. *Random House Dictionary of the English Language.* New York: Random House.

Rossi, Peter H., Richard A. Berk, David P. Boesel, Bettye K. Eidson, and W. Eugene Groves. 1968. "Between White and Black: The Faces of American Institutions in the Ghetto." In *Supplemental Studies for the National Advisory Commission on Civil Disorders.* Washington, D.C.: U.S. Government Printing Office, pp. 69–215.

Rudwick, Elliott M. 1964. *Race Riot in East St. Louis, July 2, 1917.* Carbondale: Southern Illinois University Press.

Runciman, W. G. 1966. *Relative Deprivation and Social Justice.* Berkeley: University of California Press.

Sevareid, Eric. 1967. "Dissent or Destruction?" *Look* 31 (September 5), 21ff.

Silver, Allan A. 1968. "Official Interpretations of Racial Riots." In Robert H. Connery (ed.), *Urban Riots: Violence and Social Change.* New York: Academy of Political Science.

Smelser, Neil J. 1963. *Theory of Collective Behavior.* New York: Free Press.

Tomlinson, T. M. and David O. Sears. 1967. *Los Angeles Riot Study: Negro Attitudes Toward the Riot*. Los Angeles: U.C.L.A. Institute of Government and Public Affairs.

Turner, Ralph H. 1957. "The Normative Coherence of Folk Concepts," *Research Studies of the State College of Washington* 25:127–36.

———. 1964. "Collective Behavior and Conflict: New Theoretical Frameworks," *Sociological Quarterly* 5 (Spring):122–32.

Turner, Ralph H. and Lewis M. Killian. 1957. *Collective Behavior*. Englewood Cliffs, N.J.: Prentice-Hall.

Waller, Willard and Reuben Hill. 1951. *The Family: A Dynamic Interpretation*. New York: Dryden Press.

13

Perception and Legislation:
Anti-Marihuana Laws

ALFRED LINDESMITH

In 1937 the Congress passed a Marihuana Tax Act, modeled after the Harrison Act. It was designed to curb the use of marihuana by the use of the federal police power, and like the Harrison Act imposed penalties upon both buyers and sellers. This Act was the result of a publicity campaign staged by the Federal Bureau of Narcotics under Mr. Anslinger's direction and leadership. The bill was passed with little discussion after brief hearings on the ground that marihuana was a highly dangerous drug inciting its users to commit crimes of violence and often leading to insanity.

The beliefs concerning marihuana which led to this legislation may be represented in a pure and extreme form by turning to the writing of a hyperactive reformer and alarmist of the period, Earle Albert Rowell (1939, 1937). He claimed in 1939 that he had spent fourteen years campaigning against this weed, delivering more than four thousand lectures in forty states and personally pulling up and destroying many flourishing hemp fields. Mr. Rowell's zealous opposition to marihuana was only slightly less intense than his disapproval of alcohol and tobacco. The use of tobacco, he correctly observed, invariably precedes the smoking of the deadly reefer. Mr. Rowell came into disfavor with the Bureau of Narcotics around 1938 and this agency spent considerable energy and manpower in an attempt to silence and discredit him. This may have been because of Mr. Rowell's view that opiate addiction is a disease or perhaps because of his repeated allegations that the police were not sufficiently diligent in destroying marihuana.

Mr. Rowell summarized the effects of marihuana as follows:

We know that marihuana—
1. Destroys will power, making a jellyfish of the user. He cannot say no.
2. Eliminates the line between right and wrong, and substitutes one's own warped desires or the base suggestions of others as the standard of right.
3. Above all, causes crime; fills the victim with an irrepressible urge to violence.
4. Incites to revolting immoralities, including rape and murder.
5. Causes many accidents both industrial and automobile.
6. Ruins careers forever.
7. Causes insanity as its speciality.
8. *Either in self-defense or as a means of revenue, users make smokers of others, thus perpetuating evil* (Rowell and Rowell, 1939 : 33).

In 1939 when Rowell published his book, marihuana was regarded as a relatively new drug menace in the United States. Mr. Rowell thought that he had already detected an increase of the population of mental hospitals because of it:

Asylums and mental hospitals in this country are beginning to see and feel the influence of marihuana, and are awaking to its deleterious effects on the brain. As we traveled through the various states, superintendents of these institutions told us of cases of insanity resulting from marihuana (Rowell and Rowell, 1939: 51).

"The baleful mental effects of marihuana," he said, begin soon after the first reefer is smoked" (*ibid.*).

When Mr. Anslinger appeared before the Senate subcommittee which was investigating the illicit drug traffic in 1955 under the guidance of Senator Price Daniel, there were only a few offhand discussions of marihuana. Mr. Anslinger observed that the Bureau in its national survey was "trying to keep away from the marihuana addict, because he is not a true addict." The real problem, he said, was the heroin addict.

Senator Daniel thereupon remarked: "Now, do I understand it from you that, while we are discussing marihuana, the real danger there is that the use of marihuana leads many people eventually to the use of heroin, and the drugs that do cause complete addiction; is that true?" (U.S. Congress, 1957: 16).

Mr. Anslinger agreed: "That is the great problem and our great concern about the use of marihuana, that eventually if used over a long period, it does lead to heroin addiction" (*ibid.*).

Senators Welker and Daniel pursued the subject, and Mr. Anslinger, when prompted, agreed that marihuana was dangerous. Senator Welker finally asked this question: "Is it or is it not a fact that the marihuana user has been responsible for many of our most sadistic, terrible crimes in this nation, such as sex slayings, sadistic slayings, and matters of that kind?"

Mr. Anslinger hedged: "There have been instances of that, Senator. We have had some rather tragic occurrences by users of marihuana. It does not follow that all crime can be traced to marihuana. There have been many brutal crimes traced to marihuana, but I would not say that it is a controlling factor in the commission of crimes (*ibid.:* 18).

Eighteen years earlier, in 1937, the year in which the federal antimarihuana law was passed, Mr. Anslinger had presented a very different picture of marihuana. Prior to 1937 Mr. Anslinger and the Bureau of Narcotics had spearheaded a propaganda campaign against marihuana on the ground that it produced an immense amount of violent crime such as rape, mayhem, and murder, and that many traffic accidents could be attributed to it. During the 1937 hearings before a House subcommittee, Representative John Dingell of Michigan asked Mr. Anslinger: "I am just wondering whether the marihuana addict graduates into a heroin, an opium, or a cocaine user."

Mr. Anslinger replied: "No, sir; I have not heard of a case of that kind. I think it is an entirely different class. The marihuana addict does not go in that direction" (U.S. Congress, 1937a).

A few months later in the same year, before a Senate subcommittee which was considering the antimarihuana law which the Bureau of Narcotics had asked for, Mr. Anslinger commented: "There is an entirely new class of people using marihuana. The opium user is around 35 to 40 years old. These users are 20 years old and know nothing of heroin or morphine" (U.S. Congress, 1937b).

The theme stated by the Commissioner of Narcotics in 1955, that the main threat in marihuana is that it leads to the use of heroin, is now ordinarily cited as the principal justification for applying to it the same severe penalties that are applied in the case of heroin. Reformer Rowell in 1939 was more logical and consistent than either the Senators or the Commissioner when he emphasized that cigarette smoking invariably preceded reefer smoking. Mr. Rowell told of a shrewd gangster whom he engaged in what now appears as a prophetic discussion of the prospects of the dope industry (Rowell and Rowell, 1939: 69–74).

The gangster remarked: "Marihuana is the coming thing."

"But," I protested in surprise, "marihuana is not a habit-forming drug like morphine or heroin; and, besides, it's too cheap to bother with."

He laughed. "You don't understand. Laws are being passed now by various states against it, and soon Uncle Sam will put a ban on it. The price will then go up, and that will make it profitable for us to handle."

The gangster, according to Mr. Rowell, then commented on the shrewd manner in which the tobacco companies had popularized cigarettes among the soldiers of the First World War and on the enormous increase in cigarette consumption by young persons. He grew eloquent: "Every cigarette smoker is a prospect for the dope ring via the marihuana road. Millions of boys and girls now smoke. Think of the unlimited new market!"

Mr. Rowell got the idea and commented as follows to his readers: "Slowly, insidiously, for over three hundred years, Lady Nicotine was setting the stage for a grand climax. The long years of tobacco using were but an introduction and training for marihuana use. Tobacco, which was first smoked in a pipe, then as a cigar, and at last as a cigarette, demanded more and more of itself until its supposed pleasures palled, and some of the tobacco victims looked about for something stronger. Tobacco was no longer potent enough."

Mr. Rowell was not optimistic about the future: "Marihuana will continue to be a problem for both police and educators, because it is so easy to grow, to manufacture, and to peddle, and is such a quick source of easy money. The plant can be grown anywhere; it can be harvested secretly, prepared in twenty-four hours without a penny of investment for equipment; and every cigarette user is a prospect. As our laws are enforced and the weed becomes scarcer, the price will rise, and greater profit accrue to venturesome and successful peddlers. Whereas now it is usually peddled by lone wolves, as soon as the weed becomes scarcer and the price rises, organized crime will step in and establish a monopoly" (Rowell and Rowell, 1939: 88–89).

While Mr. Rowell, in the manner of reforming alarmists, exaggerated the evil with which he was preoccupied, the above appraisal of the effects of the Marihuana Tax Act has been reasonably well borne out by subsequent events. Certainly it was a more realistic assessment of the law's effects than any that were made by the legislators who passed the bill or by the officials who promoted it. Mr. Rowell was also completely right in pointing out that virtually every marihuana smoker graduated to this practice from cigarette smoking. His gangster informant was correct in his calculation that state and federal laws prohibiting marihuana would make the weed more expensive and more profitable for peddlers to handle, and also correctly foresaw that with the same merchants handling both marihuana and heroin it would become a simple matter for marihuana users to switch from the less to the more dangerous drug, as they have done.

In the United States during the nineteenth century, and the early decades of the twentieth, addiction to opiates frequently developed from the abuse of alcohol. This still occurs to some extent and is frequently reported from other parts of the world, for morphine provides a potent means of relieving the alcoholic hangover. An American doctor once advocated as a cure of alcoholism that alcohol addicts be deliberately addicted to morphine, arguing with considerable plausibility that of the two habits the latter was obviously the lesser evil (Black, 1882). Moreover, he practiced what he preached and recommended his technique with considerable enthusiasm for use by others.

The truth of the matter, of course, is that very few cigarette smokers go on to marihuana, very few marihuana users go on to heroin, and very few alcohol users graduate to the use of heroin. Since some barbiturate and amphetamine users progress to heroin it should be added that it is also only a very small proportion who do. If all of these substances were to be prohibited because they are sometimes involved in the progression toward heroin addiction there is little doubt that the illicit traffic in marihuana and heroin would be expanded to include the other offending substances and that the movement from less to more serious habits would be greatly facilitated.

References

Black, J. R. 1882. "Advantages of Substituting the Morphia Habit for the Incurably Alcoholic," *Cincinnati Lancet-Clinic* XXII (n.s.):Pt. I, pp. 537–41.

Rowell, Earle Albert. 1937. *Dope: Adventure of David Dare*. Nashville: Southern Publishing.

Rowell, Earle Albert and Robert Rowell. 1939. *On the Trail of Marihuana, the Weed of Madness*. Mountain View, Calif.: Pacific Press.

U.S. Congress. 1937a. Taxation of Marihuana. Hearings before the Committee on Ways and Means, U.S. House of Representatives. 75th Congress, 1st session.

1937b. Taxation of Marihuana. Hearings before a subcommittee of the Committee on Finance, U.S. Senate. 75th Congress, 1st session.

1955. Illicit Drug Traffic. Hearings before the subcommittee on illicit drug traffic, Price Daniel, chairman, U.S. Senate. 84th Congress, 1st session.

14

Perception and Legislation:
The Diffusion of Sexual Psychopath Laws

EDWIN H. SUTHERLAND

This paper is an analysis of the diffusion of sexual psychopath laws from the point of view of collective behavior. Since 1937 twelve states and the District of Columbia have enacted sexual psychopath laws. With minor variations they provide that a person who is diagnosed as a sexual psychopath may be confined for an indefinite period in a state hospital for the insane. This confinement is not ordered by a criminal court as a punishment for crime but by a probate court for the protection of society against persons who are believed to have irresistible sexual impulses.[1]

Implicit in these laws is a series of propositions which have been made explicit in an extensive popular literature, namely, that the present danger to women and children from serious sex crimes is very great, for the number of sex crimes is large and is increasing more rapidly than any other crime; that most sex crimes are committed by "sexual degenerates," "sex fiends," or "sexual psychopaths" and that these persons persist in their sexual crimes throughout life; that they always give warning that they are dangerous by first committing minor offenses; that any psychiatrist can diagnose them with a high degree of precision at an early age, before they have committed serious sex crimes; and that sexual psychopaths who are diagnosed and iden-

[1] In some states conviction of a sex crime is a prerequisite to the operation of this law. Even in this case the significant characteristic of the law is that it takes the criminal out of the realm of ordinary punishment and treats him as a patient with a mental malady.

230 E. H. SUTHERLAND

tified should be confined as irresponsible persons until they are pronounced by psychiatrists to be completely and permanently cured of their malady (Hoover, 1947; Wittels, 1948; Dutton, 1937; Waldrup, 1948; Harris, 1947; Whitman, 1949).

Most of these propositions can be demonstrated to be false and the others questionable. More particularly, the concept of the "sexual psychopath" is so vague that it cannot be used for judicial and administrative purposes without the danger that the law may injure the society more than do the sex crimes which it is designed to correct. Moreover, the states which have enacted such laws make little or no use of them. And there is no difference in the trend in rates of serious crimes, so far as it can be determined, between the states which enact such laws and adjoining states which do not.[2]

These dangerous and futile laws are being diffused with considerable rapidity in the United States. Michigan first enacted such a law in 1937.[3] Illinois followed in 1938, and California and Minnesota in 1939. Thus four states have had these laws for ten years. In 1943 Vermont passed a sexual psychopath law; in 1945 Ohio; in 1947 Massachusetts, Washington, and Wisconsin; in 1948 the District of Columbia; and in 1949 Indiana, New Hampshire, and New Jersey. They continue to spread, with no indication of abatement. What is the explanation of this diffusion of laws which have little or no merit?

First, these laws are customarily enacted after a state of fear has been aroused in a community by a few serious sex crimes committed in quick succession. This is illustrated in Indiana, where a law was passed following three or four sexual attacks in Indianapolis, with murder in two. Heads of families bought guns and watchdogs, and the supply of locks and chains in the hardware stores of the city was completely exhausted.[4]

The sex murders of children are most effective in producing hysteria. Speaking of New York City in 1937, after four girls had been murdered in connection with sexual attacks, Austin H. MacCormick (1938) says:

"For a while it was utterly unsafe to speak to a child on the street unless one was well-dressed and well-known in the neighborhood. To try to help a

---

[2] These appraisals of the sexual psychopath laws have been elaborated in Sutherland (1950).

[3] This law was declared unconstitutional, but a revised law was enacted in 1939.

[4] *Time,* November 24, 1947, pp. 29–30.

lost child, with tears streaming down its face, to find its way home would in some neighborhoods cause a mob to form and violence to be threatened."

The hysteria produced by child murders is due in part to the fact that the ordinary citizen cannot understand a sex attack on a child. The ordinary citizen can understand fornication or even forcible rape of a woman, but he concludes that a sexual attack on an infant or a girl of six years must be the act of a fiend or maniac. Fear is the greater because the behavior is so incomprehensible.

A protracted man-hunt following a sex attack arouses additional fear. The newspapers report daily on the progress of the chase, and every real or imagined sex attack, from near and far, is given prominence. In the case of Fred Stroble in Los Angeles in November 1949, three days elapsed between the discovery of the multilated body of his victim and his capture. A description of the crime and of the suspected criminal was sent to all adjoining cities and counties, and blockades were set up along the Mexican border. Watches were set at hotels, motels, bus stations, railway stations, and saloons. Hundreds of reports came to the police from Los Angeles and from other cities. Timid old men were pulled off streetcars and taken to police stations for identification, and every grandfather was subject to suspicion. The body of a drowned man, recovered from the ocean, was at first reported to be Stroble. The history of Stroble's molestations of other girls was reported. A detailed description of seven other cases of sex murders of girls in Los Angeles since 1924 was published. At the end of the week, 25 other cases of molestations of girls in Los Angeles had been reported to the Los Angeles police.[5] After three days it appeared that Stroble had gone to Ocean Park, on the edge of Los Angeles, and had stayed in hotels there. He then returned to Los Angeles with the intention of surrendering to the police. He went into a bar after alighting from a bus and was recognized and pointed out to a policeman. The picture of the policeman who made the arrest was published in scores of newspapers over the United States as the "capturer of the sex fiend." After his capture, other details of the case and of related cases kept the community in a state of tension. As soon as the district attorney secured from Stroble an account of the manner of the murder, he went to the assembled reporters and repeated the story, "with beads of sweat standing on his face and neck." The psychiatrist's diagnosis of Stroble was

[5] "Molestation" is a weasel word, and can refer to anything from rape to whistling at a girl.

published: he loved this little girl because he was a timid and weak old man, insufficiently aggressive to approach grown women; the murder of the girl was merely an incident due to fear of being caught and punished.

Fear is seldom or never related to statistical trends in sex crimes. New York City's terror in 1937 was at its height in August, although that was not the month when sex crimes reached their peak. The number of sex crimes known to the police of New York City was 175 in April, 211 in May, 159 in August, and 177 in September (Citizens' Committee, 1938). Ordinarily, from two to four spectacular sex crimes in a few weeks are sufficient to evoke the phrase "sex crime wave."

Fear is produced more readily in the modern community than it was earlier in our history because of the increased publicity regarding sex crimes. Any spectacular sex crime is picked up by the press associations and is distributed to practically all the newspapers in the nation; in addition, it is often described in news broadcasts. Then weekly and monthly journals publish general articles on sex crimes. All this produces a widespread uneasiness which, given a few local incidents, readily bursts into hysteria.

Although this condition of fear has been found in all the states prior to the enactment of their sexual psychopath laws, it is not a sufficient explanation of the laws. For generations communities have been frightened by sex crimes and have not enacted sexual psychopath laws. In the present generation the states which have not enacted sexual psychopath laws have had similar fears.

A second element in the process of developing sexual psychopath laws is the agitated activity of the community in connection with the fear. The attention of the community is focused on sex crimes, and people in the most varied situations envisage dangers and see the need of and possibility for their control. When a news broadcaster, in connection with the Stroble case, expressed the belief over the radio that something should be done, he received more than 200 telegrams agreeing with him. The mother of the murdered girl demanded punishment for the daughter of Stroble, who had harbored him without notifying the parents of girls in the neighborhood that he was a dangerous criminal. A woman spoke in condemnation of striptease and other lewd shows as stimulating sex fiends and demanded that they be closed. Letters to the editors demanded that sex criminals be castrated; others recommended whipping. The City Council of Los Angeles adopted a resolution demanding that the legislature of the state be called in special session to enact laws which would punish sex crimes more severely and would make sex criminals ineligible for parole. The attorney-general of the state sent a bulletin to all sheriffs and police chiefs urging them to enforce strictly the laws which required registration of all sex criminals. The judiciary committee of the state legislature appointed a subcommittee to study the problem of sex crimes and to make recommendations to a special session of the legislature. The superintendent of city schools urged, among other things, that sex offenders who loitered around the schools should be prosecuted. The grand jury met and started a general investigation of sex crimes. The Juvenile Protective Committee urged an appropriation of $50,000 for medical and clinical treatment of sex offenders, and the County Probation Department energetically requested the authorizing of a psychiatric clinic for the study and supervision of sex offenders. It was reported that some psychiatrists in the city opposed these suggestions for psychiatric clinics as "socialized medicine" and "statism."

In the meantime, organization developed in other directions. The sheriff's office set up a special detail on sex offenses, with a staff to coordinate all police activities on sex offenses in the county. The Parent-Teacher Association sponsored mass meetings, with blanks on which interested persons could enrol as members of an organization which would continue its effort until effective action for control of sex crimes was taken. At the first mass meeting, attended by about 800 people, speakers were scheduled to explain the existing laws and procedures and to suggest programs for improvement. The news of the Stroble crime and of subsequent events was carried over the nation by the press associations and produced national reactions. J. Edgar Hoover was quoted as calling for an all-out war against sex criminals. The Associated Press's science editor wrote a syndicated column on the views of leaders in the nation regarding methods of controlling sex crimes.

The third phase in the development of these sexual psychopath laws has been the appointment of a committee. The committee gathers the many conflicting recommendations of persons and groups of persons, attempts to determine "facts," studies procedures in other states, and makes recommendations, which generally include bills for the legislature. Although the general fear usually subsides within a few days, a committee has the formal duty of following through until positive action is taken. Terror which does not result in a committee is much less likely to result in a law. The appointment of a committee is a conventional method of dealing with any problem. Even during the recent agitations in California and Michigan, which have had sexual psychopath laws for ten years, committees have been appointed to study sex crimes and to make recommendations.

These committees deal with emergencies, and their investigations are relatively superficial. Even so, the community sometimes becomes impatient. Before a committee appointed by the Massachusetts legislature had had time for even a superficial investigation, the impatient legislature enacted a sexual psychopath law. The committee report several months later recommended that the statute which had just been enacted should be repealed on the ground that sex crimes should not be considered apart from the general correctional system of the state (Massachusetts, 1948). Similarly, the legislature of New Jersey enacted a sexual psychopath law in 1949 and also appointed a committee to investigate sex crimes and to suggest a policy. In New York City, on the other hand, the mayor took certain emergency actions in 1937 and did not appoint a committee until several months after the crisis. This committee made a very thorough study of all sex crimes in New York City in the decade 1930–39 and did not report for two or three years. The result was that New York State did not enact a sexual psychopath law; and, in fact, the committee was divided in its recommendation that such a law should be enacted.

In some states, at the committee stage of the development of a sexual psychopath law, psychiatrists have played an important part. The psychiatrists, more than any others, have been the interest group back of the laws. A committee of psychiatrists and neurologists in Chicago wrote the bill which became the sexual psychopath law of Illinois; the bill was sponsored by the Chicago Bar Association and by the state's attorney of Cook County and was enacted with little opposition in the next session of the state legislature (Stewart, 1938; Haines et al., 1948). In Minnesota all of the members of the governor's committee except one were psychiatrists. In Wisconsin the Milwaukee Neuropsychiatric Society shared in pressing the Milwaukee Crime Commission for the enactment of a law. In Indiana the attorney-general's committee received from the American Psychiatric Association copies of all of the sexual psychopath laws which had been enacted in other states.

Such actions by psychiatrists are consistent in some respects with their general views. Most psychiatrists assert that serious sex crimes are the result of mental pathology, although few of them would make such unqualified statements as that attributed to Dr. A. A. Brill at the time of the panic in New York City in 1937: "Sex crimes are committed only by people of defective mentality. All mental defectives have either actual or potential sex abnormalities."[6] Also, psychiatrists almost without exception favor the view that criminals should be treated as patients. Moreover, since the sexual psychopath laws usually specify that the diagnosis for the court shall be made by psychiatrists, they have an economic interest in the extension of this procedure.

While psychiatrists have often played an important part in the promotion of sexual psychopath laws, many prominent psychiatrists have been forthright in their opposition to them. They know that the sexual psychopath cannot be defined or identified. Probably most of the psychiatrists in the nation have been indifferent to legislation; they have exerted themselves neither to promote nor to oppose enactment.

The function of the committee is to organize information. The committee, dealing with emergency conditions, customarily takes the information which is available. Much of this has been distributed through popular literature, which contains the series of propositions outlined above. The latter are customarily accepted without firsthand investigation by the committee and are presented to the legislature and the public as "science." Although these propositions are all false or questionable, they have nevertheless been very effective in the diffusion of the laws. Bills are presented to the legislature with the explanation that these are the most enlightened and effective methods of dealing with the problem of sex crimes and that the states which have sexual psychopath laws have found them effective. Very little discussion occurs in the legislature. When the bill for the District of Columbia was presented in Congress, the only question asked was whether this bill, if enacted, would weaken or strengthen the sex laws; the questioner was satisfied with a categorical reply that the bill would strengthen them (Congressional Record, 1948).

The law is similarly presented to the public as the most enlightened and effective method of dealing with sex offenders. After the sexual psychopath bill had been drafted in Indiana, the *Indianapolis Star* (December 8, 1948) had the following editorial:

[6] Quoted in *Time*, August 23, 1937. If the Kinsey Report is trustworthy, all males, whether defective or not, "have either actual or potential sex abnormalities."

Indiana today is one step nearer an enlightened approach to the growing menace of sex crimes. A proposed new law to institutionalize sexual psychopathics until pronounced permanently recovered has been drafted by a special state citizens' committee which helped the attorney general's office to study the problem. . . . Such a law should become a realistic, practical answer to the sex crime problem. This type of legislation has succeeded elsewhere and is long overdue in Indiana.

The diffusion of sexual psychopath laws, consequently, has occurred under the following conditions: a state of fear developed, to some extent, by a general, nationwide popular literature and made explicit by a few spectacular sex crimes; a series of scattered and conflicting reactions by many individuals and groups within the community; the appointment of a committee, which in some cases has been guided by psychiatrists, which organizes existing information regarding sex crimes and the precedents for their control and which presents a sexual psychopath law to the legislature and to the public as the most scientific and enlightened method of protecting society against dangerous sex criminals. The organization of information in the name of science and without critical appraisal seems to be more invariably related to the emergence of a sexual psychopath law than is any other part of this genetic process.

The most significant reason for the specific content of the proposals of these committees—treatment of the sex criminal as a patient—is that it is consistent with a general social movement (Blumer, 1946). For a century or more two rival policies have been used in criminal justice. One is the punitive policy; the other is the treatment policy. The treatment policy is evidenced by probation, parole, the indeterminate sentence, the juvenile court, the court clinic, and the facilities in correctional institutions for education, recreation, and religion. The treatment policy has been gaining, and the punitive policy has been losing, ground.

The trend toward treatment and away from punishment is based on cultural changes in the society. The trend away from punishment in criminal justice is consistent with the trend away from punishment in the home, the school, and the church. The trend toward treatment is consistent with a general trend toward scientific procedures in other fields, as illustrated by medicine, with its techniques of diagnosis and with treatment and prevention based on scientific knowledge of the causes of disease. The trend away from punishment toward treatment is not, however, based on a demonstration that treatment is more effective than punishment in protecting society against crime, for no such demonstration is available. Also, the fact that the trend in punishment is consistent with trends in other aspects of culture is not an adequate explanation of the trend in punishment. A general theory of social change must include more than a showing that one part of a culture changes consistently with other parts of a culture.

Not only has there been a trend toward individualization in treatment of offenders, but there has been a trend also toward psychiatric policies. Treatment tends to be organized on the assumption that the criminal is a socially sick person; deviant traits of personality, regarded as relatively permanent and generic, are regarded as the causes of crime. Since the time of Lombroso, at least, the logic of the typological schools of criminology has remained constant, while the specific trait used as the explanation of criminal behavior has changed from time to time. The first school held that criminals constitute a physical type, either epileptoid or degenerate in character; the second, that they are feebleminded; the third, and current, school holds that criminals are emotionally unstable. All hold that crime can be caused only by a mental pathology of some type. The professionally trained persons other than lawyers who are employed in the field of criminal justice, whether as social workers, psychologists, psychiatrists, or sociologists, tend toward the belief that emotional traits are the explanation of crime. This conclusion likewise has not been demonstrated, and the body of evidence in conflict with the conclusion is increasing.

A specific aspect of this trend toward treatment of offenders as patients is the provision for psychotic and feebleminded criminals. When such persons do the things prohibited by criminal law, they may be held to be irresponsible from the legal point of view and may still be ordered to confinement in institutions for the protection of society. All the states have some provision for psychotic criminals, and several have provisions for feebleminded criminals. In some European nations the provisions for psychotic and feebleminded criminals have been expanded and generalized under the name of "social security" laws: some have included sexual criminals under their social security measures, and the latter are the direct precedents for the sexual psychopath laws of the United States.

One of the questions in criminal law has been the criterion of responsibility. The courts have generally held that "knowledge of right and wrong" is the most satisfactory criterion. The psychiatrists have generally opposed this; they have argued that 90 percent of the inmates of state hospitals for the

insane can distinguish right from wrong but are, nevertheless, legally irresponsible. The important consideration, they argue, is that the psychotic person has impulses which he cannot control and that "irresistible impulse"
should be substituted for "knowledge of right and wrong" as the criterion.
The psychiatrists, however, have not been able to make their criterion clear
cut for practical purposes.

The trend away from punishment and toward treatment of criminals as
patients is to some extent a "paper" trend. Laws are enacted which provide
for treatment rather than punishment; but the treatment goes on within a
framework of punishment, and in many respects the punitive policies continue, despite changes in legislation. Probation, for instance, is upheld from
the constitutional point of view as a suspension of punishment rather than as a
method coordinate with punishment and is regarded by some persons as effective primarily because of the threat implied in it that punishment will
follow violation of probation.

The sexual psychopath laws are consistent with this general social
movement toward treatment of criminals as patients. Some laws define sexual psychopaths as "patients"; they provide for institutional care similar to
that already provided for psychotic and feebleminded criminals; they substitute the criterion of "irresistible impulse" for the criterion of "knowledge
of right and wrong"; and they reflect the belief that sex criminals are psychopathic. The consistency with a general social movement provides a part
of the explanation of the diffusion of sexual psychopath laws.

In the United States the connection between the enactment of sexual
psychopath laws and the development of treatment policies is, at best, vague
and loose. This is obvious from a consideration of the distribution of the
laws. Three New England states, one Middle Atlantic state, and two Pacific
Coast states have passed such laws; but the remainder—half of all the states
with sexual psychopath laws—are in the North Central region. These laws,
in fact, have been enacted in a solid block of North Central states: Ohio, Indiana, Illinois, Michigan, Wisconsin, and Minnesota. On the other hand, no
state in the southern, South Central, or Mountain regions has a sexual
psychopath law. These regions also are less committed to treatment policies
than are the regions which have sexual psychopath laws. While this association may be found when large regions are compared, it is not found when
specific states are compared; New York State, for instance, has had an ex-

tensive development of treatment policies but no sexual psychopath law. Similarly, the states which have sexual psychopath laws are not differentiated clearly from states which do not have such laws by any statistical variable which has been discovered: they are not differentiated by the rate of rape, by the racial composition of the population, by the proportion of immigrants in the population, by the sex ratio in the population, or by the extent of industrialization or urbanization.

References

Blumer, Herbert. 1946. "Social Movements." In A. M. Lee (ed.), *New Outline of the Principles of Sociology*. New York: Barnes & Noble, ch. 23.

Citizens' Committee for the Control of Crime in New York. 1938. "Sex Crimes in New York City." Quoted in *Journal of Criminal Law and Criminology* 29 (May):143–44.

Dutton, C. J. 1937. "Can We End Sex Crimes?" *Christian Century* 44 (December 22):1594–95.

Haines, W. H., H. L. Hoffman, and H. A. Esser. 1948. "Commitments under the Criminal Sexual Psychopath Law in the Criminal Court of Cook County, Illinois," *American Journal of Psychiatry* 105 (November):422.

Harris, Charles. 1947. "A New Report on Sex Crimes," *Coronet* (October):3–9.

Hoover, J. Edgar. 1947. "How Safe Is Your Daughter?" *American Magazine* 144 (July):32–33.

MacCormick, Austin H. 1938. "New York's Present Problem," *Mental Hygiene* 20 (January):4–5.

Massachussetts. 1948. "Report of the Commission for Investigation of the Prevalence of Sex Crimes," *House Reports,* Nos. 1169 and 2169.

Stewart, W. S. 1938. "Concerning Proposed Legislation for the Commitment of Sex Offenders," *John Marshall Law Quarterly* 3 (March):407–21.

Sutherland, Edwin H. 1950. "The Sexual Psychopath Laws," *Journal of Criminal Law and Criminology* 40 (January-February):534–54.

Waldrup, F. C. 1948. "Murder as a Sex Practice," *American Mercury* (February):144–58.

Whitman, Howard. 1949. "Terror in Our Cities: No. 1–Detroit," *Collier's* (November) 13–15, 64–66.

Wittels, David G. 1948. "What Can We Do About Sex Crimes?" *Saturday Evening Post* 221 (December 11):33 ff.

15

Isolation of the Police:
A Comparison of the British
and American Situations

JOHN P. CLARK

Policing in most societies exists in a state of "dynamic tension" between forces that tend to isolate it and those that tend to integrate its functioning with other social structures. In its broadest sense, the concept of isolation-integration is used here to denote the degree to which policing contributes to the overall unity and welfare of a society as measured by its own diverse sets of standards. More specifically, the police may be said to be isolated when the relationships between themselves and others involved in social control activities are less frequent or of a different nature than those thought to be desirable, or when conceptions of proper police action vary significantly between the police and some other segment of the population, or when actual police action varies from that desired by specified others. Police isolation often means the lack of social interaction on the behavioral level, but it also refers to the lack of consensus regarding proper police functioning.

It is the purpose of this paper to identify some forces that contribute to the isolation and integration of policing and to suggest their consequences to police organizations and general society. Further, the results of a study which attempted to measure the nature of police isolation in three medium-

Reprinted with permission of the *Journal of Criminal Law, Criminology, and Police Science* from "Isolation of the Police: A Comparison of the British and American Situations," *Journal of Criminal Law, Criminology, and Police Science* 56 (1965) by John P. Clark. Copyright © 1965 Northwestern University School of Law.

sized cities in Illinois are presented and compared with similar recently published data about the British police.[1]

Forces that Contribute to the Isolation of Policing

Certainly, those who have experienced restrictive action by the police (and even those who perceive themselves as potential police clients) resent this intrusion upon the pursuit of their private interests.[2] This resentment may foster efforts to neutralize further police activity and frequently sensitizes both parties involved to differences in their conceptions of desirable police work—both reactions being likely contributors to police isolation. The potency of this isolating force is probably proportional to the importance placed upon the behavior actually or potentially being curtailed, the projected social consequences of this kind of police-public contact, the availability of "isolating resources," and the predispositions of those involved regarding the proper role of formal social control agencies.

A second force that contributes to police isolation is the social reaction to recurrences of the historic problems of policing. The history of local police forces both here and in Great Britain is liberally endowed with incompetence, brutality, corruption, and the influence of private interests, although there is considerably less of this in Great Britain since about the middle of the nineteenth century.[3] The extensive documentation of policing in totalitarian countries frequently reinforces our worst fears of relatively uncontrolled police power. Our recent preoccupation with the emotion-laden issues of racial segregation, civil liberties, increased official crime rates, and corruption of those in authority (especially the police) has resensitized us to questions of the quality of police forces and their social responsiveness.[4]

[1] The data in British police-public relations are taken largely from Morton-Williams (1962: Appendix IV). Readers may also be interested in the final recommendations made in the "Final Report" by the Royal Commission.

[2] For an extremely insightful analysis concerning resentment to police activity, see Stinchcombe (n.d.).

[3] For brief histories of the development of modern police forces in the United States and Britain, see Germann (1962: 37–67) and Chapman (1962).

[4] Examples are "Our Streets of Violence," *New Republic,* Sept. 5, 1964; "How Cops Behave in Harlem," *New Republic,* Aug. 22, 1964; and "Who Cares," *Look,* Sept. 8, 1964.

The accumulative effects of fear, mistrust, and disdain overshadow relationships between the police and others and result in restricted interaction between the two factions and incomplete cooperation and distorted perceptions of police motives and operations on the part of the public.

Thirdly, police officers and their operations tend to be set apart because they are visible reminders of the seamy and recalcitrant portions of human behavior. In societies where a generalized stigmatization of the individual and perhaps his associates is the prevalent reaction to social deviance and where there is a pervasive orientation that "getting caught" is the crucial determinant of this degradation, the consequences of police detection and apprehension loom large, indeed. Lawyers, judges, probation officers, and social workers are associated with deviants, in a sense, *after* social sanction which occurs in a very real sense during the investigative and accusative operations of policing. The maneuvers and hagglings of prosecutors, defense attorneys, judges, and correctional personnel in the vast majority of cases are not primarily concerned with *whether* social sanction should be applied but *what form* formal sanctions will take. Obviously, not only does the latter depend upon the former, but "post-police" handling is likely to be less important to the actual or potential offender. Therefore, prudence demands that actual or potential police clients construct maximum insulation between themselves and the police who are the pivotal figures in the application of social sanctions. The reservoir of possible police clients has grown immensely with the proliferation of legal regulations (Gourley, 1954: 135; Parker, 1954: 5). Positive reaction notwithstanding, thoughts of policing to this segment of the population may conjure up images of surveillance, inconvenience, embarrassment, frustration, and indignation. Though the presence of police may serve as a positive socializing symbol for social control (Wenninger and Clark, n.d.: 178–191), it may also be a constant reminder that the police must be isolated in order to reduce the risk of social sanction.

The rapid growth of professional expertise in a complex industralized society has had its effect upon policing. Modern crime-detection techniques, police administrative procedures, techniques of handling mass demonstrations and riots, and communication networks have contributed to the increased differentiation of the role of policing. Good policemen must be trained and retrained. To the extent that such socialization creates an occupational structure with its own standards of behavior and a body of specialized knowledge, this occupation may be thought of as a profession. Professionalization to the point of being granted license to determine the content of policing provides both the condition and the impetus whereby the profession may become isolated from other occupations and the general public. Whereas the professionalization of other occupations might be looked upon as very desirable by the general population, its emergence here serves to aggravate an already sensitive relationship between the police and the public. Becoming more expert and unreproachable in the restriction of behavior may be interpreted quite negatively, especially by those who were not in sympathy initially with police procedures and philosophies. This same isolating force may operate to mutually isolate the police and other organizations in the social control system (e.g., social welfare agencies and schools) whose philosophy of operation is not sympathetic to the professionalization of certain police activities.

One of the most important contributions to police isolation stems from the general policy (official or unofficial) of policing organizations themselves. That is, in the interest of "good police work," officers are often advised to isolate themselves from certain segments of the public in order to avoid entangling or contaminating relationships. In fact, becoming closely identified with any segment of the public is frequently condemned because of the increased vulnerability to charges of favoritism and the fear of incurring obligations that subsequently could become detrimental to police operations.

For at least these reasons, policing in our society tends to be isolated in both the behavioral and normative sense. However, in most societies, and especially those more or less committed to democracy, numerous counterpressures contribute to the integration of policing.

Forces that Tend to Integrate Policing

First of all, a large proportion of the population accepts the legitimacy of policing as an integral part of the social structure. Though this may be an elementary observation, it is probably this basic orientation that provides the fundamental integration of police forces and their operations into most communities. To most, not having a body of functionaries who will intercede in certain social control situations that are thought to be damaging to the individual or the community, however rare the occasion, is unthinkable. Outcries against the police demand their reform, not abolition. The public and those in other parts of the social control system recognize that the police cannot be totally isolated and perform their fundamental functions. This minimum of acceptance, although variously defined, assures the police of continued existence and integration.

A second force which mediates against police isolation is the fear of what police agencies might become if they were not integrated in the sense of being responsive to the dominant will of those policed. As was mentioned above, however, this same fear may prompt police isolation, because of the possibility of negative consequences from interaction with the police who are not totally responsive to public desires. This fear of uncontrolled police activity appears to create an "approach-avoidance" situation which might better be termed a state of *social ambivalence*. The manifestations of this ambivalent orientation toward the police are numerous. For example, episodes of flirtation with the police (e.g., having them speak at service club meetings and school assemblies) alternate with widespread general condemnation of police officers and their activities and demands for investigations. At times, police are forced to be subservient to "civilian" police commissions or advisory boards to insure police integration, while at other times they are surrounded by an apathetic local government and public who may even strongly encourage them "to do whatever you think best" (Royal Commission, 1962a: 22–24, 51–55; Johnson, 1964: 440–461; Gourley, 1954: 135; Smith, 1960: 15–23; Germann, 1962: 67–133).[5] In yet another area, many communities demand that police officers be recruited only from within the local jurisdictions to assure police sensitivity to their unique circumstances, yet expect the officers to be free of any entangling social relationships that might bias their work—all this with little or no formal training in policing!

A more specific source of pressure toward the integration of policing is the process of accommodation which occurs between the police and the policed. The subversion of police activity by the policed through purposefully placing the police in a position of indebtedness or obligation to them tends to bind the two parties involved more closely together. Those at high police risk, such as tavern operators, professional criminals, cab driv-

[5] For a sample of police reaction to restriction of their power, see Wilson (1963a: 175) and Day (1963: 360).

ers, prostitutes, and drug addicts, are famous for such operations (Whyte, 1955: 111–146; Wilson, 1963b: 203–204; Deutsch, 1955: 75–84, 96–106). The police are equally renowned for their efforts to create "contacts" among these same populations. One consequence of such activity is the creation of integrative tissue between the police and their potential and actual clientele. It should be noted here that greater police integration with certain populations may result in the isolation of the police from other segments of society, as was suggested above. Therefore, this specific process may explain both the integration and isolation of the police, depending upon the portion of the citizenry or the quality of policing being considered.

Somewhat similarly, those portions of the public who are likely to request more than ordinary police services may be more solicitous than others of police personnel and may initiate relationships that in some fashion bind the police closely to them. For example, managers of financial establishments, theater owners, operators of "teen-age hangouts," certain property owners, and tavern operators, have particular need for rapid and reliable access to police services. Through their efforts to obtain these, they entwine the police into the social fabric.

Also, the occupation of policing holds considerable glamour for significant numbers of people. Characteristics of policing such as danger, public prominence, power, "being in on the know," and handling the "bad guys," appear to attract portions of the public. This probably accounts for some efforts by the public to interact with the police, and the latter's willingness to respond. A latent function of such activity is the greater integration of the police with the public.

One of the most obvious and powerful social forces of police integration is the effort of police officers themselves to keep the role they occupy in fundamental agreement with their cultural heritage and that of the community within which they work. Although the power of this pressure varies with the selection, training, and retention policies of the police, there is strain toward consistency between the work and private attitudes and values of police officers. Of course, to the extent that police recruiting, training, and retention create a body of individuals who hold a unique set of values and attitudes, consistency between private and occupational orientations may help explain the lack of police integration into the larger society.

Police officers have occupational reasons for avoiding their own isolation. Most aspects of policing require the uncoerced cooperation of the public (Parker, 1954: 5; Gourley, 1954: 135; Wilson, 1963a: 175). Since the criminal code is at best only a crude guide to police action, the major responsibility for determining when and how to activate police power lies squarely upon the shoulders of the police (Royal Commission, 1962a: 31, 34–50; LaFave, 1962, 1965). Therefore, when police initiate action, they do so with the knowledge that their action is condoned by the significant public and the legal system which may ultimately become involved, and frequently by the offenders themselves (Banton, 1964: 144–146; Goldman, 1963: 101–108). Such efforts to act safely within the boundaries of expectations of others cannot help but exert pressure toward a closer integration of policing into the larger society. On an operational level the police depend upon their working relationships with the public as sources of information, as indicators of public sentiment, and in the more informal aspects of social control, as their colleagues.

Policing leads a turbulent existence as a result of the strains imposed upon it by the various forces which tend both to isolate and integrate it within society (Wilson, 1963b : 191–193; Ehrlich, 1959; Deutsch, 1955: 21–37). Changes in the relative strength of one or more of these forces may bring about a significant change in the character of police isolation. The consequences of such isolation have been the subject of a few scientific investigations. Although these efforts have been focused primarily upon the dysfunctions of police isolation and even include suggestions as to how "the problem might be solved," several positive consequences of this isolation are identifiable.

Positive Consequences of the Isolation of Policing

Among these would be the probability that up to a certain ill-defined point the smaller the involvement of police personnel with those who are to be policed (especially the more habitual and traditional offenders), the freer the former feel to detect, harass, and apprehend the latter. Obviously, there is a real danger of overstating and distorting this point, but there is evidence to indicate that the police have some practical difficulty in restricting the behavior of those with whom they are clearly identified or by whom they have been, in a sense, co-opted (Whyte, 1955; Wilson, 1963b; Deutsch, 1955:

75–106). This is not meant to imply that good police work consists of dispassionate detection and apprehension, but merely that certain degrees of detachment from clients may be conducive to more objective evaluation and more aggressive action in police situations. When one considers the great variation in the demands placed upon municipal police forces and the equally diverse motivations for these expectations, there is a real reason to doubt whether "good police work" can be accomplished for the whole society. For example, as a practical matter, it is difficult to see how police forces in areas experiencing severe racial turmoil can retain sufficient isolation from the white population and enough integration with the Negro population to effect "good police work" with either. Here the unenviable role of the police as "the agency between" becomes sharply defined.[6]

Secondly, to the extent that police forces are used as positive agents of social change, they are likely to represent but a portion of society (likely the dominant political forces), and therefore, will be asked to force compliance with new regulations upon large segments of the population (Wenninger and Clark, undated). The relatively threat-free sanctuary of being somewhat isolated from the public, and perhaps not as vulnerable or responsive to its criticism, contributes to more aggressive action to effect social change.

In his discussion of role-set, Merton (1957: 374–376) alludes to another possible function of some degree of police isolation. He suggests that the "mechanism of insulating role-activities from observability by members of the role-set" may contribute to social stability by allowing those in the same role-set who are differently located in the social structure to play their individual roles without overt conflict. In this sense, police isolation may be said to permit the "peaceful co-existence" of police operations and anti-police sentiments and actions.

One of the most frequently offered panaceas to "police problems" is that of professionalization (Germann, 1962: 213–221; Deutsch, 1955: 226–233; Wilson, 1963b: 200–211; Smith, 1960: 14–15). To the extent that this concept implies the accumulation of practices recognized as desirable by significant numbers of policemen and serving as a major guide to police behavior, then freedom from entangling social relationships with those who do not have similar orientations is functional to its growth. At least in the short run, the detachment from certain segments of the larger society may go

---

[6] Police agencies may be viewed as standing between efforts to maximize individual desires and the need of social protection, between law breakers and their actual and potential victims.

hand-in-hand with or be a necessary precondition of increased police professionalization, given the myriad of standards for police work held within society.

Negative Consequences of Isolation of Policing

The listing of benefits derived from police isolation for either the police
themselves or other segments of the community should not overshadow the
social costs of such isolation. One prominent police chief has chastised his
fellow officers for their retreat into "minoritism" and their "near-fatal inability to recognize police dependence on public opinion" and cooperation
(Parker, 1954: 5). Police officer morale is thought to be severely damaged
by feelings of isolation, yet high morale of police forces is considered to be
a major factor in aggressive police work (Wilson, 1963b: 191–192). Gourley
(1954: 135) maintains that the lack of a "spirit of free cooperation" between
the public and the police decreases police morale and cripples their service.
He points out further that without the assistance of the public, police convictions become difficult if not impossible, a state which tends to regenerate
poor morale on the part of the police department as well as negative attitudes
on the part of the public toward the police. One might generalize such observations and predict the probable negative consequences of the isolation of
the municipal police from other community social control agencies such as
the courts, social welfare, and the schools as well.

Westley attributes much of the rationale for police violence and secrecy
to their perceived isolation. The development of a rigidly defined "in-
group," not well monitored by other social structures, allows the development and persistence of certain abuses of police power that their more
complete integration might prevent, according to this author:

> [The policeman] . . . regards the public as his enemy, feels his occupation to be
> in conflict with the community and regards himself to be a pariah. The experience
> and the feeling give rise to a collective emphasis on secrecy, an attempt to coerce re-
> spect from the public and a belief that almost any means are legitimate in completing
> an important arrest (Westley, 1953: 35).

Although such an interpretation is clearly within the tradition of suspicion of
police power and stems from the study of one metropolitan police depart-

ment, it is undeniable that the police have unique opportunities to abuse the power of the state. To the extent that forces exist that result in police malpractice if not controlled through their close integration with the larger society, isolation of the police may be looked upon as dysfunctional to society.

In a study of the discretionary power of police in their contact with juveniles, Goldman (1963) found that the more integrated the police were into the community, the greater the number of "arrests" of juveniles but the less frequently their cases resulted in official action. This conclusion suggests that the juvenile delinquency rate (as measured from court statistics) may be more a measure of police isolation than the misbehavior of youngsters. Apparently the integrative structure between the police and other facets of the local community provides avenues of informal adjustment among the offender, the offended, and the police. When such routes are not available, there is little time (and perhaps desire) to establish them and formal channels are more likely to be utilized. Once official channels have been activated, official disposition is often imminent (Scheff, 1964: 401–413). Therefore, if reduction of the official juvenile delinquency rate is a social goal, police isolation is dysfunctional.

A Study of Police Isolation

Having identified some of the forces which tend to isolate or integrate the police within society and some of the resultant consequences, questions arise as to the measurement of the degree and exact nature of such isolation. The phenomenon might be measured, using a variety of indicators depending upon the aspect of policing chosen for examination. In the research reported here data were collected on the following indicators of isolation:

1. The social isolation of police officers and their families.
2. The quality and quantity of police interaction with other agencies of social control.
3. The consensus among the public, police, and other social control agency personnel on certain moral attitudes.
4. The consensus among the public, police, and other social control agency personnel on the conception of proper police action in "police situations."

Data regarding these indicators were gathered during 1963–64 as part of a larger study of the role of the police in social control.[7] Data were collected in three Illinois cities of 80,000 to 130,000 population from three sources: (1) the total universe of municipal police, (2) a random sample of the public age 15 and over (approximately 200 from each city), and (3) the total universe of those in other social control agencies who were likely to have direct interaction with the police through the normal pursuit of their occupation. Police officers and those in the other social control agencies (operationally defined as prosecutors, school officials, court personnel, clergymen, public social workers, and private help agency personnel) responded to anonymous questionnaires.[8] The members of the public were individually

TABLE 15.1. DISTRIBUTION OF RESPONDENTS BY SOURCE IN THREE ILLINOIS COMMUNITIES

Municipal police	313
Public	598
Social control agency personnel (including)	430
Prosecutors	8
School officials	64
Court personnel	26
Clergymen	192
Public social workers	66
Private help agency personnel	74

interviewed. Part of the questionnaire to which the police and public responded was a replication of a recent survey of public-police relations conducted for the Royal Commission on the Police (1962b) in Great Britain which involved interviews of a sample of 2,605 members of the public (age 18 and upwards) and a sample of 611 police officers.[9] The recent publication by Banton of a comparative study of a few police departments in

[7] Essentially the larger study is focused upon the image the public and police have of policing, the attitudes social control agency personnel (including the police) have toward related agency personnel and the behavioral consequences of these attitudes.

[8] Police officers completed questionnaires in small groups. Other agency personnel completed their questionnaires privately. Clergymen (a two-in-three sample) responded to a mailed questionnaire with a return rate of 46 percent.

[9] All respondents in the British study were individually interviewed. The public sample was drawn randomly from sixty police administrative districts in England, Scotland, and Wales. Approximately ten police officers were drawn at random from each of these sixty districts.

Scotland and the United States provides further information for cross-cultural comparison (Banton, 1964: 144–146).

Findings and Discussion

SOCIAL ISOLATION OF THE POLICE

Perhaps the most obvious indication of the lack of integration of the police into the larger society is the isolation of the officers and their families. Although police officers may restrict their social relations with the nonpolice public for a variety of reasons, social interaction is further restricted by the public. In this study, the officers were asked if being policemen made any difference in their friendships with nonpolice persons. Forty percent replied that it did and 35 percent added that it affected their immediate family's relationships with the general public as well. In his extremely provocative study, Banton concludes that "the American policeman in his public and private roles is less set apart from society than his British counterpart" (Banton, 1964: 219). Therefore, one would expect to find a larger proportion of the British officers who felt socially isolated than was found in our study. This hypothesis is supported by the British survey results which reveal 67 percent of the police officers indicated their occupational role contributed to their social estrangement (Royal Commission, 1962b). Although these findings are not directly indicative of the *distance* between the police and the public, they provide a measure of the pervasiveness of such feelings on the part of the officers which may vary directly with the distance.

American police explain their segregation on the grounds of their peculiar working hours, other unique demands of police work, and the public dislike for those who represent arbitrary authority. British police seldom mention these factors specifically but over half (58 percent) of them felt the public to be suspicious, reserved, and guarded in their presence. (Royal Commission, 1962b). Only 7 percent of the American police noted this factor, indicating a possible difference between the two societies either in the public's reaction to police (more relaxed in America) or in the sensitivity of the police to incomplete public acceptance (more sensitive in Great Britain), or both. These findings seem to support Banton's (1964: chaps. 7, 8) contention that the British police officer is seen as a representative of the police establishment and not as an individual whereas his American counterpart is more likely to receive particularistic treatment from the public.

Responses to questions concerning social isolation suggest that police officers and immediate families are segregated from those in their own neighborhoods and social strata. For example, many of the Illinois police officers perceive their occupation to be a cause of ridicule of their children and the reason for members of the community to expect flawless behavior from the officer and his family. Probably few other occupational groups experience this isolation in social relationships from those "on their own level."

POLICE ISOLATION FROM OTHER SOCIAL CONTROL AGENCIES

If we conceive social control to be a *system* of relationships which pervade a community,[10] and if we agree that part of the policing function is to effect social control, then we might logically expect police personnel to interact with other organizations who also play social control roles. Both formal regulations and informal understandings require interaction between the municipal police and other control agencies under certain circumstances although the great majority of such contacts are left to the discretion of the agencies involved. The failure of the police to initiate interaction with another control agency when situations dictate they should, or for the other agency not to establish contact with the police in similar situations, would indicate something of the quality and quantity of police isolation in a given community.

Members of both the police department and the other social control agencies were asked to indicate the frequency with which they failed to interact with the other on official matters because the personnel of the other agency's not being "what they should be." Failure to interact was operationally defined to mean (1) avoiding or ignoring a situation which might result in the need for interaction, or (2) turning to somebody else for assistance, or (3) handling the matter themselves without the assistance of others.

The data in Table 15.2 demonstrate that a significant portion of the

[10] We stress again that the social control activities of police, although few in number when compared to total social control efforts, are important to the total efforts and must be integrated into them for greater efficiency; see Clinard (1963: 148–52).

TABLE 15.2. PERCENT OF AVOIDANCE OF INTERACTION BETWEEN POLICE AND OTHER SOCIAL CONTROL AGENCIES [a]

	Avoided or Ignored the Situation		Turned to Somebody Else		Took Care of Things Personally	
	Agency avoidance of police	Police avoidance of agency	Agency avoidance of police	Police avoidance of agency	Agency avoidance of police	Police avoidance of agency
Prosecutors	63	27	50	30	87	31
School officials	25	23	24	34	31	32
Court personnel	21	26	26	39	22	30
Clergymen	33	20	39	26	45	26
Public social workers	42	37	47	50	50	47
Private help agencies	33	27	40	39	30	40

[a] Percentages are those who failed to interact "sometimes," "often," or "almost always."

police *and* other agency personnel manage to curtail indicated interaction in official matters, and therefore, mutually isolate each other within the social control system. This phenomenon is particularly noticeable between the police and public social workers,[11] which may reflect the presence of conflicting operating ideologies, lack of professional respect, and ignorance of the other's operations.

One may only speculate on the relative isolation of the police from other control agencies in Great Britain. The greater overall integration of the British society and the commonly accepted notion of greater respect for police and their operations in Britain suggest that isolation of the police might not be as great there.

ISOLATION OF THE POLICE ON MORAL ATTITUDES

Banton (1964: chaps. 7, 8) suggests that the isolation of the British police has resulted in their espousing a value system somewhat different (more

[11] The author was impressed, as others have been, with the institutionalized hostility between those in police work and those in social work. The nature of "inter-institutional conflict" will be examined in a later article; see Miller (1958). A paper by Garabedian (1964) reports an extremely interesting study of the differential commitment these two categories of officials have to punitive reactions toward legal offenders which may have direct relevance here.

traditional) than that held by the general public. To the extent that the American police are also isolated, one might expect to discover similar differences between the police and public in this country, although of smaller magnitude if it is assumed that American police are more socially integrated than their British counterparts. Unfortunately there are no comparable British data to compare with those gathered in our research on this aspect of police isolation. However, data are available in this study to measure divergence in moral value orientations between the police and those in other social control agencies and the general public in the three Illinois communities.

All respondents were presented with six hypothetical situations which might involve police action. These situations were constructed so as to be brief, free of direct involvement of juveniles, and ranging from instances where it was thought most would agree that no police action was required to those where most would agree that police action was appropriate. These six situations were:

1. A police officer finds a grocery store illegally open for business on Sunday.
2. A Negro meets a police officer on a street and tells him that he has just been refused service in a nearby restaurant. He says that he is willing to do whatever is necessary to take action against the owner of the restaurant.
3. A police officer learns of card games being played for large amounts of money in a private home. The card games are being run by professional gamblers although the games are not crooked. No juveniles are involved.
4. A police officer discovers a couple of bums who had been drinking in the alley and are pretty drunk. The officer knows both because he has found them many times before in the same condition.
5. A police officer finds out about a woman who is charging men to sleep with her. No juveniles are involved.
6. A police officer learns that a person is in town selling obscene magazines. These magazines are written and have pictures for the purpose of being sexually exciting. As far as the officer can tell, no juveniles are involved.

All respondents were asked to reply to several questions about each of the six hypothetical situations. One such question was, "Do you believe this kind of thing is morally wrong?". As demonstrated in Table 15.3, there is

TABLE 15.3. PERCENTAGE OF RESPONDENTS WHO BELIEVED THE CON-
TENT OF HYPOTHETICAL POLICE SITUATIONS TO BE MORALLY WRONG

Situations	Police	Public	Prosecu-tors	School Officials	Court Officials	Clergy-men	Public Social Workers	Private Help Personnel
Sunday blue laws	13	28	0	19	11	58	20	25
Racial prejudice	62	71	25	81	96	87	82	92
Gambling	68	72	25	69	85	91	55	60
Drunken bums	85	86	38	78	93	93	69	68
Prostitution	90	94	63	100	96	99	89	92
Obscene literature	94	96	63	97	100	97	88	89

great similarity between the distribution of the public and police responses, indicating the absence of a unique moral orientation of policemen and suggesting no significant isolation in this regard. However, there are some interesting differences between the distributions of responses among the municipal police and certain other social control agencies. The police were more likely than any other category of respondents measured to indicate that the case of racial prejudice was not morally wrong. However, a higher proportion of police officers interpreted gambling and being a drunken bum to be moral transgressions than did the public social workers and private help agency personnel. To some extent, then, the police appear to be isolated, although cultural integration of all agencies is the predominant indication from this comparison. . . .

There is a consistent response pattern of both the public and police in both countries regarding the desirable character of the policing role. To this extent the police do not appear to be isolated. However, since such high proportions of public and particularly, the police, would suggest changes in actual policing activities, there is an overpowering suggestion that the police are isolated by the manner in which they perform their operations.

Further data pertaining to this tentative conclusion were gathered through the use of the six hypothetical situations mentioned previously. With each situation all respondents were asked several questions concerning the nature of police action dictated and usually received in their local community. Great divergence between the orientations of the police and others toward the role of the police in these circumstances would indicate police isolation from the larger society.

As the data in Table 15.4 demonstrate, the proportions of the public, police, and those in other social control agencies who would have the police take action in each situation is rather uniform. Almost all would have the police take no action in the Sunday blue-law case. Conversely, almost all would have the police take some sort of action in the situations concerning drunken bums, prostitution, and obscene literature. Nearly all categories of respondents were equally divided on the issue of police intervention in the instance of racial prejudice, and a significantly greater proportion of the police (91 percent) than the public (71 percent) believe the police should take action in the gambling situation. Once again, the data reveal the public, and other control agencies in essential agreement about the desired role of the police in these hypothetical situations. Obviously, this measure is not sensitive to the intensity of police-public or police-other control agency conflict that might occur between those of conflicting persuasions.

Knowing that the ecological distributions of the police, public, and control agencies are similar on whether action should be taken does not assure us that there is commensurate integration of orientation on the nature of the action to be taken. Cries for action do not necessarily provide useful guides to the exact police performance expected. Police officers were asked what they believed the people in the community wanted them to do, and the public was asked what they really would like the police to do in each of the situations. Although the possible responses were somewhat tailored to each

TABLE 15.4. PERCENTAGE OF RESPONDENTS WHO INDICATED THE PO-LICE SHOULD TAKE ACTION IN THE HYPOTHETICAL SITUATIONS

Situations	Police	Public	Prose-cutors	School Officials	Court Officials	Clergy-men	Public Social Workers	Private Help Personnel
1. Blue laws	2	6	0	9	4	7	0	7
2. Racial prejudice	58	55	75	48	48	54	54	63
3. Gambling	91	71	0	83	85	87	78	76
4. Drunken bums	99	94	100	97	96	96	94	100
5. Prostitution	95	89	100	98	93	98	83	93
6. Obscene literature	95	92	100	94	100	93	88	92

situation, in each case a response was available which focused upon (1) doing nothing, (2) mediating, (3) harassing, (4) warning, (5) arresting, or doing "something else." Evidence of significant discrepancies between the distribution of responses across these possible answers is submitted as evidence of a type of police isolation. Table 15.5 summarizes the results.

Again, the percentage distributions are somewhat similar in many cases, which signifies certain similarity between public desires of policing and the police perception of these desires. However, there is the noticeable tendency for the police to misperceive public desires between the warning and arresting of offenders. In almost all cases a significantly larger proportion of the public wished to have the police warn the offenders than was judged to be the case by the police, and in four of the six hypothetical situations a significantly smaller portion of the public would like to see arrests made than was perceived by the police. As mentioned previously, these data are not extremely helpful in predicting the outcome of encounters between those of different persuasions, but there is clear evidence that a greater proportion of the public than of the police is likely to wish police effort which stops short of formal arrest, however untenable this position may appear to police officials. Police officers are more likely to be aware of a series of events which precede their making an arrest, while the knowledge of the private citizen is more likely limited to the immediate incident. Based only upon the single incident the judgment that a warning is sufficient may seem to be the most appropriate action. Whatever the reason for the difference in orientation, the police can be said to be isolated in their perception of public desires regarding the arrest of certain offenders.

The final evidence regarding conceptions of the policing role as an indicator of police isolation from other aspects of society is the discrepancy between the police action desired by the public and that which the police actually perform. With each of the six situations, all police officers were asked to disclose the action usually taken by their department in such circumstances. These responses were compared to the public's declared desires for police action (see Table 15.5). In most situations the actual police performance is noticeably different than the desires of the public for it. In all cases except the racial segregation issue, reported police action becomes much more unified into a single response. Apparently police action is much more likely to be an actual arrest than public desires would dictate, and even more

TABLE 15.5 COMPARISONS AMONG POLICE PERCEPTIONS OF PUBLIC'S EX-
PECTATIONS, ACTUAL PUBLIC EXPECTATIONS, AND ACTUAL POLICE ROLE
PERFORMANCE IN SIX HYPOTHETICAL SITUATIONS

Situations	Do Nothing	Mediate	Harass	Warn	Arrest	Do Something Else
1. *Blue laws*						
Police perceive public	75	17	1	0	0	7
Public desires	67	23	3	2	1	4
Police performance	93	3	0	0	1	3
2. *Racial prejudice*						
Police perceive public	24	46	1	7	4	18
Public desires	17	52	9	10	4	8
Police performance	24	41	1	10	8	16
3. *Gambling*						
Police perceive public	10	5	14	4	61	6
Public desires	9	13	12	23	41	2
Police performance	10	2	7	3	74	4
4. *Drunken bums*						
Police perceive public	1	42	6	3	43	5
Public desires	2	15	7	31	33	12
Police performance	1	12	4	5	77	1
5. *Prostitution*						
Police perceive public	2	10	6	2	76	4
Public desires	4	5	7	24	57	3
Police performance	3	1	3	1	89	3
6. *Obscene literature*						
Police perceive public	2	8	4	5	79	2
Public desires	2	8	11	18	59	2
Police performance	5	2	3	5	83	2

likely than the police perception of community desires would suggest. The
blue-law situation is an exception, but even here, there is much greater consensus among the police on their taking no action in such cases than is warranted by expressed public desires or of the police perception of them.

When it comes to actual behavior, then, the police tend to act in a uni-
tary manner and somewhat differently from what a large segment of the
public desires in these situations. The findings are clear enough to suggest
the strong influence of separate organizational (and perhaps professional)

standards to guide police operations. As was hinted in the comparison just prior to this, the closer one's measures approach actual police operations, the greater the isolation of the police from the larger society.

Conclusion

Probably as a result of some of the forces identified at the beginning of this article, policing in the United States (Illinois) and Great Britain occupies a position of some isolation within their respective societies. The character of this isolation is somewhat peculiar to the specific society but considerable similarity between the two situations exists.

A large proportion of the policemen sampled in both countries feel socially isolated although the British officers are more likely to notice the lack of social integration.

Illinois policemen frequently avoid interaction with other social control agencies and these organizations reciprocate in kind. The quality of certain moral value orientations appears to be similarly distributed among police officers and the general public, although the police officers as an organization occasionally differ on certain moral issues from other social control agencies.

Both the British and Illinois police and public agree in principle on the content of the ideal police role, but at least in Illinois, police-role performance differs significantly from this common ideal. The data suggest that the police knowingly perform their function somewhat differently than their own individual convictions or their perception of public desires would dictate.

References

Banton, M. P. 1964. *The Policeman in the Community*. London: Tavistock.

Chapman, S. G. and T. E. St. Johnston. 1962. *The Police Heritage in England and America*. East Lansing: Michigan State University Press.

Clinard, M. B. 1963. *Sociology of Deviant Behavior*. New York: Holt.

Day, F. D. 1963. "Criminal Law Enforcement and a Free Society," *Journal of Criminal Law, Criminology, and Police Science* 54:360.

Deutsch, A. 1955. *The Trouble with Cops*. New York: Crown.

Ehrlich, Howard J. 1959. "The Analysis of Role Conflicts in a Complex Organization: The Police." Ph.D. thesis, Michigan State University.

Garabedian, Peter G. 1964. "The Control of Delinquent Behavior by Police and Probation Officers." Paper read at annual meeting of the Society for the Study of Social Problems.

Germann, A. C. et al. 1962. *Introduction to Law Enforcement*. Springfield, Ill.: C. C. Thomas.

Goldman, Nathan. 1963. *The Differential Selection of Juvenile Offenders for Court Appearance*. New York: National Council on Crime and Delinquency.

Gourley, G. D. 1954. "Police Public Relations," *The Annals* 291.

Johnson, E. H. 1964. *Crime, Correction, and Society*. Homewood, Ill.: Dorsey.

LaFave, W. R. 1962. "The Police and Non-Enforcement of the Law: Parts I and II," *Wisconsin Law Review* 104:179.

——— 1965. *Arrest: The Decision To Take a Suspect into Custody*. Boston: Little, Brown.

Merton, R. K. 1957. *Social Theory and Social Structure*. Rev. ed. Glencoe, Ill.: Free Press.

Miller, Walter B. 1958. "Inter-Institutional Conflict as a Major Impediment to Delinquency Prevention," *Human Organization* 17.

Morton-Williams, R. 1962. "Relations between the Police and the Public," Royal Commission on the Police, Appendix 14.

Parker, W. 1954. "The Police Challenge in Our Great Cities," *The Annals* 291:5.

Royal Commission on the Police. 1962a. "Final Report."

——— 1962b. Minutes of Evidence.

Scheff, T. 1964. "The Societal Reaction to Deviance: Ascriptive Elements in the Psychiatric Screening of Mental Patients in a Midwestern State," *Social Problems* 2:401–13.

Smith, B. 1960 *Police Systems in the United States*. New York: Harper.

Stinchcombe, Arthur. n.d. "The Control of Citizen Resentment in Police Work." Unpublished monograph.

Wenninger, Eugene P. and J. P. Clark. n.d. "A Theoretical Orientation for Police Studies." In Malcolm W. Klein and Barbara G. Meyerhoff (eds.), *Juvenile Gangs in Context: Theory, Research, and Action*. Los Angeles: University of Southern California, Youth Studies Center monograph.

Westley, W. A. 1953. "Violence and the Police," *American Journal of Sociology* 59 (July):34–41.

Whyte, W. F. 1955. *Street Corner Society*. Chicago: University of Chicago Press.

Wilson, James Q. 1963a. "Police Authority in a Free Society," *Journal of Criminal Law, Criminology, and Police Science* 54:175.

1963b. "The Police and their Problems: A Theory," *Public Policy* 12:203–4.

16

Police Overperception
of Ghetto Hostility

THOMAS J. CRAWFORD

Several observers of conflict between police and the residents of urban ghettos have attributed an important causal role to overperception of ghetto hostility by police as one of the factors triggering these conflicts. For example, Groves and Rossi (1970) cite several examples of ghetto violence and conclude: "There is considerable evidence that violent police overreaction to relatively slight hostile acts led what might have been minor incidents into major disorders with heavy tolls of life and property." The same authors also suggest that police overperception of ghetto hostility will affect day-to-day police-citizen encounters in a way that is highly detrimental to police-community relations.

What evidence supports the contention that police exaggerate the amount of antipathy ghetto residents feel toward them? In a questionnaire study of white officers of the Philadelphia Police Department, Kephart (1954) found that about 90 percent overestimated the Negro arrest rate in their own districts and that overestimation was related to unfavorable opinions about Negro police officers. While overperception of arrest rate cannot be automatically equated with overperception of antipolice hostility, Kephart's findings support the view that police officers, and particularly prejudiced police officers, are prone to exaggerate the lawlessness of black resi-

Reprinted with permission of the *Journal of Police Science and Administration* from "Police Overperception of Ghetto Hostility," *Journal of Police Science and Administration* 1 (1973) by Thomas J. Crawford. Copyright © 1973 Northwestern University School of Law. The author wishes to express his appreciation to Richard S. Tardanico for his assistance in analyzing and interpreting the data reported in this paper.

dents in the areas they serve. Groves and Rossi also report that more prejudiced police officers perceive greater hostility toward the police on the part of ghetto residents.

In comparing thirteen cities, Groves and Rossi note that individual differences in police officers' personal characteristics statistically account for much more of the variance in their perception of ghetto hostility than differences among the cities. The authors cite the relative unimportance of intercity differences in perceived hostility as indirect evidence in support of their argument that variations in perceived hostility reflect something more than variations in actual hostility. Nevertheless, as the title of their article suggests, the absence of data on the actual attitudes of ghetto residents leaves open the possibility that prejudiced police officers are simply more "realistic" and accurate in their perception of ghetto hostility.

In the present study an attempt was made to further explore the Groves-Rossi overperception of hostility hypothesis by asking ghetto residents to respond to questions concerning their attitudes toward the police. The actual responses of the ghetto residents were then compared with the responses police officers in the city predicted ghetto residents would make.

Method

The study was conducted in a relatively small (under 50,000 population) industrial city in California. For convenience, the city will be referred to merely as "Bay City." Bay City has a high proportion of minority residents, and, on a smaller scale, has many of the problems that confront the inner cities of large metropolitan areas. These problems include a very high unemployment rate, a high percentage of residents on welfare, residents with a low average level of formal education, and a high and evidently increasing crime rate. While reported rates of "felonious assaults on police officers" are, as with almost all crime rate statistics, difficult to interpret because of differences in departmental policies for classifying and reporting crimes, the number of reports of such assaults in Bay City is exceptionally high. The lost time due to injuries, and the number of incidents in which police officers have been injured seriously enough to require medical attention indicate that assaults on the police are not uncommon.

As the expression "the other side of the tracks" indicates, many American cities are divided into separate geographical areas along socioeconomic status or ethnic group lines by man-made or natural barriers. Such a geographical segregation clearly exists in Bay City. The low-income predominantly ethnic minority area of the city—an area clearly demarcated and recognized by both the police and the community—will be referred to as the "Eastside."

In the spring of 1971, a survey of the attitudes toward the police held by a representative sample of 397 adult residents of the Eastside area of Bay City was conducted. Immediately prior to the public opinion survey, members of the Bay City Police Department were asked to predict the responses that the Eastside public would make to five of the questions that were included on the public survey interview schedule. For example, the questionnaires which the police officers filled out included this request for a prediction of public attitudes:

If a representative sample of adults living in the Eastside area of Bay City were asked: "How much respect do you have for the Bay City police—a great deal, some, or hardly any at all?", what percentage of those asked this question would reply "A great deal" ____?; "Some" ____?; "Hardly any at all" ____?

For each of the remaining four questions the police were also asked to predict the percentage of interviewees who would make each of the available fixed-alternative responses to that particular question. In addition to the request for predictions of public attitudes toward the police, the questionnaire which Bay City police officers completed prior to the public opinion survey also included a question asking about the amount of formal education the police officer had received, as well as a five item version of the Schuman-Harding (1964) Irrational–Anti-Minority Group attitudes scale.

Results

In Table 16.1 the responses that Bay City police officers predicted that a representative sample of Eastside adults would make to five questions about the police are compared with the actual responses made by Eastside adults to these same five questions. The police predictions are based upon data fur-

TABLE 16.1 COMPARISON OF BAY CITY POLICE OFFICERS' PREDICTIONS
OF EASTSIDE RESIDENTS' RESPONSE TO FIVE POLICE ATTITUDE QUESTIONS
WITH ACTUAL EASTSIDE RESIDENTS' RESPONSE TO POLICE ATTITUDE
QUESTIONS

	Mean Police Prediction of Public Response to Survey Questions (%)	Actual Public Response to Survey Questions (%)
In general do you think the police in Bay City do an excellent, good, fair, or a poor job of enforcing the laws?		
Excellent	8	9
Good	27	34
Fair	24	30
Poor	41	27
How good a job do the police do on giving protection to people in this neighborhood?		
Excellent	6	8
Good	26	35
Fair	33	29
Poor	35	28
How much respect do you have for the Bay City police—a great deal, some, or hardly any at all?		
A great deal	24	66
Some	30	23
Hardly any at all	46	11
Do you think there is any police brutality in Bay City?		
Yes	49	32
No	51	68
Do you think there is any bribery of the police in Bay City?		
Yes	29	22
No	71	78

nished by thirteen Bay City police officers. Several other Bay City police officers completed the presurvey questionnaire but were dropped from this analysis, either because they neglected to make a prediction about one or more of the public responses, or because their predicted alternative responses to one or more of the five questions did not add up to 100 percent.

The data presented in Table 16.1 have been adjusted slightly by dropping "Don't Know" responses from both the police predictions and from the actual public responses and by treating the remaining responses and predicted responses as though they constituted 100 percent of their respective totals. This adjustment was made in order to make the comparison between predicted and obtained public responses more readily interpretable. In their predictions the police generally underestimated the percentage of "Don't Know" responses that Eastside residents would make. Since both the predicted and the actual responses must sum to 100 percent, the inclusion of the "Don't Know" data in Table 16.1 would have obscured the nature of the relationship between police predictions and public responses by artificially inflating the police prediction percentages vis-à-vis the obtained public response percentages on responses other than "Don't Know." Because of this omission, the data in Table 16.1 should be viewed as a comparison between the distribution of opinions among respondents the police predicted would express either a positive or a negative opinion (predicted "Don't Know" responses excluded) and the distribution of opinions among those respondents who actually expressed either a positive or a negative opinion (actual "Don't Know" responses excluded).

On each of the five questions the mean police predicted public response was more antipolice than the actual public response. These findings support the Groves and Rossi hypothesis that the police exaggerate the amount of antipolice hostility that exists in the urban ghettos. Although there is some variation among the five questions in the amount of overprediction of antipolice opinions, the police greatly underestimated the amount of respect Eastside respondents would claim to have for the Bay City police; moreover, the police clearly overestimated negative responses to the police brutality question. On the questions concerning enforcing the laws, bribery, and giving protection, the mean actual public responses were more positive than the police predicted, but not by so wide a margin as in the case of the "respect" and "brutality" questions.

It has been suggested that overperception of ghetto hostility may lead to police behaviors that are detrimental to both the police and the community. If so, it may be important to identify the characteristics of those police officers most likely to exaggerate ghetto hostility. As previously mentioned, the presurvey questionnaire which was administered to Bay City police officers contained measures of each police officer's attitude toward minority groups and his level of formal education. In order to determine whether either ethnic prejudice or education bears any relationship to overperception of ghetto hostility, a single index of overperception of hostility was developed for computational purposes. To construct this index the proportion of respondents that a police officer predicted would make a favorable or pro-police response to each question was subtracted from that proportion of respondents who actually made a pro-police response to that question. For example, 43 percent of the respondents replied either "Excellent" or "Good" when asked: "in general do you think the police in Bay City do an excellent, good, fair, or a poor job of enforcing the laws?" If a particular police officer predicted that 30 percent of the respondents would make either an "Excellent" or a "Good" response to this question then 13 percent would be his "underestimate of public favorability" score for this question. Similar computational procedures were followed for the remaining four questions. The sum of the five underestimate of public favorability scores was computed for each of the thirteen Bay City police officers in our study, and this sum was used as the index of overperception of ghetto hostility in our analyses. Treating the sum of the five overperception scores as a single variable seems justified in view of the fact that these five scores are highly interrelated. The ten possible correlations between the five overperception scores taken two at a time range from a high of .81 to a low of .46. Eight of the ten interitem correlations are significant at less than the .05 level. Thus the five overperception scores constitute a scale by Robinson et al.'s (1968) criterion. The correlational analyses of the relationship between this overperception of hostility variable and the measures of education and prejudice are presented in Table 16.2. Both education and the Schuman-Harding Irrational–Anti-Minority Groups attitude scale are significantly related to our index of overperception of ghetto hostility. Among the thirteen Bay City police officers in this study, those with less education and those with irrationally negative attitudes toward minority groups are most prone to exaggerate the antipolice sentiment in Bay City's Eastside. The multiple correlation of .74 suggests that education and prejudice together account for over half the variance in our index of overperception of ghetto hostility.

The single measure of overperception of ghetto hostility, constructed by summing the five "actual proportion favorable minus predicted proportion favorable" scores, enabled the author to conduct a statistical test of the prediction that the police overperceive ghetto hostility. A one-sample t test

TABLE 16.2. CORRELATIONS BETWEEN BAY CITY POLICE OFFICER'S OVER-
PERCEPTION OF GHETTO HOSTILITY AND MEASURES OF THEIR ETHNIC
GROUP PREJUDICE AND LEVEL OF EDUCATION (N = 13 FOR CORRELATIONS
EXCEPT THOSE INVOLVING EDUCATION, WHERE N = 12; ONE POLICE OF-
FICER RESPONDENT DID NOT ANSWER THE LEVEL OF EDUCATION QUES-
TION) [a]

	Correlations with Overperception of Ghetto Hostility Measure	
	r	p
A. Schuman-Harding Anti-Minority Group Attitude scale	.52	<.06
B. Education	−.59	<.04
C. Anti-Minority Group Attitude *and* Education (multiple correlation with overperception of hostility)	.74	<.02

[a] The correlation between education and the Schuman-Harding Anti-Minority Group prejudice scale was − .14. The partial correlation between education and overperception of hostility
controlling for the Schuman-Harding prejudice measure was − .61. The partial correlation between the Schuman-Harding prejudice measure and overperception of hostility controlling for
education was .55.

was conducted to test the null hypothesis that the overperception of hostility
index would not be significantly greater than zero. The results of this test indicate that the null hypothesis should be rejected at less than the .01 level of
probability ($t = 2.9$). The results of this test confirm the subjective impression obtained from an inspection of the data presented in Table 16.1.

Discussion

How can the fact be explained that Bay City police officers overestimated
the amount of antipolice sentiment which would be expressed in a survey of
residents of Bay City's Eastside—the area of the city with a low average income, a high crime rate, and a high percentage of minority group residents?
As in all opinion polls, the possibility exists that the respondents were not
reporting their true beliefs and feelings to the interviewers. It is conceivable
that respondents actually feel more negative toward the police than they are

willing to acknowledge, and consequently the police predictions and not the respondents' replies are to be believed. While this possibility cannot be completely ruled out, several factors suggest that the public responses are valid reports. The interviewers were recruited from the Eastside area, and an attempt was made to match interviewer-interviewee ethnically. The poll was a public opinion survey and not a survey sponsored by the police department, and there is no particular reason to believe that respondents interpreted the study as a police-sponsored survey. Most importantly, analyses of subgroup differences in public attitudes toward the police produced a meaningful pattern of results, and one that is consistent with findings from earlier studies. Bay City respondents in this study with the most negative reported attitudes toward the police are those who live in the Eastside area, are relatively young, and are members of ethnic minority groups. It seems unlikely that this pattern of meaningful findings would result from the analysis of false reports or attempts to misrepresent true feelings.

A more plausible explanation for the police officers' overestimate of ghetto hostility may lie in the nonrepresentative "sample" or the public with whom the police come into daily contact. It is quite possible that the police accurately perceive the antipolice sentiments of that segment of the public with which they deal. Thus the "bias" may be not in the police officer's perception, but in the sample of the public with which he interacts. In order to check on this possibility, it would be desirable to compare the attitudes of citizens who have come into contact with the local police with the attitudes of citizens who have not come into contact with the local police.

Even if it were demonstrated that the average of police predictions is an accurate estimate of the antipolice sentiment of that segment of the public which comes into contact with the police, the relationships between perception of ghetto hostility and the individual police officer's minority group prejudice and his level of education would remain to be explained. One possible explanation of the prejudice-perception of hostility relationship found in both the present study and in the Groves and Rossi research is that prejudiced police officers may be projecting their own hostility onto members of the minority groups they dislike. An alternative explanation is that of the "self-fulfilling prophecy." Prejudiced police officers who have relatively little formal education may, by their behavior, produce the very negative sentiments they expect from minority group citizens. The nature of this vicious circle has been well described by Jerome Skolnick (1968):

The situation feeds upon itself. To the extent that police are bigoted and manifest prejudices in the daily performance of their duties, to the extent that they employ different standards, to the extent that they insult black people living in the ghetto, they receive the hostility and hatred of the black man in the ghetto. This hostility and hatred, in turn, reinforces the policeman's bigotry, the policeman's hatred, the policeman's fear, and the social isolation of the policeman from those black citizens with whom he must come in daily contact.

It seems to the present author that the existence of this self-fulfilling prophecy could be most convincingly demonstrated by a combination of the public opinion survey and police officer questionnaire methods used in this study with the method of participant observation of police-citizen interaction used by Skolnick (1966), Reiss (1971), and others.

Most social science researchers strive for "objectivity" in gathering, analyzing, and reporting their data. But studies of prejudice and overperception of ghetto hostility often create strong reactions in the reader because of the emotions associated with these topics. In view of the importance of the issues, strong reactions seem appropriate to this author. In anticipation of such reactions, a word of clarification is in order at this point. The present study does *not* suggest that police officers are more prejudiced than others of similar background and characteristics. The author recently co-directed a study of a large metropolitan police department in which the attitudes of a representative sample of police officers were compared with the attitudes of a representative sample of firemen from the same city (Crawford and Crawford, 1973). There were no significant differences between policemen and firemen in cynicism, authoritarian aggression, or irrational-antiminority group prejudice, though the police appear to score somewhat higher than firemen on a measure of conventionalism. However, in view of the observed relationship between prejudice and overperception of ghetto hostility in the present study, and in view of the related findings by Kephart and by Groves and Rossi which have been previously discussed, a strong argument could be made that police officers should be recruited who are significantly *less* prejudiced than members of the general public. Furthermore, the observed relationship between the individual police officer's level of education and his overperception of ghetto hostility seems to support the President's Commission on Law Enforcement's (1968) recommendation that "The ultimate aim of all police departments should be that all personnel with general enforcement powers have baccalaureate degrees." If overperception of ghetto hostility can be convincingly demonstrated to have the negative *behavioral* consequences that Groves and Rossi and the present author attribute to such overperception, then reconsideration will have to be given to James Q. Wilson's (1968) sound observation that "It is not yet clear exactly in what ways, if at all, middle-class, college-educated men make better police officers."

References

Crawford, P. J. and T. J. Crawford. 1973. *Authoritarianism and Prejudice Among Policemen: A Comparative Study* (in preparation).

Groves, W. E. and P. H. Rossi. 1970. "Police Perceptions of a Hostile Ghetto," *American Behavioral Scientist* 13:728.

Kephart, W. H. 1954. "Negro Visibility," *American Sociological Review* 19:462–67.

President's Commission on Law Enforcement and Administration of Justice, 1968. *The Challenge of Crime in a Free Society*. Washington, D.C.: U.S. Government Printing Office.

Reiss, A. J., Jr. 1971. *The Police and the Public*. New Haven: Yale University Press.

Robinson, J. P. et al. 1968. *Measures of Political Attitudes*. Ann Arbor: University of Michigan Institute for Social Research.

Schuman, H. and J. Harding, 1964. "Prejudice and the Norm of Rationality," *Sociometry* 27:353–71.

Skolnick, J. H. 1966. *Justice without Trial*. New York: Wiley.

1968. "The Police and the Urban Ghetto," *Research Contributions of the American Bar Foundation* 3:1–29.

Wilson, J. Q. 1968. *Varieties of Police Behavior: The Management of Law and Order in Eight Communities*. Cambridge, Mass.: Harvard University Press.

17

Police Perception and Selective Enforcement

WAYNE R. LAFAVE

There are not sufficient resources available to the police for them to proceed against all the conduct which the legislature may actually desire subjected to enforcement. As a consequence, discretion must be exercised in deciding how to allocate the resources that do exist. As Thurman Arnold (1935: 153) has said, to deny discretion at this point would be "like directing a general to attack the enemy on all fronts at once." The police and other enforcement agencies are given the general responsibility for maintaining law and order under a body of criminal law defining the various kinds of conduct against which they may properly proceed. They are then furnished with enforcement resources less than adequate to accomplish the entire task. Consequently, discretionary enforcement occurs in an attempt to obtain the best results from these limited means. In this sense, the budgetary appropriation is an establishment of policy (the general level of enforcement for which the public is willing to pay) and an indirect delegation of power by the legislative to the administrative branch (Wilson, 1957: 20).

Much of the criminal conduct coming to the attention of the police does not lead to arrest. Often a warning is given; this is the form of action least demanding on available enforcement resources.[1] Though warnings are gen-

Reprinted by permission of Little, Brown and Company, Inc., from chapter five of *Arrest: The Decision To Take a Suspect into Custody* by Wayne R. LaFave. Copyright © 1965, Little, Brown and Company, Inc.

[1] In this analysis, warning is not considered a form of invocation of the process. Warning might be viewed as one kind of invocation, inasmuch as the offender learns that his violation has

erally issued on a haphazard basis, they are regularly used in some situations where the conduct is thought not serious enough to justify an arrest.

Even more serious offenses do not necessarily lead to arrest, however. This may occur, for example, when the police view the conduct as conforming to the normal standards of the group involved; when the victim is not seriously interested in prosecution; or when the victim's plight, considering his own misconduct, is not thought worthy of official attention. Factors such as these influence the police in their adjustment of enforcement priorities.[2]

Before discussing the particular criteria employed, one general observation can be made. Although police decisions not to arrest do lessen the burden upon the prosecutor's office, the courts, the prisons, and the correctional agencies, there is no evidence to indicate that they are especially prompted by this consideration.[3] Rather, the practice of not arresting is generally adopted to conserve *police* resources, either those which would be used to arrest, book, and detain the suspect or those necessarily involved later in the process, such as for police testimony at the trial.

This is not to say that the predictable action at later stages of the process has no bearing on police allocation of enforcement resources. Police may not arrest if they believe that there is no likelihood of prosecution or conviction. Also, if the predictable punishment is thought to be either too strict or too lenient, arrest is less likely unless the police have means of influencing the nature of the penalty.[4] Finally, if the conduct is such that it

come to official attention and the warning, hopefully, serves to prevent future offenses. However, no established policy exists with regard to the issuance of a warning, except that some police manuals state that a warning may be given for "minor offenses" (see footnote 6). It is generally quite an arbitrary matter whether a decision not to invoke, as the phrase is used here, is accompanied by a warning. Thus any attempt to select for separate discussion decisions to invoke by warning would tend to give a distorted picture of current practice.

[2] Of course, not all police attempts to allocate law enforcement resources take the form of decisions on whether or not to arrest a particular offender. Priorities of enforcement are largely set by the manner in which a particular police agency is organized. An examination of the distribution of manpower among specialized subagencies may be particularly revealing in this respect.

[3] Criticism of police lack of consideration for these other agencies was noted only once. A judge of Recorder's Court, Detroit, was critical of the police going into a bar to arrest a drunk, and said: "If the police did this in every bar in Detroit they would have time for nothing else, and if they did the jails would not hold all the drunks."

[4] Thus if the officer views the punishment as too severe, he may attempt to have a lesser offense charged. In Wisconsin, the officer can often significantly alter the possible punishment by

is thought that the criminal process cannot provide the appropriate punishment, deterrence, or rehabilitation, the police may again devote their resources to other cases.[5] Combinations of these factors will appear in the situations which follow.

Trivial Offenses

Police manuals often advise the officer that warning rather than arrest is appropriate when only minor violations are concerned.[6] This has the effect of conserving enforcement resources for more serious conduct. . . .

---

channeling the case through the ordinance violation process rather than the state statute process. Since city ordinance violations in Wisconsin are not criminal, they involve no jail sentence, and the fines are correspondingly lower than those for violations of state statutes. Conversely, in more serious cases, particularly in those involving second offenders, the person may be charged under the state statutes because the officer thinks that time in jail will be beneficial.

The Michigan State Police indicated that they were able to influence the penalty by their choice of the justice of the peace to whom they sent the violator. Thus, if they felt the violation was not serious enough to warrant the usual penalty, they would send the violator to a lenient justice. Conversely, if they desired a more severe penalty, the offender would be sent to a justice who usually imposed such penalties.

[5] The police may consider the alternative methods available. The conduct may be best dealt with by a private agency of a civic, recreational, religious, educational, or welfare nature, or by a governmental agency not under the criminal justice system.

Where the conduct calls for penal treatment, it would appear that it could be effectively dealt with by the criminal administration process. However, the distinction between penal treatment and the administration of welfare services is often not clear, even in theory (see Allen, 1958: 107). Even when welfare services are called for, law enforcement agencies may have to handle the situation because of a lack of appropriate public or private welfare facilities. Thus Allen (1958: 109) notes that unmarried pregnant women were convicted when they were unable to pay for the necessary hospital expenses and the subsequent care of the child, so that the burden was shifted to the state.

[6] Detroit and Milwaukee police are cautioned that "a polite warning" will suffice for "minor offenses" and that arrests should not be made in such cases unless the violations are "willful or repeated." Detroit Police Dept., *Revised Police Manual,* chaps. 16, 34 (1955); Milwaukee Police Dept., *Rules & Regulations,* Rules 30, 31 (1950). Wichita police, in their "square deal code," are cautioned to "save unfortunate offenders from unnecessary humiliation, inconvenience and distress" and "never to arrest if a summons will suffice; never to summons if a warning would be better." Wichita Police Dept., *Duty Manual i* (undated). Similarly, Kansas City police are instructed, "Don't make trivial arrests when a warning will suffice." Kansas City Police Dept., *Rules & Regulations,* Reg. 121 (2) (1956). Pontiac (Michigan) police are told to use warnings, but are then "enjoined against the indiscriminate use of this rule to the

Conduct Thought to Reflect the Standards of a Community Subgroup

Illustration: A report that a stabbing had taken place came in to the station of a precinct predominantly Negro in population. An officer reported to the address and learned that a Negro woman had seriously stabbed her husband with a pair of scissors. The husband commented that there had been a little argument and requested transportation to the hospital. The officer, who had served in the precinct for some time, had reported to such calls in the past and had received similar responses. Although the conduct constituted a felonious assault, no official action was taken.

Differential treatment of racial groups may take many forms in law enforcement. One possibility is that members of minority groups may be arrested or may have even more serious action taken against them when they have not in fact engaged in criminal conduct.[7] This quite obviously is improper. A second possibility is that laws which generally are not enforced may be enforced only when violated by members of certain minority groups. Such a practice is not so easy to evaluate, and it is harder for the individual defendant to establish, because it is almost impossible to present adequate proof of the discrimination.[8] A third possibility, and the one of concern here, is the failure to enforce certain laws which are enforced when members of certain minority groups are not involved. This obviously is not thought disadvantageous by the offender himself, but it may be of concern to the victim or to other members of the minority group.[9]

---

detriment of the peace and order of the city, and will be held accountable for undue leniency toward offenders." Pontiac Police Dept., *Rules & Regulations* 237 (undated).

[7] E.g., Thompson v. City of Louisville, 362 U.S. 199, 80 Sup. Ct. 624, 4 L. Ed. 2d 654 (1960).

[8] In People v. Winters, 171 Cal. App. 2d Supp. 876, 342 P.2d 538 (Super Ct. 1959), when a Negro trial judge dismissed a case on the basis of discriminatory enforcement of the gambling laws against Negroes, the court reversed his decision but without prejudice to the defendant's right to prove intentional or deliberate discriminatory enforcement. This would appear a formidable task, however.

  While no instances of this kind of discriminatory law enforcement were observed, allegations to this effect were made. A Negro attorney objected to a police lieutenant in one Michigan community that while Negro gambling was proceeded against, a horse racing book for whites only two blocks from the police station was not. The lieutenant offered to make an arrest if the attorney would make a formal complaint, but the attorney declined the offer. These same charges were repeated in the Negro press shortly thereafter.

[9] "Equality of treatment implies also that there will be one standard of law enforcement in all areas within the community. Respectable members of a minority group do not appreciate the

This kind of unequal enforcement of the law frequently occurs when Negroes are involved, particularly in large metropolitan areas such as Detroit. Such offenses as bigamy and open and notorious cohabitation are overlooked by law enforcement officials,[10] and arrests often are not made for carrying knives [11] or for robbery of other Negroes.[12] However, the practice is most strikingly illustrated by the repeated failure of the police to arrest Negroes for a felonious assault upon a spouse or acquaintance unless the victim actually insists upon prosecution.

This practice is most apparent in one predominantly Negro precinct in Detroit. The average officer, after spending several months in that precinct, becomes accustomed to the offenses which he is regularly called upon to handle; he accepts the double standard and applies it without question.[13] He does not look upon a stabbing, for example, with the same degree of seriousness as would an officer in one of the other precincts. While settling differences with a knife cannot properly be called the established standard of behavior for Negroes, the officer repeatedly called to cases of this kind is apt to conclude that it is, particularly since his contacts with Negroes are usually confined to the law-breaking, and not the law-abiding, Negro. Thus what might appear to be an aggravated assault to an officer assigned elsewhere would, to the officer in this precinct, be looked upon merely as a family disturbance.

---

fact that minor criminals in their areas are sometimes treated like children, or are laughed at, when their violations are the type that run down the minority community, but do not seriously annoy the police or local complainants. It becomes particularly galling to them when, on the other hand, they feel that excessive police attention is given to other violations by their members. They sometimes allege the police make or fail to make arrests of their members to suit police convenience rather than the ends of justice.'' This is from a pamphlet distributed by the National Conference of Christians and Jews. It is prepared by a retired inspector of the New York City Police Department who had 22 years of service (Brown, 1962: 19–20).

[10] These offenses came to official attention principally when aid to dependent children was sought or when a domestic dispute was being dealt with.

[11] A car occupied by ten Negro youths was stopped and switchblade knives were found on each of them. The knives were taken, but no arrests were made.

[12] Only one such case was observed, and the facts are unusual because the offender recouped his losses at gunpoint from his co-gamblers but then returned the money before the police located him.

[13] One exception was the officer who reflected that perhaps the department should begin signing complaints in these cases despite the protest of the victim. This officer appeared principally concerned with decreasing the number of calls to the police. This proposal would seem to approve the present lower standard of enforcement in Negro communities, since, if successful, it would result not in less crime being committed, but in less crimes coming to police attention.

Usually the victim of such an assault does not wish to have the offender prosecuted. Even arrest is not usually desired; the police are called because they are able to provide the victim with ambulance service to the hospital. While the attitude of the victim is an important factor in the exercise of police discretion generally, the assault cases between Negroes are the only apparent situations in which the victim controls the arrest decision when the offense is a serious one. Although the reluctance of the victim to cooperate makes successful prosecution difficult and in many cases impossible, the willingness of the police to accept the decision of the victim indicates that they are not greatly concerned about the problem.

The Negro press sometimes accuses the police of discrimination solely on the grounds that more Negroes are being arrested than whites.[14] Nonenforcement in Negro assault cases has the effect of keeping down Negro arrest statistics and thus is sometimes thought to have the added benefit of deterring criticism. While there is no reason to believe that this is the only cause of the practice, the attitude of the Negro press is hardly conducive to the adoption of a nondiscriminatory policy.[15]

[14] Frequent criticism of the Negro press was heard. Similarly, one Philadelphia policeman is quoted in another study as saying, "I don't know what the answer is. I think the Negro press plays up the wrong angle. Sometimes they hurt things instead of helping. It's got so now some white cops hate to arrest a Negro. They know if there's any trouble the press will play it up to look bad for the cop" (Kephart, 1957: 66). Similarly, a Negro patrolman, when asked if he was discouraged by the high Negro crime rate, replied, "No, I don't get discouraged. It's just being handled all wrong. The cops, the magistrates, the judges—everybody's afraid to crack down, especially with the Negro press yelling discrimination all the time" (Kephart, 1957: 119). Kephart (p. 147) reports that police of all ranks and both races were interviewed and all condemned local Negro newspapers.

[15] Chief Parker of Los Angeles, in one of a series of interviews on the American character published by the Center for the Study of Democratic Institutions (1962: 15–16), said, "One of the real problems has been the resentment of some minority groups because of the publication of the high amount of crime attributed to these groups. From the police standpoint, however, that incidence of crime is a fact. The social and economic conditions that contribute to this high rate of criminal activity is another matter. . . . In the last meeting with the commission on human rights I made it clear that I was disturbed about the consistently inflammatory criticism of the police in the press published by one of these minority groups. I challenged this group. . . . They accepted the challenge. A little later there was a most amazing editorial in the leading newspaper of this group. It stated, calmly and objectively, that their people must stop blaming the police for their own criminal activity. It admitted that there was a great deal of crime and it went on to say that a man who holds up another person with a gun must expect vigorous and prompt action by the police, regardless of whether he is a member of a minority group or not. It was a magnificent, thorough treatise on the subject and represents a real breakthrough in this matter. We had never seen such an editorial."

The fact that the practice of not arresting in Negro assault cases is more prevalent in Detroit than elsewhere [16] undoubtedly reflects the higher concentration of Negro population there.[17] In such areas, there is apt to be more of a disparity between Negro crime and the resources which the police administrator has to deal with the problem.

The basic question is: To what extent, if at all, is it ever justifiable to take into account the customs, practices, and prevailing standard of conduct of an identifiable subcultural group in determining whether the process should be invoked against a member of that group? [18] The problem was defined by a Negro assistant prosecutor in these terms:

Negroes have been struggling for many years to secure their civil and legal rights through such organizations as the NAACP, but there has been too little emphasis placed upon the Negro's duty to assume responsibility for acts of violence and not to expect differential treatment. But it will take cooperation by the white people as well. There is too much of a tendency on the part of police officers, juries, and even judges to dismiss Negro crimes of violence with the saying, "It's only Negroes, and they've always been like that." Too many Negroes expect to escape lightly in crimes of this nature, and with some justification, as those in authority have actually condoned such offenses by taking them so lightly.

The obvious dilemma is that the Negro continues to be judged by a different standard because it is assumed that he has a greater tolerance for certain kinds of antisocial conduct, and existing differences in attitude are probably

[16] In Milwaukee a definite attempt has been made to eliminate any prejudice against, and unfair treatment of, the Negro section of the community. Great care is taken in the selection of officers for duty in Negro areas. Police commanders said that if a policeman was believed to be prejudiced against Negroes, he was assigned to an area where he was not likely to be called upon to deal with them; and cases of overt prejudice would be grounds for disciplinary action. "The Negro in Milwaukee VII," *Milwaukee Journal,* May 30, 1960, p. 22. On more than one occasion observation was made of the courteous manner in which these officers treated Negroes.

It might be argued that the double standard can still prevail despite these highly successful attempts to combat the other manifestations of discrimination. The data from Milwaukee do not allow a conclusive judgment, as noninvocation against Negroes was observed only with regard to lesser assaults. But in some of the instances it appeared likely that an arrest would have resulted had the parties been white.

[17] Detroit had a population 16.2 percent Negro in the 1950 census, while Milwaukee had only 3.4 percent (see Kephart, 1957: 135).

[18] The criminal law has rarely considered cultural differences, although the problem has arisen when a given set of laws has been imposed upon territories with a population unlike that of the lawmakers (see Howard, 1961: 41; Marsack, 1959: 697).

reinforced by the fact that different standards are applied by enforcement agencies.

Victim Does Not or Will Not Request Prosecution

Police nonenforcement is also the rule when the victim of a minor offense does not wish to expend his own time in the interests of successful prosecution. This occurs not only with minor property crimes, when the victim is concerned primarily with restitution, but also with many offenses arising out of family relationships or other associations, such as that between landlord and tenant or employer and employee.

The reluctance of the victim to prosecute makes conviction difficult or impossible and is at least some indication that the offense is not serious enough to justify the expenditure of time and effort of the police and prosecutor.[19] In those cases arising out of a private relationship, resolution of the difficulty without prosecution may appear to be a more desirable alternative. For these reasons, the police frequently decide to apply their resources to other offenses. . . .

[19] The fact that the victim does not desire prosecution will be disregarded in some offenses where the damage is minor if the police consider the conduct serious. The following excerpt, from a newspaper report on enforcement against the hit-and-run offender, is particularly revealing. "Often his offense is minor, but affects the owner of the other car disproportionately. In a routine case handled in the traffic court last week, for example, the owner of a damaged parked car spent an entire morning 'doing nothing,' he said, 'but following the policeman around.'

"In this case, the other driver pleaded not guilty, said he did not think he had damaged the other car much, accepted a fine of $10 (with costs, it came to $24.50) and went home. The owner of the damaged car received assurances that his car would be fixed, collected a witness fee of $5.50, but lost $25 in wages because he had to appear in court instead of at his job.

"Some car owners, not wanting to be bothered with the lengthy process of justice, refuse to sign complaints against hit-run drivers if they know their own damages will be taken care of.

"This attitude, needless to say, does not serve the cause of justice. Investigating officers, questioning a witness reluctant to give information about a hit-runner, ask: 'How would you feel if it had been your car—or your child—that was hit?' The witnesses usually come through." *Milwaukee Journal,* Dec. 10, 1959, pt. Im, p. 4, col. 3.

Victim Involved in Misconduct

Illustration: A man entered a precinct station and complained that he had just been cheated of $20. Asked to explain, he said that he had given the money to a prostitute who had agreed to meet him at a certain time and place, but that she had failed to appear. The police, although familiar with this kind of racket, subjected the complainant to some ridicule, suggested that he had learned his lesson, and sent him on his way.

In some situations a crime is committed upon a person who is himself engaged in criminal conduct at the time. Indeed, the person's misconduct often increases the likelihood that he will become a victim of criminal action. Such is the case, for example, when a prostitute is mistreated as a direct result of her illegal activity,[20] or when both parties to a fight are at fault. Despite the fact that the criminal activity of the victim would not be a defense in a criminal prosecution of the other party, the police are reluctant to arrest in such cases. . . .[21]

References

Allen, Francis A. 1958. "The Borderland of the Criminal Law: Problems of 'Socializing' Criminal Justice," *Social Service Review* 32:107.

Arnold, Thurman. 1935. *The Symbols of Government.* New Haven: Yale University Press.

Brown. 1962. "The Police and Community Conflict." National Conference of Christians and Jews.

Center for the Study of Democratic Institutions. 1962. "The Police."

[20] One case of this kind in which the police will take action is that in which a prostitute is beaten or otherwise mistreated by her pimp. The police strongly desire to prosecute panderers, and such a situation is about the only one in which they can hope to have the prostitute testify against her pimp.

[21] No similar police reaction is to be found regarding the multitude of offenses which involve what might be termed a "willing victim," such as prostitution, gambling, and the illegal sale of liquor or narcotics.

Howard, Colin. 1961. "What Colour Is the "Reasonable Man?" *Criminal Law Review* (England).

Kephart, W. M. 1957. *Racial Factors and Urban Law Enforcement*. Philadelphia: University of Pennsylvania Press.

Marsack, C. C.. 1959. "Provocation in Trials for Murder," *Criminal Law Review* (England).

Wilson, O. W. 1957. *Police Planning*. 2d ed. Springfield, Ill.: C. C. Thomas.

18

Jurors' Assessment
of Criminal Responsibility

RITA JAMES SIMON

This paper will report some qualitative impressions of jurors' assessments of criminal responsibility. The materials discussed here are part of a much larger study of jury decision-making, the full results of which will be published in a series of separate volumes.[1] One of these volumes will deal with jurors' reactions to alternative legal criteria of responsibility in a sequence of experimental cases involving a plea of insanity. The present discussion will be limited to comments and impressions relevant to jurors' assessment of responsibility in the first of these jury experiments. The problem as we have approached it may be divided into three sections: the legal and historical background, the research design, and the data.

   The belief that a criminal should be held responsible because he is capable of exercising choice is derived from a view of human nature which sees the individual as a rational being, socialized by the norms of society, and capable of controlling his own conduct. It rejects the deterministic view that an individual is controlled by psychic, divine, or social forces which render him helpless to abstain from antisocial behavior. The individual is seen not as the victim of his society, his environment, his class, or his God but as a true controller and engineer of his own destiny. As Dean Pound

Reprinted with permission of the Society for the Study of Social Problems from "Jurors' Assessment of Criminal Responsibility," *Social Problems* 7 (Summer 1959) by Rita James.

[1] Research on the jury system has been the concern of lawyers and social scientists at the University of Chicago Law School since 1953 under the general direction of Fred L. Strodtbeck. Materials already published include Strodtbeck and Mann (1956), Strodtbeck et al. (1957), James (1959), and Kalven (1957).

suggested: "Our traditional law thinks of the offender as a moral agent who, having before him the choice whether to do right or wrong, intentionally chooses to do wrong." [2]

This does not imply that criminal law fails totally to recognize the effects of environment—e.g., poverty, broken homes, etc.—on individual behavior. It does imply that the law does not believe that these environmental influences can totally overwhelm the individual. The law has traditionally taken into account exceptional circumstances or observed special categories. Neither infants nor persons acting under a form of coercion or compulsion nor the insane can be convicted of a crime, because they fail to fulfill the expectations of responsible human behavior. [3] As Herbert Wechsler (1955: 367) pointed out: "Responsibility criteria define a broad exception: the theory of this exception is that it is futile to threaten and condemn persons who through no fault of their own are wholly beyond the range of influence of threatened sanctions of this kind."

Thus, the nature of the penal law is derivable from the foregoing view of human capacity. A person is liable to punishment if he commits a legally proscribed act because it is assumed that he is accountable as a competent person for voluntary conduct. The act of punishment, as has been observed by many students of law and society, expresses a formal condemnation, the aim of which is not only to punish and deter the offender but "to give concrete effect and publicity to the communities' standards of right and wrong" (Hall, 1958: 272). Thus the act of punishment serves to impress upon the law-abiding public the fact that persons who commit legal transgressions do not go unnoticed or unpunished. When the society is remiss and the offender is allowed to go unpunished, this may have latent disfunctional consequences for the system. The law-abiding public may feel that it is not being suitably rewarded for its own conforming behavior. In a later section of the paper we shall note the uneasy manner in which jurors talk about persons they knew who received "Section 8" discharges from the armed services and yet who seemed to adjust with no difficulty to civilian life. . . .

[2] Cited in Glueck (1925: 109).

[3] There is a substantial legal literature concerned with criminal responsibility as it is related to a plea of insanity. A partial bibliography on this subject includes Biggs (1955), East (1954), Guttmacher and Weihofen (1952), *Insanity and the Criminal Law* (1955), Overholser (1953), Radzinowicz and Turner (1949), Ray (1871), Roche (1958), Weihofen (1956), and Zilboorg (1954).

The rule of law applicable to a plea of insanity which has been in effect in the United States since 1851 is the M'Naghten rule, which provides that

> To establish a defense on the grounds of insanity, it must be clearly proved that, at the time of the committing of the act, the party accused was laboring under such a defect of reason, from disease of the mind, as not to know the nature and the quality of the act he was doing; or, if he did know it, that he did not know he was doing what was wrong (M'Naghten Case, 1843).

Thus, the "right-from-wrong" criterion restates the premise that the offender is a rational being capable of voluntary conduct, of distinguishing right from wrong; capable, that is, unless he is suffering from a disease which incapacitates his cognitive faculties.

Almost from the moment of its adoption the M'Naghten rule has been the object of considerable criticism.[4] In recent years the critics of the rule have intensified their attacks and have specified the following points as its major sources of weakness. The M'Naghten formulation fails to take into account the importance of noncognitive processes in human behavior and restricts the scope of expert testimony. They argue that, as the rule is currently interpreted, it does not permit the psychiatrist to testify on matters in which considerable knowledge has been gained since the M'Naghten decision was handed down in 1843. Despite the criticisms, however, there was no break in the uniform acceptance of the rule in the United States until very recently. . . .[5]

In 1954 the Circuit Court of the District of Columbia, in an opinion by Judge Bazelon, provided a dramatic stimulus to the controversy by introducing still another criterion for assessing responsibility in cases involving a plea of insanity. This new rule repudiated the traditional right-wrong and irresistible-impulse tests and adopted a criterion which was believed to be more in keeping with modern psychiatric knowledge. The Durham rule states:

> If from all the evidence in the case you believe beyond a reasonable doubt that the defendant committed the crime of which he is accused in manner and form as

---

[4] The judges sitting on the case establishing the M'Naghten rule in England in 1843 were accused by Queen Victoria of participating in a miscarriage of justice, and by the newspapers of the day as being "soft-headed."

[5] In New Hampshire in 1869, another criterion was introduced in *State v. Pike* (1869). This rule, however, was neither adopted elsewhere nor tested extensively in the state of New Hampshire.

charged in the indictment, and if you believe beyond a reasonable doubt that the accused was not suffering from a diseased or defective mental condition at the time he committed the criminal act, you may find him guilty. If you believe he was suffering from a diseased or defective mental condition when he committed the act, but beyond a reasonable doubt that the act was not the product of such mental abnormality, you may find him guilty. If you believe he was suffering from a mental disorder at the time he committed the act and the criminal act was a product of mental abnormality, you must find the accused not guilty by reason of insanity (*Durham v. United States,* 1954).

The Durham rule has as yet not been adopted outside the District of Columbia. However, unlike the New Hampshire standard, which attracted little attention, the Durham rule has been reviewed many times in the brief period since its adoption in 1954.

Even those who have been critical of the M'Naghten rule because of its emphasis on cognition and have generally applauded the direction of the Durham standard are not completely satisfied with the rule as it is now formulated. They see in its wording ambiguities and vagueness so great as to impair seriously its application by a jury of laymen. Where, in the above phrasing, they ask, are jurors to find suitable guides for defining when an impairment is severe enough to confer immunity and for establishing the relationship between the impairment and the act? Those who are generally sympathetic to the M'Naghten formulation, although they agree that the phrase "to know" needs to be revised or more broadly interpreted, are critical of the Durham test because "it ignores cognition; it ignores the rational element of purposive conduct; it ignores the question that is crucial from the perspective of the law—whether the accused was competent to make the moral decision" (Hall, 1958: 288). Thus, whereas M'Naghten is criticized for overemphasizing the cognitive aspects of human behavior, Durham is criticized for underemphasizing those same aspects. . . .

The foregoing discussion has made some attempt to set the legal tone of the problem. Members of the bench and bar have shown that they are well aware of the difficulty of capturing a meaningful and, at the same time, functional principle of responsibility. The direction of their efforts is the increasingly sympathetic exploration of the underlying principles of human behavior, from which it is hoped that adequate criteria may be derived for assessing criminal responsibility.

It was shortly after the announcement of the Durham decision that the Jury Project at the Law School of the University of Chicago designed an experiment for studying "jurors' reactions to alternative definitions of legal insanity." The following steps are involved in the experimental procedure:

1. The experimental transcript is modeled after a real trial from which repetitious sections have been condensed or deleted. The experimental trial is recorded, the parts of the attorneys and the principals in the case being read by members of the law school staff.

2. Regular jurors are used, drawn from the jury pools of metropolitan areas. The experiment is conducted in the court house.

3. Before the trial, each juror is asked to fill out a questionnaire which elicits much the same information as that acquired during an extensive *voir dire* or pretrial examination.

4. The jurors then listen to a recorded trial.

5. After the trial, but before the deliberation, each juror is asked to state his own verdict.

6. The jurors then begin their deliberation. They are told at the outset that their deliberation is being recorded and that while their verdict can in no way effect the principles of the case, the judges of this court are interested in the result of the experiment for guidance in policy-making decisions.

7. After the deliberation, each juror is asked to fill out another questionnaire concerning his reactions to the trial and the deliberation.

The transcript used for this experiment was adapted from the case of *The People v. Monte Durham,* heard originally in the Circuit Court of the District of Columbia in 1954. The recorded trial, renamed *The People v. Martin Graham,* was played before twenty juries. The alternative instructions for guiding the deliberations were M'Naghten, "right from wrong," and Durham, "product of mental illness" with ten juries deliberating under each rule. Later ten of the twenty deliberations were transcribed and their content analyzed.[6] A brief summary of the trial appears below.

At approximately 3 A.M. in the morning, the defendant, Martin Graham, was caught by the local police in the act of rummaging through the upstairs apartment of a house he had illegally entered. The police found him kneeling in the corner of the room holding a cap and T-shirt in his hand with about $50.00 worth of merchandise in his pockets. He offered no resistance to arrest.

---

[6] These deliberations were selected so as to maintain the same proportion of "Guilty" and "Not Guilty by Insanity" verdicts that were obtained under the alternative forms for the full set of deliberations.

The defendant was charged with housebreaking. In his opening statement at the trial, the defense attorney maintained that the question of whether or not the defendant committed the act was not in dispute. The question was: was the defendant's mental state at the time of the offense such that he should be held responsible for his criminal act? Graham had a long history of mental illness and hospitalization. At the age of seventeen he was discharged from the Navy after a psychiatric examination had shown that he suffered "from a profound personality disorder which renders him unfit for naval service." A few years later he attempted suicide and was taken to a hospital for observation, where he was diagnosed as suffering from "psychosis with psychopathic personality." Graham's last internment in a mental hospital occurred four months before he committed the crime for which he is now standing trial. At the time of this last internment the diagnosis was "without mental disorder, psychopathic personality" and he was discharged two months later.

During the trial the defense called two psychiatrists to testify concerning Graham's mental condition. One of the psychiatrists was familiar with Graham's mental history over a seven-year period; the other since his indictment. Both doctors testified that in their opinion the defendant was of unsound mind at the time of the crime. When asked to describe for the court the nature of the patient's mental state, Dr. Barton described Graham's condition in this manner:

"The patient's condition has been diagnosed as reactive psychoneurosis, emotional immaturity, and a general psychopathic personality. The symptoms ordinarily associated with psychopathic personalities are irrational thinking, general unreliability, untruthfulness, insincerity, and lack of shame. Such patients usually exhibit poor judgment, although they have a superficial charm and good intelligence. They tend to engage in fantastic and uninviting behavior which may or may not be induced by alcohol. Their interpersonal relations are poor. They do things to get their own ends, and show little concern for the effect it may have on others. These people are frequently liars and their demands on others are usually excessive."

The defendant and the defendant's father and mother were called to testify. Except for brief periods of lucidity, Graham's testimony was incoherent. He was unable to account for his activities during the periods when he was not in a mental hospital; he did not remember where he lived; and he answered one question by saying: "People get all mixed up in machines." Graham's parents testified that their son was a model child until the age of thirteen, when he suddenly became ill with rheumatic fever. From that time on he had difficulty in school, paid no attention to his parents' attempts at discipline, and would wander off, sometimes for days, without informing his parents of his whereabouts.

Throughout the trial the prosecutor directed his arguments toward two points: (1) This case is a simple criminal action. The evidence presented incontrovertibly proves that the defendant broke into the "Harris home on Aspen Street" and was arrested in the act of burglary. The defense has made no effort to rebut these facts. (2) The defendant is feigning mental illness in order to escape responsibility for his crime. He has learned to depend on mental illness to extricate himself from difficult situations, be they at home, in military service, or when he is facing criminal charges. Martin Graham should be found guilty as charged.

The content of the ten deliberations will be the concern of the remainder of this paper.[7] The discussion of jurors' views of criminal responsibility can be divided into the following questions: (1) How is sane behavior differentiated from insane behavior? (2) How is the testimony of the expert witness evaluated? (3) How are the instructions interpreted? Concerning questions (1) and (2), it is possible to lump together the deliberations from both instruction versions because, in fact, the jurors' discussion of these problems is the same under both versions. For the third question, the discussion obviously will be different and will be treated individually.

In making the differentiation between sane and insane behavior, the most frequent argument supporting the defendant's insanity referred to the nature of the items he was attempting to steal. The fact that they were small and of little value indicated that he was not robbing for profit—i.e., there was no rational purpose behind his behavior. As one juror said:

Look at it this way. If you were going to go out and break into someone's house, would you take the chance of breaking into somebody's house and getting caught and spending a couple of years in jail just to steal a cigarette lighter or a pair of cufflinks?

The second most frequently cited fact indicating insanity was the defendant's position or behavior when caught by the police.

The defendant was hiding in such a childish way, in a corner holding something over his face like an ostrich. His failure to resist arrest by fighting or running away was not the behavior of the normal criminal, who would have been aware of his situation and the consequences of being caught.

These were two major points used by jurors who argued that the defendant was insane. In addition, there were those who cited the defendant's past history, indicating that he had been previously committed to a mental institution, and that during one commitment he had received shock treatments. The mention of shock treatments was the decisive point in one jury for arriving at a verdict of not guilty by reason of insanity, because it was argued:

[7] Obviously, what the jurors say in the deliberation is related to who the jurors are: their sex, age, socioeconomic status, religious background, etc.; the individual vote before the deliberation began; the initial alignment in each jury; and many other factors. These problems, although they are certainly pertinent, will not be treated in this article but will be extensively discussed in a volume to appear at a later time. The jurors' discussion of responsibility was also obviously influenced by the nature of the case they heard; and it may well be that had they heard a murder or rape case involving a plea of insanity, the discussion would have emphasized quite different points.

"shock treatments are given only as a last resort to people who are very ill mentally." The defendant's apparent "low mentality" was inferred by the slowness and dazed quality of his speech. There were brief comments by a few jurors that one could not consider the commission of any crime without immediately raising doubts as to the defendant's sanity.

Surprisingly, jurors who argued in favor of finding the defendant sane emphasized essentially the same facts as the NGI jurors [8] the defendant's behavior at the scene of the crime and the items he attempted to steal. The fact that he committed a crime against property rather than person indicated sanity. The implication is that when the insane commit antisocial acts, they commit acts of violence and not those in which personal gain might be a factor. In this case, not only did the defendant commit a crime for which personal gain might be a factor but he carried it out in a typically criminal fashion. Parenthetically, it might be noted that the jurors in this case used as their standard the "reasonable criminal." This is an interesting transformation of the model—used by economists, lawyers, or jurors on a negligence case—of the "reasonable" or "rational" man. As one juror observed:

If in broad daylight, with people watching him, he had thrown a brick through the window and then tried to enter the house, that would have indicated insanity (i.e., uncontrollable, compulsive behavior). But here we have a case in which the defendant broke into an empty house in the middle of the night by fiddling with the lock.

These actions indicated the defendant's ability to plan and carry out purposive behavior—i.e., "he must have been watching the house for some time and knew that it would be unoccupied."

When he entered, he did so quietly and at a time when an ordinary burglar would think it safe to break in. Once he was in the house, he didn't turn on any lights, which again is normal for a burglar; and he was selective in the articles he stole; that is, he took small pieces that were easy to carry and negotiable.

Later, when confronted by the police, the defendant acted like a "normal criminal." "Hiding, cowering, playing dumb when you know you're caught is what they all do." In addition, the fact that he was hiding indicated shame, and "if you're ashamed, it means that you are aware that you have done wrong." With this interpretation of the defendant's action at the scene of the crime, the guilty-prone jurors had little difficulty in placing

[8] NGI refers to jurors who believe the defendant should be found not guilty by reason of insanity.

reports of his previous behavior in context. The defendant had consistently and effectively used insanity to gain the things he wanted and could not achieve any other way. When he wanted to be released from the Army and later from the Navy, "he began acting queerly." [9] When the defendant did not receive the affection and attention he demanded from his mother, he threatened suicide. When he wanted to gain release from an institution, "he knew how to act." The guilty-prone jurors saw these actions as consistent instances of malingering behavior.

The striking point about the discussion is the general agreement between NGI and Guilty jurors concerning the crucial facts in the case. For both groups the important points are the details of the crime: the defendant's motive for entering the house, his manner of entry, his behavior when confronted by the police, and the items he attempted to steal. They agree on what the crucial acts are but disagree on their significance as criteria for determining responsibility. The jurors' emphasis on events at the scene of the crime may provide a serious obstacle to their use of expert testimony, since the experts were more concerned with explaining the causes for the defendant's behavior than in discussing his actual behavior at the scene of the crime.

During the trial, jurors heard the testimony of two psychiatrists. Both were called by the defense and both testified, in some detail, that the defendant had a long history of mental disorder and in their opinion was mentally unsound at the time of the crime. In response to the question of whether the defendant could distinguish right from wrong at the time of the crime, the first doctor stated:

If the question of right and wrong were propounded to him, he could give the right answer.

At this point the court interrupted.

No. I don't think that is the question, Doctor; not whether or not he could give the right answer to a question, but whether he himself knew the difference between right and wrong in connection with governing his own actions. If you are unable to answer, why you can say so; I mean if you are unable to form an opinion.

To this the witness responded:

[9] References to the defendant's period in the armed forces, it might be noted, always stimulated a story about someone he knew, on the part of at least one of the male jurors. There was always "a guy who was released on a Section 8, or shipped back to the States and later told his buddies how he planned it all." These stories were usually told by jurors urging a guilty verdict.

I can't tell how much the abnormal thinking and the abnormal delusions of persecution had to do with his antisocial behavior. I don't know how anyone can answer that question categorically, except as one's experience leads him to know that most mental cases can give you a categorical answer of right and wrong. But what influence these symptoms have on abnormal or antisocial behavior—

The court interrupted and stated:

"Well, your answer is that you are unable to form an opinion, is that it?"

To which the witness replied:

"I would say that that is essentially true for the reasons I have given."

In the "Durham," or "product," version, the following testimony was given.

Attorney: "Doctor, directing your attention specifically to July 3, 1953, will you give your opinion as to the mental condition of the patient at the time?"
Witness: "It would be my opinion that Graham was suffering from a diseased mental condition at the time he was found housebreaking."
Attorney: "And now, Doctor, would you say that the crime was the product of such a diseased mental condition?"
Witness: "Well, I can definitely say this: the diseased mental condition did affect Graham's capacity to control his conduct."

There is little doubt that the jurors paid careful attention to the testimony of the two experts. In each of the deliberations, references were made to the testimony, and strong opinions were expressed concerning it. With few exceptions, all jurors, regardless of their individual verdicts, seemed to consider their own views on the mental state of the defendant as more moderate than that of the prosecuting attorney but less extreme than that of the two psychiatrists. For example, this is a statement by a NGI juror:

I think we can all agree that insanity has been abused a lot. But here, this boy has a past record, we've got record of a man who over a period of years has had that psychotic tendency; he's definitely a mental case. It isn't something that a man would come up to you and say, "Well I was insane," and then he'd get out of the institution, and then he'd say, "Well I'm sane now." Of course people do get disgusted with that type of stuff. But here, I think it's pretty clear that this man had a mental condition over a period of years. Since we're not psychiatrists ourselves, we'll just have to use our own judgments of whether he was sane at the time he committed this burglary. In absence of the prosecution absolutely showing that this man was sane, I think we've got to go along with the psychiatrists, that this man had a mental condition.

A juror who believed the defendant should be found guilty observed:

The thing we are trying to do now is determine the defendant's sanity. On this sanity deal, the psychiatrists said they found a mental disorder. Well, I'm not too much on the psychological aspect of life, but I can say this. I don't think there is a person sitting in this room that if they were tried by a psychiatrist, with their background of education and their approach that they couldn't find some kind of quirk in all of us.

In the same vein another juror commented:

As far as the psychiatric testimony, I would say that a psychiatrist could pick up any dozen people and make up some sort of examination, the type that they give you; and they'll find something wrong with you. They'll turn up some kind of nervous state. Why you or I could be in a bad condition while we're sitting here now.

On the other hand, the typical NGI response, exemplified by one juror, was:

The doctor from the Municipal Hospital found him insane. He said he had mentally diseased, psychopathic tendencies with a psychosis. He also said that these people, though they are mentally unbalanced, a lot of the time they can be rational; they can give you a rational answer to a question that you ask them; that doesn't necessarily mean in itself they are not diseased.

There were few jurors who believed that the testimony of the psychiatrists should determine the verdict. The best expression of this atypical position is the following:

I don't know anything about this technically; but if a doctor said you had appendicitis, and you said no, I haven't got appendicitis, who would you believe? Now, it's true that you might go to another doctor, but if he said the same thing, who would you believe? Your own feelings that you just had a pain in your side, or the doctors', that you had appendicitis?

The guilty-prone jurors found that aspect of the doctors' testimony which was directly relevant to the rule of law particularly helpful for defending their own position. The experts' inability to state explicitly the relevance of the rule to the defendant's behavior was commented upon in the following manner:

You guys [jurors voting NGI] are disregarding the testimony of the two psychiatrists. Neither of the two doctors when asked specifically if the crime was caused because of the illness, neither doctor would admit that insanity prompted him to commit the crime.

Or, for those who heard the right-from-wrong version:

The psychiatrist could not answer whether the defendant could tell right from wrong. He wouldn't commit himself on that one.

From the general tenor of the deliberations it may be concluded that the jurors neither wholeheartedly adopted the opinions of the medical experts as directives for their own behavior nor did they completely discount them. They did, however, clearly differentiate their own role in this procedure. Although the psychiatrists as experts may present their views for consideration, it is the jurors who are concerned with weighing the evidence, accepting or rejecting testimony, deciding on the meaningfulness of the defendant's previous medical history, and assessing responsibility.

There was one point on which it appeared that all jurors were in agreement. There was something wrong with the defendant; he was "a little peculiar," "somewhat unbalanced," "slightly retarded"; the difference arose concerning the extent of his incapacity and its relationship to the legal criterion. The psychiatric evidence was accepted, at least to the extent of establishing opinions concerning the defendant's mental state. But the jurors' problem of reaching a decision which had legal implications still remained. In this sense the jurors' dilemma mirrors the controversy of the forensic experts. The jurors were not faced with the relatively easy problem of the "raving maniac" or the "drooling idiot"; they were required to explore that fuzzy area between the extremes of sanity and insanity. In that area they had to decide whether the extent of the mental incapacity and its relationship to the crime were sufficiently established to warrant a finding of not guilty on grounds of insanity.

Jurors who have been instructed under the M'Naghten rule discuss the application of the rule of law to the facts in the following manner:

There is no doubt that the boy was mentally deficient; but the definition of sanity or insanity is whether he [the defendant] knew the difference between right and wrong. Whether he knew he was doing something wrong by his actions. . . .

His [the defendant's] mind was retarded; but I wouldn't say he was or wasn't insane. It seems to me that he had the mind of a thirteen-year-old and if a child of thirteen committed a crime, he'd know right from wrong and he'd be punished in some way. . . .

I think he is a little insane, but I think he knew the nature of the act, knew he was doing something wrong. The judge's instructions point out that even though the man may have had perverted notions, if he knew what he was doing at the time he committed the act, if he knew he was doing wrong, that's all we have to pass on. That's really our decision.

Many of the jurors urging a verdict of guilty gave to the instructions the narrowest interpretation. Under M'Naghten, the term "to know" was regarded as exclusively a matter of cognition. As one juror summed it up, "If the defendant doesn't know right from wrong, how is it that he knows what day of the month it is?" It was a rare instance when a broader interpretation, such as the one included below, was ventured:

He [the defendant] knew what he was doing in the sense that he knew how to get into the house, where to find the bedroom, what articles he wanted to take, but, he still didn't know the full significance of what he was doing.

In juries deliberating under the Durham instructions, the term "product" was frequently given as limited and precise an interpretation as was the phrase "to know" in the M'Naghten formula. "Product" was believed to mean an exclusive and exhaustive result of mental disease.

We don't want to leave the impression that the boy in this case doesn't need medical attention; but, we're trying to decide whether this robbery was the result of his mental condition.

He [the defendant] could be insane, but so long as the robbery is not the product of that insanity, then we have to find him guilty. . . .

I agree he's mentally sick, but our problem is did he know what he was doing. In other words, was the crime caused by him being sick?

In one jury instructed under Durham, both criteria were operative, "product" and "right from wrong." The following comments made during the discussion aptly capture the confusion concerning the two instructions.[10]

Now, there's no doubt that the defendant had a defective mental condition; but, the law says if he knew he was doing wrong even though he was in a psychotic condition, he could be found guilty. . . .

Everyone admits he's mentally abnormal; but did he know he was committing an act against society? That's the whole point.

Many of the jurors, in their interpretation of the Durham instructions, appeared to bypass one of its basic tenets. They did not ". . . view the total personality of the individual and his ability to function in society"; instead the jurors ". . . enumerate[d] particular symptoms of insanity in order to

[10] A possible explanation for the confusion of instructions is that although the jurors had been instructed only under Durham, some members may have sat on another case in which a plea of insanity had been entered and the instructions given were "right from wrong." More probably the right-from-wrong criterion is so commonly cited a standard that it is everyday knowledge to jurors.

see if they add[ed] up to mental incapacity" (Wechsler, 1955: 373). As previous quotations indicate, they analyzed each of the defendant's actions at the scene of the crime and asked, "Is this a symptom of disease?" When the jurors found a particular action which might be deemed a symptom, they probed: could the behavior have any other meaning and what is the relationship between the behavior and the commission of the crime? For example: "While it is true that holding a T-shirt over one's face is silly and irrational, perhaps the defendant was one step ahead of the police." This act, then, was interpreted as a cunning maneuver for escaping responsibility.

Two points emerge from the discussion above. The first is that all jurors, those instructed under M'Naghten as well as those instructed under Durham, believed that cognition was the crucial factor in determining responsibility. The second point is that the Durham jurors appeared to have no more difficulty than the M'Naghten jurors in construing the instructions to suit their beliefs concerning the centrality of cognition.

Although replications may negate the conclusions, a study of these ten deliberations indicates that the fear expressed by some members of bench and bar that instructions are ignored or not given serious consideration in the jury room is not justified. However, the fear that jurors either out of ignorance or partisanship misinterpret portions of the instructions cannot be wholly dismissed. For example, one juror holding out for a guilty verdict argued:

We're not here to reform this guy; we're here to punish him. [*Other:* We're not here to punish.] When he's punished, you put him in a jail, not in a hospital. Under normal conditions, if a man is guilty and he's been proved that way, he goes to jail. There's no talk about sending him to a hospital instead of a jail. We're here to enforce the laws of the city. [*Others:* No, we're not here to enforce the laws of the city, we're here to decide whether that boy is insane or not. We're here to do justice, we're not here to decide or enforce the law.] You don't solve a crime by putting him in the hospital; you're not supposed to do that.

When one juror asked him:

Do you think you would be disqualified from serving on a jury later because a verdict of insanity is not legal? Do you believe in any case, a plea of insanity is legal, I mean that it has a place in our system of jurisprudence?

The juror was not directly responsive in his reply:

You can say anything you want to, it's a free country. All I do is go by the instructions. There it says that the man was arrested for burglary by two policemen.

You people want to cure or coddle him, all I want to do is punish him for that one little crime. And if the judge turned him loose because it's his first offense that would be all right. That's the law.

Returning to the three questions posed earlier: sane behavior is differentiated from insane behavior by the defendant's ability to act rationally and to commit legally proscribed acts in which personal gain might be a consideration. Although careful attention is paid to the expert testimony, the bases for the jurors' assessment of the defendant's mental state seem to derive primarily from their recounting of the details of his behavior at the scene of the crime and from piecing together what must have taken place before the police arrived. The view that psychiatrists have a certain investment in finding something wrong with everybody also appears to have rather wide acceptance. With the jurors' criterion of insanity so dependent on cognition, it is not surprising that the discussions in the deliberations relevant to instructions are similar for both groups. The particular phrasing of the legal formulation does not appear to interfere with preconceived beliefs that the criminal who is insane cannot plan or carry out seemingly rational but legally proscribed acts.

Considerable progress has been made since the turn of the century in dealing more generously with persons who are insane. This progress is linked with the popular image and public understanding of the nature and manifestation of mental disease. The opportunity of conducting jury experiments in trials involving a plea of insanity provides a remarkably good way of polling public opinion when it is mobilized around a given problem.

References

Biggs, J. 1955. *The Guilty Mind*. New York: Harcourt, Brace.

Durham v. United States. 1954. 214 F. 2d. 862 (D.C. Cir.).

East, N. 1954. *The Roots of Crime*. London: Butterworth.

Glueck, S. 1925. *Mental Disorder and the Criminal Law*. Boston: Little, Brown.

Guttmacher, M. and H. Weihofen. 1952. *Psychiatry and the Law*. New York: Norton.

Hall, J. 1958. *Studies in Jurisprudence and Criminal Theory*. New York: Oceana Publications.

Insanity and the Criminal Law. 1955. Vol. 22 of *University of Chicago Law Review*. Chicago: University of Chicago Press.

James, R. M. 1959. "Competency in Jury Deliberations," *American Journal of Sociology* 64 (May):563–70.

Kalven, H. 1957. "The Jury, the Law and Personal Damage Award," *Ohio State Law Journal* 19 (Winter):158–78.

M'Naghten's Case. 1843. 10 Cl. & Fin. 200, 210, 8 Eng. Rep. 718, 722, (H. L.).

Overholser, W. 1953. *The Psychiatrist and the Law*. New York: Harcourt, Brace.

Radzinowicz, L. and J. W. C. Turner (eds.). 1949. *Mental Abnormality and Crime*. London: Macmillan.

Ray, I. 1871. *Medical Jurisprudence of Insanity*. Boston: Little, Brown.

Roche, P. 1958. *The Criminal Mind*. New York: Farrar, Straus and Cudahy.

State v. Pike. 1869. 49 N. H. 399.

Strodtbeck, F. L., R. M. James, and C. Hawkins. 1957. "Social Status in Jury Deliberations," *American Sociological Review* 22 (December):713–19.

Strodtbeck, F. L. and R. D. Mann. 1956. "Sex Role Differentiation in Jury Deliberations," *Sociometry* 19 (March):1–11.

Wechsler, H. 1955. "The Criteria of Criminal Responsibility," *University of Chicago Law Review* 22 (Winter):367–76.

Weihofen, H. 1956. *The Urge to Punish*. New York: Farrar, Straus and Cudahy.

Zilboorg, G. 1954. *The Psychology of the Criminal Act and Punishment*. New York: Harcourt, Brace.

19

Perception of Cases and Judicial Sentencing Behaviour

JOHN HOGARTH

[EDITORS' NOTE: In order for readers not familiar with Hogarth to get full benefit from the following two pieces, some of the background of the study should be presented. Hogarth interviewed and included in his sample most of the magistrates in Ontario in 1965. Of the 83 magistrates in the province in that year, 71 (all who had adjudicated 700 or more Criminal Code cases) constituted the final sample. For a period of eighteen months magistrates completed sentencing study sheets with regard to seven indictable offences. Magistrates were required to rate the seriousness of offences, indicate how they perceived offenders, identify and place in order factors which were considered to be of overriding importance in the case, and to give reasons for the sentences imposed. This instrument was filled in at the time of determination of sentence (Hogarth, p. 19). Additional information about magistrates was obtained by a personal interview and an attitude questionnaire.]

The Research Problem

The amount of consistency between "what magistrates perceive" and "what they decide" is tested by means of prediction equations. In the scheme of analysis, two types of prediction problems are dealt with. The first relates to predicting the type of sentence that will be imposed in qualitative terms, i.e., will it be a fine, suspended sentence, probation, or an institutional sentence? The second relates to the amount, length, or severity of the sentence imposed in quantitative terms. Different statistical models were required for these respective tasks. For the first set of problems the statistical technique used was multiple discriminant analysis and for the second, regression analysis. . . .

An attempt will be made to see whether knowledge of the complexity of thought processes in sentencing adds significantly to the power of prediction equations which already incorporate variables concerned with the attitudes of magistrates and their definitions of the operative social and legal constraints in the situations facing them. Towards the end of the chapter, an attempt will be made to draw together various aspects of the overall research scheme. . . .

In this study, the problem is to predict the separation of cases into types of sentence, on the basis of the perceptions magistrates have of these cases. There are four types of sentence into which the case can fall: fine, suspended sentence, probation, and institution. In all, some 2,340 cases were used in the analysis. The original variables used were magistrates' perceptions of various features of the cases as revealed from sentencing study sheets. Twenty-five variables were used in the analysis. They relate to the magistrate's assessment of the offence, his perception of the offender, his assessment of the determining or overriding considerations in the case, and his purpose.

The analyses were based on the case rather than on the magistrate. Differences among magistrates were controlled for by accepting their individual interpretation of the cases as revealed by relevant sections of the sentencing study sheet. . . .

Results

The findings suggest that in the selection of sentences among alternatives available, a high level of consistency exists among magistrates once variation in perceptions have been accounted for. This means that once magistrates perceive cases in a particular way, there is a strong tendency for them to select the same type of sentence. The difficulty arises from the fact that different magistrates tend to perceive similar cases differently. But the data suggest that if means could be found to develop greater uniformity among magistrates in the way in which they assess information in sentencing, a great deal more consistency in sentencing practice could be achieved.

Prediction of Length of Sentence

There appears to be a high level of consistency between magistrates' perceptions of facts and the *types* of sentences they select; the analysis now turns to an examination of the degree to which these perceptions are associated with the length or severity of sentences imposed. First of all, correlations between perceived facts and lengths of institutional sentence were calculated. A series of regression equations were then calculated which regressed magistrates' perceptions of the facts and their purposes against the length of institutional sentences imposed (in days). Seven equations were derived, one for each type of offence for which sentencing study sheets were completed.

CORRELATIONAL ANALYSIS

The results of initial correlational analysis indicated that there was significant association between the lengths of institutional sentence imposed and most aspects of magistrates' assessments of the cases. Magistrates' assessments of offences, their perceptions of offenders, their selection of determining factors, and the purposes attempted were all found to be significantly associated with the severity of the penalties imposed.

While there were slight differences with respect to individual offences, the general pattern which emerged was of a tendency to select longer sentences if the crime was assessed as being serious, if the offender was seen to have participated fully in it and to lack remorse, if the offender was seen to have a great many problems in his background, and if the magistrate attached particular importance to the factors concerning the offence, the criminal record, and social control.

Different patterns with respect to purposes attempted appeared for each offence. In cases of robbery, long sentences were associated with giving emphasis to punishment and to incapacitation. In cases of breaking and entering, long sentences were associated with giving great weight to general deterrence and incapacitation and little weight to reformation. In cases of fraud, long sentences were associated with giving great weight to general deterrence and incapacitation. On the other hand, long sentences for taking a motor vehicle without consent were associated with attaching little weight to punishment and great weight to both reformation and incapacitation. Lengthy sentences in cases of assault occasioning bodily harm were associated with attaching great weight to incapacitation. Over all, the pattern which emerged is that the longer the sentence, the more likely was the magistrate concerned with preventing crime by removing the offender from society, and the less likely was he concerned with reformation or individual deterrence. . . .

While there were many statistically significant correlations between various features of the cases as perceived by magistrates and the length of sentence imposed, they were not particularly high. The highest correlations achieved were with respect to magistrates' assessments of the gravity of the acts committed and their assessments of the length of the offender's criminal record. Even in these areas, however, correlations ranged from a low of 0.3 to a high of 0.7. One should not expect correlations between these individual factors and the sentences imposed to be much higher. Sentences are based on the combination of a great many facts as perceived and understood by magistrates. While individual correlations shed some light on the decision-making process, the appropriate statistical model is one that allows for an assessment of the magistrate's total response to various features of the case. This is a situation which calls for multivariate procedures, and in this case stepwise multiple regression was used.

Regression Analysis

In the analysis the dependent variable in all cases was the length of institutional sentence given (in days). Seven regression equations were calculated, one for each offence for which sentencing study sheets were completed. A computer was instructed to roam freely among the independent variables, selecting those which best predicted the severity of the penalty given. The seven regression equations derived can be seen in Table 19.1 (pp. 303–304).

The size of the correlation coefficients range from a low of 0.638 to a high of 0.834, with an average of 0.716. This means that about 50 percent of the total variation in length of institutional sentences imposed can be ac-

TABLE 19.1. REGRESSION OF LENGTHS OF INSTITUTIONAL SENTENCES (IN DAYS) AGAINST MAGISTRATES' ASSESSMENTS OF CASES

Constant	Assessment of Offence	Assessment of Offender	Determining Factors	Purposes
1. *Robbery* (*r* at final step = 0.705)				
−2140.7	+394.4 gravity	+375.2 criminal record	+414.4 control	+87.5 incapacitation
				+158.7 punishment
				−182.0 deter potential offender
				−121.6 deter this offender
2. *Breaking and entering* (*r* at final step = 0.668)				
−255.1	+147.1 gravity	+100.9 criminal record		+55.9 incapacitation
	+70.7 premeditation	−25.6 criminal associations		+15.9 deter potential offender
				−23.2 reform
				−14.2 deter this offender
3. *Fraud* (*r* at final step = 0.828)				
−1000.8	+220.4 gravity	+36.4 criminal record	−58.7 diagnosis	+34.5 incapacitation
	+101.5 participation	+100.5 criminal associations		+26.6 deter potential offender
		−34.8 adjustment at work		

TABLE 19.1. *(continued)*

Constant	Assessment of Offence	Assessment of Offender	Determining Factors	Purposes
4. *Assault and bodily harm* (r at final step = 0.728)				
−284.7	+94.1 gravity	+42.6 criminal record	+50.8 diagnosis	+30.2 incapacitation
	+25.2 premeditation		+12.5 control	−9.3 punishment
5. *Indecent assault on a female* (r at final step = 0.834)				
+123.14	+157.3 premeditation	+173.3 criminal record	+41.4 control	+99.0 incapacitation
		+217.8 finance		+60.5 punishment
		−131.4 adjustment at work		
6. *Take motor vehicle* (r at final step = 0.638)				
122.9	+64.2 participation		−20.5 offence	+25.3 incapacitation
	+37.7 premeditation			+177.7 reformation
	+25.1 lacks remorse			−6.6 punishment
				−7.7 deter this offender
7. *Dangerous driving* (r at final step = 0.809)				
177.7		+47.4 criminal record	+26.9 offence	+64.8 incapacitation
		−27.9 attitude to authority		+15.1 reformation
		−27.3 family relations		
		+48.1 finance		

counted for by variations in magistrates' perceptions of the facts in the cases.

It is interesting to see the variables which appear frequently in the regression equations. As far as magistrates' assessments of offences are concerned, their assessments of the degree of premeditation appears in five out of seven regression equations, the gravity of the criminal act in three, the offender's present attitude towards his involvement in only two, and the degree of participation in none. From this it would appear that the degree of premeditation is a somewhat more important factor in the determination of length of sentence than any other aspect of the offence.

As far as assessments of offender's problems are concerned, the length of criminal record appears in each of the seven regression equations. Moreover, in each case it is the first variable selected by the computer. This means that it explains more variance than any other factor. Adjustment at work and school appears in three equations, criminal associates and financial standing appear in two each, family relationships and attitude to authority appear only once, and the other four factors appear in nine. It would seem from this that, as far as length of institutional sentences is concerned, a small number of factors related to the background and the history of the offender are relevant, the most important being the criminal record.

As far as the determining factors in the case are concerned, different patterns emerge with respect to individual offences. For cases of assault occasioning bodily harm, indecent assault on a female, and robbery (both serious offences against the person), lengths of institutional sentences are positively associated to the weights attached to factors concerning the control of further criminal behaviour by the offender. With respect to dangerous driving and taking a motor vehicle without consent, lengths of institutional sentences are associated with weights given to factors concerning the offence; in cases of fraud, long sentences are associated with a tendency to minimize factors concerning a diagnosis of the offender's problems. This shows that magistrates will not impose long sentences of imprisonment on offenders convicted of relatively minor offences unless they ascribe particular importance to the severity of the offence and minimize the importance of the offender's problems.

Turning to purposes in sentencing, it is interesting that the prevention of crime through incapacitation appeared in all seven regression equations, whilst punishment appeared in four, the deterrrence of potential offenders in three, and both the deterrence of the individual offender and reformation in only two. This suggests that while magistrates tend to give low overall weights to retributive punishment and incapacitation, these two purposes play a more important role in the actual behaviour of magistrates than do any of the others. It would appear, therefore, that despite verbal support given to the more acceptable purposes, such as reformation and deterrence, sentencing is to a significant extent centred around the more traditional purposes of retribution and short term protection of society through incapacitation.

The relationships between purposes and length of institutional sentences is rather complex. In regression equations, each variable makes an independent contribution to the prediction equation, i.e., a separate contribution to that of other variables already in the equation. Thus, it can be seen that after controlling for the other purposes involved, attaching weight to reformation is negatively associated with length of institutional sentences in cases of breaking and entering, while being positively associated with length of institutional sentences in cases of dangerous driving and taking a motor vehicle without consent. Similarly, attaching great weight to punishment is positively associated with length of institutional sentences in cases of robbery and cases of indecent assault on a female (serious cases), while being negatively associated with length of institutional sentences in cases of assault occasioning bodily harm and taking a motor vehicle without consent (less serious cases). In all cases, the weights attached to incapacitation and the deterrence of potential offenders are positively associated with the length of institutional sentences imposed.

It is interesting to note that in relatively minor cases long institutional sentences are associated with attaching great weight to reformation and individual deterrence and little weight to punishment. In serious cases, severe sentences are associated with attaching great weight to incapacitation and general deterrence. This suggests that when the offence itself does not warrant a severe penalty, magistrates will only impose such a penalty if they can justify it on the grounds of preventing further crime in the individual through reformation or intimidation.

The general conclusion is that there is a high level of consistency among magistrates in the lengths of institutional sentences imposed once variation in their perceptions of cases is controlled for.

The Relationship of How Magistrates Perceive to What They Decide

Having demonstrated that the relationship between magistrates' perceptions of the facts and their decisions is a close one, the analysis now returns to the complexity of thought processes in decision-making. In the analyses described below, the basic unit is the magistrate. Each magistrate received three scores representing his level of cognitive-complexity. These scores related to his capacity to discriminate in a complicated fact situation, the amount of information he is capable of bringing to bear on a given problem, and the effort he expends in problem-solving. The purpose of the analysis was to determine the degree to which knowledge of these three factors could lead to successful prediction of sentencing behaviour. Sixty-seven different measures of sentencing behaviour were used. They represented the proportion of sentences of particular kinds given for specific types of offence. Thus, the analysis begins with an examination of the general breakdown of sentences for all indictable cases. The cases are then divided into specific types and finally an examination is made of the sentencing behaviour of magistrates with respect to individual offences.

The cognitive-complexity variables were created from magistrates' responses to sentencing study sheets with respect to seven offences dealt with over an eighteen-month period. These cases were not used in this part of the analysis. It was deemed desirable to test the validity of the cognitive-complexity concept against further data, independent to that from which the original variables were derived. In a sense, the use of new behavioural variables provides an opportunity to validate the original study and thus strengthens the cogency of the findings.

The judicial section of the Dominion Bureau of Statistics provided a special print-out of sentencing behaviour by magistrates in the Province of Ontario for the year 1965. For each magistrate the proportion of his sentences falling within the main categories of fine, suspended sentence, probation, and institution were determined. The mean lengths of institutional sentences imposed were also calculated. These variables became the dependent variables. The first step in the analysis was to calculate correlations between the three complexity scores and the sentencing behaviour of magistrates. The next step was to determine the degree to which knowledge of the complexity of thought processes adds significantly to the prediction equations which already took into account the attitudes of magistrates, and their definitions of the operative constraints in their social environments.

Results

CORRECTIONAL ANALYSIS

A large number of statistically significant correlations were found between cognitive-complexity and sentencing behaviour (see Table 19.2). Magistrates who use suspended sentence frequently in indictable cases, particularly suspended sentence with probation, tend to discriminate better in complicated fact situations, are capable of bringing a larger body of information to bear on a given problem and expend more effort in problem solving. In contrast, magistrates who rely heavily on fines do not appear to be as subtle in discriminating among information. Magistrates who use institutional measures frequently tend to bring less information to bear on sentencing problems and are rather more rigid in their approach to sentencing problems.

Cognitive-complexity was associated not only with the *frequency* with which institutional sentences were used, but also with the *type* of institutional sentence selected. Thus, magistrates who rely heavily on short-term institutional sentences expend less effort in problem-solving. Magistrates who tend to use gaol as opposed to reformatory or penitentiary sentences do not discriminate so well in assessing information, and magistrates who rely heavily on penitentiary sentences tend to bring less information to bear on sentencing problems. In contrast, magistrates who use reformatory sentences frequently tend to have a greater capacity to discriminate.

The main conclusion that can be drawn is that the frequent use of both very short and very long institutional sentences is associated with a simpler and more rigid way of dealing with information.

Turning to specific offences, a number of different patterns emerge. While it is generally true that magistrates whose decision-behaviour is characterized by cognitive-complexity tend to rely more heavily on suspended sentence and less heavily on fines and institutions, different patterns emerged with respect to individual offences. The most striking fact which appeared is that there is a tendency for magistrates who often give sentences which depart from the norm to be rather more complex in their thought processes. Thus, the use of both probation and suspended sentence in serious cases is associated with cognitive-complexity. On the other hand, the more frequent use of these sentences in relatively minor cases is associated with cognitive-simplicity. . . .

TABLE 19.2.   CORRELATIONS OF SENTENCING BEHAVIOUR AGAINST COGNITIVE- COMPLEXITY VARIABLES ($N = 50$ MAGISTRATES)

Sentencing Behaviour	Cognitive-Complexity Variables		
	Discrim-ination	Size of information space	Effort
All indictable			
Suspended sentence with probation	0.310	–	0.278
Suspended sentence without probation	0.453	–	–
Suspended sentence combined	0.643	0.335	–
Fine	−0.57	–	–
Institution	–	−0.287	–
Average gaol sentence (days)	−0.509	−0.332	–
Average reformatory (days)	–	–	–
Average penitentiary (days)	–	–	0.284
Average all institutions (days)	−0.257	−0.515	0.239
Gaol: percentage of total disposition	–	–	–
Less than 6 months	–	–	−0.316
More than 6, less than 24 months	−0.303	–	–
Total gaol	–	–	–
Reformatory: percentage of total disposition	–	–	–
Less than 12 months	0.327	–	–
More than 12, less than 24 months	0.332	–	–
Total reformatory	0.382	–	–
Total penitentiary: percentage of total disposition	–	−0.383	–
Gaol: percentage within all institutions	–	–	–
Less than 6 months	–	–	−0.241
More than 6, less than 24 months	−0.377	–	–
Total gaol	−0.327	–	–
Reformatory: percentage within all institutions	–	–	–
Less than 12 months	0.320	–	–
More than 12, less than 24 months	0.321	0.264	–
Total reformatory	0.381	–	–
Total penitentiary: percentage within all institutions	–	−0.438	–

20

Magistrates' World Views and Sentencing Behaviour

JOHN HOGARTH

[EDITORS' NOTE: Readers not familiar with Hogarth's study should refer to the Editors' Note preceding Chapter 19.]

The approach taken differs in several respects from classical research orientations in this area, all of which assume that the only significant variables affecting sentencing are those externally visible "facts" available from judicial records. This is the familiar stimulus-response or input-output model of behaviour in which the facts of the case comprise the stimulus or input and the sentencing decision the output or response. It should also be noted that this approach is consistent with the traditional legal view of the process which makes the assumption that the only "legally significant" variables governing judicial decisions, within a given legal framework, are differences in the factual makeup of the cases, the law being a constant and the personality of the judge being legally irrelevant. The black box or legal model is schematically presented in Figure 20.1.

The point of departure in this study is in its attempt to show how magistrates interpret their factual, legal, and social environments. . . . Magistrates tend to interpret their environments differently, depending on their personal values and subjective ends. In a variety of ways . . . the decision-making process in sentencing is not a neutral or mechanical one. It is highly charged affectively and motivationally. It is not neutral because it relates to matters touching on each magistrate's values, sentiments and commitments;

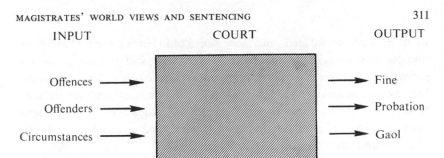

Figure 20.1 Black Box Model

in short, the very material out of which his self-identity is composed. The centre of the social space of a magistrate, therefore, is seen as his concept of self, expressed in his attitudes.

As Murphy (1947) observes: "Whatever the self is, it becomes a centre, an anchorage point, a standard of comparison, an ultimate real. Inevitably it takes its place as the supreme value."

The concept of self as the centre of the social space of the magistrate leads to these propositions: (1) the development of relationships to judicial task that are consistent and enduring, including sets of attitudes which define their relationships to that task, is an integral aspect of the development of a judicial self concept; (2) there is a tendency for magistrates to maintain adequate self-images in their perceptions and responses to the objects and persons they define as being significant; and (3) self is a valued object and is protected and enhanced in the face of influences which are perceived as tending to destroy or minimize it. . . .

Considerable mental energy is expended by magistrates in protecting their self-concepts from all threatening influences. . . . Magistrates interpret the law, the expectations of others, and the facts of the cases in selective ways which maximize concordance with their concept of self. The medium through which the world is selectively perceived (and the self-concept protected) are the attitudes of magistrates. Attitudes were studied as information-processing structures and it was shown that these attitudes were closely associated with all aspects of the sentencing process. The end result is a remarkably high level of internal consistency between magistrates' perceptions of the world and their behaviour on the bench.

The model which emerges from the analysis is one that sees sentencing as a dynamic process in which the facts of the cases, the constraints arising out of the law and the social system and other features of the external world are interpreted, assimilated, and made sense of in ways compatible with the attitudes of the magistrate concerned. In the process of judgement, the objective, external world is transformed into a subjective, definitional world. The results are sentencing decisions which are consistent with magistrates' definitions of the situations facing them. Relationships between the external world, magistrates' interpretation of that world, and their behaviour on the bench is presented schematically in Figure 20.2.

It would be interesting to compare the above model with one that ignored the conscious definitions, intentions, and purposes of magistrates, concentrating on "objectively" defined facts concerning the cases and situations faced by magistrates, i.e., a black box model. Data for such a comparison have been collected, and the findings will be described immediately below.

Two Models of Sentencing

THE BLACK BOX MODEL

The first step in testing the black box model was to collect as much information as possible concerning the facts of the cases (the input or stimulus) coming before the court. In choosing variables the research was guided by findings in previous studies, particularly those of Green (1961) and Hood (1962), which showed statistical relationships between certain fact patterns and sentencing decisions. We also added additional variables in the hope that they might add to the predictive power of the model. These additional variables were not available to previous researchers, and it was felt that a fair test of the black box model would require a more complete analysis of the differences in fact patterns of cases appearing before the courts. The following list of twelve variables were eventually included:

1. The severity of the crime is measured by the Sellin-Wolfgang severity scale.
2. The type of victim categorized as (a) a private person, (b) a private business or corporation, (c) a government agency or department, and (d) the public at large.
3. The sex of the victim.

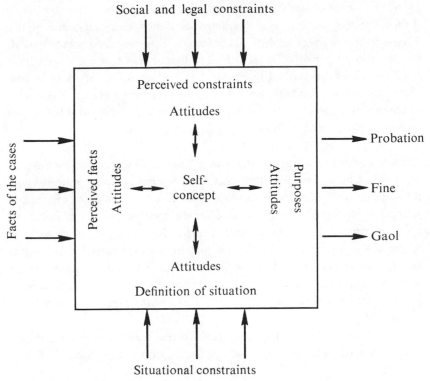

Figure 20.2 A Model of Sentencing Behavior

4. The offender's relationship to the victim, classified as: related by marriage, known to victim, and unknown to victim.

5. Number of separate counts or charges.

6. The plea.

7. The age of the offender.

8. The sex of the offender.

9. The marital status of the offender.

10. The occupation of the offender.

11. The length of the offender's criminal record.

12. The recency of the offender's previous conviction.

Variables were created representing each of these factors, and analyses were performed to determine the relationship of these factors, both individually and collectively, to the sentencing behaviour of the courts.

The first set of analyses concerned the relationship between objectively defined facts of the case and the choice of sentence, in qualitative terms. The purpose was to reveal the extent to which different fact combinations affect the type of penalty. The statistical technique was multiple discriminant function analysis, described in chapter 19. The second set of analyses concerned the relationship between objectively defined variables and the lengths or amount of sentence given in quantitative terms. The statistical techniques included correlational analysis and multiple regression.

Relationship between Fact Patterns and Type of Sentence   Discriminant function analysis revealed that there were statistically significant relationships between fact patterns in individual cases and the types of sentence selected by the court. This held true for the total population of indictable cases for which magistrates completed sentencing study sheets and for each of the seven individual offences. The pattern which emerged was roughly similar with respect to each offence studied, and the detailed findings of the analyses are summarized in Technical Appendix 13 [Ed. note: Not included in this excerpt]. A summary of the findings with respect to all offences (combined) is included below.

On a sample of approximately 1,500 cases, the computer program extracted three discriminant functions, the first two accounting for over 90 per-

TABLE 20.1. RANKED CORRELATIONS BETWEEN OBJECTIVELY DEFINED VARIABLES AND DISCRIMINANT FUNCTION 1

Rank Order	Original Variable	Correlation Coefficients
1.	length of criminal record	0.85
2.	recency of previous conviction	0.80
3.	type of victim	0.24
4.	occupation score	−0.24
5.	number of counts	0.22
6.	age	0.14
7.	sex of offender	−0.14
8.	relationship to victim	0.09
9.	severity score	0.09
10.	plea	−0.06
11.	marital status	−0.05
12.	sex of victim	0.03

cent of the explained variance. The probability that these functions could have occurred solely by chance was less than one in a thousand. From this it was concluded that among various fact patterns in the cases, two underlying factors relate to the choice of sentence selected by the court.

In order to determine what these factors are, an examination was made of the loadings of each original variable on each of the discriminant functions. Tables 20.1 and 20.2 contain such loadings, ranked in order of significance.

Original variables with high loadings on discriminant function 1 include: length of criminal record, recency of previous conviction, type of victim, occupation of offender, and number of counts, in that order. This function appears to measure the criminality of the offender as expressed by the nature of his crime and his previous criminal activity.

Original variables with high loading on discriminant function 2 include: the plea of the offender, the age of the offender, the sex of the victim, the offender's relationship to the victim, the number of counts, the marital status of the offender, and the severity of the crime. This discriminant function appears to measure the culpability of the offender in the particular offence charged. It would appear, therefore, that the choice of sentence among alternatives available is influenced by (1) whether or not the background and history of the offender reveal a pattern of criminality, and (2) whether the

TABLE 20.2. RANKED CORRELATIONS BETWEEN OBJECTIVELY DEFINED VARIABLES AND DISCRIMINANT FUNCTION 2

Rank Order	Original Variables	Correlation Coefficients
1.	plea	0.76
2.	age	0.67
3.	sex of victim	0.35
4.	relationship to victim	−0.28
5.	number of counts	−0.27
6.	marital status score	0.27
7.	severity score	0.23
8.	type of victim	−0.08
9.	occupation score	0.06
10.	sex of offender	0.03
11.	recency of previous conviction	−0.02
12.	length of criminal record	0.00

facts surrounding the commission of the offence suggest a high level of culpability or moral blameworthiness on the part of the offender.

The analyses then turned to an examination of the degree to which the
original variables discriminated among the four types of sentence selected.
Dealing first with overall discrimination, it appeared that the length of the
criminal record was the most important factor influencing a court in the
choice of sentence. The second was the recency of the last conviction. The
third was the age of the offender, followed by the type of victim and the severity of the crime as measured by the Sellin-Wolfgang Scale.

Now let us turn to the way in which the two general functions discriminate among sentences selected. Table 20.3 contains loadings on discriminant
functions 1 and 2 for each type of sentence. A high loading indicates that the
selection of this type of penalty is associated with fact patterns suggesting a
history of criminality or a high level of culpability in the commission of the
offence, as the case may be.

The results showed that the selection of institutional sentences was associated with fact patterns which revealed both a background of previous
criminality and a high level of culpability in the commission of the offence.
The selection of fines was associated with backgrounds which revealed no
previous pattern of criminality but at the same time a high level of culpability of the offender in the present offence. The selection of suspended
sentence with and without probation was linked to no previous history of
criminality and low culpability in the present offence. A similar pattern
emerged with each individual offence studied, and a full description of the

TABLE 20.3.   DISCRIMINANT FUNCTION LOADINGS ON TYPES OF SENTENCE

	Centroids	
Type of Sentence	Previous criminality	Culpability
	1	2
Institution (1,393 cases)	3.75	5.33
Fine (533 cases)	2.67	6.15
Suspended sentence (204 cases)	2.60	3.50
Probation (775 cases)	2.44	4.92

analyses is included in Technical Appendix 13 [Ed. note: Not included in this excerpt].

These data suggested that in the selection of sentences among alternatives available, fact patterns in the cases are significant, at least in a statistical sense. It remains to be determined whether or not these "objectively defined" facts are more powerful predictors of sentencing than the facts of the cases as perceived by magistrates. It was not possible to compare the predictive power of the two kinds of variables to predict choice of sentence in qualitative terms, as the statistical techniques used would not allow for such a comparison. All that can be said is that both classes of variables are closely enough associated to the decisions of the courts to make highly remote the possibility of such associations being due solely to chance. When we turn, however, to predicting the length or amount of sentence in quantitative terms, an adequate test of strength between the two models becomes possible. The next section will deal with this.

Relationship between Objectively Defined Facts and Lengths of Sentence Imposed   The analyses began with simple correlations between the twelve objectively defined variables and the lengths of sentence imposed for each of the seven indictable cases examined. It was immediately discovered that the correlations between these variables and length of sentence (in days) were, in all instances, either nonsignificant or very low. Dealing with all offences (combined), only two variables were statistically at the .05 level. These were severity of the crime and the length of the criminal record. The size of these correlation coefficients were 0.201 and 0.231, respectively. None of the other variables was significantly associated with the length of sentence imposed. Turning to individual cases, in no instance were more than three variables significantly associated with the length of sentence imposed and in no case did the correlations exceed 0.4. Individual correlation coefficients for each offence are included in Technical Appendix 13 [Ed. note: not included]. Table 20.4 shows the correlations between lengths of institutional sentences and these variables for the total sample of cases studied.

The following conclusions may be drawn. Correlational analysis indicates that the facts most closely associated with length of sentence are the length of criminal record and the severity of the crime. Occasionally the age of the offender, his occupation, and the number of counts in the indictment

TABLE 20.4.   CORRELATIONS OF LENGTHS OF INSTITUTIONAL SENTENCE WITH OBJECTIVE VARIABLES

Number of Cases = 771	Correlation Coefficient
Occupational variable	−0.033
Marital status	−0.028
Age	0.089
Sex	−0.052
Plea	−0.066
Number of counts	0.100
Sex of victim score	0.088
Relationship to victim	0.071
Type of victim	0.142
Severity	0.201
Recency of previous conviction	0.050
Length of criminal record	0.231

were associated with the length of the sentence imposed. However, none of these variables accounts for very much of the variation in lengths of sentence imposed and in no case did the contribution of any one variable exceed 6 percent.

Turning to regression analysis, we sought to determine the combined predictive power of these variables. Regression equations were calculated for all offences (combined) and for each of the seven indictable offences concerned. The computer program selected the best combination of variables and weighted them to maximize their predictive power. The results indicated that in no case was the computer program able to develop an equation that could account for more than 20 percent of the total variation in length of sentence imposed. Individual correlation coefficients of the resulting equations ranged from a low of 0.17 in cases of taking a motor vehicle without consent, to a high of 0.485 in cases of breaking and entering, with an average correlation of approximately 0.3. On average, the facts of the cases account for 9 percent of the variation in practice. This means that while these facts bear some relationship to the decisions of the court they do not account for very much of the total variation in sentencing practice. Using tests of significance one may be tempted to conclude that one has "explained" sentencing through an exhaustive analysis of the facts before the court. However, in using measures of association it must be concluded that this type of analysis gives only a partial and inadequate explanation of the processes involved. Let us compare the predictive and explanatory power of the black box model to that of the phenomenological model upon which the bulk of our research was based.

THE PHENOMENOLOGICAL MODEL

We have already seen that correlations between the facts of the cases as perceived and understood by the judge and their sentencing behaviour on the bench yielded correlation coefficients ranging from a low of 0.638 to a high of 0.834 with an average of 0.716. This means that about 50 percent of the total variation in length of institutional sentence imposed could be accounted for by variations among magistrates in their perceptions of the facts of the cases. It can therefore be concluded that analysis based on "facts" as perceived and understood by judges is five or six times more powerful in the predictive sense than analysis based on "facts" as defined by the researcher himself. Of course, it may be expected that both classes of variables make an independent contribution to these decisions and that better prediction could be achieved by combining them. This was done, and it was learned that, in most instances, the size of correlation coefficients were not significantly increased, while in a few a marginal improvement was achieved. From this it was concluded that once one knows how a magistrate defines the case before him, it becomes unnecessary to seek additional information about that case. In fact, it appears from the analysis that one can explain more about sentencing by knowing a few things about the judge than by knowing a great deal about the facts of the case. . . .

Sentencing is not a rational, mechanical process. It is a human process and is subject to all the frailties of the human mind.

References

Campbell, J. 1967. "Studies in Attitude Formation." In M. Sherif (ed.), *Attitude, Ego-Involvement, and Change*. New York: Wiley.

Green, E. 1961. *Judicial Attitudes in Sentencing*. London: Macmillan.

Hood, R. 1962. *Sentencing in Magistrates' Courts*. London: Stevens.

Mead. G. 1934. *Mind, Self, and Society*. Chicago: University of Chicago Press.

Murphy, G. 1947. *Personality*. New York: Harper.

Rose, A. 1961. *Human Behavior and Social Processes: An Interactionist Approach*. New York: Houghton Mifflin.

Rosenberg, H. 1957. "Psychological Selectivity in Self-Esteem Formation." In M. Sherif (ed.), *Attitude, Ego-Involvement and Change*. New York: Wiley.

Wylie, R. 1961. *The Self Concept*. Lincoln: University of Nebraska Press.

21

Perception, Optimism, and Accuracy in Correctional Decision-Making

JOSEPH W. ROGERS
AND NORMAN S. HAYNER

"If men define situations as real, they are real in their consequences." Such was the theorem set forth by W. I. Thomas. As Merton (1957: 421) emphasizes, this theorem "provides an unceasing reminder that men respond not only to the objective features of a situation, but also, and at times primarily, to the meaning this situation has for them." Whereas previous researches have emphasized the relation between various facts about the offender and his success or failure on parole, in this paper we are stressing the importance of the *perception* by correctional decision-makers concerning this relationship. Regardless of the results of empirical research, the treatment of an offender is affected by any *imagined* relationship between a given parole prediction item and the probable success or failure of the offender on parole.

One of the authors (Hayner, 1958) has indicated in an earlier article that under the influence of several strongly established attitudes, parole board members are reluctant to make use of experience tables growing out of success and failure studies. Like all human beings, correctional personnel are products of distinctive personal and social backgrounds, and tend to structure situations and establish norms. Although specific parole board members, judges, or police chiefs vary in the extent to which they have insight regarding the criteria that influence them in reaching the decisions they make about offenders, we are assuming here that some response is made to various items in the criminal's record at all points in the correctional sequence.

As one aspect of a larger study (Rogers), our respondents were asked to assess "the relative merit or worth" of twenty items for predicting a man's success on parole. The respondents consisted of incumbents in ten correctional occupations with a total N of 415. They were asked to rate each item on a seven-point scale ranging from "very favorable to parole success" to "very unfavorable." Table 21.1 shows the identity of these items, the identity and sample size of each correctional group participating in the research, the rank-order of success favorability assigned to each item by the respective position incumbents, and (in the last column) overall mean ratings for each item. The higher the rank (i.e, rank 1 is high; rank 20 is low), the more favorable the item is thought to be and the more optimistic of success is the rating group.

The rankings and mean values of Table 21.1 reflect the degree of optimism with which a particular item is held for parole success as that item is extracted from the offender background. For example, our representatives of the correctional world are most optimistic about an offender who had "a good work record prior to imprisonment" or who is the receiver of "active interest by his family during imprisonment." In contrast they are most pessimistic about the success chances of a parolee who possesses a "long juvenile delinquency record" or "a history of frequent intoxication." As we shall show in a later table, these ratings at the two extremes are supported by evidence from empirical research. The comparative ordering within each group may be inspected easily. For instance, it will be seen that the correctional treatment staff ratings result in a lower, i.e., less optimistic, ranking of the family-interest item than that of the parolee's being a "first-time felony offender." Police chiefs, on the other hand, seem especially optimistic about inmates who make "constructive use of prison time."

The principal focus of this paper is on the congruency of respondent perceptions with the research evidence connecting certain prediction items to

TABLE 21.1. RANK-ORDER OF PAROLE PREDICTION ITEMS ACCORDING TO MEAN RATINGS BY EACH SELECTED GROUP [a]

Parole Prediction Items [b]	Corr. Inst. Staff Custody (N = 92)	Corr. Inst. Staff Treat- ment (N = 19)	Corr. Inst. Staff Other (N = 25)	Parole Board Mem- bers (N = 14)	Prob. and Parole Staff (N = 56)	Prose- cuting At- torneys (N = 19)
Good work record prior to imprisonment	3	1	3	3	1	3
Active interest by family during imprisonment	2	5	4	1	2	2
First-time felony offender	1	2	1	4	3	1
Constructive use of prison time	4	3	2	2	5	4
Committed for homicide	5	4	5	5	4	6
Committed crime alone	7	6	10	6	7	5
More than 2 yrs. imprison- ment	9	9	9	7	6	10
Negro	6	11.5	6	9	10	11
Divorced from spouse	8	7	7	11.5	11	8
Parents divorced	12	9	8	11.5	8	9
Committed for burglary	10	13.5	11	8	14	12
Left parental home at an early age	11	11.5	12	10	13	13
Committed crime with 3 or more associates	16	15	13	14	12	7
Committed for armed robbery	14	16	15	15	16	17.5
Committed for forgery	13	18	14	19.5	19	16
Inadequate job on parole	15	17	17	17	17	14
Committed for forcible rape	19	13.5	19	13	15	17.5
Committed for other sex offense	20	9	20	16	9	15
Long juvenile delinquency record	18	19	18	18	18	20
History of frequent intoxication	17	20	16	19.5	20	19

[a] Ranks range from *1* to *20* reading vertically. Conventional procedures were used for tied ranks.

[b] The items are presented here in the order based upon *all* respondents with the favorable items at the top and the unfavorable at the bottom.

TABLE 21.1 (*continued*). RANK-ORDER OF PAROLE PREDICTION ITEMS ACCORD-
ING TO MEAN RATINGS BY EACH SELECTED GROUP

Parole Prediction Items	Law-Enforcement Officers (N = 113)	Police Chiefs (N = 19)	Superior Court Judges (N = 44)	Citizens Council (N = 14)	Prof. Resp. Total (N = 415)	Over-all Item Means [c]
Good work record prior to imprisonment	1	3	1	2.5	1	1.96
Active interest by family during imprisonment	2	4	3	1	2	2.02
First-time felony offender	4	2	4	4	3	2.18
Constructive use of prison time	3	1	2	2.5	4	2.29
Committed for homicide	12	5	5	5	5	3.42
Committed crime alone	7	7	6	8	6	3.76
More than 2 yrs. imprisonment	8	9.5	9.5	9	7	3.94
Negro	9	11	9.5	11.5	8	3.96
Divorced from spouse	6	9.5	11	13	9.5	4.00
Parents divorced	5	8	13	6	9.5	4.00
Committed for burglary	11	6	7	7	11	4.20
Left parental home at an early age	10	12	12	10	12	4.28
Committed crime with 3 or more associates	13	17	8	14.5	13	4.75
Committed for armed robbery	14	13	16	14.5	14	4.91
Committed for forgery	15	14.5	19	11.5	15	5.13
Inadequate job on parole	16	14.5	17	18.5	16	5.23
Committed for forcible rape	19	16	15	16.5	17	5.36
Committed for other sex offense	20	18	14	16.5	18	5.38
Long juvenile delinquency record	17.5	19	18	18.5	19	5.66
History of frequent intoxication	17.5	20	20	20	20	5.77

[c] These means are based upon seven-point scales and were computed with nonrespondents omitted.

parole success. Such congruency will be referred to as "perceptual accuracy."[1] Fortunately for the task of determining accuracy, clear and comparable empirical findings were available on eleven of our twenty items from three parole prediction studies within the state of Washington.[2]

Since average favorableness in the rating of a prediction-item by the incumbents of a position fails to reveal the extent of accuracy, three-way tables were prepared for each of the eleven items. Utilizing the method partially illustrated by Table 21.2, positional accuracy measures were obtained. This table shows the percentage of Parole Board and Citizens Council members who rated commitment for forgery as favorable, not significantly related (i.e., relatively neutral), or unfavorable to parole success. This particular item was gauged as *unfavorable* to parole success since all three of

TABLE 21.2 PERCENTAGE OF PAROLE BOARD AND CITIZENS COUNCIL MEMBERS RATING COMMITMENT FOR FORGERY CORRECTLY AND INCORRECTLY AS DETERMINED BY EMPIRICAL FINDINGS

Respondents' Rating [a]	Correct Ratings	Incorrect Ratings
Favorable:		
1 and 2		7
		14
Relatively neutral:		
3, 4, and 5		21
		57
Unfavorable:		
6 and 7	71	
	21	

[a] Parole Board percentages are above; Citizens Council percentages below. Seven percent of the latter group did not rate this item.

[1] It is important to be clear on the meaning here. Respondents were not asked whether they knew of the research connections nor were they asked if they agreed with such results. The perceptual focus was on the linkage itself between the predictive item, e.g., forgery commitment, and parole success.

[2] These consisted of Clarence Schrag's two unpublished 1954 studies, one dealing with parolees from the penitentiary, one with parolees from the reformatory. (We are indebted to Dr. Schrag for permission to use his data.) The third, entitled *Adult Parole Study* (1960) was conducted by the Section of Research and Program Analysis, Washington State Department of Institutions in cooperation with the State Board of Prison Terms and Paroles. A. R. Little was at that time supervisor of research for the Board.

the empirical studies mentioned above agree on this point. The first of the Schrag series at the Washington State Penitentiary which followed through on 527 parolees (in Washington State 99 percent of the inmates are released on parole) had an overall average violation rate of 42.7; the forgers, a rate of 64.5. The first of the Schrag series at Washington State Reformatory, checking on 688 cases, showed an overall average violation rate of 41.4; the forgers, 58.5.[3] The *Adult Parole Study* followed 1,731 parolees, reporting an overall average violation rate of 38 percent while that of the forgers alone was 50 percent. As a criterion for item classification, the decision was made to let a deviation of 5 percent from the overall average violation rate determine the category. Using this criterion, commitment for forgery is clearly classified as unfavorable.[4] Table 21.2 shows that 71 percent of the Parole Board members compared with 21 percent of the Citizens Council members were correct in their ratings.[5]

Table 21.3 presents the perceptual accuracy ratings for each respondent position for the eleven items in terms of the method outlined above. A composite index is also shown providing a somewhat crude measure of overall

---

[3] In the Schrag research, the parolees were followed for a period of two years, with a "pink" violation report in the file constituting a violation although the offender was not in all cases returned to prison. In the *Adult Parole Study,* which followed parolees released during the period July 1957 through June 1959, three types of violation (between time of release from prison and December 31, 1959) were counted: absconding, i.e. parolee's whereabouts unknown (47.4 percent); technical, i.e., in custody for a technical violation of parole conditions or charged with a misdemeanor (18.4 percent); and commission of a felony, i.e., in custody charged with a new serious crime (34.2 percent).

[4] In other words:

Study	Average Viol. Rate	Forgers Viol. Rate	Difference	>5%?
Schrag penitentiary	42.7	64.5	+21.8	yes
Schrag reformatory	41.4	58.5	+17.1	yes
Adult parole study	38.0	50.0	+12.0	yes

Since all three studies agree in showing forgers to have a failure rate in excess of the criterion of 5 percent from the overall averages of the respective studies, the item is classified as *unfavorable*.

[5] Correctness of response was determined by dividing the items which were constructed on a seven-point basis into favorable, neutral, and unfavorable, which are common points of reference in parole-prediction studies. The occupational positions were then rated on the basis of the percentage of positional incumbents correctly rating each item. Finally an index score of average percentage accuracy was obtained for each position.

accuracy. Utilizing the null hypothesis of no interpositional differences, chi-square tests of significance were computed and are reported in the right margin of Table 21.3. In brief, these tests indicate significant distinctions in perceptual accuracy by position at the 5-percent level or better on seven items. No significant differences occurred in the evaluation of the two items dealing with frequent intoxication or with a long delinquency record.[6]

A Set of Concepts and a Rationale for Exploring the Correlates of Perceptual Accuracy

Persons occupying various positions in a social system are expected by others to behave in certain ways, and they define for themselves certain appropriate ways of behaving. In short, they have roles to perform. Within the correctional system the roles are presumably defined largely in professional terms. The incumbents of the various positions are expected to deal with one another and with their central object of mutual concern, the criminal offender, on a knowledgeable and objective basis. Arrest, prosecution, trial, incarceration, or parole are not matters of personal whim to be treated frivolously or subjectively. It is to be anticipated that serious errors of justice, sanction, and treatment will be few since they involve such core values as human life, liberty, and welfare. However, correctional persons, no matter how dedicated to professional standards or how well trained, do not possess a sure body of knowledge for executing their tasks. It is no indictment of dedicated personnel to assert that errors are made in job performance throughout the correctional continuum.

The characteristics of the offender are of interest to most correctional personnel. Some of these are more visible, of course, than others. The status of Negro, for instance, would be more obvious than the status of murderer. Yet, if the latter is known it may take on more saliency for the observer than the former. Such an ideal is hardly to be achieved in any full sense. In a

[6] By reason of inadequate expected cell frequencies, the chi-square test was inappropriate for the two items pertaining to sex offenders. As to those which disclosed significant differences, careful inspection of Table 21.3 should disclose the sources contributing to the chi-square formula. For example, on the forgery commitment item, the Parole Board, the parole staff, and the superior court judge positions contribute to the accuracy side of the formula, while the institutional custody position and that of the Citizens Council contribute to the inaccuracy side.

TABLE 21.3.   PERCENTAGE OF ACCURACY FOR EACH RESPONDENT POSITION ON

		Respondent Positions				
Parole Prediction Items		*Superior Court Judges* (N = 44)	*Parole Board* (N = 14)	*Prosecuting Attorneys* (N = 19)	*Parole Staff* (N = 56)	*Corr. Inst. Staff Other* (N = 25)
Good work record prior to imprisonment (1) (2)	F	98	86	79	70	84
Negro (1) (2) (3)	NS	89	71	94	87	56
Active interest by family during imprisonment (2)	F	84	86	79	64	76
First-time felony offender (1) (2) (3)	F	70	71	79	48	76
History of frequent intoxication (1) (2) (3) b	U	64	64	79	79	60
Constructive use of prison time (1) (2)	F	84	71	63	48	80
Long juvenile delinquency record (1) (2)	U	63	57	84	62	52
Commitment for forgery (1) (2) (3)	U	64	71	58	70	32
Commitment for homicide	F	34	71	11	57	60
Commitment for other sex offenses (1) (2) (3)	F	4	0	0	14	0
Commitment for forcible rape (3)	F	5	7	0	14	0
Average percentage of accuracy		59.9	59.5	56.9	55.7	52.4

[a] Arranged from highest to lowest percentage of accuracy.
[b] "Excessive drinkers" only 4 percent (instead of 5) above average violation rate in Adult Parole Study.
[c] Chi-square inappropriate.
F = Favorable as a predictive item
NS = Not significant
U = Unfavorable

ELEVEN PAROLE PREDICTION ITEMS AS DETERMINED BY EMPIRICAL FINDINGS [a]

			Respondent Positions			
Citizens Council ($N = 14$)	Corr. Inst. Staff Trtmt. ($N = 19$)	Corr. Inst. Staff Custody ($N = 92$)	Law Enf. Officers ($N = 113$)	Police Chiefs ($N = 19$)	Prof. Resp. Total ($N = 415$)	Chi-Square $p <$
86	74	76	71	68	77	.05
78	90	65	77	58	76	.001
86	37	82	68	63	73	.01
71	63	80	55	74	66	.01
57	58	55	65	58	64	NS
86	58	58	61	74	64	.01
50	58	63	63	47	62	NS
21	53	29	54	37	49	.001
21	52	38	18	32	36	.001
14	16	4	2	5	5	c
0	5	4	3	5	5	c
51.8	51.3	50.4	48.8	47.4	52.5	

(1) Schrag Washington State Penitentiary Study
(2) Schrag Washington State Reformatory Study
(3) Washington State Adult Parole Study

world of human interaction, of which the correctional system is only a part, men categorize one another in such terms as sex, age, skin color, marital status, and occupation. When a known offender interacts with others, his employment record, his offense, his interpersonal relationships may also serve as classifying bases and be responded to accordingly. Assessments are made and decisions are reached as the offender moves through the correctional sequence.

It is assumed here that certain position characteristics are relevant for better understanding the management of the offender at different stages in his correctional experience.[7] Preparation for some positions, for example, entails a longer period of training than that needed for others. Utilizing three indicators of training, we hypothesize:

1. *The greater the socialization implied by incumbency in an occupational group, the greater will be the perceptual accuracy of position incumbents (in respect to parole prediction items).* Indicators: (a) education, (b) age, (c) position tenure.

Positions within a social system may be assumed to have social status, and as such, possess differential rankings relative to one another. George Homans (1961: 149–150) uses the term to refer to the ''stimuli'' (including the kinds of reward he receives) that a person presents to other persons and to himself. It refers to ''what men perceive about one of their fellows.'' Incumbents of higher status positions would be expected to possess higher morale, perhaps fewer internal conflicts, and possibly to occupy more strategic communication points within the system. This suggests the following hypothesis:

2. *The higher the social status of a position, the greater will be the perceptual accuracy of position incumbents (in respect to parole prediction items).* Indicator: income (occupational).

Position occupancy, of course; involves much more than socialization and status. How one evaluates himself relative to other incumbents of his own or of similar posts may be of parallel import. There has been research

---

[7] It is important to note that throughout this paper the principal unit of analysis is the position rather than the person. This has been referred to as macroscopic analysis, the utility of which has been supported by Gross et al. (1958: 95–115); also see Wagner (1964) and Martindale (1960).

evidence to suggest the relevance of a favorable self-concept to the ability to judge others correctly.[8] Hence, the hypothesis:

3. The more favorable the concept of self characteristic of position incumbents, the greater will be their perceptual accuracy (in respect to parole prediction items). Indicator: self-ranking (occupational).

Just as self-esteem may be relevant to the judgment of others, so may other forms of adjustment. If large numbers of positional occupants are dissatisfied, unhappy, uninterested in their work, it would tend to steer perception toward self-concern rather than concern with others. Conversely we might expect that occupational satisfaction would tend to "free" position incumbents to carry out role performances more effectively.[9] Thus, we hypothesize:

4. The greater the occupational satisfaction of a position, the greater will be the perceptual accuracy of position incumbents (in respect to parole prediction items). Indicator: position satisfaction.

Situational definitions and human perception are hardly limited to being simple functions of demographic characteristics, nor are they likely to be imposed in complete detail by requirements of the system itself. Rather, from a social interactionist point of view, they emerge through interchange of viewpoints, ideas, complaints, aspiration, etc., which leads to the following hypothesis:

5. The greater the breadth of contact which position incumbents have throughout their social system, the greater will be their perceptual accuracy (in respect to parole prediction items). Indicator: contact (throughout correctional system).

Likewise:

[8] Perhaps a number of readers have wondered why we have not made more use of material from research in the realm of interpersonal perception. Actually, much of our thinking has resulted from this literature. But as Secord and Backman (1964: 79) observe: "Unfortunately, the assessment of accuracy has raised such difficult methodological problems that the definitive research necessary to provide conclusive answers to these questions has not yet been carried out. . . ." For good summaries of perception research, we have found the following most helpful: Hare (1962), Newcomb et al. (1965: 155–84), and Bruner and Tagiuri (1954: 634–54).

[9] The research relevant to the above has rendered contradictory results as indicated in the sources cited in the preceding footnote.

6. The greater the amount of contact position incumbents have with the central object of their role (parolees, prison inmates), the greater will be their perceptual accuracy (in respect to parole prediction items). Indicator: contact (inmates and parolees).

Homans (1961: 33–35) sees sentiments as general reinforcers through which rewards or punishments may be rendered. He speaks especially of social approval as a sentiment and "liking" as a form of social approval. Even in the face of professional disagreements, differing role expectations, or opposing commitments (e.g., prosecuting attorneys and defense attorneys; or, captor *vis-à-vis* captive), positive feelings of respect or affection may emerge.[10] The more persons like one another, not only are they apt to spend more time together, but it is plausible to assume they will devote more effort to maintain established friendships—positive relationships; and to understand—to "see" (if not agree to)—the others' point of view (or the basis for that view).[11] Hence the hypothesis:

7. The greater the positive sentiment which incumbents of a given position express for other incumbents in their social system, the greater will be their perceptual accuracy (in respect to parole prediction items). Indicator: liking (throughout correctional system).

Similarly:

8. The greater the amount of positive sentiment position incumbents express for the central object of their role (parolees, prison inmates), the greater will be their perceptual accuracy (in respect to parole prediction items). Indicator: liking (inmates and parolees).

General frames of reference, attitudes, or ways of approaching social phenomena have been of demonstrable relevance in interpersonal perception. A high degree of authoritarianism, for instance, reportedly reduces perceptual accuracy whereas a low degree of authoritarianism tends to enhance it. Newcomb and his associates (1965: 178–179) point to a component of nonauthoritarianism, namely *intraceptiveness* which may provide a clue to

[10] The modern approach to deviancy seems to be one of disapproving the act, not the actor; the deed rather than the doer. This is, of course, an abstraction not always easy to make, yet the history of criminology is filled with accounts of "lovable rogues."

[11] Within the prison community life is not simply a matter of "screws" versus "cons"—the network of relationships is more intricate than this (see Sykes 1958).

these results. Intraceptiveness, they say, is in many ways the opposite of projectiveness, and highly intraceptive persons are "open" to information from others, and thus make themselves accessible to the observations and interpretation of cues that others present. While we do not have a direct equivalent of either authoritarianism or intraceptiveness, our concepts of punitiveness, progressivism, and permissiveness are in a similar vein and probably possess common ingredients. By the concept of *punitiveness* we mean the extent to which a person uses or recommends the use of punishment in response to deviancy. *Progressivism* is defined as the degree of favorability to the acceptance of new ideas, methods, etc., in a given field, in this instance, the field of corrections (Gross et al., 1958: 183–186). Its opposite might be called "traditionalism," which means rejection of the new in favor of retaining the old or "status quo." *Permissiveness* means flexibility in the extent to which conformity to role expectations is demanded. In the therapeutic setting, it can be thought of as social tolerance of deviation. It seeks to maintain the link to institutional structures while expressing disapproval of a person's deviant tendencies or acts (Bredemeier and Stephenson, 1962). Hence, we hypothesize:

9. *The greater the (a) nonpunitiveness, or (b) progressiveness (correctional), or (c) permissiveness characteristic of a position, the greater will be the perceptual accuracy of position incumbents (in respect to parole prediction items).*

In the correctional system, some positions are relatively removed from the commission of criminal acts or from victims. On the other hand the incumbents of some positions are in close proximity to both. It is to be supposed that emotions influence perceptions and attitudes, and that emotions are intensified by viewing a murdered corpse, speaking with a recent rape victim, or being injured by or threatened with an assault. In the performance of his role the rank-and-file police officer is more exposed to such influences than the Parole Board member who is several steps removed.[12] The prose-

---

[12] In our opinion, one must take care to avoid personal value judgements. Our statement must not be construed in terms of "good" and "bad" or "right" and "wrong." Police officers and Parole Board members have different roles. While the policeman may think he is exposed to the reality of the firing line and that the Parole Board member is in an "ivory-tower" of sorts, the Board member may retort that this enables him to be more objective and to calmly take into account "all the facts." Interestingly enough, it is not unusual for police officers to serve on Parole Boards. Among our fourteen Board members, two were former police chiefs. In a recent

cuting attorney and superior court judge are closer than the Board member, while the member of a lay Citizens Council is still further away.[13] It seems reasonable to venture that those who must deal more *directly* and more *immediately* [14] with the consequences of criminal behavior are more apt to suffer perceptual difficulties, and we are thus led to hypothesize:

10. The greater the distance (in terms of the correctional sequence) between a position and the commission of the criminal behavior, the greater will be the perceptual accuracy of position incumbents (in respect to parole prediction items). Indicator: correctional sequence.

Testing the Hypothesized Relationships

The tests of the above hypotheses are presented in Table 21.4, where the positional rank on each variable is shown. As previously stated, our principal dependent variable is perceptual accuracy; a secondary one, optimism.[15] The Spearman rank-order correlation coefficients (*Rho*) which relate accuracy and optimism to fourteen independent indicators (of variables) [16] are given at the base of this table.[17]

---

television interview, former California Governor Pat Brown publicly accounted for his current liberal position on capital punishment in similar terms. He explained that while he was a public prosecutor he was simply too close to the victims of the crime to oppose capital punishment. The position of Governor permitted him distance and perspective ("The Joey Bishop Show," ABC Television Network, May 3, 1967).

[13] The Citizens Council is a group of lay people sponsored by the National Council on Crime and Delinquency.

[14] We are thinking here in terms of both time and location. The parole officer may know many victims and yet the time factor is more apt to shield him than the policeman who sees identical persons, but under different circumstances.

[15] While similar hypotheses to those presented above might have been formulated for the optimism variable, we have not done this formally.

[16] Perhaps it should be reiterated that the rankings of Table 21.4 reflect grouped data and arithmetic means derived from questionnaire responses. Some were single items, others represent indexes. For a full account of methodological concerns including nominal and operational definitions, see Rogers, pp. 36–65.

[17] Using the *conventional* significance test, with ten positions, a Spearman rank correlation coefficient of .564 or above is significant at the .05 level or .746 at the .01 level (one-tailed tests);

Hypothesis One, the socialization hypothesis, is supported on the indicator of education ($+.59$); more modestly so on age ($+.32$). However, job tenure not only failed to receive expected substantiation but, rather, turned out to be negatively correlated ($-.49$) to perceptual accuracy.

Examination of the data reveals that the Parole Board and the parole staff, while among the positions that perceived more accurately, were the two lowest in job tenure. Similar findings have been reported in the literature on interpersonal perception. Renato Tagiuri, in discussing observations by Theodore Newcomb (made in his 1956 address to the American Psychological Association) cogently remarked:

This relative absence of improvement in awareness is surprising and, at first, rather difficult to understand. We developed, however, the following speculative explanation for it. Groups do not start "from scratch" in an absolute sense of the word. A "new" group is new only to the extent that the persons in it are unknown to each other. But these persons have characteristics in common with members of other groups with which most people have had experience. Thus, upon entering into interaction in a new group, the member engages in activities and assumes relationships that are not, strictly speaking, new—no more new than an unfamiliar automobile is to the man who drives it for the first time. Only a small portion of the essential characteristics are "new." So, too, a group settles down in terms of the major formal features quickly and on the basis of foreknowledge (Tagiuri, 1958).

In our study, the positions were in existence prior to the entry of the individual respondents, and represent particular occupational choices. It seems likely that the role expectations, when applied to parole positions, plus the educational backgrounds, help to account for the ability of position incumbents to overcome the presumed handicaps of shorter job tenure.

Hypothesis Two, the social status hypothesis, is supported by a substantial relationship ($+.53$). Naturally, income and education (the latter could also be used as an index of status) are intercorrelated ($+.83$). It is noteworthy, however, that income and education relate differentially to the optimism variable with rank correlation coefficients of $+.20$ and $-.20$, respectively. In brief, while both variables seem to contribute to perceptual

---

see Siegel (1956). However, Herbert Costner points out that in using the conventional test, the magnitude of the *rho* necessary to reject the hypotheses of no correlation is a function only of the number of "items" ranked and is in no way affected by the number of persons who contributed the judgments that are summarized in the ranks nor by the magnitude of the difference in those judgments that lead one item to be ranked higher than another. Since our rankings summarize data for positions (groups), the conventional test tends to *understate* the significance of the correlations.

TABLE 21.4. RANK CORRELATIONS BETWEEN ACCURACY AND OPTIMISM IN UTILIZING TEN POSITIONS [a]

Position	Accuracy	Optimism	Education	Age	Job Tenure	Income	Self-Rank
Judges	1	7	2	2	5	2	3
Parole board	2	3	5	1	10	3	5
Prosecuting attorneys	3	10	1	8	6	4	4
Parole staff	4	8	6	10	9	7	9
Other corr. inst. staff	5	2	9	5	4	9	10
Citizens council	6	1	4	3	2	1	1
Corr. inst. staff tr.	7	5	3	7	8	5	2
Corr. inst. staff cust.	8	6	10	6	7	10	7
Law enf. officers	9	9	8	9	1	8	8
Chiefs of police	10	4	7	4	3	6	6
Acc. Spearman *Rho*	x	−.09	+.59	+.32	−.49	+.53	+.20
Opt. Spearman *Rho*	−.09	x	−.22	+.67	+.09	+.20	+.18

[a] The top rank is *1;* the low, *10.* Thus they are read, for example, as the higher the rank, the higher the average age of position incumbents. With two exceptions, all variables were measured by the arithmetic mean from index scores. Accuracy was measured as indicated in text. Correctional sequence was based on arbitrarily assigned ranks.

accuracy, income seems more conducive than does education to a favorable view of the offenders chances of success on parole.

   Hypotheses Three and Four, which deal with self-ranking and job satis-faction, respectively, are in the predicted directions, but the coefficients are low (*+.20* and *+.16*). Both variables, job satisfaction especially (*+.53*), are associated with parole optimism. It is not unlikely that "the leniency ef-fect" may be operating here. According to Bruner and Tagiuri (1954: 641) this consists of the tendency of respondents to rate others and also himself high in favorable traits and low in unfavorable traits.[18]

   Hypotheses Five and Six, the contact hypotheses, provide interesting results. Interprofessional contact throughout the correctional system varies directly with accuracy (*+.38*) but inversely with optimism (*−.16*); contact with inmates and parolees leads to the reverse: accuracy is negatively as-

[18] This concept is akin to the concept of projection.

THE PERCEPTION OF PAROLE PREDICTION ITEMS AND TEN SELECTED VARIABLES

Job Satisfaction	Overall Contact	Offender Contact	Overall Liking	Offender Liking	Nonpunitiveness	Progressivism	Permissiveness	Correctional Sequence
2	5	9	3	9	6	6	6	4
5	1	3	4	5	4.5	3	4.5	9
6	4	10	1.5	6	3	7	8	3
10	2	1	7	2	1	2	1	8
4	10	6	8	7	7	5	3	6
1	6	8	9	3	4.5	1	4.5	10
9	8	2	6	4	2	4	2	6
8	9	4	10	10	9	8	7	6
7	7	7	5	8	10	10	9	10
3	3	5	1.5	1	8	9	10	2
+.16	+.38	−.20	+.21	−.18	+.53	+.50	+.41	−.36
+.53	−.16	+.18	−.39	+.30	−.05	+.48	+.30	−.58

sociated with offender contact (−.20), but optimism is positively associated (+.18). And *Hypotheses Seven and Eight, dealing with sentiment,* receive similar support. Interprofessional sentiment reveals a positive coefficient (+.21) with accuracy, and a negative coefficient (−.39) with optimism; while sentiment toward the inmate leads to the opposite (accuracy, −.18; optimism, +.30).

These data suggest reformulation of this subset of four hypotheses, especially those involving professional-offender sentiment and contact since only one (interprofessional contact) is clearly supported. The size *and* direction of the above coefficients suggest a strain toward professional objectivity in the face of cross-pressures or perceived cross-pressures emanating from "colleagues" and "clients." Several major studies make this observation plausible. Paul F. Lazarsfeld and his associates (1948) in their voting-behavior research observe the crucial nature of cross-pressures on both re-

duced interest in and delay of voting in election campaigns. Gresham M.
Sykes (1958: 55), in his insightful chapter entitled "The Defects of Total
Power," takes careful note of the "good Joe" pressure and the conflict of
loyalties within a correctional system. Stanton Wheeler (1958), in his detailed study of a correctional institution reports that the most consistent finding concerning role perception and role expectation is that inmate and staff
expectations are perceived to be in greater conflict than they actually are.

Hypothesis Nine, involving three orientations, is supported on each
dimension: (a) nonpunitiveness (+ .53), (b) progressivism (+ .50), and (c)
permissiveness (+ .41).[19] While they are highly intercorrelated with one
another, the fact that they were separately measured on three very different
types of instrument leads to some confidence that a common element (possibly intraceptiveness) is involved and that the above coefficients collectively
possess an added degree of reliability. While punitiveness (− .05) appears to
be independent of optimism, the association of both permissiveness (+ .30)
and progressiveness (+ .48) with optimism is higher. It would be of particular interest to pursue through research the meaning of this latter correlation.
It may possibly mean that the correctional traditionalist is committed to the
status quo since he sees little "hope" for the parolee anyway. This notion
will surely remind many readers of the "self-fulfilling prophecy," about
which Merton (1957: 421–436) has spoken so eloquently.

Hypothesis Ten, the proximity hypothesis, is adequately supported
(− .36), although the stronger relationship is to the optimism variable
(− .58). Indeed, the closer the position to the offense the less the accuracy
and the greater the pessimism.

Summary, Conclusions, and Recommendations

A summary of our data reveals macroscopically that the greater the educational level, age, income, interprofessional contact, and orientations of nonpunitiveness, correctional progressivism and permissiveness characteristic of a
position; and the greater the distance (in terms of the correctional sequence)
between a position and the criminal offense, the greater will be the positional
perceptual accuracy measured in terms of the correct assessment of parole-

[19] Rhos for a and b = + .75; a and c, + .70; b and c, + .83.

prediction-item relationships. On the other hand, position tenure was negatively related to accuracy, while the variables of inmate contact and liking, occupational satisfaction, and interprofessional liking were found to be statistically independent.

Our secondary dependent variable, parole optimism, seems to bear a positive relationship to age, job satisfaction, inmate liking, permissiveness, progressivism, and distance from the offense. With the lone exception of interprofessional liking, which bears a negative association, the remainder of the indicators were not significantly related to optimism about the chances of success for the parolee. Further, our two dependent variables, optimism and accuracy, are statistically unrelated.

Since throughout our focus has been upon an interlocking set of positions utilizing group data, it must be explicitly recognized that the above conclusions are subject to the well-known "ecological fallacy" (Robinson, 1950; Menzel, 1950; Tannenbaum and Bachman, 1964; Gold, 1964; Selvin and Hagstrom, 1964). Thus, it is of paramount import that we make reference to some checks on this liability, although our remarks shall be abbreviated rather than exhaustive.

Concerning the correlates of accuracy, wherein the unit of analysis is the individual in exchange for the position, substantial support was received for the above generalizations, especially those relating to education, income, and correctional sequence.[20] The age indicator which was of modest size macroscopically was clearly nonsignificant microscopically although, nevertheless, in the hypothesized direction. Additional light is cast on the influence of differential contact, for the greatest contribution to accuracy seems to emanate from interaction with parole components and superior court judges; also, consistent with the above, offender contact and sentiment seem to be as detrimental as they are conducive to accuracy. Further, as noted macroscopically, occupational satisfaction and interprofessional contact appear relatively independent of accuracy, although the data "flow" remains consistent with the hypotheses.[21]

[20] The tests utilized for microscopic analysis utilized a combination of gamma coefficients and sign tests. For a more complete description of some of these procedures, see Rogers (forthcoming). In contrast to the present treatment, that article is concerned with items themselves, especially as related to the sociological theories from which the items are derived.

[21] Unfortunately, through a computer programming oversight our comparable data are not available on the orientations-accuracy relationships. More extensive use of these particular items was made in conjunction with a paper by Rogers (1967).

Microscopically, the optimism correlates also reveal a reasonably consistent pattern. Those of job satisfaction, offender liking, offense proximity, and orientation received expected support. Further, those cited above as macroscopically unrelated were microscopically neutral. However, there were two notable modifications. One, involving age, the coefficients of which while in the same direction, were reduced considerably in size. The interprofessional liking variable underwent an actual sign reversal, winding up with small positive coefficients in all four correctional domains (i.e., law enforcement, legal, institutional, and parole). And of course, this type of happening was precisely the concern of Robinson and the thrust of his arguments concerning the ecological fallacy. In this particular instance our attention, though *ad hoc,* is drawn to the probable source of discrepancy. Most of the *Rho* variance can be accounted for by a combination of the prosecutors' position and that of the Citizens Council. The former expressed considerable positive feeling for other system incumbents but were the least optimistic about their clients' parole chances; in contrast, the council is more optimistic as a group than any other, yet comparatively low in their expressed liking of correctional representatives.

Pertinent to the theoretical rationale employed, it seems reasonable to infer that location within a correctional system influences perception. Accordingly patterns of interaction, socialization, status distinctions, and other related concepts point to at least a partial accounting for such linkage. While all of the foregoing must necessitate further research, perhaps of particular interest is the nature of professional-offender interaction and sentiment. Here, these were shown to be less conducive to perceptual accuracy than to optimism about an offender's chances on parole. As such, they bear further intensive scrutiny as they relate not only to these particular dependent variables but to others of relevance in the correctional world.

By way of conclusion, Table 21.5 is offered as a typological device for classifying each position in the correctional system in respect to the two major dependent variables which have been trichotomized. The three most accurate positions, judges, Parole Board members and prosecuting attorneys, have in common a strong norm for possession of an "open mind" and for "seeing both sides." Even the prosecuting attorney, while serving in an adversary relationship to the offender, is by training and by practice required to know defense and is expected to give justice precedence over conviction.

It is of parallel interest to observe the two most optimistic positions. In

TABLE 21.5. A CLASSIFICATION OF TEN POSITIONS BY THEIR COMBINED ACCURACY AND OPTIMISM IN THE PERCEPTION OF PAROLE PREDICTION ITEMS [a]

Optimism in Perception of Parole	Accuracy in Perception of Parole		
	High (1, 2, 3)	Medium (4, 5, 6, 7)	Low (8, 9, 10)
High (1, 2, 3)	parole board (2, 3)	corr. inst. staff other (5, 2); citizens council (6, 1)	
Medium (4, 5, 6, 7)	judges (1, 7)	corr. inst. staff treatment (7, 5)	corr. inst. staff custody (8, 6); police chiefs (10, 4)
Low (8, 9, 10)	prosecuting attorneys (3, 10)	parole staff (4, 8)	law enforcement officers (9, 9)

[a] In the rankings after each respondent, group accuracy is given first and optimism second.

certain respects these are removed from the more intense relationships characterizing the other positions. The Citizens Council and the "other" members of the correctional institution staff which includes clerical persons and work supervisors, probably occupy the most neutral positions with regard to involvement in decisions affecting offenders. In contrast, the three positions least optimistic are those most in the line of fire. When parolees violate, it is the rank-and-file personnel, the law enforcement and parole officers who receive the most immediate and direct impact of failure, and the prosecutors are not far away.

Lastly, the three positions marked as least accurate, police chiefs, law enforcement officers and institutional custody staff, occupy those positions that are most protective in character. Their roles are to arrest and to hold and to do so at some personal risk. Given these roles and their positional location within the correctional system, resultant misperceptions appear both predictable and understandable.[22]

[22] If cells HH and LL of Table 21.5 were considered in terms of ideal polar types and, further, were we to *dichotomize* all of the independent indicators of Table 21.4 in terms of high and low the following contrast emerges: The Parole Board position (managing to be both highly accurate while simultaneously optimistic) is characterized by being *high* on all indicators except one, job tenure. At the other extreme, the law enforcement officer position (inaccurate and pessimistic) is characterized by being *low* on every indicator but two, job tenure and interprofessional liking.

References

Bredemeier, Henry C. and Richard M. Stephenson. 1962. *The Analysis of Social Systems.* New York: Holt, Rinehart, & Winston, pp. 116–74.

Bruner, Jerome S. and Renato Tagiuri. 1954. "The Perception of People." In Gardner Lindzey (ed.), *The Handbook of Social Psychology.* Cambridge, Mass.: Addison-Wesley, Vol. 2.

Gold, David. 1964. "Some Comments on 'The Empirical Classification of Formal Groups,' " *American Sociological Review* 29 (October):736–39.

Gross, Neal, Ward S. Mason, and Alexander W. McEachern. 1958. *Explorations in Role Analysis.* New York: Wiley.

Hare, A. Paul. 1962. *Handbook of Small Group Research.* New York: Free Press of Glencoe, pp. 79–100.

Hayner, Norman S. 1958. "Why Do Parole Boards Lag in the Use of Prediction Scores?" *Pacific Sociological Review* (Fall), pp. 73–76.

Homans, George C. 1961. *Social Behavior: Its Elementary Forms.* New York: Harcourt.

Lazarsfeld, Paul F., Bernard Berelson, and Hazel Gaudet. 1948. *The People's Choice.* New York: Columbia University Press, pp. 60–64.

Martindale, Don. 1960. *The Nature and Types of Sociological Theory.* Boston: Houghton Mifflin, pp. 464–521.

Menzel, Herbert. 1950. "Comment on Robinson's 'Ecological Correlations and the Behavior of Individuals,' " *American Sociological Review* 15 (October):674.

Merton, Robert K. 1957. *Social Theory and Social Structure.* Rev. ed. Glencoe, Ill.: Free Press.

Newcomb, Theodore M., Ralph H. Turner, and Philip E. Converse. 1965. *Social Psychology: The Study of Human Interaction.* New York: Holt, Rinehart & Winston.

Robinson, W. S. 1950. "Ecological Correlations and the Behavior of Individuals," *American Sociological Review* 15 (June):351–57.

Rogers, Joseph W. 1967. "Correctional Progressivism: A Study of Liberals and Traditionalists within the Correctional Realm." Paper given at the annual meeting of the American Sociological Association, San Francisco.

"The Parole Board: An Analysis of Role within the Correctional Setting." Ph.D. dissertation, University of Washington.

"Parole Prediction in Three Dimensions: Theory, Prediction and Perception," *Sociology and Social Research*. Forthcoming.

Secord, Paul F. and Carl W. Backman. 1964. *Social Psychology*. New York: McGraw-Hill, p. 79.

Selvin, Hanan C. and Warren O. Hagstrom. 1964. "Reply to Gold," *American Sociological Review* 29 (October):739.

Siegel, Sidney. 1956. *Nonparametric Statistics for the Behavioral Sciences*. New York: McGraw-Hill, p. 284.

Sykes, Gresham M. 1958. *The Society of Captives*. Princeton: Princeton University Press.

Tagiuri, Renato. 1958. "Social Preference and Its Perception." In Renato Tagiuri and Luigi Petrullo (eds.), *Person Perception and Interpersonal Behavior*. Stanford: Stanford University Press, p. 326.

Tannenbaum, Arnold S. and Jerald Bachman. 1964. "Structural versus Individual Effects," *American Journal of Sociology* 69 (May):571–84.

Wagner, Helmut. 1964. "Displacement of Scope: A Problem of the Relationship Between Small-Scale and Larger-Scale Sociological Theories," *American Journal of Sociology* 69 (May):571–84.

PART THREE:

Labeling:
Secondary
Criminogenic
Perception

Although the labeling perspective is not new to sociology, it has in recent years generated a great deal of sociological analysis. The relevance of the perceptual dimension to the labeling perspective would appear to be obvious. Whether we discuss the labeling of self, of others, or of acts, using positive or negative labels, we at least tacitly assume that the perception of the labeler and of the "labeled"—as well as that of third parties—is an important component of the analysis.[1] It is perception that leads to the invocation of the criminal justice process and to all the concomitant consequences of labeling.

[1] See the introduction to Part Two for a discussion of the labeling of acts.

Discussions of the perceptual aspects of labeling have so far been surprisingly limited. We suspect that to some extent this situation is a result of the historical development of the theory itself. Criminological theories have most often been associated with one name (Merton with anomie, Sutherland with differential association, Sellin with culture conflict), while labeling has evolved through the work of numerous theorists. The sociologist has been faced with statements by many authors, each with its own special nuances, and this has made dealing with the theory a somewhat more difficult task. Given labeling's early developmental history and the numerous avenues it has opened to exploration, it is perhaps not surprising that the perceptual dimension has been somewhat neglected. But beginning with Scheff (1966), attempts have been made to place the perspective into a systematic framework (e.g., Schur, 1969, 1971), and we also now have available sophisticated critiques of the theory (Gibbs, 1966; Glaser, 1971; Mankoff, 1971, among others).[2] It is interesting that studies of stereotyping—the older tradition from which labeling theory draws so much, at least implicitly—have been quite aware of their links with the perception of persons in social psychology.

Even though the word itself rarely appears in discussions, the notion of perception is ubiquitous in the labeling framework. In fact, as we noted in the general Introduction, it plays a dual role, appearing first in the initial application of the label and then again in the subsequent change of self-image. And we might have added yet a third occasion: the perception of the "product" by the community.

W. I. Thomas' classical dictum—"if men define situations as real, they are real in their consequences"—lays the foundation for a discussion of the linkage of labeling and perception. In the beginning it is perception on the part of the public or the police that leads first to the labeling of individuals as deviant or criminal. Often, the objective reality of a situation may become manifest too late to overcome the effects of labeling. Even if a trial finds an individual innocent, and even if, speaking objectively, he did not commit the offense, much harm may be done by the arrest, pretrial confinement, and the judicial procedure itself, and it may be irreversible. (The best discussion of these "early" components of the labeling process is found in Matza, 1969.) Hence, to repeat, it is perception on the part of the public or the police that precipitates the process.

---

[2] Scheff's work is, unfortunately, outside of criminological concerns, but it represents what may be the clearest introduction to the labeling point of view.

Perception also plays a part in the development of a new self-label by the deviant. An individual who feels that he has been labeled, that society (or at least the offended majority) will henceforth react to him negatively regardless of his subsequent behavior, may begin to internalize the components of the role that parallels the stereotype and move from primary to secondary deviance. Typically, of course, he is also welcomed by new associates as well as rejected, and this exerts a considerable influence upon a person already in a highly anxious state. Considerations of role modeling, choice of reference group, and rationalizations ("neutralizations") of stigma are relevant here. At last the other actors in the drama look in upon what they have themselves helped to create, and pronounce it, not suprisingly, in line with their expectations. Thus is stereotypy self-fulfilling—and indeed self-perpetuating.[3]

While perception has remained in the background as a component of analysis in labeling, the theory itself has reached a state of respectability and far-reaching application. The perspective has been used to analyze such diverse topics as political deviance (Schervish, 1973), mental illness (Scheff, 1966), juvenile rehabilitation (Schur, 1973), and the police (Young, chapter 23). It has even been coupled with systems analysis (Wilkins, 1965: 85–100).[4]

Since we hope to stimulate the study of perception among investigators of labeling, the articles and excerpts in this section have been chosen from that standpoint. We have tried to place the articles in a sequence useful to the student, in that the earlier articles contain the basic concepts of labeling as well as a perceptual component, while the later entries take up various important refinements.

Frank Tannenbaum's *Crime and Community* (1938) is often cited as the original work in labeling theory.[5] In this excerpt, "The Dramatization of Evil," Tannenbaum concisely explicates the nature of the labeling process, and its potentially damaging consequences (chapter 22). It is this notion of labeling that Matza has followed to its logical conclusion in *Becoming Deviant* (1969). When Tannenbaum discusses the existence of "two opposing definitions of the situation" he is of course referring to conflicting perceptions on the part of two groups. These perceptual conflicts are at the center of the processes that lead to the labeling of individuals as deviant.

[3] For a discussion of self-perpetuating labeling, see Katz, 1973, and Sagarin, 1974.

[4] See also the Introduction to this volume.

[5] Classical writings include Becker (1963), Erikson (1962), and Kitsuse (1962), among others.

Jock Young's "The Police as Amplifiers of Deviance" (chapter 23) provides an excellent fit to the perspective outlined in the Introduction to this volume. In his analysis of the British experience, Young provides us with examples of perception directly resulting in labeling, and how this in turn results in the amplification of deviant behavior. This piece is written in the style of the phenomenological orientation that is presently developing in criminology.[6]

Richard Quinney, Howard Becker, and Kai Erikson offer theoretical statements that illuminate the labeling-perceptual orientation. In "The Social Reality of Crime," Quinney emphasizes the ways in which a social reality of crime is constructed (chapter 24). When he discusses the formation of criminal definitions he is referring to the way in which perceptions are formulated (propositions one and two), while in propositions three through six the consequences of such formulations within his theoretical framework are portrayed.

In his classic statement on labeling, Becker indicates the process by which individuals come to be viewed as deviant (chapter 25). As he concludes, "Whether an act is deviant, then, depends on how other people react to it." Becker goes on to illustrate differing consequences resulting from essentially the same act. While he does not specify perception as a causal agent, it is not difficult to discern this element in his examples.

Erikson's selection emphasizes the role of the audience in labeling (chapter 26). The audience rarely manages to sift through all of the elements of an individual's behavior and personality; it tends instead to perceive only a few "important details" by which it identifies a whole character. Erikson goes on to delineate variables that are likely to enter into this decision-making process, and he rightly questions the possible consequences of such labeling for society.

The next four articles in the collection are empirical examples of the perceptual-labeling frame. "Two Studies of Legal Stigma" by Schwartz and Skolnick (chapter 27) is included as an empirical investigation of the consequences of legal sanctions, which simultaneously illuminates the role of the perception of the public in such consequences.[7] Mary Owen Cameron, in

[6] For another application see Atkinson (1971). He indicates that coroners label events as suicide at least partially on the basis of their perception of the "facts" of a case.

[7] There is an exchange of opinions between the authors and H. Lawrence Ross in *Social Problems* (Spring, 1963), pp. 390–92.

what was originally titled *The Booster and the Snitch,* takes up the self-perception aspect of labeling, discussing the mechanisms by which pilferers
who do not have an impression of themselves as deviants begin to acquire
such a self-image (chapter 28).[8] In "Public Stereotypes of Deviants," Simmons states that "stereotyping . . . is an inherent aspect of perception and
cognition." In chapter 29 he analyzes both the correlates of a tendency to
stereotype and the consequences of such public stereotyping.

The final article in the section is a critical overview by Edwin Schur
(chapter 30). After a lengthy and sophisticated discussion of labeling theory
(reactions analysis), Schur formulates a new working definition of deviance
that explicitly takes the importance of the perceptual dimension into account.[9]

References

Atkinson, J. Maxwell. 1971. "Societal Reactions to Suicide: The Role of
Coroners' Definitions." In S. Cohen (ed.), *Images of Deviance,* Harmondsworth: Penguin.

Becker, Howard. 1963. *Outsiders.* New York: Free Press.

1973. "Labeling Theory Reconsidered." In Howard Becker, *Outsiders* (enlarged ed.). New York: Free Press. chap. 10.

Erikson, Kai T. 1962. "Notes on the Sociology of Deviance," *Social
Problems* 9 (Spring):307–14.

Gibbs, Jack P. 1966. "Conceptions of Deviant Behavior: The Old and the
New," *Pacific Sociological Review* 9 (Spring):9–14.

Glaser, Daniel. 1971. *Social Deviance.* Chicago: Markham.

Goffman, Erving. 1959. *The Presentation of Self in Everyday Life.* New
York: Doubleday/Anchor.

1963. *Stigma: Notes on the Management of Spoiled Identity.* Englewood
Cliffs, N.J.: Prentice-Hall.

[8] Readers intrigued by the selection from Cameron might also wish to examine Gould (1969) on
the development of self-perceived delinquency from official labeling.

[9] See also a very insightful overview recently published by Becker (1973).

Gould, Leroy. 1969. "Who Defines Delinquency: A Comparison of Self-Reported and Officially-Reported Indices of Delinquency for Three Racial Groups," *Social Problems* 16 (Winter):325–36.

Kitsuse, John I. 1962. "Societal Reaction to Deviant Behavior: Problems of Theory and Method," *Social Problems* 9 (Winger):247–56.

Mankoff, Milton. 1971. "Societal Reaction and Career Deviance: A Critical Analysis," *Sociological Quarterly* 12 (Spring):204–18.

Katz, Jack. 1973. "Essences as Moral Identities." Paper presented at the meetings of the Society for the Study of Social Problems, New York.

Matza, David. 1969. *Becoming Deviant*. Englewood Cliffs, N.J.: Prentice-Hall.

Sagarin, Edward. 1974. "The Tyranny of Isness." In Edward Sagarin, *Deviants and Deviance: An Introduction to the Study of Disvalued People and Behavior*. New York: Praeger.

Scheff, Thomas J. 1966. *Being Mentally Ill*. Chicago: Aldine.

Schervish, Paul. 1973. "The Labeling Perspective: Its Bias and Potential in the Study of Political Deviance," *The American Sociologist* 8 (May):47–57.

Schur, Edwin. 1971. *Labeling Deviant Behavior: Its Sociological Implications*. New York: Harper and Row.

1973. *Radical Non-Intervention*. Englewood Cliffs, N.J.: Prentice-Hall.

Wilkins, Leslie T. 1965. *Social Deviance: Social Policy, Action and Research*. Englewood Cliffs, N.J.: Prentice-Hall.

22

The Dramatization
of Evil

FRANK TANNENBAUM

A Matter of Definition

In the conflict between the young delinquent and the community there develop two opposing definitions of the situation. In the beginning the definition of the situation by the young delinquent may be in the form of play, adventure, excitement, interest, mischief, fun. Breaking windows, annoying people, running around porches, climbing over roofs, stealing from pushcarts, playing truant—all are items of play, adventure, excitement. To the community, however, these activities may and often do take on the form of a nuisance, evil, delinquency, with the demand for control, admonition, chastisement, punishment, police court, truant school. This conflict over the situation is one that arises out of a divergence of values. As the problem develops, the situation gradually becomes redefined. The attitude of the community hardens definitely into a demand for suppression. There is a gradual shift from the definition of the specific acts as evil to a definition of the individual as evil, so that all his acts come to be looked upon with suspicion. In the process of identification his companions, hang-outs, play, speech, income, all his conduct, the personality itself, become subject to scrutiny and question. From the community's point of view, the individual who used to do bad and mischievous things has now become a bad and unredeemable human being. From the individual's point of view there has taken place a similar change. He has gone slowly from a sense of grievance and injustice, of being unduly mistreated and punished, to a recognition that the definition of him as a human being is different from that of other boys in his neighborhood, his school, street, community. This recognition on his part becomes a process of self-identification and integration with the group which shares his activities. It becomes, in part, a process of rationalization; in part, a simple response to a specialized type of stimulus. The young delinquent becomes bad because he is defined as bad and because he is not believed if he is good. There is a persistent demand for consistency in character. The community cannot deal with people whom it cannot define. Reputation is this sort of public definition. Once it is established, then unconsciously all agencies combine to maintain this definition even when they apparently and consciously attempt to deny their own implicit judgment.

Early in his career, then, the incipient professional criminal develops an attitude of antagonism to the regulated orderly life that he is required to lead. This attitude is hardened and crystallized by opposition. The conflict becomes a clash of wills. And experience too often has proved that threats, punishments, beatings, commitments to institutions, abuse and defamation of one sort or another, are of no avail. Punishment breaks down against the child's stubbornness. What has happened is that the child has been defined as an "incorrigible" both by his contacts and by himself, and an attempt at a direct breaking down of will generally fails.

The child meets the situation in the only way he can, by defiance and escape—physical escape if possible, or emotional escape by derision, anger, contempt, hatred, disgust, tantrums, destructiveness, and physical violence. The response of the child is just as intelligent and intelligible as that of the schools, of the authorities. They have taken a simple problem, the lack of fitness of an institution to a particular child's needs, and have made a moral issue out of it with values outside the child's ken. It takes on the form of war between two wills, and the longer the war lasts, the more certainly does the child become incorrigible. The child will not yield because he cannot yield—his nature requires other channels for pleasant growth; the school system or society will not yield because it does not see the issues involved as between the incompatibility of an institution and a child's needs, sometimes physical needs, and will instead attempt to twist the child's nature to the institution with that consequent distortion of the child which makes an unsocial career inevitable. The verbalization of the conflict in terms of evil, delinquency, incorrigibility, badness, arrest, force, punishment, stupidity, lack of intelligence, truancy, criminality, gives the innocent divergence of the child from the straight road a meaning that it did not have in the beginning and makes its continuance in these terms by so much the more inevitable.

The only important fact, when the issue arises of the boy's inability to acquire the specific habits which organized institutions attempt to impose upon him, is that this conflict becomes the occasion for him to acquire another series of habits, interests, and attitudes as a substitute. These habits become as effective in motivating and guiding conduct as would have been those which the orderly routine social institutions attempted to impose had they been acquired.

This conflict gives the gang its hold, because the gang provides escape, security, pleasure, and peace. The gang also gives room for the motor activity which plays a large role in a child's life. The attempt to break up the gang by force merely strengthens it. The arrest of the children has consequences undreamed of, for several reasons.

First, only some of the children are caught though all may be equally guilty. There is a great deal more delinquency practiced and committed by the young groups than comes to the attention of the police. The boy arrested, therefore, is singled out in specialized treatment. This boy, no more guilty than the other members of his group, discovers a world of which he knew little. His arrest suddenly precipitates a series of institutions, attitudes, and experiences which the other children do not share. For this boy there suddenly appear the police, the patrol wagon, the police station, the other delinquents and criminals found in the police lock ups, the court with all its agencies such as bailiffs, clerks, bondsmen, lawyers, probation officers. There are bars, cells, handcuffs, criminals. He is questioned, examined, tested, investigated. His history is gone into, his family is brought into court. Witnesses make their appearance. The boy, no different from the rest of his gang, suddenly becomes the center of a major drama in which all sorts of unexpected characters play important roles. And what is it all about? about the accustomed things his gang has done and has been doing for a long time. In this entirely new world he is made conscious of himself as a different human being than he was before his arrest. He becomes classified as a thief, perhaps, and the entire world about him has suddenly become a different place for him and will remain different for the rest of his life.

The Dramatization of Evil

The first dramatization of the "evil" which separates the child out of his group for specialized treatment plays a greater role in making the criminal than perhaps any other experience. It cannot be too often emphasized that for the child the whole situation has become different. He now lives in a different world. He has been tagged. A new and hitherto nonexistent environment has been precipitated out for him.

The process of making the criminal, therefore, is a process of tagging, defining, identifying, segregating, describing, emphasizing, making conscious and self-conscious; it becomes a way of stimulating, suggesting, emphasizing, and evoking the very traits that are complained of. If the theory of relation of response to stimulus has any meaning, the entire process of dealing with the young delinquent is mischievous insofar as it identifies him to himself or to the environment as a delinquent person.

The person becomes the thing he is described as being. Nor does it seem to matter whether the valuation is made by those who would punish or by those who would reform. In either case the emphasis is upon the conduct that is disapproved of. The parents or the policeman, the older brother or the court, the probation officer or the juvenile institution, insofar as they rest upon the thing complained of, rest upon a false ground. Their very enthusiasm defeats their aim. The harder they work to reform the evil, the greater the evil grows under their hands. The persistent suggestion, with whatever good intentions, works mischief, because it leads to bringing out the bad behavior that it would suppress. The way out is through a refusal to dramatize the evil. The less said about it the better. The more said about something else, still better.

The hard-drinker who keeps thinking of not drinking is doing what he can to initiate the acts which lead to drinking. He is starting with the stimulus to his habit. To succeed he must find some positive interest or line of action which will inhibit the drinking series and which by instituting another course of action will bring him to his desired end.[1]

The dramatization of the evil therefore tends to precipitate the conflict situation which was first created through some innocent maladjustment. The child's isolation forces him into companionship with other children similarly

[1] John Dewey, *Human Nature and Conduct* (New York: Holt, 1922), p. 35.

defined, and the gang becomes his means of escape, his security. The life of the gang gives it special mores, and the attack by the community upon these mores merely overemphasizes the conflict already in existence, and makes it the source of a new series of experiences that lead directly to a criminal career.

In dealing with the delinquent, the criminal, therefore, the important thing to remember is that we are dealing with a human being who is responding normally to the demands, stimuli, approval, expectancy, of the group with whom he is associated. We are dealing not with an individual but with a group.

23

The Police as
Amplifiers of Deviancy

JOCK YOUNG

The starting point of this article is W. I. Thomas's famous statement that a situation defined as real in a society will be real in its consequences. In terms, then, of those individuals whom society defines as deviants, one would expect that the stereotypes that society holds of them would have very real consequences on both their future behaviour and the way they perceive themselves.

I wish to describe the manner in which society's stereotypes of the drug-taker fundamentally alter and transform the social world of the marihuana smoker. To do this I draw from a participant observation study of drug-taking in Notting Hill which I carried out between 1967 and 1969. I will focus on the effect of the beliefs and stereotypes held by the police about the drug-taker, as important characteristics of our society are that there is an increasing segregation between social groups, and that certain individuals are chosen to mediate between the community and deviant groups. Chief of these individuals are the police, and I want to suggest:

1. The policeman, because of his isolated position in the community, is peculiarly susceptible to the stereotypes, the fantasy notions that the mass media carry about the drug-taker.

2. In the process of police action—particularly in the arrest situation, but continuing in the courts—the policeman because of his position of power

inevitably finds himself negotiating the evidence, the reality of drug-taking, to fit these preconceived stereotypes.

3. In the process of police action against the drug-taker, changes occur within drug-taking groups involving an intensification of their deviance and in certain important aspects a self-fulfillment of these stereotypes; that is, there will be an amplification of deviance, and a translation of stereotypes into actuality, of fantasy into reality.

I am concerned in this article not with the origins of drug-taking—I have dealt with this in detail elsewhere (Young, 1971)—but with the social reaction against drug use. The position of the police is vital in this process, for they man the barricades which society sets up between itself and the deviant.

There are two interrelated factors necessary to explain the reaction of the police against the drug-taker: the motivations behind the conflict, and the manner in which they perceive the typical drug-user.

The Conflict between Police and Marihuana Smoker

It is essential for us to understand the basis of the conflict between police and drug-user. It is not sufficient to maintain that the policeman arrests all those individuals in a community who commit illegalities, for if such a course of action were embarked upon the prisons would be filled many times over and a gigantic police force would become necessary. For as criminal acts occur widely throughout society, and the police are a limited fluid resource, they must to some extent choose, in terms of a hierarchy of priority, which groups warrant their attention and concern. There are three major reasons why one group should perceive another as a "social problem" necessitating intervention.

CONFLICT OF INTERESTS

This is where either a deviant group is seen as threatening the interests of powerful groups in society, or reaction against the offenders is seen as advantageous in itself. The marihuana smoker represents a threat to the police to the extent that, if the occurrence of the habit becomes over large and its practice unashamedly overt, considerable pressure will be put on them by both local authorities and public opinion to halt its progress, and in particular, to clean up the area in question. At the same time, marihuana smokers form a criminal group which has the advantage as far as the policeman on the beat—and more particularly members of the drug squads—is concerned of providing a regular source of fairly easily apprehendable villains. But to eliminate the problem—especially in areas such as Notting Hill where drug-taking is widespread—would demand the deployment of considerable forces, and severely strain the capacity of the police to deal with other more reprehensible forms of crime. It would also be institutional suicide on the part of drug squads, and bureaucracies are not well known for their capacity to write themselves out of existence. The solution therefore is to contain the problem rather than to eliminate it. In this fashion public concern is assuaged, regular contributions to the arrest statistics are guaranteed, and the proportion of police time channelled against the drug-taker is made commensurate with the agreed gravity of the problem.

MORAL INDIGNATION

We have explained in part the way in which the bureaucratic interests of the police shape their action against the drug-taker, but we have not explored the degree of fervour with which they embark on this project. To do this we must examine the moral indignation the policeman evidences towards the drug-taker.

A. K. Cohen (1965) writes of moral indignation:

The dedicated pursuit of culturally approved goals, the eschewing of interdicted but tantalizing goals, the adherence to normatively sanctioned means—these imply a certain self-restraint, effort, discipline, inhibition. What is the effect of others who, though their activities do not manifestly damage our own interests, are morally undisciplined, who give themselves up to idleness, self-indulgence, or forbidden vices? What effect does the propinquity of the wicked have on the peace of mind of the virtuous?

There is a very real conflict between the values of the police and those of the bohemian marihuana smoker. For whereas the policeman values upright masculinity, deferred gratification, sobriety, and respectability, the bohemian embraces values concerned with overt expressivity in behaviour and clothes, and the pursuit of pleasure unrelated to—and indeed disdaining—work. The bohemian in fact threatens the *reality* of the policeman. He lives without work, he pursues pleasure without deferring gratification, he enters sexual relationships without undergoing the obligations of marriage, he dresses freely in a world where uniformity in clothing is seen as a mark of respectability and reliability.

At this point it is illuminating to consider the study made by R. Blum and associates (1965) of American policemen working in the narcotics field. When asked to describe the outstanding personal and social characteristics of the illicit drug-user, the officers most frequently mentioned moral degeneracy, unwillingness to work, insecurity and instability, pleasure orientation, inability to cope with life problems, weakness, and inadequate personality. They rated marihuana users as being a greater community menace than the Mafia. The following quote by an intelligent and capable officer is illustrative:

I tell you there's something about users that bugs me. I don't know what it is exactly. You want me to be frank? OK. Well, I can't stand them; I mean I *really* can't stand them. Why? Because they bother me personally. They're *dirty,* that's what they are, filthy. They make my skin crawl.

It's funny but I don't get that reaction to ordinary criminals. You pinch a burglar or a pickpocket and you understand each other; you know how it is, you stand around yacking, maybe even crack a few jokes. But Jesus, these guys, they're a danger. You know what I mean, they're like Commies or some of those CORE people.

There are some people you can feel sorry for. You know, you go out and pick up some poor chump of a paper hanger [bad-cheque writer] and he's just a drunk and life's got him all bugged. You can understand a poor guy like that. It's different with anybody who'd use drugs.

Similarly, a British policeman—Detective Inspector Wyatt, formerly head of Essex drugs squad—is quoted as saying about cannabis users: "Never in my experience have I met up with such filth and degradation which follows some people who are otherwise quite intelligent. You become a raving bloody idiot so that you can become more lovable" (Devlin, 1970).

Thus the drug-user evokes an immediate gut reaction, while most criminals are immediately understandable in both motives and life style. For the criminal is merely cheating at the rules of a game which the policeman himself plays, whereas the bohemian is sceptical of the validity of the game itself and casts doubts on the world view of both policemen and criminal.

HUMANITARIANISM

This occurs where a powerful group seeks to curb the activities of another group in their own better interests. They define them as a social problem and demand that action be taken to ameliorate their situation. This is complicated in the case of marihuana smoking, insofar as those individuals who make up the social problem would deny that any real problem exists at all.

I would argue that the humanitarian motive is exceedingly suspect; for it is often—though not necessarily—a rationalization behind which is concealed either a conflict of interests or moral indignation. For example Alex Comfort (1967), in *The Anxiety Makers,* has charted the way in which the medical profession have repeatedly translated their moral indignation over certain "abuses" into a clinically backed humanitarianism. For example, masturbation was once seen as causing psychosis, listlessness, and impotence, and various barbaric clinical devices were evolved to prevent young people from touching their genital organs.

I suggest that there is a tendency in our society to cloak what amounts to moral or material conflicts behind the mantle of humanitarianism. This is because serious conflicts of interest are inadmissible in a political order which obtains its moral legitimacy by invoking the notion of a widespread consensus of opinion throughout all sections of the population. Moreover, in this century, because of a ubiquitous liberalism, we are loathe to condemn another man merely because he acts differently from us, providing that he does not harm others. Moral indignation, then, the intervention into the affairs of others because we think them wicked, must necessarily be replaced by humanitarianism, which, using the language of therapy and healing, intervenes in what it perceives as the best interests and well-being of the individuals involved. Heresy or ungodliness become personal or social pathology. With this in mind, humanitarianism justifies its position by invoking the notion of an in-built justice mechanism which automatically punishes the wrong-doer. Thus premarital intercourse is wrong because it leads to V.D., masturbation because it causes impotence, marihuana smoking because a few users will step unawares on the escalator which leads to heroin addiction.

The policeman, then, is motivated to proceed against the drug-taker in terms of his direct interests as a member of a public bureaucracy, he acts with a fervour rooted in moral indignation, and he is able to rationalize his conduct in terms of an ideology of humanitarianism.

The Marihuana Smoker as a Visible and Vulnerable Target

It is not sufficient to argue that the marihuana smoker is on paper a member of a group with which the police are likely to conflict. Two intervening variables determine whether such a conflict will actually take place: the visibility and the vulnerability of the group. The drug-taker, because of his long hair and—to the police—bizarre dress, is an exceedingly visible target for police action. The white middle-class dropout creates for himself the stigmata out of which prejudice can be built, he voluntarily places himself in the position in which the Negro unwittingly finds himself. Moreover, he moves to areas such as Notting Hill where he is particularly vulnerable to apprehension and arrest, unlike the middle-class neighbourhoods he comes from where he was to some extent protected by "good" family and low police vigilance.

The Amplification of Deviancy

We have examined the reasons for police action against the drug-taker. We must now examine the manner in which this proceeds. It is not a question merely of the police reacting in terms of their stereotypes and the drug-using groups being buffeted once and for all by this reaction. The relationship between society and the deviant is more complex than this. It is a tight knit in teraction process which can be most easily understood in terms of a myriad changes on the part of both police and drug-user:

1. The police act against the drug-users in terms of their stereotypes.
2. The drug-user group finds itself in a new situation, which it must interpret and adapt to in a changed manner.
3. The police react in a slightly different fashion to the changed group.
4. The drug-users interpret and adapt to this new situation.
5. The police react to these new changes; and so on.

One of the most common sequences of events in such a process is what has been termed deviancy amplification. The major exponent of this concept is the criminologist Leslie Wilkins (1965), who notes how, when society defines a group of people as deviant, it tends to react against them so as to isolate and alienate them from the company of "normal" people. In this situation of isolation and alienation, the group—because of various reasons which I will discuss later—tends to develop its own norms and values, which society perceives as even more deviant than before. As a consequence of this increase in deviancy, social reaction increases even further, the group is even more isolated and alienated, it acts even more deviantly, society acts increasingly strongly against it, and a spiral of deviancy amplification occurs. See Figure 23.1.

It should not be thought that the deviant group is, so to speak, a pinball inevitably propelled in a deviant direction, or that the police are the cushions of the machine that will inevitably reflex into a reaction triggered by the changing course of the deviant. To view human action in such a light would be to reduce it to the realm of the inanimate, the nonhuman. For although Leslie Wilkins himself uses a mechanistic model there is no need for us to limit ourselves to such an interpretation. As David Matza (1969) has forcefully argued, the human condition is characterized by the ability of a person to stand outside the circumstances that surround him. "A subject actively addresses or encounters his circumstances; accordingly, his distinctive capacity is to reshape, strive toward creating, and actually *transcend* circumstances." The drug-taking group creates its own circumstances to the extent that it interprets and makes meaningful the reactions of the police against it; both the police and the group evolve theories which attempt to explain each other and test them out in terms of the actual course of events: the arrest situation, encounters on the street, portrayals in the mass media, and conversations with friends. These hypotheses of the police about the nature of drug-use, and of the drug-taker about the mentality of the police, determine the direction and intensity of the deviancy amplification process.

Deviancy Amplification in Industrial Societies

The determining factor in our treatment of individuals is the type of information we receive about them. In modern urban societies there is extreme social segregation between different groups which leads to information being obtained at second hand through the mass media rather than directly by face-to-face contact. The type of information which the mass media portray is that which is "newsworthy." They select events which are *atypical,* present

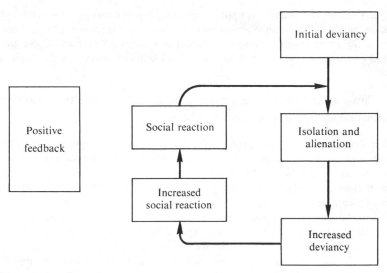

Figure 23.1

them in a *stereotypical* fashion, and contrast them against a backcloth of normality which is *overtypical*.

The atypical is selected because the everyday or humdrum is not interesting to read or watch—it has little news value. As a result of this, if one has little face-to-face contact with young people one's total information about them would be in terms of extremes: drug-taking, sex, and wanton violence on one hand, and Voluntary Services Overseas and Outward Bound courses on the other. But the statistically unusual alone is not sufficient to make news. The mass-circulation newspapers in particular have discovered that people read avidly news which titillates their sensibilities and confirms their prejudices. The ethos of "give the public what it wants" involves a constant play on the normative worries of large segments of the population; it utilizes outgroups as living Rorschach Blots on to which collective fears and doubts are projected. The stereotypical, distorted image of the deviant is then contrasted with the overtypical, hypothetical "man in the street," that persistent illusion of consensual sociology and politics. Out of this, simple moral directives are produced demanding that something must be done about it; the solitary deviant faces the wrath of all society epitomized by its moral conscience, the popular newspaper. For instance, if we consider the headline in the *People* of 21 September 1969, the atypical, the stereotypical, and the overtypical are fused into two magnificent sentences:

HIPPIE THUGS—THE SORDID TRUTH: Drugtaking, couples making love while others look on, rule by a heavy mob armed with iron bars, foul language, filth and stench, THAT is the scene inside the hippies' Fortress in London's Piccadilly. These are not rumours but facts—sordid facts which will shock ordinary decent family loving people.

Christopher Logue (1969) came nearest to describing the distortion of information by the mass media when he wrote:

Somehow, but how I am not sure, popular newspapers reflect the attitudes of those whose worst side they deepen and confirm. Pinning their influence exactly, by example or image, is difficult: they use common words cleverly; certain public figures nourish their vocabulary; in a few years we have seen "permissive" and "immigrant" gain new meanings.

One technique for worsening ourselves seems to go like this: Take a genuine doubt, formulate it as a question whose words emphasize its worst possible outcome, pop the question into print or into the mouths of respectable scaremongers as many times as you can, package this abstract with a few examples of judicial guilt; thus, when reiterated, the question becomes an argument certifying the delusory aspect of the original, true doubt.

The twin factors of social segregation and the mass media introduce into the relationship between deviant groups and society an important element of misperception; and the deviancy amplification process is initiated always in terms of, and often because of, incorrect perceptions.

Moreover, one of the characteristics of complex societies is that certain people are allocated special roles in the process of social control. The roles—such as those of the policeman, the magistrate and the judge—tend to involve people who themselves exist in specially segregated parts of the system. I suggest that the particular individuals assigned to administrating the legal actions against deviants inhabit their own particular segregated spheres, and that the processes of arrest, sentencing, and imprisonment take place within the terms of their own particular misperceptions of deviancy.

Furthermore, our knowledge of deviants not only is stereotypical because of the distortions of the mass media but is also, unlike in small-scale societies, one-dimensional. For example, we know very little of the methylated-spirits drinker as a person in terms of his attitudes to the world. We know him merely by the label "meths-drinker," and the hazy stereotype of activities which surrounds this phrase. Rarely—or not at all—have we even seen or talked to him in the early hours of the morning.

We are immensely aware of deviants in modern societies because of the constant bombardment of information via the mass media. Marshall McLuhan (1967) pictures the world as first expanding through the growth of the city and transport systems, and then imploding as the media bring the world close together again. "It is this implosive factor," he writes, "that alters the position of the Negro, the teenager, and some other groups. They can no longer be contained in the *political* sense of limited association. They are now *involved* in our lives as we in theirs, through electric media." We can no longer have no knowledge of or conveniently forget the deviant. He is brought to our hearth by the television set, his picture is on our breakfast table in the morning newspaper. Moreover, the mass media do not purvey opinions on all deviant groups, they create a universe of discourse for our segregated social world in which many groups are ignored; they simply do not exist in the consciousness of most men. "Cathy Come Home" is shown on television, and suddenly, dramatically, the public are aware of a new social problem. The "homeless" have become a problem to them. Methylated-spirits drinkers, however, although numerically quite a large group, are largely outside the universe of discourse of the mass media; they exist in a limbo outside the awareness of the vast majority of the population.

The media, then—in a sense—can create social problems, they can present them dramatically and overwhelmingly, and, most important, they can do it suddenly. The media can very quickly and effectively fan public indignation and engineer what one might call a "moral panic" about a certain type of deviancy. Indeed because of the phenomenon of overexposure— such a glut of information in a short time on one topic that it becomes uninteresting—there is institutionalized into the media the need to create moral panics and issues which will seize the imagination of the public. For instance, we may chart the course of the great panic over drug abuse which occurred during 1967 by examining the amount of newspaper space devoted to this topic. The number of column inches in *The Times* for the four-week period beginning 29 May was 37; because of the Jagger trial this exploded to 709 in the period beginning 27 June; it continued at a high level of 591 over the next four weeks; and then began to abate from 21 August onwards, when the number of column inches was 107.

To summarize: the type of information available as regards deviants in modern urban societies is as follows:

1. There is a gross misperception of deviants because of social segregation and stereotyped information purveyed via the mass media. This

leads to social reaction against deviants which is phrased in terms of a stereotyped *fantasy,* rather than an accurate empirical knowledge of the behavioural and attitudinal *reality* of their life styles.

2. A one-dimensional knowledge of the deviant in terms of the stereotyped *label* which we have fixed to him leads to a low threshold over which we will expel him from our society and begin a process of deviancy amplification. It is much more unlikely in a small-scale society with multidimensional knowledge of individual members that expulsion would occur.

3. Instead of utilizing informal modes of social control, we have special roles manned by people who are often particularly segregated from the rest of society, and thus especially liable to misperception.

4. Because of the *implosion* of the mass media, we are greatly aware of the existence of deviants, and because the criterion of inclusion in the media is newsworthiness it is possible for moral panics over a particular type of deviancy to be created by the *sudden* dissemination of information about it.

So, when compared to other societies, the modern urban community has a peculiar aptitude to initiate deviancy amplification processes, and to base the gradual expulsion of the deviant from the community on rank misperceptions.

The Position of the Policeman in a Segregated Society

The police occupy a particularly segregated part of the social structure. This is because of five factors.

1. A policy of limited isolation is followed, based on the premise that if you become too friendly with the community you are liable to corruption.

2. Public attitudes range from a ubiquitous suspicion to, in areas such as Notting Hill, downright hostility.

3. In terms of actual contacts, the Royal Commission Survey on the police found that just under half of city police and three-quarters of country police thought they would have had more friends if they had a different job. Two-thirds of all police thought their job adversely affected their outside friendships.

4. A fair proportion of policemen are residentially segregated. Thus a quarter of city police live in groups of six or more police houses.

5. That in the particular instance of middle-class drug-takers in Notting Hill, the police have very little direct knowledge, outside the arrest situation, of the normal behaviour of middle-class youth.

Because of this segregation the police are particularly exposed to the sterotypical accounts of deviants prevalent in the mass media. They have, of course, by the very nature of their role, a high degree of face-to-face contact with deviants; but these contacts, as I will argue later, are of a type which, because of the policeman's position of power, make for a reinforcement rather than an elimination of mass-media stereotypes. Indeed a person in a position of power *vis-à-vis* the deviant tends to negotiate reality so that it fits his preconceptions. As a consequence of the isolation of the police and their awareness of public suspicion and hostility, there is a tendency for the police officer to envisage his role in terms of enacting the will of society, and representing the desires of a hypothesized "normal" decent citizen. In this vein, he is sensitive to the pressures of public opinion as represented in the media, and given that the police are grossly incapable because of their numbers of dealing with all crime, he will focus his attention on those areas where public indignation would seem to be greatest and which at the same time are in accord with his own preconceptions. He is thus a willing instrument—albeit unconsciously—of the type of moral panics about particular types of deviancy which are regularly fanned by the mass media. The real conflict between police and drug-taker in terms of direct interests and moral indignation is thus confirmed, distorted, and structured by the specified images presented in the mass media.

The Fantasy and Reality of Drug-Taking

I wish to describe the social world of the marihuana smoker in Notting Hill, as it was in 1967, contrasting it with the fantasy stereotype of the drug-taker available in the mass media.

1. It is a typical bohemian "scene," that is, it is a highly organized community involving tightly interrelated friendship nets and especially intense patterns of visiting.

The stereotype held in the mass media is that of the isolated drug-taker living in a socially disorganized area, or at the best, a drifter existing in a loose conglomeration of misfits.

2. The values of the hippie marihuana smoker are relatively clear-cut and in opposition to the values of the wider society. The focal concerns of the culture are short-term hedonism, spontaneity, expressivity, disdain for work. These are similar to what Matza and Sykes (1961) have called the subterranean values of society.

The stereotype held is of a group of individuals who are essentially asocial, who *lack* values, rather than propound alternative values. An alternative stereotype is of a small group of ideologically motivated antisocial individuals (the corruptors) who are seducing the innocent mass of young people (the corrupted). I will elaborate this notion of the corruptors and the corrupted later on.

3. Drug-taking is—at least to start with—essentially a peripheral activity of hippie groups. That is, it does not occupy a central place in the culture: the central activities are concerned with the values outlined above (for example dancing, clothes, aesthetic expression). Drug-taking is merely a vehicle for the realization of hedonistic, expressive goals.

Drugs hold a great fascination for the non-drug-taker, and in the stereotype drugs are held to be the primary concern of such groups. That is, a peripheral activity is misperceived as a central group activity.

4. The marihuana user and the marihuana seller are not fixed roles in the culture. At one time a person may sell marihuana, at another he may be buying it. This is because at street level supply is irregular, and good ''connexions'' appear and disappear rapidly. The supply of marihuana derives from two major sources: tourists returning from abroad, and ''hippie'' or immigrant entrepreneurs. The latter are unsystematic, deal in relatively small quantities, and make a restricted and irregular profit. The tourists' total contribution to the market is significant. Both tourists and entrepreneurs restrict their criminal activities to marihuana importation. The dealer in the street buys from these sources and sells in order to maintain himself in drugs and sustain subsistence living. He is well thought of by the group, is part of the ''hippie'' culture, and is not known as a ''pusher.'' The criminal underworld has little interest in the entrepreneur, the tourist, or the dealer in the street.

The stereotype, in contrast, is on the lines of the corruptor and the corrupted, that is the "pusher" and the "buyer." The pusher is perceived as having close contacts with the criminal underworld and being part of a "drug pyramid."

5. The culture consists of largely psychologically stable individuals. The stereotype sees the drug-taker essentially as an immature, psychologically unstable young person corrupted by pushers who are criminals with weak superegos, and a near psychopathic nature.

6. The marihuana user has in fact a large measure of disdain for the heroin addict. There is an interesting parallel between the marihuana user's perception of the businessman and of the heroin addict. Both are considered to be "hung up," obsessed and dominated by money or heroin, respectively. Hedonistic and expressive values are hardly likely to be realized by either, and their way of life has no strong attraction for the marihuana user. Escalation, then, from marihuana to heroin is a rare phenomenon which would involve a radical shift in values and life style.

In the stereotype the heroin addict and the marihuana user are often indistinguishable, the values of both are similar, and escalation is seen as part of a progressive search for more effective "kicks."

7. The marihuana user is widely prevalent in Notting Hill. A high proportion of young people in the area have smoked pot at some time or another.

The stereotype based on numbers known to the police is small compared to the actual number of smokers, yet is perceived as far too large at that and increasing rapidly.

8. The effects of marihuana are mildly euphoric; psychotic effects are rare and only temporary.

The stereotypical effects of marihuana range from extreme sexuality, through aggressive criminality, to wildly psychotic episodes.

The Policeman as a Negotiator of Reality

We live in a world which is, as I have suggested, segregated in terms not so much of distance but of meaningful contact and empirical knowledge. The stereotype of the drug-taker–drug-seller relationship is available to the public via the mass media. This stereotype is constructed according to a typical explanation of deviancy derived from consensual notions of society: namely, that the vast majority of individuals in society share common values and agree on what is conformist and what is deviant. In these terms the deviant is a fringe phenomenon consisting of psychologically inadequate individuals who live in socially disorganized or anomic areas. The emergence of large numbers of young people indulging in deviant activities such as drug-taking in particular areas such as Notting Hill would seem to clash with this notion, as it is impossible to postulate that all of them are psychologically inadequate and that their communities are completely disorganized socially. To circumvent this, consensual theories of society invoke the notion of the corrupted and the corruptor: healthy youngsters are being corrupted by a few psychologically disturbed and economically motivated individuals. This is a subtype of the type of conspiracy theory that suggests all strikes are caused by a few politically motivated, psychologically disturbed individuals. Thus the legitimacy of alternative norms—in this case drug-taking—arising of their own accord in response to certain material and social pressures is circumvented by the notion of the wicked drug-pusher corrupting innocent youth. This allows conflicts of direct interest and moral indignation to be easily subsumed under the guise of humanitarianism. The policeman—like the rest of the public—shares this stereotype, and his treatment of individuals suspected of drug-taking is couched in terms of this stereotype.

The individual found in possession of marihuana is often—and in Notting Hill frequently—ignored by the police. They are after the real enemy, the drug-pusher. In order to get at him they are willing to negotiate with the individual found in possession. Thus they will say, "We are not interested in you, you have just been stupid, we are interested in the person who sold you this stuff. Tell us about him and we will let you off light." Moreover, if the individual found in possession of marihuana actually finds himself in the courts he is in a difficult position: if he tells the truth and says that he smokes marihuana because he likes it and because he believes that it does no harm and that therefore the law is wrong, he will receive a severe sentence. If, on the other hand, he plays the courts' game and conforms to their stereotype—say, he claims that he had got into bad company, that somebody (the pusher) offered to sell him the stuff, so he thought he would try it out, that he knows he was foolish and won't do it again—the courts will let him off light. He is not then in their eyes the true deviant. He is not the dangerous individual whom the police and the courts are really after. Thus the fantasy stereotypes of drug-taking available to the police and the legal profession are reinforced and reenacted in the courts, in a process of negotiation between the accused and the accusers. T. Scheff (1968) has described this as the process of "negotiating reality." The policeman continues with evangelical zeal to seek the pusher, with the forces of public opinion and the mass media firmly behind him. As a result the sentences for possession and for sale become increasingly disparate. In a recent case that I know of, the buyer of marihuana received a fine of £5 while the seller received a five-year jail sentence. A year previously the individual who in this case was buying, was selling marihuana to the person who was sentenced in this case for selling.

The negotiation of reality by the policeman is exhibited in the widespread practice of perjury. This is not due to policemen's Machiavellianism, but rather to their desire, in the name of administrative efficiency, to jump the gap between what I will term theoretical and empirical guilt. For example a West Indian who wears dark glasses, who has no regular employment, and who mixes with beatniks would quite evidently conform to their idea of a typical drug-pusher. If he is arrested, then it is of no consequence that no marihuana is found in his flat, nor is it morally reprehensible to plant marihuana on his person. For all that is being done is to aid the course of justice by providing the empirical evidence to substantiate the obvious theoretical guilt. That the West Indian might really have sold marihuana only a few times in the past, that he mixes with hippies because he likes their company, and that he lives on his national assistance payments, all this is ignored; the stereotype of the pusher is evident, and the reality is unconsciously negotiated to fit its requirements.

The Amplification of Deviance and the Translation of Fantasy in Reality

Over time, police action on the marihuana smoker in Notting Hill results in (1) the intensification of the deviancy of the marihuana user—that is, the consolidation and accentuation of his deviant values in the process of de-

viancy amplification; and (2) a change in the life style and reality of marihuana use, so that certain facets of the stereotype become actuality—that is,
a translation of fantasy into reality.

I wish to consider the various aspects of the social world of the marihuana user which I outlined earlier, and note the cumulative effects of intensive police action:

1. Intensive police action serves to increase the organization and cohe-
sion of the drug-taking community, uniting its members in a sense of injustice felt at harsh sentences and mass-media distortions. The severity of the
conflict compels bohemian groups to evolve theories to explain the nature of
their position in society, thereby heightening their consciousness of themselves as a group with definite interests over and against those of the wider
society. Conflict welds an introspective community into a political faction
with a critical ideology, and deviancy amplification results.

2. A rise in police action increases the necessity for the drug-taker to
segregate himself from the wider society of non-drug-takers. The greater his
isolation the less chance there is that the informal face-to-face forces of
social control will come into operation, and the higher his potentiality for
further deviant behaviour. At the same time, the creation by the bohemian of
social worlds centring around hedonism, expressivity, and drug use makes it
necessary for the non-drug-taker, the "straight" person, to be excluded not
only for reasons of security but also to maintain definitions of reality unchal-
lenged by the outside world. Thus after a point in the process of exclusion of
the deviant by society, the deviant himself will cooperate in the policy of
separation.

3. The further the drug-taker evolves deviant norms, the less chance
there is of his reentering the wider society. Regular drug use, bizarre dress,
long hair, and lack of a workaday sense of time, money, rationality, and
rewards, all militate against his reentry into regular employment. To do so
after a point would demand a complete change of identity; besides modern
record systems would make apparent any gaps which have occurred in his
employment or scholastic records, and these might be seen to indicate a personality which is essentially shiftless and incorrigible. Once he is out of the
system and labelled by the system in this manner, it is very difficult for the
penitent deviant to reenter it especially at the level of jobs previously open
to him. There is a point therefore beyond which an ossification of deviancy
can be said to occur.

4. As police concern with drug-taking increases, drug-taking becomes more and more a secret activity. Because of this, drug-taking in itself becomes of greater value to the group as a symbol of their difference, and of their defiance of perceived social injustices. Simmel (1906), writing on the "Sociology of Secrecy," has outlined the connexion between the social valuation of an activity and the degree of secrecy concerned with its prosecution.

This is what Goffman (1968) referred to as overdetermination. "Some illicit activities," he notes, "are pursued with a measure of spite, malice, glee and triumph and at a personal cost that cannot be accounted for by the intrinsic pleasure of consuming the product." That is, marihuana comes to be consumed not only for its euphoric effects but as a symbol of bohemianism and rebellion against an unjust system. In addition to this, given that a desire for excitement is one of the focal concerns of the community, the ensuing game of cops and robbers is positively functional to the group. What the "fuzz" are investigating, who they have "busted" recently, become ubiquitous topics yielding unending interest and excitement.

Drug-taking and trafficking thus move from being peripheral activities of the groups, a mere vehicle for the better realization of hedonistic, expressive goals, to become a central activity of great symbolic importance. The stereotype begins to be realized, and fantasy is translated into reality.

5. The price of marihuana rises, the gains to be made from selling marihuana become larger, and the professional pusher begins to emerge as police activity increases. Importation becomes more systematized, long-term, and concerned with large regular profits. Because of increased vigilance at the customs, the contribution of returning tourists to the market declines markedly. International connexions are forged by importers linking supply countries and profitable markets and involving large sums of capital. Other criminal activities overlap with marihuana importation, especially those dealing in other saleable drugs. On the street level the dealer becomes more of a "pusher," less part of the culture, and motivated more by economic than social and subsistence living considerations. The criminal underworld becomes more interested in the drug market, overtures are made to importers; a few pushers come under pressure to buy from them and to sell a wider range of drugs, including heroin and methedrine. A drug pyramid, as yet embryonic, begins to emerge. Once again fantasy is being translated into reality.

6. The marihuana user becomes increasingly secretive and suspicious of those around him. How does he know that his activities are not being observed by the police? How does he know that seeming friends are not police informers? Ugly rumours fly around about treatment of suspects by the police, long terms of imprisonment, planting and general social stigmatization. The effects of drugs are undoubtedly related to the cultural milieu in which drugs are taken. A Welsh rugby club drinks to the point of aggression, an all-night party to the point of libidinousness; an academic sherry party unveils the pointed gossip of competitiveness lurking under the mask of a community of scholars. Similarly, the effects of marihuana being smoked in the context of police persecution invite feelings of paranoia and semipsychotic episodes. As Allen Ginsberg (1968) astutely notes:

> It is no wonder . . . that most people who have smoked marihuana in America often experience a state of anxiety, of threat, of paranoia in fact, which may lead to trembling or hysteria, at the microscopic awareness that they are breaking a Law, that thousands of Investigators all over the country are trained and paid to smoke them out and jail them, that thousands of their community are in jail, that inevitably a few friends are "busted" with all the hypocrisy and expense and anxiety of that trial and perhaps punishment—jail and victimage by the bureaucracy that made, propagandized, administers, and profits from such a monstrous law.
>
> From my own experience and the experience of others I have concluded that most of the horrific effects and disorders described as characteristic of marihuana "intoxication" by the US Federal Treasury Department's Bureau of Narcotics are quite the reverse, precisely traceable back to the effects on consciousness not of the narcotic but of the law and the threatening activities of the US Bureau of Narcotics itself. Thus, as Buddha said to a lady who offered him a curse, the gift is returned to the giver when it is not accepted.

This relates to Tigani el Mahi's (1962) hypothesis that making a drug illegal, and failing to institutionalize its use through controls and sanctions, produce adverse psychic effects and bizarre behaviour when the drug is taken. Thus stereotypical effects become in part reality.

7. As police activity increases, the marihuana user and the heroin addict begin to feel some identity as joint victims of police persecution. Interaction between heroin addicts and marihuana users increases. The general social feeling against all drugs creates a stricter control of the supply of heroin to the addict. He is legally bound to obtain his supplies from one of the properly authorized clinics. Lack of personnel who are properly trained, or who even have an adequate theoretical knowledge of dealing with the

withdrawal problems of the heroin addict, results in the alienation of many from the clinics. The addict who does attend either is kept on maintenance doses or else has his supply gradually cut. Either way euphoria becomes more difficult to obtain from the restricted supply, and the "grey market" of surplus National Health heroin, which previously catered for addicts who required extra or illicit supplies, disappears. In its place a sporadic black market springs up, often consisting of Chinese heroin diluted with adulterants. This provides a tentative basis for criminal underworld involvement in drug selling and has the consequence of increasing the risks of overdosage (because the strength is unknown) and infection (because of the adulterants).

But the supply of black-market heroin alone is inadequate. Other drugs are turned to in order to make up the scarcity; the precise drugs varying with their availability, and the ability of legislation to catch up with this phenomenon of drug displacement. Chief of these are methadone, a drug addictive in its own right and which is used to wean addicts off heroin, and freely prescribed barbiturates. As a result of displacement, a body of methadone and barbiturate addicts emerges; the barbiturates are probably more dangerous than heroin and cause even greater withdrawal problems. For a while the overprescription by doctors creates, as once occurred with heroin, an ample grey market of methadone and barbiturates. But pressure on the doctors restricts at least the availability of methadone, and the ranks of saleable black-market drugs are increased in the process. Because many junkies share some common bohemian traditions with hippies (they often live in the same areas, smoke pot, and affect the same style of dress), the black market of heroin, methadone, barbiturates, *and* marihuana will overlap. The heroin addict seeking money in order to maintain his habit at a desirable level and the enterprising drug-seller may find it profitable to make these drugs available to marihuana smokers.

Some marihuana users will pass on to these hard drugs, but let me emphasize *some,* as, in general, *heavy* use of such drugs is incompatible with hippie values. For full-blown physical addiction involves being at a certain place at a certain time every day, it involves an obsession with one substance to the exclusion of all other interests, it is anathema to the values of hedonism, expressivity, and autonomy. But the number of known addicts in Britain is comparatively small (just over 2,000 heroin addicts in March 1970), while the estimates of the marihuana smoking population range up to one million and beyond. Thus it would need only a minute proportion of marihuana smokers to escalate for the heroin addiction figures to rise rapidly. Besides, the availability of methodone and barbiturates gives rise to alternative avenues of escalation. Methadone, once a palliative for heroin addicts, becomes a drug of addiction for individuals who have never used heroin. To this extent increased social reaction against the drug-taker would make real the stereotype held by the public about escalation. But the transmission of addiction, unlike the transmission of disease, is not a matter of contact, it is a process that is dictated by the social situation and values of the person who is in contact with the addict. The values of marihuana smokers and the achievement of subterranean goals are not met by intensive heroin use. Escalation to heroin (or methadone and the barbituates) will occur only in atypical cases where the structural position of the marihuana user changes sufficiently to necessitate the evolution of values compatible with heroin use as solutions to his newly emergent problems. I have discussed this problem elsewhere (Young, 1971); suffice it to say here that it is a product of contradictions between the subterranean goals and the limited economic and material base of the bohemian culture, which are considerably aggravated in situations where social reaction is particularly intensive. On the face of things, escalation to other, equally dangerous drugs, especially intravenous amphetamine use, is a more likely occurrence. Amphetamines, particularly methedrine or "speed," are particularly appropriate to hedonistic and expressive cultures. It is to drugs such as these that the deviancy amplification of marihuana users might well result in escalation in the type of drugs taken.

8. As the mass media fan public indignation over marihuana use, pressure on the police increases: the public demands that they solve the drug problem. As I have mentioned previously, the number of marihuana users known to the police is a mere tip of the iceberg of actual smokers. Given their desire to behave in accordance with public opinion and to legitimize their position, the police will act with greater vigilance and arrest more marihuana offenders. All that happens is that they dig deeper into the undetected part of the iceberg; the statistics for marihuana offenders soar; the public, the press, and the magistrates view the new figures with even greater alarm. Increased pressure is put on the police, the latter dig even deeper into the iceberg, the figures increase once again, and public concern becomes even greater. We have entered what I term a fantasy crime wave, which does not necessarily involve at any time an actual increase in the number of

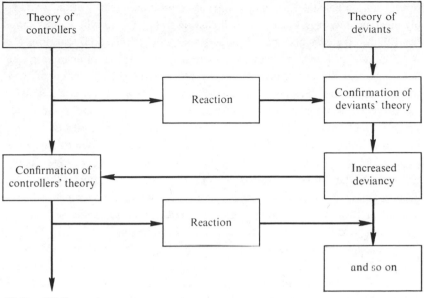

Figure 23.2

marihuana smokers. Because of the publicity, however, the notion of marihuana smoking occurs for the first time to a larger number of people, and
through their desire to experiment there will be some slight real increase.
We must not overlook here the fact that moral panic over drug-taking results
in the setting up of drug squads which by their very bureaucratic creation
will ensure a regular contribution to the offence figures which had never
been evidenced before.

Police action not only has a deviancy amplification effect because of
the unforeseen consequences of the exclusion of the marihuana smoker from
"normal" society; it has also an effect on the content of the bohemian culture within which marihuana smoking takes place.

I have discussed a process which has been going on over the last three
years, to some extent accentuating the contrasts in an ideal typical fashion in
order to make more explicit the change. The important feature to note is that
there has been change, and that this has been in part the product of social reaction. For many social commentators and policy makers, however, this
change has merely reinforced their initial presumptions about the nature of
drug-takers: individuals with near psychopathic personalities, a weak su-

perego, an unrealistic ego, and inadequate masculine identification. Inevitably these people, it is suggested, will pass on to heroin, and the figures show that this has actually occurred. Similarly the police, convinced that drug-use is a function of a few pushers, will view the deviancy amplification of the bohemian and the emergence of a drug pyramid as substantiation of their theory that we have been too permissive all along. False theories are evolved and acted upon in terms of a social reaction, resulting in changes which, although merely a *product* of these theories, are taken by many to be a proof of their initial presumptions. Similarly, the drug-taker, evolving theories as to the repressive nature of the police, finds them progressively proven as the gravity of the situation escalates. As Figure 23.2 shows, there can occur a spiral of theoretical misperceptions and empirical confirmations very similar to the spiral of interpersonal misperceptions described by Laing, Phillipson, and Lee (1966) in *Interpersonal Perception*.

What must be stressed is that we are dealing with a delicately balanced system of relationships between groups, and between values and social situations, which can be put, so to speak, out of gear by the overreaction of public and police. It is my contention that the tendency to unnecessary overreaction is part of the nature of modern large-scale urban societies, and that a proper understanding of the nature of deviancy amplification and moral panic is a necessary foundation for the basis of rational social action. We could quite easily launch ourselves, through faulty mismanagement of the control of drug-taking, into a situation which would increasingly resemble that pertaining in the United States.

References

Blum, R. 1965. *Utopiates*. London: Tavistock.

Cohen, A. K. 1965. "The Sociology of the Deviant Act," *American Sociological Review* 30:5–14.

Comfort, A. 1967. *The Anxiety Makers*. London: Nelson.

Devlin, T. 1970. "Drug Talk Makes Sixth Formers Queasy," *Times Educational Supplement,* January 30.

Ginsberg, A. 1968. "First Manifesto To End the Bringdown." In D. Soloman (ed.), *The Marijuana Papers*. New York: Signet, p. 242.

Goffman, E. 1968. *Asylums*. Harmondsworth: Penguin, p. 274.

Laing, R., H. Phillipson, and A. Lee. 1966. *Interpersonal Perception*. London: Tavistock.

Logue, Christopher. 1969. "A Feir Feld Ful of Folk," *The Times,* September 13.

Mahi, Tigani I. 1962. "The Use and Abuse of Drugs," World Health Organization Reg. Off. Eastern Mediterranean, EM/RC 12/6XVI.

Matza, D. 1969. *Becoming Deviant*. Englewood Cliffs, N.J.: Prentice-Hall, p. 93.

and G. Sykes. 1961. "Juvenile Delinquency and Subterranean Values," *American Sociological Review* 26:712 ff.

McLuhan, M. 1967. *Understanding Media*. London: Sphere.

Scheff, T. 1968. "Negotiating Reality," *Social Problems* 16 (Summer).

Simmel, G. 1906. "The Sociology of Secrecy and of Secret Societies," *American Journal of Sociology* 11:441 ff.

Wilkins, L. 1965. "Some Sociological Factors in Drug Addiction Control." In D. Wilner and G. Kassebaum (eds.), *Narcotics*. New York: McGraw-Hill.

Young, J. 1971. *The Drugtakers: The Social Meaning of Drug Use*. London: McGibbon, Kee & Paladin.

24

The Social Reality of Crime

RICHARD QUINNEY

Much of what we have been discussing thus far in theoretical criminology can be summarized in the form of a theory of the *social reality of crime*. The world of crime is conceived of as a social construction, whereby definitions of crime (primarily through the criminal law) are established and subsequently related to the behavior patterns and actions of the members of society. The theory of the social reality of crime integrates the diversity of theoretical criminology into a theory of crime. The following propositions constitute the basis of this theory.[1]

The Official Definition of Crime

Crime is a legal definition of human conduct created by agents of the dominant class in capitalist society.

The essential starting point in the theory is a definition of crime which itself is based on the legal definition. Crime, as *officially* determined, is a *definition* of behavior that is conferred on some persons by those in power. Agents of the law (such as legislators, police, prosecutors, and judges), as

[1] This is a revision of the theory of the social reality of crime as originally presented in Quinney (1970).

representatives of the ruling class in a capitalist society, are responsible for the formulation and administration of criminal law. Persons and behaviors, therefore, become criminal because of the *formulation* and *application* of these definitions of crime.

Crime, according to the first proposition of the social reality of crime, then, is not inherent in behavior, but is rather a judgment made by some about the actions and characteristics of others. This proposition allows us to focus upon the formulation and administration of the criminal law in relation to the behaviors that become defined as criminal in a capitalist society. Crime is seen as a result of the class-dynamic processes that culminate in the defining of persons and behaviors as criminal. It follows, then, that the greater the number of definitions of crime, formulated and applied, the greater the amount of crime.

The Formulation of Definitions of Crime

Definitions of crime are composed of behaviors that conflict with the class interests of the dominant economic class.

Definitions of crime are formulated according to the interests of the dominant class that has the power to translate its particular interests into public policy. According to a Marxian analysis, the class interests that are ultimately incorporated into the criminal law are those treasured by the dominant class in capitalist society (Quinney, 1973). Furthermore, definitions of crime in a society change with changes in the interests of the dominant class. In other words, those who have the ability to have their class interests represented in public policy regulate the formulation of definitions of crime.

The formulation of definitions of crime is one of the most obvious manifestations of *class conflict* in society. The formulation of criminal law, including legislative statutes, administrative rulings, and judicial decisions, allows the ruling class to protect and perpetuate its own interests. Definitions of crime exist, therefore, because of class struggle. Through the formulation of definitions of crime the dominant economic class is able to control the behavior of persons in the subordinate class. It follows that the greater the class struggle, the greater the probability that the ruling class will formulate definitions of crime.

The interests of the ruling class are reflected not only in the content of the definitions of crime and the kinds of penal sanctions attached to the definitions but also in the *legal policies* regarding the handling of those defined as criminals. Hence, procedural rules are created for the enforcement and administration of the criminal law. Policies are also established in respect to programs for the treatment and punishment of the criminally defined and programs for the control and prevention of crime. In all cases, whether in regard to the initial definitions of crime or the subsequent procedures, correctional and penal programs, or policies of crime control and prevention, the class that has the dominant power is the class that regulates the behavior of those without power.[2]

Finally, since law is formulated within the context of the class structure of capitalist society, it follows that law changes with modifications in that structure. New and shifting demands require new laws. When the class interests that underlie a criminal law are no longer relevant to those in power, the law will be reinterpreted or altered in order to incorporate the dominant class interests. Hence, the probability that definitions of crime will be formulated is increased by such factors as (1) changing social structure, (2) emerging class interests, and (3) increasing concern with the protection of class interests. The social history of law can thus be written in terms of changes in the class structure of capitalist society.

The Application of Definitions of Crime

Definitions of crime are applied by the class that has the power to shape the enforcement and administration of criminal law.

The interests of the dominant class intervene in all the stages in which definitions of crime are created. Since class interests cannot be effectively protected through the mere formulation of criminal law, there must be enforcement and administration of the law. The interests of the powerful, therefore, also operate in the *application* of the definitions of crime. Consequently, as Vold (1958) has argued, crime is "political behavior and the criminal becomes in fact a member of a 'minority group' without sufficient

[2] Considerable support for this proposition is found in Chambliss and Seidman (1971); also see Rusche and Kirchheimer (1939).

public support to dominate the control of the police power of the state." [3] Those whose interests conflict with the interests represented in the law must either change their behavior or possibly find it defined as criminal.

The probability that definitions of crime will be applied varies according to the extent to which the behaviors of the powerless conflict with the interests of those in power. Law-enforcement efforts and judicial activity are likely to be increased when the interests of the dominant class are being threatened. Fluctuations and variations in applying definitions of crime reflect shifts in class relations.

Obviously, the criminal law is not applied directly by the dominant class. Rather, the actual enforcement and administration of the law are delegated to authorized *legal agents*. These authorities, nevertheless, represent the interests of the dominant economic class. In fact, the legal agents' security of office is dependent upon their ability to represent ruling class interests.

Because of the physical separation of the groups responsible for the creation of the definitions of crime from the groups delegated the authority to enforce and administer law, local conditions affect the actual application of definitions (Banton, 1964; Bittner, 1967; Clark, 1965; Goldman, 1963; Wilson, 1968). In particular, communities vary from one another in their expectations of law enforcement and the administration of justice. The application of definitions is also influenced by the visibility of offenses in a community and by the norms in respect to the reporting of possible violations by the public. And especially important in the enforcement and administration of the criminal law are the occupational organization and ideology of the legal agents. (Blumberg, 1967; Bordua and Reiss, 1966; Cicourel, 1968; Neiderhoffer, 1967; Skolnick, 1966; Stinchcombe, 1963; Sudnow, 1965; Westley, 1953; Wood, 1967). Thus, the probability that definitions of crime will be applied is influenced by such community and organizational factors as (1) community expectations of law enforcement and administration, (2) the visibility and public reporting of offenses, and (3) the occupational organization, ideology, and actions of the legal agents delegated the authority to enforce and administer criminal law. On the basis of such factors, the dominant interests of society are implemented in the application of definitions of crime.

The probability that these definitions will be applied in specific situa-

[3] Also see Horowitz and Liebowitz (1968).

tions is dependent upon the actions of the legal agents who have been given the authority to enforce and administer the law. In the final analysis, the application of a definition of crime is a matter of evaluation on the part of persons charged with the authority to enforce and administer the law. As Turk (1966) has argued, in the course of "criminalization," a criminal label may be affixed to persons because of real or fancied attributes: "Indeed, a person is evaluated, either favorably or unfavorably, not because he *does* something, or even because he *is* something, but because others react to their perceptions of him as offensive or inoffensive." [4] Evaluation by the definers is affected by the way in which the suspect handles the situation, but ultimately the evaluations and subsequent decisions of the legal agents are the crucial factors in determining the criminality of human acts. Hence, the more legal agents evaluate behaviors and persons as worthy of definitions of crime, the greater the probability that definitions of crime will be applied.

The Development of Behavior Patterns in Relation to Definitions of Crime

Behavior patterns are structured in relation to definitions of crime, and within this context persons engage in actions that have relative probabilities of being defined as criminal.

Although the substance of behavior varies, all behaviors are similar in that they represent behavior patterns within the society. Therefore, all persons—whether they create definitions of crime or are the objects of these definitions—act in reference to *normative systems* learned in relative social and cultural settings.[5] Since it is not the quality of the behavior but the action taken against the behavior that gives it the character of criminality, that which is defined as criminal is relative to the behavior patterns of the class that formulates and applies definitions. Consequently, persons whose behavior patterns are not represented in the formulation and application of the def-

[4] For research on the evaluation of suspects by policemen, see Piliavin and Briar (1964).

[5] Assumed within the theory of the social reality of crime is Sutherland's (1967) theory of differential association. An analysis of the differential association theory is found in De Fleur and Quinney (1966).

initions of crime are more likely to act in ways that will be defined as criminal than those in the class that formulate and apply the definitions.

Once behavior patterns become established with some degree of regularity within the different segments of society, individuals are provided with a framework for the creation of *personal action patterns*. These action patterns continually develop for each person as he moves from one life experience to another. It is the development of certain action patterns that gives the behavior of persons an individual substance in relation to the definitions of crime.

People construct their own patterns of action in participating with others. It follows, then, that the probability that persons will develop action patterns that have a high potential of being defined as criminal is dependent upon the relative substance of (1) structured opportunities, (2) learning experiences, (3) interpersonal associations and identifications, and (4) self-conceptions. Throughout the course of experiences, each person creates a conception of self as a human social being. Thus prepared, persons behave in terms of the anticipated consequences of their actions (Burgess and Akers, 1966; Jeffery, 1965).

In the course of the shared experiences of the definers of crime and the criminally defined, personal action patterns develop among the latter as a consequence of being so defined. After such persons have had continued experience in being defined as criminal, they learn to manipulate the application of criminal definitions (Lorber, 1967).

Furthermore, those who have been defined as criminal begin to conceive of themselves as criminal. As they adjust to the definitions imposed upon them, they learn to play the role of the criminal (Lemert, 1951, 1964; Tannenbaum, 1938). As a result of the reactions of others, therefore, persons may develop personal action patterns that increase the likelihood of their being defined as criminal in the future. That is, increased experience with definitions of crime increases the probability of the development of actions that may be subsequently defined as criminal.

Thus, both the definers of crime and the criminally defined are involved in reciprocal action patterns. The personal action patterns of both the definers and the defined are shaped by the interrelation of their common, continued, and interrelated experiences. The fate of each is bound to that of the other.

The Construction of an Ideology of Crime

*An ideology of crime is constructed and diffused in the course of establishing
the hegemony of the ruling class.*

An ideology is created by the ruling class for the purpose of maintaining the hegemony of the capitalistic order. The construction of an ideology
is related to the kinds of ideas people are exposed to, the manner in which
they select information to fit the world they are in the process of shaping,
and the manner in which they interpret the information. People behave in
reference to the *social meanings* they attach to their experiences.

Among the conceptions that develop in a society are those relating to
what people regard as crime. Whenever the concept of crime exists, conceptions of the nature of crime also exist. Images develop concerning the relevance of crime, the characteristics of the offender, the appropriate reaction
to crime, and the relation of crime to the social order (Clark and Gibbs, 1965;
Dow, 1967; Lentz, 1966; McIntyre, 1967; Mylonas and Reckless, 1963;
Rooney and Gibbons, 1966). These conceptions are constructed through the
process of communication. In fact, the construction of conceptions of crime
is dependent upon the portrayal of crime in all personal and mass communication. Through such means, conceptions of what is criminal are diffused throughout a society.

One of the most concrete ways in which conceptions of crime are
formed and transmitted is through official investigations of crime. The President's Commission on Law Enforcement and Administration of Justice
(1967) is the best contemporary example of the role of the state in shaping
conceptions of crime. Not only do we as citizens have a greater awareness
of crime today because of the activities of the President's Commission, but
official policy regarding crime has been established in a crime bill (the Om-
nibus Crime Control and Safe Streets Act of 1968). The crime bill, which
itself was a reaction to the growing fears of class conflict in American society, creates an image of the severity of the crime problem and, in the course
of so doing, negates some of our basic constitutional guarantees in the name
of crime control. Our current social reality of crime has thus been shaped by
the communication of the ideas and interests of the ruling class.

Consequently, the conceptions that are most critical in the actual formulation and application of the definitions of crime are those held by the
dominant class. These are the conceptions of crime that are certain to be-

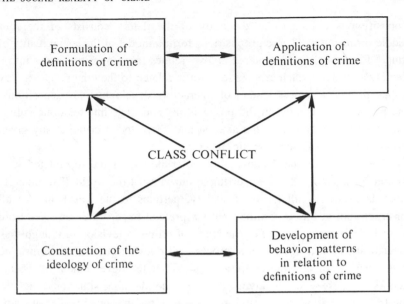

Figure 24.1 The Social Reality of Crime

come incorporated into the social reality of crime. Furthermore, the more the dominant class is concerned about crime, the greater the probability that definitions of crime will be created and that behavior patterns will develop in opposition to the definitions. The formulation of definitions of crime, the application of the definitions, and the development of behavior patterns in relation to the definitions are thus joined in full circle by the construction of an ideological hegemony regarding crime.

Construction of the Social Reality of Crime

The social reality of crime is constructed by the formulation and application of definitions of crime, the development of behavior patterns in relation to these definitions, and the construction of an ideology of crime.

The first five propositions can be collected into a final composite proposition. The theory of the social reality of crime, accordingly, postulates the creation of a series of phenomena that increase the probability of crime in a capitalist society. The result, in holistic terms, is the construction of the social reality of crime (Fig. 24.1).

Since the first proposition of the theory is a definition and the sixth proposition is a composite, the body of the theory consists of the four middle propositions. These propositions form a model of the social reality of crime. The model, as diagramed below, relates the proposition units into a theoretical system. Each proposition unit is related to the others. The theory is thus in the form of a system of interacting developmental propositions. The phenomena denoted in the propositions and their interrelations culminate in what is regarded as the amount and character of crime at any given time—that is, in the social reality of crime.

The theory of the social reality of crime as I have formulated it is inspired by a change that is occurring in our view of the world. This change, which is pervading all levels of society, pertains to the world that we all construct and, at the same time, that we pretend to separate ourselves from in our human experiences. For the study of crime, a revision in thought has directed attention to the criminal process: all relevant phenomena contribute to the process of creating definitions of crime, the development of the behaviors of those who are involved in criminal-defining situations, and the construction of an ideology of crime. The result is the social reality of crime that is constantly being constructed in society.

References

Banton, Michael. 1964. *The Policeman in the Community*. London: Tavistock.

Bittner, Egon. 1967. "The Police on Skid-Row: A Study of Peace Keeping," *American Sociological Review* 32 (October):699–715.

Blumberg, Abraham S. 1967. *Criminal Justice*. Chicago: Quadrangle.

Bordua, David J. and Albert J. Reiss, Jr. 1966. "Command, Control, and Charisma: Reflections on Police Bureaucracy," *American Journal of Sociology* 72 (July):68–76.

Burgess, Robert L. and Ronald L. Akers. 1966. "A Differential Association-Reinforcement Theory of Criminal Behavior," *Social Problems* 14 (Fall):128–47.

Chambliss, William J. and Robert B. Seidman. 1971. *Law, Order, and Power*. Reading, Mass.: Addison-Wesley.

Cicourel, Aaron V. 1968. *The Social Organization of Juvenile Justice*. New York: Wiley.

Clark, John P. 1965. "Isolation of the Police: A Comparison of the British and American Situations," *Journal of Criminal Law, Criminology and Police Science* 56 (September):307–19.

Clark, John P. and Jack P. Gibbs. 1965. "Social Control: A Reformulation," *Social Problems* 12 (Spring):398–415.

DeFleur, Melvin L. and Richard Quinney. 1966. "A Reformulation of Sutherland's Differential Association Theory and a Strategy for Empirical Verification," *Journal of Research in Crime and Delinquency* 3 (January):1–22.

Dow, Thomas E., Jr. 1967. "The Role of Identification in Conditioning Public Attitude toward the Offender," *Journal of Criminal Law, Criminology and Police Science* 58 (March):75–79.

Goldman, Nathan. 1963. *The Differential Selection of Juvenile Offenders for Court Appearance*. New York: National Council on Crime and Delinquency.

Horowitz, Irving L. and Martin Liebowitz. 1968. "Social Deviance and Political Marginality: Toward a Redefinition of the Relation between Sociology and Politics," *Social Problems* 15 (Winter):280–96.

Jeffery, C. Ray. 1965. "Criminal Behavior and Learning Theory," *Journal of Criminal Law, Criminology and Police Science* 56 (September):294–300.

Lemert, Edwin M. 1951. *Social Pathology*. New York: McGraw-Hill, pp. 3–98.

1964. *Human Deviance, Social Problems, and Social Control*. Englewood Cliffs, N.J.: Prentice-Hall, pp. 40–64.

Lentz, William P. 1966. "Social Status and Attitudes toward Delinquency Control," *Journal of Research in Crime and Delinquency* 3 (July):147–54.

Lorber, Judith. 1967. "Deviance as Performance: The Case of Illness," *Social Problems* 14 (Winter):302–10.

McIntyre, Jennie. 1967. "Public Attitudes toward Crime and Law Enforcement," *Annals of the American Academy of Political and Social Science* 374 (November):34–46.

Mylonas, Anastassios D. and Walter C. Reckless, 1963. "Prisoners' Attitudes toward Law and Legal Institutions," *Journal of Criminal Law, Criminology and Police Science* 54 (December):479–84.

Niederhoffer, Arthur. 1967. *Behind the Shield: The Police in Urban Society.* Garden City, N.Y.: Doubleday.

Piliavin, Irving and Scott Briar. 1964. "Police Encounters with Juveniles," *American Journal of Sociology* 70 (September):206–14.

President's Commission on Law Enforcement and Administration of Justice. 1967. *The Challenge of Crime in a Free Society.* Washington, D.C.: U.S. Government Printing Office.

Quinney, Richard. 1970. *The Social Reality of Crime.* Boston: Little, Brown, pp. 15–25.

1973. "Crime Control in Capitalist Society: A Critical Philosophy of Legal Order," *Issues in Criminology* 8 (Spring):75–99.

Rooney, Elizabeth A. and Don C. Gibbons. 1966. "Social Reactions to 'Crimes without Victims.' " *Social Problems* 13 (Spring):400–10.

Rusche, George and Otto Kirchheimer. 1939. *Punishment and Social Structure.* New York: Columbia University Press.

Skolnick, Jerome H. 1966. *Justice Without Trial.* New York: Wiley.

Stinchcombe, Arthur L. 1963. "Institutions of Privacy in the Determination of Police Administrative Practice," *American Journal of Sociology* 69 (September):150–60.

Sudnow, David. 1965. "Normal Crimes: Sociological Features of the Penal Code in a Public Defender Office," *Social Problems* 12 (Winter):255–76.

Sutherland, Edwin H. 1947. *Principles of Criminology* (4th ed.). Philadelphia: Lippincott.

Tannenbaum, Frank. 1938. *Crime and the Community.* New York: Columbia University Press, pp. 3–81.

Turk, Austin T. 1966. "Conflict and Criminality," *American Sociological Review* 31 (June):338–52.

Vold, George B. 1958. *Theoretical Criminology.* New York: Oxford University Press, p. 202.

Westley, William A. 1953. "Violence and the Police," *American Journal of Sociology* 59 (July):34–41.

Wilson, James Q. 1968. *Varieties of Police Behavior: The Management of Law and Order in Eight Communities*. Cambridge: Harvard University Press.

Wood, Arthur Lewis. 1967. *Criminal Lawyer*. New Haven: College and University Press.

25

Deviance
and the Responses of Others

HOWARD S. BECKER

[We can define] deviance as the infraction of some agreed-upon rule. [We can then] ask who breaks rules, and . . . search for the factors in their personalities and life situations that might account for the infractions. This assumes that those who have broken a rule constitute a homogeneous category, because they have committed the same deviant act.

Such an assumption seems to me to ignore the central fact about deviance: it is created by society. I do not mean this in the way it is ordinarily understood, in which the causes of deviance are located in the social situation of the deviant or in "social factors" which prompt his action. I mean, rather, that *social groups create deviance by making the rules whose infraction constitutes deviance,* and by applying those rules to particular people and labeling them as outsiders. From this point of view, deviance is *not* a quality of the act the person commits, but rather a consequence of the application by others of rules and sanctions to an "offender." The deviant is one to whom that label has successfully been applied; deviant behavior is behavior that people so label.[1]

Since deviance is, among other things, a consequence of the responses of others to a person's act, students of deviance cannot assume that they are dealing with a homogeneous category when they study people who have

[1] The most important earlier statements of this view can be found in Tannenbaum (1951) and Lemert (1951). A recent article stating a position very similar to mine is Kitsuse (1962).

been labeled deviant. That is, they cannot assume that these people have actually committed a deviant act or broken some rule, because the process of labeling may not be infallible; some people may be labeled deviant who in fact have not broken a rule. Furthermore, they cannot assume that the category of those labeled deviant will contain all those who actually have broken a rule, for many offenders may escape apprehension and thus fail to be included in the population of "deviants" they study. Insofar as the category lacks homogeneity and fails to include all the cases that belong in it, one cannot reasonably expect to find common factors of personality or life situation that will account for the supposed deviance.

What, then, do people who have been labeled deviant have in common? At the least, they share the label and the experience of being labeled as outsiders. I will begin my analysis with this basic similarity and view deviance as the product of a transaction that takes place between some social group and one who is viewed by that group as a rule-breaker. I will be less concerned with the personal and social characteristics of deviants than with the process by which they come to be thought of as outsiders and their reactions to that judgment. . . .

Whether an act is deviant, then, depends on how other people react to it. You can commit clan incest and suffer from no more than gossip as long as no one makes a public accusation; but you will be driven to your death if the accusation is made. The point is that the response of other people has to be regarded as problematic. Just because one has committed an infraction of a rule does not mean that others will respond as though this had happened. (Conversely, just because one has not violated a rule does not mean that he may not be treated, in some circumstances, as though he had.)

The degree to which other people will respond to a given act as deviant varies greatly. Several kinds of variation seem worth noting. First of all, there is variation over time. A person believed to have committed a given "deviant" act may at one time be responded to much more leniently than he would be at some other time. The occurrence of "drives" against various kinds of deviance illustrates this clearly. At various times, enforcement officials may decide to make an all-out attack on some particular kind of deviance, such as gambling, drug addiction, or homosexuality. It is obviously much more dangerous to engage in one of these activities when a drive is on than at any other time. (In a very interesting study of crime news in Colorado newspapers, Davis (1952) found that the amount of crime reported in Colorado newspapers showed very little association with actual changes in the amount of crime taking place in Colorado. And, further, that peoples' estimate of how much increase there had been in crime in Colorado was associated with the increase in the amount of crime news but not with any increase in the amount of crime.)

The degree to which an act will be treated as deviant depends also on who commits the act and who feels he has been harmed by it. Rules tend to be applied more to some persons than others. Studies of juvenile delinquency make the point clearly. Boys from middle-class areas do not get as far in the legal process when they are apprehended as do boys from slum areas. The middle-class boy is less likely, when picked up by the police, to be taken to the station; less likely when taken to the station to be booked; and it is extremely unlikely that he will be convicted and sentenced (Cohen and Short, 1961, p. 87). This variation occurs even though the original infraction of the rule is the same in the two cases. Similarly, the law is differentially applied to Negroes and whites. It is well known that a Negro believed to have attacked a white woman is much more likely to be punished than a white man who commits the same offense; it is only slightly less well known that a Negro who murders another Negro is much less likely to be punished than a white man who commits murder (Garfinkel, 1949). This, of course, is one of the main points of Sutherland's (1940) analysis of white-collar crime: crimes committed by corporations are almost always prosecuted as civil cases, but the same crime committed by an individual is ordinarily treated as a criminal offense.

Some rules are enforced only when they result in certain consequences. The unmarried mother furnishes a clear example. Vincent (1961) points out that illicit sexual relations seldom result in severe punishment or social censure for the offenders. If, however, a girl becomes pregnant as a result of such activities the reaction of others is likely to be severe. (The illicit pregnancy is also an interesting example of the differential enforcement of rules on different categories of people. Vincent notes that unmarried fathers escape the severe censure visited on the mother.)

Why repeat these commonplace observations? Because, taken together, they support the proposition that deviance is not a simple quality, present in some kinds of behavior and absent in others. Rather, it is the product of a process which involves responses of other people to the behavior. The same behavior may be an infraction of the rules at one time and not at another, or it may be an infraction when committed by one person, but not when committed by another; some rules are broken with impunity, others are not. In short, whether a given act is deviant or not depends in part on the nature of the act (that is, whether or not it violates some rule) and in part on what other people do about it.

Some people may object that this is merely a terminological quibble, that one can, after all, define terms any way he wants to and that if some people want to speak of rule-breaking behavior as deviant without reference to the reactions of others they are free to do so. This, of course, is true. Yet it might be worthwhile to refer to such behavior as *rule-breaking behavior* and reserve the term *deviant* for those labeled as deviant by some segment of society. I do not insist that this usage be followed. But it should be clear that insofar as a scientist uses "deviant" to refer to any rule-breaking behavior and takes as his subject of study only those who have been *labeled* deviant, he will be hampered by the disparities between the two categories.

If we take as the object of our attention behavior which comes to be labeled as deviant, we must recognize that we cannot know whether a given act will be categorized as deviant until the response of others has occurred. Deviance is not a quality that lies in behavior itself but in the interation between the person who commits an act and those who respond to it.

References

Cohen, Albert K. and James F. Short, Jr. 1961. "Juvenile Delinquency." In Robert Merton and Robert Nisbet (eds.), *Contemporary Social Problems*. New York: Harcourt, Brace.

Davis, F. James. 1952. "Crime News in Colorado Newspapers," *American Journal of Sociology* 58 (January):325–30.

Garfinkel, Harold. 1949. "Research Notes on Inter- and Intra-Racial Homocides," *Social Forces* 27 (May):369–81.

Kitsuse, John. 1962. "Societal Reaction to Deviant Behavior: Problems of Theory and Method," *Social Problems* 9 (Winter): 247–56.

Lemert, E. M. 1951. *Social Pathology*. New York: McGraw-Hill.

Sutherland, Edwin H. 1940. "White Collar Criminality," *American Sociological Review* 5 (February):1–12.

Tannenbaum, Frank. 1938. *Crime and the Community*. New York: Columbia University Press.

Vincent, Clark. 1961. *Unmarried Mothers*. New York: Free Press of Glencoe, pp. 3–5.

26

The Tyranny
of the Label

KAI T. ERIKSON

One of the earliest problems the sociologist encounters in his search for a
meaningful approach to deviant behavior is that the subject itself does not
seem to have any natural boundaries. Like people in any field, sociologists
find it convenient to assume that the deviant person is somehow "different"
from those of his fellows who manage to conform, but years of research into
the problem have not yielded any important evidence as to what, if anything, this difference might be. Investigators have studied the character of
the deviant's background, the content of his dreams, the shape of his skull,
the substance of his thoughts—yet none of this information has enabled us to
draw a clear line between the kind of person who commits deviant acts and
the kind of person who does not. Nor can we gain a better perspective on the
matter by shifting our attention away from the individual deviant and looking instead at the behavior he enacts. Definitions of deviance vary widely as
we range over the various classes found in a single society or across the
various cultures into which mankind is divided, and it soon becomes apparent
that there are no objective properties which all deviant acts can be said to
share in common—even within the confines of a given group. Behavior
which qualifies one man for prison may qualify another for sainthood, since
the quality of the act itself depends so much on the circumstances under
which it was performed and the temper of the audience which witnessed it.

   This being the case, many sociologists employ a far simpler tactic in
their approach to the problem—namely, to let each social group in question

provide its own definitions of deviant behavior. In this study, as in others dealing with the same general subject,[1] the term "deviance" refers to conduct which the people of a group consider so dangerous or embarrassing or irritating that they bring special sanctions to bear against the persons who exhibit it. Deviance is not a property *inherent in* any particular kind of behavior; it is a property *conferred upon* that behavior by the people who come into direct or indirect contact with it. The only way an observer can tell whether or not a given style of behavior is deviant, then, is to learn something about the standards of the audience which responds to it.

This definition may seem a little awkward in practice, but it has the advantage of bringing a neglected issue into proper focus. When the people of a community decide that it is time to "do something" about the conduct of one of their number, they are involved in a highly intricate process. After all, even the worst miscreant in society conforms most of the time, if only in the sense that he uses the correct silver at dinner, stops obediently at traffic lights, or in a hundred other ways respects the ordinary conventions of his group. And if his fellows elect to bring sanctions against him for the occasions when he does misbehave, they are responding to a few deviant details scattered among a vast array of entirely acceptable conduct. The person who appears in a criminal court and is stamped a "thief" may have spent no more than a passing moment engaged in that activity, and the same can be said for many of the people who pass in review before some agency of control and return from the experience with a deviant label of one sort or another. When the community nominates someone to the deviant class, then, it is sifting a few important details out of the stream of behavior he has emitted and is in effect declaring that these details reflect the kind of person he "really" is. In law as well as in public opinion, the fact that someone has committed a felony or has been known to use narcotics can become the major identifying badge of his person: the very expression "he is a thief" or "he is an addict" seems to provide at once a description of his position in society and a profile of his character.

The manner in which a community sifts these telling details out of a person's overall performance, then, is an important part of its social control apparatus. And it is important to notice that the people of a community take a number of factors into account when they pass judgment on one another which are not immediately related to the deviant act itself: whether or not a

[1] See particularly the works of Edwin M. Lemert, Howard S. Becker, and John I. Kitsuse.

person will be considered deviant, for instance, has something to do with his social class, his past record as an offender, the amount of remorse he manages to convey, and many similar concerns which take hold in the shifting mood of the community. Perhaps this is not so apparent in cases of serious crime or desperate illness, where the offending act looms so darkly that it obscures most of the other details of the person's life, but in the day-by-day sifting processes which take place throughout society this feature is always present. Some men who drink heavily are called alcoholics and others are not, some men who behave oddly are committed to hospitals and others are not, some men with no visible means of support are charged with vagrancy and others are not—and the difference between those who earn a deviant title in society and those who go their own way in peace is largely determined by the way in which the community filters out and codes the many details of behavior which come to its attention.

Once the problem is phrased in this manner we can ask: how does a community decide which of these behavioral details are important enough to merit special attention? And why, having made this decision, does it build institutions like prisons and asylums to detain the persons who perform them? The conventional answer to that question, of course, is that a society creates the machinery of control in order to protect itself against the "harmful" effects of deviation, in much the same way that an organism mobilizes its resources to combat an invasion of germs. Yet this simple view of the matter is apt to pose many more problems than it actually settles. As both Emile Durkheim and George Herbert Mead pointed out long ago, it is by no means evident that all acts considered deviant in society are in fact (or even in principle) harmful to group life. It is undoubtedly true that no culture would last long if its members engaged in murder or arson among themselves on any large scale, but there is no real evidence that many other of the activities considered deviant throughout the world (certain dietary prohibitions are a prominent example) have any relationship to the group's survival. In our own day, for instance, we might well ask why prostitution or marihuana smoking or homosexuality are thought to endanger the health of the social order. Perhaps these activities *are* dangerous, but to accept this conclusion without a thoughtful review of the situation is apt to blind us to the important fact that people in every corner of the world manage to survive handsomely while engaged in practices which their neighbors regard as extremely abhorrent. In the absence of any surer footing, then, it is quite reasonable for sociologists to return to the most innocent and yet the most basic question which can be asked about deviation: why does a community assign one form of behavior rather than another to the deviant class? . . .

References

Becker, Howard S. 1963. *Outsiders*. New York: Free Press.

Kitsuse, John I. 1962. "Societal Reaction to Deviant Behavior: Problems of Theory and Method," *Social Problems* 9 (Winter):247–56.

Lemert, Edwin M. 1951. *Social Pathology*. New York: McGraw-Hill.

1967. *Human Deviance, Social Problems, and Social Control*. Englewood Cliffs, N.J.: Prentice-Hall.

27

Two Studies
of Legal Stigma

RICHARD SCHWARTZ
AND JEROME SKOLNICK

Legal thinking has moved increasingly toward a sociologically meaningful view of the legal system. Sanctions, in particular, have come to be regarded in functional terms.[1] In criminal law, for instance, sanctions are said to be designed to prevent recidivism by rehabilitating, restraining, or executing the offender. They are also said to be intended to deter others from the performance of similar acts and, sometimes, to provide a channel for the expression of retaliatory motives. In such civil actions as tort or contract, monetary awards may be intended as retributive and deterrent, as in the use of punitive damages, or may be regarded as a *quid pro quo* to compensate the plaintiff for his wrongful loss.

While these goals comprise an integral part of the rationale of law, little is known about the extent to which they are fulfilled in practice. Lawmen do not as a rule make such studies, because their traditions and techniques are not designed for a systematic examination of the operation of the legal system in action, especially outside the courtroom. Thus, when extra-legal consequences—e.g., the social stigma of a prison sentence—are taken into account at all, it is through the discretionary actions of police, prosecutor, judge, and jury. Systematic information on a variety of unanticipated outcomes, those which benefit the accused as well as those which hurt him,

Reprinted with permission of the Society for the Study of Social Problems from "Two Studies of Legal Stigma," *Social Problems* 10 (Fall 1962) by Richard D. Schwartz and Jerome H. Skolnick.

[1] Legal sanctions are defined as changes in life conditions, imposed through court action.

might help to inform these decision makers and perhaps lead to changes in substantive law as well. The present paper is an attempt to study the consequences of stigma associated with legal accusation.

From a sociological viewpoint, there are several types of indirect consequences of legal sanctions which can be distinguished. These include differential deterrence, effects on the sanctionee's associates and variations in the degree of deprivation which sanction imposes on the recipient himself.

First, the imposition of sanction, while intended as a matter of overt policy to deter the public at large, probably will vary in its effectiveness as a deterrent, depending upon the extent to which potential offenders perceive themselves as similar to the sanctionee. Such "differential deterrence" would occur if white-collar antitrust violators were restrained by the conviction of General Electric executives, but not by invocation of the Sherman Act against union leaders.

The imposition of a sanction may even provide an unintended incentive to violate the law. A study of factors affecting compliance with federal income tax laws provides some evidence of this effect (Schwartz, 1959). Some respondents reported that they began to cheat on their tax returns only *after* convictions for tax evasion had been obtained against others in their jurisdiction. They explained this surprising behavior by noting that the prosecutions had always been conducted against blatant violators and not against the kind of moderate offenders which they then became. These respondents were, therefore, unintentionally educated to the possibility of supposedly "safe" violations.

Second, deprivations or benefits may accrue to nonsanctioned individuals by virtue of the web of affiliations that join them to the defendant. The wife and family of a convicted man may, for instance, suffer from his arrest as much as the man himself. On the other hand, they may be relieved by his absence if the family relationship has been an unhappy one. Similarly, whole groups of persons may be affected by sanctions to an individual, as when discriminatory practices increase because of a highly publicized crime attributed to a member of a given minority group.

Finally, the social position of the defendant himself will serve to aggravate or alleviate the effects of any given sanction. Although all three indirect consequences may be interrelated, it is the third with which this paper will be primarily concerned.

Endings

The subjects studied to examine the effects of legal accusation on occupational positions represented two extremes: lower-class unskilled workers charged with assault, and medical doctors accused of malpractice. The first project lent itself to a field experiment, while the second required a survey design. Because of differences in method and substance, the studies cannot be used as formal controls for each other. Taken together, however, they do suggest that the indirect effects of sanctions can be powerful, that they can produce unintended harm or unexpected benefit, and that the results are related to officially unemphasized aspects of the social context in which the sanctions are administered. Accordingly, the two studies will be discussed together, as bearing on one another. Strictly speaking, however, each can, and properly should, stand alone as a separate examination of the unanticipated consequences of legal sanctions.

STUDY I. THE EFFECTS OF A CRIMINAL COURT RECORD ON THE EMPLOYMENT OPPORTUNITIES OF UNSKILLED WORKERS

In the field experiment, four employment folders were prepared, the same in all respects except for the criminal court record of the applicant. In all of the folders he was described as a 32-year-old single male of unspecified race, with a high school training in mechanical trades, and a record of successive short-term jobs as a kitchen helper, maintenance worker, and handyman. These characteristics are roughly typical of applicants for unskilled hotel jobs in the Catskill resort area of New York State where employment opportunities were tested.[2]

The four folders differed only in the applicant's reported record of criminal court involvement. The first folder indicated that the applicant had been convicted and sentenced for assault; the second, that he had been tried

[2] The generality of these results remains to be determined. The effects of criminal involvement in the Catskill area are probably diminished, however, by the temporary nature of employment, the generally poor qualifications of the work force, and the excess of demand over supply of unskilled labor there. Accordingly, the employment differences among the four treatment groups found in this study are likely, if anything, to be smaller than would be expected in industries and areas where workers are more carefully selected.

for assault and acquitted; the third, also tried for assault and acquitted, but
with a letter from the judge certifying the finding of not guilty and reaffirm-
ing the legal presumption of innocence. The fourth folder made no mention
of any criminal record.

A sample of one hundred employers was utilized. Each employer was
assigned to one of four "treatment" groups.[3] To each employer only one
folder was shown; this folder was one of the four kinds mentioned above,
the selection of the folder being determined by the treatment group to which
the potential employer was assigned. The employer was asked whether he
could "use" the man described in the folder. To preserve the reality of the
situation and make it a true field experiment, employers were never given
any indication that they were participating in an experiment. So far as they
knew, a legitimate offer to work was being made in each showing of the
folder by the "employment agent."

The experiment was designed to determine what employers would do in
fact if confronted with an employment applicant with a criminal record. The
questionnaire approach used in earlier studies seemed ill-adapted to the
problem, since respondents confronted with hypothetical situations might be
particularly prone to answer in what they considered a socially acceptable
manner (Rubin, 1958: 151–158). The second alternative—studying job opportunities of individuals who had been involved with the law—would have
made it very difficult to find comparable groups of applicants and potential
employers. For these reasons, the field experiment reported here was utilized.

Some deception was involved in the study. The "employment
agent"—the same individual in all hundred cases—was in fact a law student
who was working in the Catskills during the summer of 1959 as an insurance adjuster. In representing himself as being both an adjuster and an
employment agent, he was assuming a combination of roles which is not uncommon there. The adjuster role gave him an opportunity to introduce a
single application for employment casually and naturally. To the extent that

---

[3] Employers were not approached in preselected random order, due to a misunderstanding of instructions on the part of the law student who carried out the experiment during a 3½-week
period. Because of this flaw in the experimental procedure, the results should be treated with
appropriate caution. Thus, chi-square analysis may not properly be utilized. (For those used to
this measure, $p < .05$ for Table 27.1.)

the experiment worked, however, it was inevitable that some employers should be led to believe that they had immediate prospects of filling a job opening. In those instances where an offer to hire was made, the "agent" called a few hours later to say that the applicant had taken another job. The field experimenter attempted in such instances to locate a satisfactory replacement by contacting an employment agency in the area. Because this procedure was used and since the jobs involved were of relatively minor consequence, we believe that the deception caused little economic harm.

As mentioned, each treatment group of 25 employers was approached with one type of folder. Responses were dichotomized: those who expressed a willingness to consider the applicant in any way were termed positive; those who made no response or who explicitly refused to consider the candidate were termed negative. Our results consist of comparisons between positive and negative responses, thus defined, for the treatment groups.

Of the 25 employers shown the "no record" folder, nine gave positive responses. Subject to reservations arising from chance variations in sampling, we take this as indicative of the "ceiling" of jobs available for this kind of applicant under the given field conditions. Positive responses by these employers may be compared with those in the other treament groups to obtain an indication of job opportunities lost because of the various legal records.

Of the 25 employers approached with the "convict" folder, only one expressed interest in the applicant. This is a rather graphic indication of the effect which a criminal record may have on job opportunities. Care must be exercised, of course, in generalizing the conclusions to other settings. In this context, however, the criminal record made a major difference.

From a theoretical point of view, the finding leads toward the conclusion that conviction constitutes a powerful form of "status degradation" which continues to operate after the time when, according to the generalized theory of justice underlying punishment in our society, the individual's "debt" has been paid. (Garfinkel, 1956). A record of conviction produces a durable if not permanent loss of status. For purposes of effective social control, this state of affairs may heighten the deterrent effect of conviction—though that remains to be established. Any such contribution to social control, however, must be balanced against the barriers imposed upon rehabilitation of the convict. If the ex-prisoner finds difficulty in securing menial kinds of legitimate work, further crime may become an increasingly attractive alternative.[4]

Another important finding of this study concerns the small number of positive responses elicited by the "accused but acquitted" applicant. Of the 25 employers approached with this folder, three offered jobs. Thus, the individual accused but acquitted of assault has almost as much trouble finding even an unskilled job as the one who was not only accused of the same offense, but also convicted.

From a theoretical point of view, this result indicates that permanent lowering of status is not limited to those explicitly singled out by being convicted of a crime. As an ideal outcome of American justice, criminal procedure is supposed to distinguish between the "guilty" and those who have been acquitted. Legally controlled consequences which follow the judgment are consistent with this purpose. Thus, the "guilty" are subject to fine and imprisonment, while those who are acquitted are immune from these sanctions. But deprivations may be imposed on the acquitted, both before and after victory in court. Before trial, legal rules either permit or require arrest and detention. The suspect may be faced with the expense of an attorney and a bail bond if he is to mitigate these limitations on his privacy and freedom. In addition, some pretrial deprivations are imposed without formal legal permission. These may include coercive questioning, use of violence, and stigmatization. And, as this study indicates, some deprivations not under the direct control of the legal process may develop or persist after an official decision of acquittal has been made.

Thus two legal principles conflict in practice. On the one hand, "a man is innocent until proven guilty." On the other, the accused is systematically treated as guilty under the administration of criminal law until a functionary or official body—police, magistrate, prosecuting attorney, or trial judge or jury—decides that he is entitled to be free. Even then, the results of treating him as guilty persist and may lead to serious consequences.

The conflict could be eased by measures aimed at reducing the depriva-

[4] Severe negative effects of conviction on employment opportunities have been noted by Rubin (1958). A further source of employment difficulty is inherent in licensing statutes and security regulations which sometimes preclude convicts from being employed in their preconvict occupation or even in the trades which they may have acquired during imprisonment. These effects may, however, be counteracted by bonding arrangements, prison associations, and publicity programs aimed at increasing confidence in, and sympathy for, ex-convicts; see also McSally (1960), Lasswell and Donnelly (1959), and Andeneas (1952).

tions imposed on the accused, before and after acquittal. Some legal attention has been focused on pretrial deprivations. The provision of bail and
counsel, the availability of habeas corpus, limitations on the admissibility of
coerced confessions, and civil actions for false arrest are examples of measures aimed at protecting the rights of the accused before trial. Although
these are often limited in effectiveness, especially for individuals of lower
socioeconomic status, they at least represent some concern with implementing the presumption of innocence at the pretrial stage.

By contrast, the courts have done little toward alleviating the postacquittal consequences of legal accusation. One effort along these lines has
been employed in the federal courts, however. Where an individual has been
accused and exonerated of a crime, he may petition the federal courts for a
"Certificate of Innocence" certifying this fact.[5] Possession of such a docu-
ment might be expected to alleviate postacquittal deprivations.

Some indication of the effectiveness of such a measure is found in the
responses of the final treatment group. Their folder, it will be recalled, contained information on the accusation and acquittal of the applicant, but also
included a letter from a judge addressed "To whom it may concern" certifying the applicant's acquittal and reminding the reader of the presumption of
innocence. Such a letter might have had a boomerang effect, by reempha-
sizing the legal involvement of the applicant. It was important, therefore, to
determine empirically whether such a communication would improve or
harm the chances of employment. Our findings indicate that it increased
employment opportunities, since the letter folder elicited six positive responses. Even though this fell short of the nine responses to the "no
record" folder, it doubled the number for the "accused but acquitted" and
created a significantly greater number of job offers than those elicited by the
convicted record. This suggests that the procedure merits consideration as a
means of offsetting the occupational loss resulting from accusation. It should
be noted, however, that repeated use of this device might reduce its effectiveness.

The results of the experiment are summarized in Table 27.1. The differences in outcome found there indicate that various types of legal records
are systematically related to job opportunities. It seems fair to infer also that
the trend of job losses corresponds with the apparent punitive intent of the
authorities. Where the man is convicted, that intent is presumably greatest.

[5] 28 United States Code, Secs. 1495, 2513.

TABLE 27.1. EFFECT OF FOUR TYPES OF LEGAL FOLDER ON JOB OPPOR-
TUNITIES

	No Record	Acquitted With Letter	Acquitted Without Letter	Convicted	Total
(in percent)					
	(N = 25)	(N = 25)	(N = 25)	(N = 25)	(N = 100)
Positive response	36	24	12	4	19
Negative response	64	76	88	96	81
Total	100	100	100	100	100

It is less where he is accused but acquitted and still less where the court makes an effort to emphasize the absence of a finding of guilt. Nevertheless, where the difference in punitive intent is ideally greatest, between conviction and acquittal, the difference in occupational harm is very slight. A similar blurring of this distinction shows up in a different way in the next study.

STUDY II: THE EFFECTS ON DEFENDANTS OF SUITS FOR MEDICAL MALPRACTICE

As indicated earlier, the second study differed from the first in a number of ways: method of research, social class of accused, relationship between the accused and his "employer," social support available to accused, type of offense and its possible relevance to occupational adequacy. Because the two studies differ in so many ways, the reader is again cautioned to avoid thinking of them as providing a rigorous comparative examination. They are presented together only to demonstrate that legal accusation can produce unanticipated deprivations, as in the case of Study I, or unanticipated benefits, as in the research now to be presented. In the discussion to follow, some of the possible reasons for the different outcomes will be suggested.

The extralegal effects of a malpractice suit were studied by obtaining the records of Connecticut's leading carrier of malpractice insurance. According to these records, a total of 69 doctors in the state had been sued in 64 suits during the post World War II period covered by the study, September 1945 to September 1959.[6] Some suits were instituted against more

[6] A spot-check of one county revealed that the Company's records covered every malpractice suit tried in the courts of that county during this period.

than one doctor, and four physicians had been sued twice. Of the total of 69 physicians, 58 were questioned. Interviews were conducted with the approval of the Connecticut Medical Association by Robert Wyckoff, whose extraordinary qualifications for the work included possession of both the M.D. and LL.B. degrees. Dr. Wyckoff was able to secure detailed response to his inquiries from all doctors contacted.

Twenty of the respondents were questioned by personal interview, 28 by telephone, and the remainder by mail. Forty-three of those reached practiced principally in cities, eleven in suburbs, and four in rural areas. Seventeen were engaged in general practice and 41 were specialists. The sample proved comparable to the doctors in the state as a whole in age, experience, and professional qualifications.[7] The range was from the lowest professional stratum to chiefs of staff and services in the state's most highly regarded hospitals.

Of the 57 malpractice cases reported, doctors clearly won 38; nineteen of these were dropped by the plaintiff and an equal number were won in court by the defendant doctor. Of the remaining nineteen suits, eleven were settled out of court for a nominal amount, four for approximately the amount the plaintiff claimed, and four resulted in judgment for the plaintiff in court.

The malpractice survey did not reveal widespread occupational harm to the physicians involved. Of the 58 respondents, 52 reported no negative effects of the suit on their practice, and five of the remaining six, all specialists, reported that their practice *improved* after the suit. The heaviest loser in court (a radiologist), reported the largest gain. He commented, ''I guess all the doctors in town felt sorry for me because new patients started coming in from doctors who had not sent me patients previously.'' Only one doctor reported adverse consequences to his practice. A winner in court, this man suffered physical and emotional stress symptoms which hampered his later effectiveness in surgical work. The temporary drop in his practice appears to have been produced by neurotic symptoms and is therefore only indirectly traceable to the malpractice suit. Seventeen other doctors reported varying degrees of personal dissatisfaction and anxiety during and after the suit, but none of them reported impairment of practice. No significant relationship was found between outcome of the suit and expressed dissatisfaction.

A protective institutional environment helps to explain these results. No

---

[7] No relationship was found between any of these characteristics and the legal or extralegal consequences of the lawsuit.

cases were found in which a doctor's hospital privileges were reduced following the suit. Neither was any physician unable later to obtain malpractice insurance, although a handful found it necessary to pay higher rates. The State Licensing Commission, which is headed by a doctor, did not intervene in any instance. Local medical societies generally investigated charges through their ethics and grievance committees, but where they took any action, it was almost always to recommend or assist in legal defense against the suit.

Discussion

Accusation has different outcomes for unskilled workers and doctors in the two studies. How may these be explained? First, they might be nothing more than artifacts of research method. In the field experiment, it was possible to see behavior directly, i.e., to determine how employers act when confronted with what appears to them to be a realistic opportunity to hire. Responses are therefore not distorted by the memory of the respondent. By contrast, the memory of the doctors might have been consciously or unconsciously shaped by the wish to create the impression that the public had not taken seriously the accusation leveled against them. The motive for such a distortion might be either to protect the respondent's self-esteem or to preserve an image of public acceptance in the eyes of the interviewer, the profession, and the public. Efforts of the interviewer to assure his subject of anonymity—intended to offset these effects—may have succeeded or may, on the contrary, have accentuated an awareness of the danger. A related type of distortion might have stemmed from a desire by doctors to affect public attitudes toward malpractice. Two conflicting motives might have been expected to enter here. The doctor might have tended to exaggerate the harm caused by an accusation, especially if followed by acquittal, in order to turn public opinion toward legal policies which would limit malpractice liability. On the other hand, he might tend to underplay extralegal harm caused by a legally insufficient accusation in order to discourage potential plaintiffs from instituting suits aimed at securing remunerative settlements and/or revenge for grievances. Whether these diverse motives operated to distort doctors' reports and, if so, which of them produced the greater degree of distortion is a matter for speculation. It is only suggested here that the interview method is more subject to certain types of distortion than the direct behavioral observations of the field experiment.

Even if such distortion did not occur, the results may be attributable to differences in research design. In the field experiment, a direct comparison is made between the occupational position of an accused and an identical individual not accused at a single point in time. In the medical study, effects were inferred through retrospective judgment, although checks on actual income would have no doubt confirmed these judgments. Granted that income had increased, many other explanations are available to account for it. An improvement in practice after a malpractice suit may have resulted from factors extraneous to the suit. The passage of time in the community and increased experience may have led to a larger practice and may even have masked negative effects of the suit. There may have been a general increase in practice for the kinds of doctors involved in these suits, even greater for doctors not sued than for doctors in the sample. Whether interviews with a control sample could have yielded sufficiently precise data to rule out these possibilities is problematic. Unfortunately, the resources available for the study did not enable such data to be obtained.

A third difference in the two designs may affect the results. In the field experiment, full information concerning the legal record is provided to all of the relevant decision makers, i.e., the employers. In the medical study, by contrast, the results depend on decisions of actual patients to consult a given doctor. It may be assumed that such decisions are often based on imperfect information, some patients knowing little or nothing about the malpractice suit. To ascertain how much information employers usually have concerning the legal record of the employee and then supply that amount would have been a desirable refinement, but a difficult one. The alternative approach would involve turning the medical study into an experiment in which full information concerning malpractice (e.g., liable, accused but acquitted, no record of accusation) was supplied to potential patients. This would have permitted a comparison of the effects of legal accusation in two instances where information concerning the accusation is constant. To carry out such an experiment in a field situation would require an unlikely degree of cooperation, for instance by a medical clinic which might ask patients to choose their doctor on the basis of information given them. It is difficult to conceive of an experiment along these lines which would be both realistic enough to be valid and harmless enough to be ethical.

If we assume, however, that these methodological problems do not invalidate the basic finding, how may it be explained? Why would unskilled workers accused but acquitted of assault have great difficulty getting jobs, while doctors accused of malpractice—whether acquitted or not—are left unharmed or more sought after than before?

First, the charge of criminal assault carries with it the legal allegation and the popular connotation of intent to harm. Malpractice, on the other hand, implies negligence or failure to exercise reasonable care. Even though actual physical harm may be greater in malpractice, the element of intent suggests that the man accused of assault would be more likely to repeat his attempt and to find the mark. However, it is dubious that this fine distinction could be drawn by the lay public.

Perhaps more important, all doctors and particularly specialists may be immune from the effects of a malpractice suit because their services are in short supply.[8] By contrast, the unskilled worker is one of many and therefore likely to be passed over in favor of someone with a "cleaner" record.

Moreover, high occupational status, such as is demonstrably enjoyed by doctors,[9] probably tends to insulate the doctor from imputations of incompetence. In general, professionals are assumed to possess uniformly high ability, to be oriented toward community service, and to enforce adequate standards within their own organization (Parsons, 1951; Hughes, 1958). Doctors in particular receive deference, just because they are doctors, not only from the population as a whole but even from fellow professionals (Zander et al., 1957).

Finally, individual doctors appear to be protected from the effects of accusation by the sympathetic and powerful support they receive from fellow members of the occupation, a factor absent in the case of unskilled,

---

[8] Freidson's (1960) point is that general practitioners are more subject to client control than specialists are. Our findings emphasize the importance of professional as compared to client control, and professional protection against a particular form of client control, extending through both branches of the medical profession. However, what holds for malpractice situations may not be true of routine medical practice.

[9] National Opinion Research Center (1947). More recent studies in several countries tend to confirm the high status of the physician; see Inkeles (1960).

unorganized laborers.[10] The medical society provides advice on handling
malpractice actions, for instance, and referrals by other doctors sometimes
increase as a consequence of the sympathy felt for the malpractice suit victim. Such assistance is further evidence that the professional operates as "a
community within a community," (Goode, 1957), shielding its members
from controls exercised by formal authorities in the larger society.

In order to isolate these factors, additional studies are needed. It would
be interesting to know, for instance, whether high occupational status would
protect a doctor acquitted of a charge of assault. Information on this question is sparse. Actual instances of assaults by doctors are probably very rare.
When and if they do occur, it seems unlikely that they would lead to publicity
and prosecution, since police and prosecutor discretion might usually be
employed to quash charges before they are publicized. In the rare instances
in which they come to public attention, such accusations appear to produce a
marked effect because of the assumption that the pressing of charges, despite the status of the defendant, indicates probable guilt. Nevertheless, instances may be found in which even the accusation of first degree murder
followed by acquittal appears to have left the doctor professionally un-
scathed.[11] Similarly, as a test of the group protection hypothesis, one might
investigate the effect of an acquittal for assault on working men who are
union members. The analogy would be particularly instructive where the
union plays an important part in employment decisions, for instance in industries which make use of a union hiring hall.

In the absence of studies which isolate the effect of such factors, our
findings cannot readily be generalized. It is tempting to suggest after an initial look at the results that social class differences provide the explanation. But subsequent analysis and research might well reveal significant in-
traclass variations, depending on the distribution of other operative factors.
A lower-class person with a scarce specialty and a protective occupational
group who is acquitted of a lightly regarded offense might benefit from the
accusation. Nevertheless, class in general seems to correlate with the rele-

---

[10] Unions sometimes act to protect the seniority rights of members who, discharged from their
jobs upon arrest, seek reemployment following their acquittal.

[11] For instance, the acquittal of Dr. John Bodkin Adams after a sensational murder trial, in
which he was accused of deliberately killing several elderly women patients to inherit their es-
tates, was followed by his quiet return to medical practice. *New York Times,* Nov. 24, 1961,
p. 28. Whether the British regard acquittals as more exonerative than Americans is uncertain.

vant factors to such an extent that in reality the law regularly works to the disadvantage of the already more disadvantaged classes.

Conclusion

Legal accusation imposes a variety of consequences, depending on the nature of the accusation and the characteristics of the accused. Deprivations occur, even though not officially intended, in the case of unskilled workers who have been acquitted of assault charges. On the other hand, malpractice actions—even when resulting in a judgment against the doctor—are not usually followed by negative consequences and sometimes have a favorable effect on the professional position of the defendant. These differences in outcome suggest two conclusions: one, the need for more explicit clarification of legal goals; two, the importance of examining the attitudes and social structure of the community outside the courtroom if the legal process is to hit intended targets, while avoiding innocent bystanders. Greater precision in communicating goals and in appraising consequences of present practices should help to make the legal process an increasingly equitable and effective instrument of social control.

References

Andeneas, J. 1952. "General Prevention—Illusion or Reality? *Journal of Criminal Law, Criminology, and Police Science* 43 (July-August):176–98.

Freidson, Eliot. 1960. "Client Control and Medical Practice," *American Journal of Sociology* 65 (January):374–82.

Garfinkel, Harold. 1956. "Conditions of Successful Degradation Ceremonies," *American Journal of Sociology* 61 (March):420–24.

Goode, William J. 1957. "Community within a Community: The Professions," *American Sociological Review* 22 (April):194–200.

Hughes, Everett C. 1958. *Men and Their Work*. Glencoe, Ill.: Free Press.

Inkeles, Alex. 1960. "Industrial Man: The Relation of Status to Experience, Perception, and Value," *American Journal of Sociology* 66 (July):1–31.

Lasswell, Harold D. and Richard C. Donnelly. 1959. "The Continuing Debate over Responsibility: An Introduction to Isolating the Condemnation Sanction," *Yale Law Journal* 68 (April):869–99.

McSally, B. F. 1960. "Finding Jobs for Released Offenders," *Federal Probation* 24 (June):12–17.

National Opinion Research Center. 1947. "Jobs and Occupations: A Popular Evaluation," *Opinion News* 9 (September):3–13.

Parsons, Talcott. 1958. *The Social System*. Glencoe, Ill.: Free Press, pp. 454-73.

Rubin, Sol. 1958. *Crime and Juvenile Delinquency*. New York: Oceana.

Schwartz, Richard D. 1959. "The Effectiveness of Legal Contracts: Factors in the Reporting of Minor Items of Income on Federal Income Tax Returns." Paper presented at the annual meeting of the American Sociological Association, Chicago.

Zander, Alvin, Arthur R. Cohen, and Ezra Stotland. 1957. *Role Relations in the Mental Health Professions*. Ann Arbor, Mich.: Institute for Social Research.

28

Self-Perception
and the Shoplifter

MARY OWEN CAMERON

It seems probable that most adult pilferers start their careers as children or adolescents in groups where the techniques of successful pilfering are learned from other more experienced children. Later, as group activity is abandoned, some of the group members continue the practices they learned as adolescents. The lavish displays of merchandise which department stores exhibit to encourage "impulse buying" are, for the experienced pilferer, there for the taking.

Adult women pilferers, generally belonging to families of rather modest income, enter department stores with a strong sense of the limitations of their household budgets. They do not steal merchandise which they can rationalize purchasing: household supplies, husband's clothes, children's wear. But beautiful and luxury goods for their personal use can be purchased legitimately only if some other member of the family is deprived. Although pilferers often have guilt feelings about their thefts, it still seems to them less wrong to steal from a rich store than to take from the family budget. Pilferers seem to be, thus, narcissistic individuals in that they steal for their own personal use, but, on the other hand, they do not use the limited family income for their own luxury goods.

Pilferers differ in one outstanding respect, at least, from other thieves: They generally do not think of themselves as thieves. In fact, even when arrested, they resist strongly being pushed to admit their behavior is theft. This became very clear as I observed a number of interrogations of shoplifters by the store detective staff, and it was supported in conversations with the detectives who drew on their own wider experience. It is quite often difficult for the store staff to convince the arrested person that he has actually been arrested, even when the detectives show their licenses and badges. Again and again store police explain to pilferers that they are under arrest as thieves, that they will, in the normal course of events, be taken in a police van to jail, held in jail until bond is raised, and tried in a court before a judge and sentenced. Much of the interview time of store detectives is devoted to establishing this point; in making the pilferer understand that what happens to him from the time of his arrest is a legal question, but it is still a question for decision, first of all, by the store staff.

Store detectives use the naiveté of pilferers as an assistance in arrest procedures while the pilferer is in the presence of legitimate customers on the floor of the store. The most tactful approach possible is used. The store detective will say, for example, "I represent the store office, and I'm afraid the office will have to see what's in your shopping bag. Would you care to come with me, please?" If the pilferer protests, the detective adds, "You wouldn't want to be embarrassed in front of all these people, would you? In the office we can talk things over in private."

Edwards (1958: 134) states that the method of making an arrest is important in preventing excitement and even disorder.

A gentle approach will usually disarm any shoplifter, amateur or professional, while a rough seizure or loud accusation may immediately put him on the defensive. At other times it may result in a nervous or hysterical condition accompanied by an involuntary discharge which may be embarrassing to both the arrestor and the arrested.

Inbau (1952) adds the thought that the gentle approach is helpful too in forestalling suits for false arrest.

The finesse with which defendant accosts plaintiff is a definite factor also affecting the temper with which the court approaches a case. The defendant acting in good faith with probable cause, whose attitude is quiet, non-threatening, and deferential to the plaintiff's feelings can weather an honest mistake much more cheaply than otherwise. At the most it may induce a court to find there was no imprisonment at all. At the least, it will relieve defendant of punitive damages and reduce the amount of actual damages.

The "deference" of the arresting detective combined with the already existing rationalizations of the pilferer sustain in him the belief that whereas his behavior might be reprehensible, the objects taken were, after all, not of great value; he would be glad to pay for them and be on his way. "Yes, I took the dress," one woman sobbed as she was being closely interrogated, "but that doesn't mean I'm a thief."

Arrest forces the pilferer to think of himself as a thief. The interrogation procedure of the store is specifically and consciously aimed at breaking down any illusions the shoplifter may have that his behavior is regarded as merely "naughty" or "bad." The breakdown of illusions is, to the store detective staff, both a goal in itself and a means of establishing the fact that each innocent-appearing pilferer is not, in fact, a professional thief "putting on an act." In the interrogation the shoplifter is searched for other stolen merchandise and for identification papers. Pockets and pocketbooks are thoroughly examined. All papers, letters, tickets, bills, etc., are read in detail in spite of considerable protest from the arrested person. Each person is made to explain everything he has with him. If suspect items such as public locker keys, pawn tickets, etc., are found, he will have to explain very thoroughly indeed and agree to have the locker examined and the pawned merchandise seen to avoid formal charge. In any event, once name, address, and occupation have been established (and for women, the maiden name and names in other marriages), the file of names and identifying material of all persons who have, in the past years, been arrested in any of the State Street department stores is consulted. The shoplifter is questioned at length if similarities of names or other identifying data are encountered.

While identification and prior record are being checked, store detectives, persons in charge of refunds, and even experienced sales clerks may be summoned to look at the arrested person to determine if he has been previously suspected of stealing merchandise or has been noted as behaving suspiciously.

In the course of all this investigation, it becomes increasingly clear to the pilferer that he is considered a thief and is in imminent danger of being hauled into court and publicly exhibited as such. This realization is often accompanied by a dramatic change in attitudes and by severe emotional disturbance. Occasionally even hysterical semi-attempts at suicide result.

The professional shoplifter who has been arrested and knows he is recognized, on the other hand, behaves quite differently. He does, of course, make every effort possible to talk his way out of the situation. But once he finds that this is impossible, he accepts jail and its inconveniences as a normal hazard of his trade.

"This is a nightmare," said one woman pilferer who had been formally charged with stealing an expensive handbag. "It can't be happening to me! Why, oh why can't I wake up and find that it isn't so," she cried later as she waited at a store exit, accompanied by a city and a store policemen, for the city police van to arrive. "Whatever will I do? Please make it go away," she pleaded with the officer. "I'll be disgraced forever. I can never look anyone in the face again."

Pilferers expect no "in-group" support for their behavior. As they become aware of the possible serious consequences of their arrest (trial, jail, etc.), pilferers obviously feel isolated from all supporting relationships. Store detectives report that the most frequent question women ask is, "Will my husband have to know about this?" Men, they say, express immediate fear that their employers will be informed of their arrest when questions about employment are raised. Children are apprehensive of parental reaction. Edwards (1958: 135–136) says,

> The composure of juveniles being detained has never ceased to amaze me, that is, until notified that they must tell a parent of their misdemeanor. Then the tears flow and pleadings begin. The interviewer must be firm in his denial that notification will "kill" the parent, and he must sell the child on the idea that any deviation from accepted practice must be discussed with the person most interested in his welfare.

Pilferers feel that if their family or friends learn about their arrest they will be thoroughly disgraced. The fear, shame, and remorse expressed by arrested pilferers could not be other than genuine and a reflection of their appraisal of the attitudes they believe others will take toward them. One woman was observed who, thoroughly shaken as the realization of her predicament began to appear to her, interrupted her protestations of innocence from time to time, overwhelmed at the thought of how some particular person in her "in-group" would react to her arrest. Her conversation with the interrogator ran somewhat as follows: "I didn't intend to take the dress. I just wanted to see it in daylight. [She had stuffed it into a shopping bag and carried it out of the store.] Oh, what will my husband do? I *did* intend to pay for it. It's all a mistake. Oh, my God, what will my mother say! I'll be glad to pay for it. See, I've got the money with me. Oh, my children! They can't find out I've been *arrested!* I'd never be able to face them again."

Pilferers not only expect no in-group support, but they feel that they have literally *no* one to turn to. The problem of being embroiled in a wholly unfamiliar legal situation is obviously not only frightening but unexpected. Apparently they had anticipated being reprimanded; they had not anticipated being searched by a licensed detective, identified, etc., and on the whole, placed in a position in which the burden of argument for keeping out of jail is theirs.

The contrast in behavior between the pilferer and the recognized and self-admitted thief is striking. The experienced thief either already knows what to do or knows precisely where and how to find out. His emotional reactions may involve anger directed at himself or at features in the situation around him, but he is not at a loss for reactions. He follows the prescribed modes of behavior, and knows, either because of prior experience or through the vicarious experiences of acquaintances, what arrest involves by way of obligations and rights. He has some familiarity with bonding practice and either already has or knows how to find a lawyer who will act for him.

Because the adult pilferer does not think of himself, prior to his arrest, as a thief and can conceive of no in-group support for himself in that role, his arrest forces him to reject the role (at least insofar as department store shoplifting is concerned). The arrest procedure, even though not followed by prosecution, is in itself sufficient to cause him to redefine his situation. He is, of course, informed that subsequent arrest by any store will be followed by immediate prosecution and probably by a considerable jail sentence. But since this does not act as a deterrent to the self-admitted thief nor could this kind of admonition deter the compulsive neurotic, neither the fear of punishment nor the objective severity of the punishment in itself is the crucial point in relation to the change from criminal to law abiding behavior. Rather the threat to the person's system of values and prestige relationships is involved. Social scientists who have investigated criminal activities which have subcultural support are unanimous in pointing out the persistence of criminal activity, the high rate of recidivism and the resistance to reform shown by law violators. Pilfering seems to be the other side of the coin. Not having the support of a criminal subculture, pilferers are very "reformable" individuals.

References

Edwards, Loren. 1958. *Shoplifting and Shrinkage Protection for Stores*. Springfield, Ill.: C. C. Thomas.

Inbau, Fred E. 1952. "Protection and Recapture of Merchandise from Shoplifters," *Illinois Law Review* 46.

29

Public Stereotypes
of Deviants

J. L. SIMMONS
WITH THE ASSISTANCE OF
HAZEL CHAMBERS

The idea that publics "create" deviance through the same symbolic processes by which they invent "baseball," "flags," and "niggers" existed *passim* in the writings of Durkheim (1938) and has recently been set forth in a more explicit and systematic manner by Lemert (1951), Erikson (1962), Kitsuse (1962), and Becker (1963), among others. Put simply, the assertion is that "deviance" is not an intrinsic attribute of any behavior, but is instead the distilled result of a social process of labelling.[1]

One of the most provocative outgrowths of this approach is that it has focused attention upon the labelling and imputing social audience as well as on the deviate himself. But the approach still remains a promising orientation rather than a full-blown theory.[2] With a few notable exceptions (Kitsuse, 1962; Scheff, 1964), there has been remarkably little explicit investigation of public attitudes toward deviant behavior. And for almost all the questions arising from this perspective, we have little more than intelligent guesses as answers.

Reprinted with permission of the Society for the Study of Social Problems from "Public Stereotypes of Deviants," *Social Problems* 13 (1965) by J. L. Simmons with the assistance of Hazel Chambers. This research was carried out under a grant from the University Research Board, Graduate College, University of Illinois. The writer is indebted to Daniel Glaser for his advice and constructive criticism.

[1] This does not mean there is "really" no such thing as deviance, or that society is the villain and the deviate an innocent bystander.

[2] This is, of course, also true of most other "theories" in sociology; c.f. Zetterberg (1963).

This paper is a report on four pilot studies which were carried out as an attempt to provide a more empirical grounding for the perspective sketched above. The aim was to explore this labelling process and its consequences by modifying techniques previously developed for studying attitudes toward racial and cultural minorities. These studies yielded some preliminary and "soft" data on the following questions: (1) How much agreement is there about what is deviant? (2) Does the public hold stereotyped images of deviants? (3) If so, what are some of the consequences? Some differences between those who stereotype and those who don't will also be noted.

Public Consensus on What is Deviant

In the first pilot study the following question was asked of 180 subjects selected by a quota formula designed to produce variation in age, sex, education, occupation, religion, race, and census region within the sample: [3]

In the following spaces please list those things or types of persons whom you regard as deviant.

In response, the 180 subjects listed a total of 1,154 items (mean of 6.4 responses per subject). Even with a certain amount of grouping and collapsing, these included no less than 252 different acts and persons as "deviant." The sheer range of responses included such expected items as homosexuals, prostitutes, drug addicts, beatniks, and murderers; it also included liars, democrats, reckless drivers, atheists, self-pitiers, the retired, career women, divorcees, movie stars, perpetual bridge-players, prudes, pacifists, psychiatrists, priests, liberals, conservatives, junior executives, girls who wear makeup, and know-it-all professors.

The most frequently mentioned acts or persons, together with the percent of respondents who mentioned them, are given in Table 29.1. No type was mentioned by as many as half of the subjects, and only 14 of the 252 different types were mentioned by as many as 10 percent of the sample. Examination of the percentages in Table 29.1 shows, further, that the proportion *spontaneously* subscribing to a given thing as deviant falls off sharply.

[3] The questionnaires were administered by members of an advanced research methods class who had been previously trained in interviewing.

TABLE 29.1.   MOST FREQUENT RESPONSES TO THE QUESTION "WHAT IS DE-VIANT" ($N = 180$)

Response	Percent
Homosexuals	49
Drug addicts	47
Alcoholics	46
Prostitutes	27
Murderers	22
Criminals	18
Lesbians	13
Juvenile delinquents	13
Beatniks	12
Mentally ill	12
Perverts	12
Communists	10
Atheists	10
Political extremists	10

But the data from this study must be interpeted in the light of the weaknesses inherent in all open-ended responses. We can more or less assume that the respondent means what he *says,* but we can assume nothing about what he happened *not* to say. For instance, we can assume that at least 47 percent of the subjects regard drug addiction as deviant, but it does not follow that the other 53 percent do not. Given a list, we would expect 80 percent or 90 percent of a sample to check drug addiction as deviant.[4] When you ask persons to list "what is deviant," you get primarily the denotative definition of a word.

In light of this qualification, the data from this study suggest that there is wide consensus that some types of acts and persons are deviant, but also that a tremendous variety of things are considered deviant by at least some people.

The respondents were subdivided by age, sex, and education but there were few significant differences between these subgroups in frequency of mentioning types. Thirty-six percent of the females, as opposed to 18 percent of the males, mentioned prostitute; 54 percent of those with some college, as opposed to 34 percent of those who had finished high school or

[4] A further study using a list to be checked deviant-nondeviant would be useful in providing more accurate data on percentages of respondents who regarded various acts as deviant.

less, mentioned drug addicts; and 19 percent of those over 40 years old, as opposed to 7 percent of those under 40, said beatniks were deviant. But all other subgroup variations were too slight to be reliable. Thus, no clear between-group differences emerged, at least with these variables, and within-group variations remained very high.

Because of sample inadequacies [5] the data from this pilot study must be regarded as tentative and exploratory, but they do suggest and lend support to the following generalizations. The fact that even this small number of respondents—all contemporary Americans—named so many different things as deviant, and that there was much within-group variation even among those with the same social background, suggest that almost every conceivable dimension of human behavior is considered deviant from the normative perspective of some existing persons and groups. A fascinating corollary of this is that most individuals would be labelled deviant from someone's point of view.

The range of items mentioned seems to defy content analysis; that is, the items do not seem to have any characteristics in common except that they are regarded as deviant by someone. Thus, *there may be only one sense in which all deviants are alike: very simply, the fact that some social audience regards them and treats them as deviant.*

A further implication of the above variation in responses is that, by embracing and conforming to the normative standards of some groups, the individual will *automatically* be violating the standards of other groups and persons. To the extent that this is true, questions of deviance and conformity become questions of intergroup divergence and conflict. And to the extent that the individual is mobile, he will tend to experience normative cross-pressures. Hence, as mobility rates increase within a pluralistic society, the amount of such cross-pressures and the amount of ambivalence resulting from it will likely increase. As one of our informants said: "I'm not sure what's right anymore so how can I say who's doing wrong?"

This may indeed be one important sense in which our society and perhaps other modern industrial societies are "pluralistic." It seems that

[5] Actually, since such quota samples almost always underrepresent the heterogeneity of the population from which it is drawn a representative sample would, almost certainly, produce even greater variation of response on what is deviant. Also, response biases—tendencies not to write down "unspeakable" things and tendencies to omit one's more idiosyncratic dislikes— would lead to a spurious reduction in variation of response.

there are not one but several publics and normative standards. As a result, societal definitions of deviance become somewhat blurred and standards of right and wrong become issues in themselves. This would seem to call into question the assumption, so pervasive among "social structure" theorists, that American society is composed of a large majority who more or less conform to a broad normative standard and a fraction of "boat-rockers" who deviate grossly from this standard. "Social system" is a devised abstraction, several steps removed from concrete social life, and when we observe conflicts and accommodations among groups and cliques in every milieu, the degree of normative integration within society seems quite problematic.

Stereotyped Conceptions of Deviants

The "overcategorization" of objects seems to be a necessary and ubiquitous aspect of human thought processes—a necessary means of organizing the infinite detail and complexity of the "outside" world (Bruner, 1958). But such coding is necessarily a simplification of incoming stimuli, a *selective* simplification in which information is lost, and misinformation may be added. It must be emphasized that such stereotypes about people and things often contain some freight of truth. But they lead to distorted appraisals because they overestimate within-group similarity and between-group differences, and they tend to be unresponsive to objective evidence.

The other three pilot studies were designed to explore the content of public stereotypes of several kinds of deviants, the extent of consensus on these stereotypes, and some possible corollaries of tendency to stereotype. The types chosen were those usually considered deviant by social scientists and laymen, and they were further picked to represent something of a range of behaviors. The research designs were an elaboration of techniques developed by Katz and Braly (1933) to explore stereotypes of racial and ethnic groups.

First, we asked a sample of 89 students enrolled in a social problems class to answer the following question with regard to homosexuals, beatniks, adulterers, and marijuana smokers: "Characterize each type. What are they like and what kind of life do they lead?" (Simmons, 1969).

In response, more than half of the students wrote a highly stereotyped characterization of every deviant type. The responses of those who presented stereotypes were remarkably similar in content; the only major variation among the student protocols was between those who stereotyped and those who didn't. This variation appeared to be something of a natural dichotomy; the former group expressing an image of the deviate as a dark haunted creature beyond the pale of ordinary life, the latter describing deviates as just people. Illustrative of the stereotyped response is the following description of the marijuana smoker by a male sociology major.

. . . a greasy Puerto Rican boy or the shaky little Skid Row bum . . . As for the life led, it is shiftless, unhappy, dog eat dog for survival. I guess marijuana is used as a means of avoiding reality. The pleasure that comes from the drug outweighs the pleasure of life as it really is.

The following portrayal of homosexuals by a female sophomore illustrates the nonstereotyped responses.

As far as I know the homosexual is not like anything. They are merely people who have different ideas about sex than I do. They probably lead lives which are normal and are different only in the way they receive sexual gratification. They have no distinguishing characteristics.

Emotional reactions toward the deviants ranged from revulsion to benevolent contempt among the stereotyping group, and from mild sympathy to no apparent reaction among the nonstereotypers. The only exceptions were in the responses to beatniks, in which a moderate fraction of both groups expressed some ambivalence.

The two groups of respondents were not distinguishable by any of the social category variables included in the questionnaire. Some other facets of the open-ended responses will be drawn upon in the final section of this paper, dealing with the consequences of stereotypes.

Following the procedures developed by Katz and Braly and similar studies of racial and ethnic stereotypes, we constructed a second questionnaire listing 70 traits extracted from content analysis of the first open-ended questionnaire. The list included a variety of positive, negative, and neutral attributes from which respondents could choose in building their portraits. Respondents were asked to select those words and phrases they considered necessary to adequately characterize each of the following groups: marijuana smokers, adulterers, beatniks, homosexuals, and political radicals. They were encouraged to add any words they considered descriptively important, but only a very few did so. They were asked then to go back and encircle those five words which they considered the most important in describing each group. As with earlier studies, our analysis is based largely on the encircled words, although as a reliability check we analyzed the entire lists chosen, with comparable results.

The questionnaire was administered to a sample of 134 subjects selected again on the basis of a quota sampling formula designed to guarantee variation in age, education, census region, sex, occupation, and race.

The most frequently chosen traits and the proportion who encircled them for each of the five deviant types are presented in Table 29.2. Examination of the table shows that, for each deviant type, a handful of traits accounts for a large proportion of the responses and that a large number of traits were chosen not at all or only once or twice. Thus, as in the open-ended questionnaire, a fair degree of stereotyping is evidenced.

From further examination of the table, we see that the stereotypic portrait of each deviant type is somewhat distinct in content. The marijuana smoker stereotype emerges as an insecure escapist, lacking self-control and looking for kicks; the beatnik is a sloppy, immature nonconformist; the adulterer is immoral, promiscuous, and insecure; the homosexual is perverted and mentally ill; the political radical is ambitious, aggressive, stubborn, and dangerous. The only characteristic imputed frequently to all five types was irresponsible–lacking self-control. All but the radicals were described as lonely and frustrated. Immaturity was encircled by at least some fraction of respondents for each of the types.

The word portraits are almost unequivocally negative for the marijuana smoker, homosexual, and adulterer. The only differences of opinion seem to revolve around whether they should be pitied or condemned. Characterizations of the beatnik and political radical were more ambivalent and respectful. Each was considered clearly beyond the pale of the ordinary citizen, but a number of positive and neutral traits were imputed to each with a good deal of frequency. The beatnik image included artistic, imaginative, and happy-go-lucky, and the radical was considered imaginative and intelligent. Both were conceived as individualistic by over one-fourth of the respondents. But the preponderant image of both these types was also negative; the positive and neutral imputations were only an attenuation of a basically pariah image.

In order to get a more quantitative idea of the degree of agreement

TABLE 29.2. TRAITS ENCIRCLED AS DESCRIPTIVELY MOST IMPORTANT FOR EACH OF THE FIVE DEVIANT GROUPS (N = 134)

Marijuana Smokers	(%)	Beatniks	(%)	Adulterers	(%)	Homosexuals	(%)	Political Radical	(%)
Looking for kicks	59	Sloppy	57	Immoral	41	Sexually abnormal	72	Ambitious	61
Escapist	52	Nonconformist	46	Promiscuous	36	Perverted	52	Aggressive	47
Insecure	49	Escapist	32	Insecure	34	Mentally ill	40	Stubborn	32
Lacking self-control	41	Immature	28	Lonely	32	Maladjusted	40	Nonconformist	32
Frustrated	34	Individualistic	27	Sinful	31	Effeminate	29	Impulsive	28
Excitement seeking	29	Lazy	27	Self-interested	29	Lonely	22	Dangerous	28
Nervous	26	Insecure	26	Lacking self-control	28	Insecure	21	Individualistic	26
Maladjusted	24	Irresponsible	20	Passionate	24	Immoral	16	Self-interested	23
Lonely	22	Self-interested	18	Irresponsible	22	Repulsive	14	Intelligent	22
Immature	21	False lives	16	Frustrated	21	Frustrated	14	Irresponsible	21
Weakminded	17	Artistic	16	Immature	16	Weakminded	12	Conceited	15
Irresponsible	15	Maladjusted	14	Sensual	14	Lacking self-control	12	Imaginative	14
Mentally ill	13	Harmless	13	Oversexed	13	Sensual	11	Excitement-seeking	9
Pleasure-loving	11	Imaginative	12	Sexually abnormal	12	Secretive	11		
Dangerous	11	Lonely	11	Pleasure-loving	12	Oversexed	10		
		Imitative	10	False lives	11	Dangerous	10		
		Frustrated	10	Maladjusted	11	Sinful	10		
		Happy-go-lucky	9			Sensitive	10		

among the respondents in imputing traits to the deviant types, we calculated what proportion of the total encirclings was covered by the one most frequent, by the five most frequent, and by the ten most frequent traits for each deviant type. When there was no agreement, any one word received less than 2 percent of the responses; any five words accounted for 7 percent of the responses; and any ten words, for 14 percent. When there was a completely consensual image, every respondent encircled the same five words, and these would account for 100 percent of the responses. The results are presented in Table 29.3.

TABLE 29.3. AMOUNT OF AGREEMENT AMONG RESPONDENTS IN IMPUTING TRAITS TO DEVIANTS
(N = 134)

| | Percent of All Responses Covered By: | | |
Deviant Type	Most Frequent Trait	Five Most Frequent Traits	Ten Most Frequent Traits
Marijuana smokers	12	47	71
Adulterers	8	35	60
Beatniks	11	38	59
Homosexuals	14	47	64
Political radicals	12	40	64
Expected by chance	1.5	7	14

This table shows a fair degree of consensus among the respondents in imputing traits to each deviant type. One-twelfth to one-seventh of all responses were accounted for by the first trait; from a third to half of all responses were covered by the five most frequent traits; and the ten most frequent traits accounted for three-fifths or more of the encirclings. Since a number of the words overlap each other in meaning, the actual degree of consensus among the sample is somewhat higher. That is, if the traits were distinct, the consensus figures would have been even higher.

It appears that the deviant types are far more similar than different in the degree to which a consensual stereotype of them exists. Hence an attempt to rank the types on amount of consensus would be exaggerating the significance of slight variations.

In summary, the data lend preliminary support to the contention that discernable stereotypes of at least several kinds of deviants do exist in our society and that there is a fair amount of agreement on the content of these stereotypes.

Some Correlates of Tendency to Stereotype

Like the respondents on the open-ended questionnaire, the subjects of the third pilot study seemed to fall into a natural dichotomy of those who stereotyped and those who didn't. We therefore classified the subjects into this high-low dichotomy by the extent to which their encircled words corresponded with the group of most frequently chosen words (those negative words chosen by at least 10 percent of the respondents). This classification was then run against the other variables in the questionnaire and a fourth pilot study, using exactly the same procedures and based on a judgment sample of 78 students, was conducted to explore the possible correlates of tendency to stereotype deviants.[6]

To see the extent to which stereotyping was a generic tendency, we computed the associations between scores on each possible pairing of deviant types. All ten of the resulting associations (Q) were significant beyond the .001 level, and positive, suggesting that tendency to stereotype deviants is a general characteristic of the appraiser himself. The associations ranged from .80 to .22, and eight of them were above .50.

There was also a rather marked relationship between educational level and tendency to stereotype deviants. When the high-low dichotomy was run against an education trichotomy (less than high school grad, high school grad, some college) the resulting associations (gamma) ranged from .38 to .64. When respondents' scores for each of the five deviant types were summed, the relationship between these composite stereotype scores and education was .63. Thus a strong inverse association between amount of education and tendency to stereotype was found.

But this finding cannot be taken at face value. For one thing, the associations are largely one-way. The majority of even the most highly educated group expressed unequivocally negative stereotypes toward most or all of the deviant types. The associations were produced by the fact that *none* of

---

[6] As a reliability check, we "intuitively" coded tendencies to stereotype and ran this variable against the others. All associations were as high or higher than those here reported. For example, the gamma between education and this intuitive coding was .75.

those low in education scored low in tendency to stereotype. The "success" of education in teaching more thoughtfulness in appraising social objects is therefore only relative.

In the second place, the response protocols suggest that the more educated groups expressed what might be termed a "secondary stereotype" of each deviant type, derived from the currently fashionable psychiatric explanations of human behavior so rampant in the high- and middle-brow mass media. Albeit, these images are more liberal than the traditional stereotypes and psychoanalytic pity is a softer stance than rigid rejection, these protocols suggest that many of the educated are merely more subtle in their stereotyping.

Sex, age, and the other background variables bore no significant relationship to tendency to stereotype deviants.

In the fourth pilot study, stereotyping tendencies were compared with a number of attitudinal variables. Since this study was also a pretest of other measures and since the sample size was small, analysis problems are complex and only one of the associations will be presented here.[7]

For this student sample, a moderate inverse relationship was found between tendencies to stereotype and a composite liberalism scale.[8] The associations (gamma) between these scores and stereotyping of the specific deviant types ranged from .22 to .58 and the relation between composite liberalism and composite stereotyping tendency was .57. These associations are fairly modest, but unlike the education findings they are more reliable because they are two-way. Liberals stereotyped less and conservatives stereotyped more often than moderates.

Consequences of Public Stereotypes of Deviants

The major generalization suggested by the data from these pilot studies is that empirically discernible stereotypes of at least several major types of

[7] The other findings and many details from the other pilot studies will be presented in Simmons (forthcoming).

[8] The liberalism scale is a composite index including questions pertaining to politics, economics, international affairs, sex, divorce, child-rearing, and religion. Copies will be sent upon request.

deviance do exist among the populace. But this finding is important only to the extent that it has consequences for deviants or for society, or both. The finding that stereotypes exist immediately poses the question: what effects do they have?

In the first place, it should be noted that stereotypes may provide useful information for evaluating and behaving toward deviants. To the extent that they contain some descriptive validity, they may provide the same kind of utility as generalizations like "policemen can be trusted to help when you're in trouble" or "wildcats are vicious and unfriendly." Stereotypes of deviants probably do contain some fraction of truth; certainly the populace does better than chance in recognizing deviants and predicting their behavior. However, as Merton (1957) and others have pointed out, even those aspects of the stereotype which have some *descriptive* validity may be the self-fulfilling result of the stereotype in the first place.

Second, as Becker (1963: 41–78) has suggested, the stereotype is a major mechanism of social control. The baleful image, learned in socialization, prevents a large proportion of the populace from engaging in that type of deviance or even seriously contemplating it. Becker pointed out that this negative stereotype must be overcome before an individual will become a marijuana smoker. And in our open-ended questionnaire, three-fourths of the respondents—enrolled in an advanced sociology course—characterized the marijuana smoker as physiologically enslaved by the drug.

Third, the negative stereotype results in a virtual *a priori* rejection and social isolation of those who are labelled, wrongly or rightly, deviant. In this sense the person so labelled is literally prejudged and is largely helpless to alter the evaluations or treatments of himself. The force of such negative stereotypes is not necessarily attenuated even when the individual is aware that his image is a stereotypic one. As one student wrote in the open-ended questionnaire:

> I realize that this is a stereotypical picture, but nevertheless it is my conception. For me homosexuality is repulsive. It is inconceivable to me how anyone can physically love someone of the same sex.

The negative stereotype may imprison or freeze the individual so labelled into willy-nilly adopting and continuing in a deviant role. This "role imprisonment" occurs because the stereotype leads to social reactions which may considerably alter the individual's opportunity structure, notably, impeding his continuation or readoption of conventional roles. The reaction of others, based on stereotypes, is thus a major aspect of the link between performing deviant acts and systematically adopting deviant roles.

It should be noted that this reaction may be somewhat realistic in terms of the self-interests of those reacting. Even the enlightened reformer is realistic in hesitating to let his children become involved with youths who have delinquent records, and we cannot entirely damn a businessman for hesitating to hire an ex-mental patient on an important deadline job. But the sum of these personal behavioral decisions—many of them made by liberal and kindhearted people—is to make it more than ordinarily difficult for one labelled deviant to perform conventional roles.

Finally, among those known to have committed deviant acts, stereotypes have a selective influence upon who is labelled "deviant." Studies have shown that a sizeable proportion of the populace has committed deviant acts, yet only a small fraction of this proportion is labelled deviant (Wallerstein and Wyle, 1947). The fraction so labelled is not a random subset of the larger group. With type and frequency of offense held constant, it has been shown that minority groups, lower class persons, and men, for most offenses, are differentially susceptible to the labelling process.[9] Among those who are known to have committed a deviant act, those who seem to possess additional qualities concurring with the stereotypic image of that kind of deviance are far more likely to be labelled and processed a deviate. Again, to the extent that the stereotype is a valid generalization about a class of elements, this labelling by stereotype may have diagnostic and prognostic value. But to the extent that the stereotype is invalid, it serves no useful purpose and does positive damage by imprisoning innocent people, and people no more guilty than a large proportion of the populace, in deviant roles.

We noted earlier that stereotyping, in the broad sense of building up inferential generalizations about classes of phenomena, is an inherent aspect of perception and cognition. In the light of this, an injunction to eliminate stereotypic thinking is facile and impossible, and it is based, if you will, on stereotyped thinking about stereotypes. We are, it would seem, stuck with stereotypes. But stereotypes are variable: at one extreme they may be myths invented from superstition and misinformation; at the other, verified scientific generalizations. They may be rigid prejudgments immune to reality test-

[9] For a summary discussion of this point, see the monograph by Cressey (1961).

ing, or they may be tentative appraisals with the built-in notion that their validity and applicability to all class members is problematic.

Rather than try to eliminate stereotypes about deviants and other social objects, it would seem, then, that social scientists should aim at gathering and communicating valid knowledge, in the hope that this knowledge will form the basis for future public attitudes.

References

Becker, Howard S. 1963. *Outsiders,* New York: Free Press; London: Macmillan.

Bruner, Jerome. 1958. "Social Psychology and Perception." In Eleanor Maccoby et al. (eds.), *Readings in Social Psychology* (3d ed.). New York: Holt, Rinehart and Winston, Inc., pp. 85–94.

Cressey, Donald. 1961. "Crime." In Robert Merton and Robert Nisbet (eds.), *Contemporary Social Problems*. New York: Harcourt, Brace, pp. 21–76.

Durkheim, Emile. 1938. *The Rules of Sociological Method*. Glencoe, Ill.: Free Press.

Erikson, Kai. 1962. "Notes on the Sociology of Deviance," *Social Problems* 9 (Spring):307–14.

Katz, Daniel and Kenneth Braly. 1933. "Racial Stereotypes of One Hundred College Students," *Journal of Abnormal and Social Psychology* (October–December):280–90.

Kitsuse, John. 1962. "Societal Reaction to Deviant Behavior: Problems of Theory and Method," *Social Problems* 9 (Winter):247–57.

Lemert, Edwin. 1951. *Social Pathology*. New York: McGraw-Hill, pp. 3–101.

Merton, Robert. 1957. "The Self-Fulfilling Prophecy." In Robert Merton, *Social Theory and Social Structure* (rev. ed.). Glencoe, Ill.: Free Press, pp. 421–39.

Scheff, Thomas. 1964. "The Societal Reaction to Deviance: Ascriptive Elements in the Psychiatric Screening of Mental Patients in a Midwestern State," *Social Problems* 11 (Spring):401–13.

Simmons, J. L. 1969. *Deviants*. Berkeley, Calif.: Glendessary Press.

—— *The Deviant in Society*. Forthcoming.

Wallerstein, James and Clement Wyle. 1947. "Our Law-Abiding Law Breakers," *Federal Probation* (April):107–12.

Zetterberg, Hans. 1963. *On Theory and Verification in Sociology*. Totowa, N.J.: Bedminster.

30

A Critical Assessment of Labeling

EDWIN SCHUR

The central tenet of the labeling orientation is quite straightforward: Deviance and social control always involve processes of social definition. Howard Becker's (1963: 9) comments, widely taken to be the most important recent statement of the position, make this point succinctly:

> . . . *social groups create deviance by making the rules whose infraction constitutes deviance,* and by applying these rules to particular people and labeling them as outsiders. From this point of view, deviance is *not* a quality of the act the person commits, but rather a consequence of the application by others of rules and sanctions to an "offender." The deviant is one to whom that label has successfully been applied; deviant behavior is behavior that people so label.

Key Themes

Given the important place granted to processes of social definition in sociological analysis (represented, for example, by W. I. Thomas' dictum, "if men define situations as real, they are real in their consequences"—surely a truism among most present-day sociologists), it is remarkable that so much fuss has greeted Becker's remarks. The tendency to consider them unusual and to "argue" about them is largely the result of several misunderstandings, especially of what the labeling school does and does not claim and of its technical standing as a mode of explanation.

At the heart of the labeling approach is an emphasis on *process;* deviance is viewed not as a static entity but rather as a continuously shaped and reshaped *outcome* of dynamic processes of social interaction.[1] It is in this general theme of process, in concentration on deviant roles and the development of deviant self-conceptions, and in use of such concepts as "career" and "commitment" that we see most clearly the indebtedness of labeling analysis to the theoretical perspective of symbolic interactionism. Discussing George H. Mead's theory of the social self, Herbert Blumer has noted that "Mead saw the self as a process and not as a structure." Schemes that seek to explain the self through structure alone, Blumer has pointed out, ignore the reflexive process that Meade recognized as central to social interaction. For Mead, human action could not be viewed simply as a product of determining factors operating upon the individual. Rather, as Blumer has put it, "the human being is seen as an active organism in his own right, facing, dealing with, and acting toward the objects he indicates." Social patterns are believed to reflect a continuous process "of fitting developing lines of conduct to one another" (Blumer, 1969: 62, 65, 66). A major implication of this mode of analysis has been succinctly noted by Norman Denzin (1969) in his recent reference to "an emergent quality that may not have existed before the parties came together."

By attending to the "social history" and ramifications of deviant behavior, rather than to the supposed basic "characteristics" of deviating acts or actors (as determined by examination of associations with standard sociological variables), the labeling approach represents a major exception to what Albert Cohen has called the "assumption of discontinuity" in deviance studies. As he has pointed out, until recently "the dominant bias in American sociology has been toward formulating theory in terms of variables that describe initial states, on the one hand, and outcomes, on the other, rather than in terms of processes whereby acts and complex structures of action are built, elaborated, and transformed" (Cohen, 1965). The same point has been made perhaps even more directly by Becker, who has emphasized a distinction between simultaneous and sequential models of deviance: ". . .

---

[1] Schur (1960). We have drawn heavily on this earlier paper for several sections of the present chapter.

all causes do not operate at the same time, and we need a model which takes into account the fact that patterns of behavior *develop* in orderly sequence" (Becker, 1963: 23).

Yet, though labeling analysis represents something of a break with the rather static statistical comparisons that have tended, despite recognition of severe sampling problems, to dominate research into the "causes" of deviating behavior, it is well to keep in mind that even in the specific study of deviance and control concern with process is not entirely new. It is thus significant that Edwin Sutherland, in his classic definition of criminology, referred to knowledge of "the processes of making laws, of breaking laws, and of reacting toward the breaking of laws." Sutherland (1939) saw these processes as constituting "three aspects of a somewhat unified sequence of interactions" and concluded that "this sequence of interactions is the object-matter of criminology." Another classic statement, more explicit in its recognition of the direct impact of labeling processes, was offered by Frank Tannenbaum (1938) in his discussion of the role that early stigmatization plays in generating delinquent and criminal careers:

> The process of making the criminal, therefore, is a process of tagging, defining, identifying, segregating, describing, emphasizing, making conscious and self-conscious; it becomes a way of stimulating, suggesting, emphasizing and evoking the very traits that are complained of. . . .
> The person becomes the thing he is described as being. Nor does it seem to matter whether the valuation is made by those who would punish or by those who would reform. . . . The harder they work to reform the evil, the greater the evil grows under their hands. The persistent suggestion, with whatever good intentions, works mischief, because it leads to bringing out the bad behavior that it would suppress. The way out is through a refusal to dramatize the evil.

In his more systematic effort at theoretical elaboration Edwin Lemert laid much of the basis for the current labeling approach. In 1951 he wrote:

> . . . we start with the idea that persons and groups are differentiated in various ways, some of which result in social penalties, rejection, and segregation. These penalties and segregative reactions of society or the community are dynamic factors which increase, decrease, and condition the form which the initial differentiation or deviation takes. . . .
> The deviant person is one whose role, status, function and self-definition are importantly shaped by how much deviation he engages in, by the degree of its social visibility, by the *particular* exposure he has to the societal reaction, and by the nature and strength of the societal reaction (Lemert, 1951: 22, 23).

It is Lemert (1951: 75–76; 1967 chap. 3), furthermore, who developed the distinction between *primary* and *secondary* deviation, a distinction that has been central to the work of recent labeling analysts. We shall shortly explore the problem of defining the term "deviance." At this juncture let us simply stress the importance of always distinguishing, for purposes of analysis, between a primary or initial act of deviation, on one hand, and deviant roles, deviant identities, and broad situations involving deviance—as shaped by societal definitions and responses—on the other. As we shall see, some of the misunderstandings underlying certain criticisms of the labeling orientation result from failure to keep such a distinction in mind.

Although we have stated that the labeling approach preeminently involves process, we have made relatively little effort so far to indicate more precisely just which processes. Very generally, as is probably already clear, the labeling school asserts that *deviance outcomes* reflect complex processes of action and reaction, of response and counterresponse. The notion of deviance "outcomes" may be useful, for it encompasses both individual consequences of societal reactions (as represented by the secondary deviant, recently defined by Lemert (1967: 41) as "a person whose life and identity are organized around the facts of deviance") and situational consequences for society at large (for example, the economic consequences of labeling certain forms of deviating behavior as criminal). At times the labeling perspective has seemed to be concerned only with the former type of outcome, that is, with the production of deviant identities or characters in individuals. There is good reason to believe, however, that a considerably broader interpretation of labeling is warranted. . . . Processes of social definition, or labeling, that contribute to deviance outcomes are actually found on at least three levels of social action, and all three require analysis. Such processes—as they occur on the levels of *collective rule-making, interpersonal reactions,* and *organizational processing*—all constitute important concerns of the labeling school: *stereotyping, retrospective interpretation,* and *bargaining and negotiation* appear to be crucial ingredients in the production of deviance outcomes.

It should be apparent, then, that interest in labeling suggests at least several focal points for research on deviance and control. Paradoxically this approach seems both to emphasize the individual deviator (at least his personal and social characteristics) less than did previous approaches and at the

same time to focus on him more intensively, seeking the meaning of his behavior to him, the nature of his self-concept as shaped by social reactions,
and so on. We shall return to this paradox when we consider issues of responsibility and freedom. To the extent that the individual "offender" remains an object of direct investigation, clearly the dominant, or favored,
mode of research has shifted from statistical comparison of "samples" of
supposed deviants and nondeviants, aimed at unearthing the differentiating
"causal factors," to direct observation, depth interviews, and personal accounts, which can illuminate subjective meanings and total situational contexts.

    In line, however, with the implicit argument that "deviant" is in large
measure an *ascribed status* (reflecting not only the deviating individual activities but the responses of other people as well), research attention has
shifted from the deviator himself to the *reactors*. Kai Eirkson (1962) has
nicely described this shift:

> Deviance is not a property *inherent* in certain forms of behavior; it is a property
> *conferred upon* these forms by the audiences which directly or indirectly witness
> them. Sociologically, then, the critical variable is the social *audience* . . . since it is
> the audience which eventually decides whether or not any given action or actions will
> become a visible case of deviation.

In this connection, several related but different meanings can be given to the
term "audience." Both direct and indirect "audiences" react to either a
given deviating individual or a particular deviance problem-situation in a
given society. All three levels of analysis mentioned come into play. One
"audience" is the society at large, the complex of interwoven groups and
interests from which emerge general reactions to (and therefore labelings of)
various forms of behavior. Another "audience" comprises those individuals
(including significant others) with whom a person has daily interaction and
by whom he is constantly "labeled" in numerous ways, positive and negative, subtle and not so subtle. A third "audience" includes official and organizational agents of control. They are among the most significant of the
direct reactors or labelers, for they implement the broader and more diffuse
societal definitions through organized structures and institutionalized procedures. It is on this third audience that the labeling approach has especially
focused until now, but, as we shall see, this audience is only one of several
important research targets suggested by a labeling orientation.

Criticisms and Misunderstandings

FAILURE TO DISTINGUISH ADEQUATELY BETWEEN
DEVIANCE AND NONDEVIANCE

An alleged failure to distinguish adequately between deviance and non-deviance is the source of several related criticisms of the labeling approach. Jack Gibbs (1966: 9–14) has claimed that labeling analysts fail to specify what kind of social reaction and how much social reaction are required before an act or an individual can be considered "deviant." Gibbs is particularly troubled by the "secret" deviant (the undiscovered violator of rules) and the "falsely accused" (who has not violated a rule but is believed to have done so and is reacted to accordingly), both of which categories have been explicitly recognized by Becker (1963: 20–21). Gibbs has asserted that, if labeling theorists were to be consistent, they

would have to insist that behavior which is contrary to a norm is not deviant unless it is discovered and there is a particular kind of reaction to it. Thus, if persons engage in adultery but their act is not discovered and reacted to in a certain way (by the members of the social unit), then it is not deviant! Similarly, if a person is erroneously thought to have engaged in a certain type of behavior and is reacted to "harshly" as a consequence, a deviant act has taken place! (Gibbs, 1966: 13)

Gibbs is correct in his charge that no unequivocal basis for distinguishing what is deviant from what is not has been established, yet as labeling's proponents would rightly insist the attempt to make such a clear-cut distinction is misguided. It is a central tenet of the labeling perspective that neither acts nor individuals are "deviant" in the sense of immutable, "objective" reality without reference to processes of social definition. Gibbs is in fact not far off the mark in his allegation that the approach is "relativistic in the extreme" (Gibbs, 1966: 11), yet this relativism may be viewed as a major strength, rather than as a weakness. John Kitsuse (1962) has properly noted that it is necessary "that the sociologist view as problematic what he generally assumes as given—namely, that forms of behavior are *per se* deviant." Actually, it has long been recognized among sociologists that definitions of crime and other deviant behavior are relative, varying according to time and place. Indeed, relativism is central to various classic sociological formulations on problematic behavior, for example, some early comments by Willard Waller: "In spite of all attempts to define social problems objectively and denotatively, value judgments must be brought in somehow, for there is no other way of identifying a condition as a social problem than by passing a value judgment upon it.'' As Waller (1936) concluded, the only common aspect of all social problems is "the fact that someone has passed a value judgment upon them.'' Empirical evidence tends to support the relativistic stance. It is true that within a given society there may be widespread consensus on negative evaluations of certain forms of behavior, though not necessarily on the intensity and methods of implementing such evaluations. It is also true, as J. L. Simmons (1965, 1969) has put it, that "almost every conceivable dimension of human behavior is considered deviant from the normative perspective of some existing persons and groups.''

Similarly, it is unrealistic to expect to be able to neatly categorize individuals as either "deviant" or "nondeviant," with no reference to how they have been perceived and treated. Although some labeling analysts may have been less than fully clear on this point, it seems most acceptable to insist that there is no single point at which an individual "becomes" deviant for once and for all. It is true that we may wish at times to refer to "full-fledged" or "secondary" deviants (as Lemert has described the individual whose self-concept and activities have come to conform substantially to the deviant image that others have of him). And labeling analysts undoubtedly have emphasized the importance of public labeling, especially of "deviant identity." [2] Although labeling analysis does also stress an individual's difficulty in "shaking off" a well-developed deviant identity once it has been successfully imputed to him, nothing in this approach denies either the possibility that he may do so or the likelihood of significant (and patterned) variations in individuals' susceptibility and resistance to such labeling. Furthermore, it is well to remember, in connection with the demand that individuals be classified as either deviant or nondeviant, that acts construed as deviant (according to a particular set of standards) always constitute only one segment of an individual's behavior. Commitment to (or involvement in) "deviant" roles is likely to vary greatly among individuals exhibiting similarly deviating behavior and to undergo considerable change over time for any one such individual. It thus seems clear that our characterization of deviating individuals must refer to the set of standards from which they are said to deviate and must always be expressed in terms of degree, variation,

[2] See Garfinkel (1956); see also Strauss (1962).

and circumstance, rather than in simplistic "either-or" classifications.

Critics have tended to overstate their criticism of the labeling approach with respect to its treatment of both deviating acts and deviating individuals. In neither instance does the labeling analyst deny the reality of deviance, as the critics often seem to suggest that he does. Nobody argues that the behavior that we call "homicide," "mental illness," "homosexuality," and "theft" would not occur if it were not defined as "deviant." Rather, it seems simply meaningless to try to understand and "explain" such deviations without taking into account the fact that in a given social order they are inevitably defined and reacted to in various specific ways. Such reaction processes affect the nature, distribution, social meaning, and implications of the behavior, *whatever* other factors may help to account for the initial acts of such deviation by particular individuals. The focus, then, is on *what is made of an act socially;* this matter is to some extent related to the issue of why individual acts of deviation occur in the first place, but at the same time it transcends such narrow concerns. Similarly, the labeling theorist is clearly aware that acts of deviation, as well as societal reactions to them, are necessary in the production of deviant outcomes. He stresses, however, that the patterns of deviance and control that we find in a given social system are significantly determined by the reciprocal relations between the two. He no longer finds acceptable the "assumption of differentiation" (Matza, 1964) that underlay earlier analysis and that took for granted that some basic "differentness" of the deviating individuals (apart from the mere act of deviating) can fully explain these patterns. He is more interested in the total social context of the behavior and its subjective meaning for the actor (which cannot help but involve direct or indirect, actual or anticipated reactions of others) than in the initial precipitants of the acts.

The critic of labeling often fails to consider the important distinction between "primary deviation" (the sheer act of rule-violation) and "deviance" (in which there has been a secondary elaboration of such rule-violation, in terms of both individual self-concept and behavior, as well as of broader situational ramifications). The critic ignores the fact that social action, as Max Weber (1947) correctly emphasized, is not merely externally observable, "objective" behavior; attached to it is a highly significant component of subjective meaning. Appreciation of the subjective meaning (and, for that matter, the total social patterning) of deviation is impossible without attention to processes of societal definition and labeling. The experience of stealing from a neighborhood fruit stand is simply not the same for the boy who is undiscovered as it is for the boy who is caught. The meaning and consequences of an adulterous relationship change when it has been disclosed, even to significant others, let alone to the community. Similarly, a false accusation of wrongdoing can have very serious consequences indeed for the accused individual; that he has not actually engaged in the alleged deviation is not the sole determinant of the situation in which he finds himself and of the meaning it has for him. Nor does "being caught" or formally dealt with (or the opposite) alone shape the subjective meaning of deviating behavior. Mere knowledge of the rule and anticipation of likely reactions can also shape self-concepts and behavior. A homosexual's concealment and self-contempt, the embarrassment attending a breach of etiquette as yet unreacted to, and subterfuge by a political deviator who seeks to avoid the likely reactions to open activity are examples. Proponents of the labeling perspective are vitally concerned with explaining such *varieties of deviant experience,* considering a qualitative understanding of them as more meaningful sociologically than mere counting and classifying of deviating acts and individuals.

NARROW FOCUS

There are several alternative forms of the criticism that the focus of the labeling approach is too narrow. According to one version, labeling analysts are so preoccupied with the social psychology of deviant identity and with the impact of labeling upon the individual deviator that they unwisely neglect structural and systemic "causes" of deviance. This criticism is essentially the one that Gibbs had in mind when he claimed that the labeling approach does not explain variations in the incidence of deviating acts in different populations. He went on to ask:

   . . . are we to conclude that the incidence of a given act is in fact a constant in all populations and that the only difference is in the quality of reactions to the act? Specifically, given two populations with the same kind of reaction to a particular act, can the new perspective explain why the incidence of the act is greater in one population than in the other? Not at all! On the contrary, even if two populations have the same legal and social definition of armed robbery and even if instances of the crime are reacted to in exactly the same way, it is still possible for the armed robbery rate to be much higher in one population than in the other (Gibbs, 1966: 12).

Although it could be argued that reactions never occur "in exactly the same way" in differing social contexts, nevertheless it is undoubtedly true that labeling analysts are less concerned with rates of deviation (which have, of course, been a major preoccupation of traditional sociological work on deviance). They are likely, as we shall see, to view rates as partly reflecting reaction processes, rather than as merely reflecting underlying "causes" of the deviation. As we shall also discover, however, nothing in the labeling approach is contradictory to or incompatible with approaches that do focus on rates; indeed in some respects labeling and the other approaches complement each other.

Preoccupation with the labeling school's social-psychological focus may also underlie the claim that even on its own terms labeling analysis provides an inadequate explanatory framework. Gibbs has insisted that labeling analysts like Becker have provided no means for explaining "why a given act is considered deviant and/or criminal in some but not all societies . . . a certain kind of reaction may identify behavior as deviant . . . it obviously does not explain why the behavior is deviant" (Gibbs, 1966: 12). This argument, like the more general complaint that labeling analysis is so intent upon reaction processes that it slights the significance of norms, seems overstated. As has already been mentioned, a broadly conceived labeling approach proceeds simultaneously on several different levels of analysis, including the crucial level of collective rule-making. After all, Becker's comment that "social groups create deviance by making the rules" is every bit as germane as is his stress on deviance as a consequence of the application of such rules to particular individuals. True, the latter aspect has been more thoroughly researched by proponents of labeling, and it must be admitted that we do not yet have a generally accepted and full-fledged systematic theory explaining variations in societal definitions of behavior as deviant. Yet the labeling approach has in fact called attention to the importance of rule-making much more forcibly than has the other sociological approaches to the study of deviance. . . .

A rather different sort of "narrow focus" objection to labeling analysis is directed at its stress upon the ascribed aspects of deviant status, at its supposed failure to consider deviant motivation adequately. To the extent that proponents of this perspective pay more attention to the consequences of engaging in deviating acts than to the precipitating "causes" of such acts, the charge has some validity. The authors of one recent labeling-oriented anthol-

ogy have indeed remarked in their introduction that "this book takes relatively little notice of the motivations for deviance, but instead pays closer attention to the sociology of deviance." [3] An ambivalence in the labeling
view of the individual deviator as social actor has already been noted. On
one hand, the actor is viewed as largely at the mercy of the reaction processes; what they are determines what he is to become. At the same time,
the approach incorporates from symbolic interactionism a view of the actor
as significantly shaping his own projects and lines of action. . . .

FAILURE TO EXPLAIN SOME DEVIANCE

Critics who complain that not all deviance can be explained by labeling are
also concentrating unduly on only one of the several levels at which labeling
processes operate to produce deviant outcomes. In this narrow view, labeling theory involves only the cumulative impact of successive negative reactions (largely public or official ones) in the shaping of individual deviant careers. Certainly this problem has been a major focus of labeling analysts, but
again we emphasize that there is a great deal more to a perspective based on
broadly conceived societal reactions or social definitions. If we accept rule-
making itself as one level at which relevant "labeling" processes occur,
then clearly no explanation of any form of deviance can dispense with
labeling entirely. Even if we are concerned more narrowly with the social
psychology of the deviating individual, some labeling or definition is going
to have to be considered for a qualitative understanding of the meaning of
the deviant experience to the actor. In most instances we shall find that negative labeling is a prerequisite of the individual's acquisition of those special
qualities of behavior and outlook that we usually mean by "deviant career"
or "deviant identity." It is true that sometimes there are instances of even
prolonged involvement in deviating behavior in which the deviator has not
felt the impact of direct or official labeling (as, for example, when his rule-
violating has gone unrecognized). Even such hidden or secret deviators, of
course, fall prey to certain indirect and subtle definitional influences that are
likely to affect their behavior and self-concepts. But the important point is
that all behavior takes its meaning from the definitional processes in which it
is enmeshed. Comprehensive understanding of any course of deviating ac-

[3] Rubington and Weinberg (1968). On the relation between motivational explanations and
sociological approaches, see Cohen (1966).

tion thus always requires appreciation of the definitional context—of the labeling processes in all their variety and likely combinations (formal and informal, intense and subdued, negative and positive).

Often when it is argued that some deviance cannot be explained by labeling, the critics have lost sight of the distinction between primary and secondary deviation and think only of discrete or initial deviating acts of particular sorts. Actually in some instances negative labeling does seem to come close to "causing" initial, or primary, deviation, as when an act of deviation appears to represent a kind of behavioral compliance with the prior expectations of significant others. Labeling analysis does not, however, require that it be possible to specify negative labeling as a necessary condition for any single deviating act. No labeling theorist has advanced such an argument, and it seems in no way necessary for recognition of the vital significance of labeling, in the broad sense of social definitions, of whatever sort, in shaping what we have called the "varieties of deviant experience."

Some specific forms of deviation may, it is true, lend themselves less readily to labeling analysis than do others. It should be clear from the preceding comments that, by and large, types of deviation that tend not to be repeated or to undergo elaboration are difficult to "explain" in labeling terms. A discrete act of homicide, for example, seems to incorporate fewer labeling processes than does long-term addiction to drugs. At the same time, it must be recognized that the social meaning and consequences of even such usually unrepeated acts as homicides are significantly shaped by processes of societal definition in the broadest sense. Social judgments on the conditions under which killing is "justifiable" or "excusable" clearly affect the consequences of homicidal acts and to some extent their occurrence. (The frequent comparison between ordinary homicides and killing in wartime reveals the influence of broad definitional processes.) The value of labeling analysis in explaining a particular form of deviance may be related to the degree of consensus on its social definition. It could be argued that Becker's analysis of drug use, for example, has held up particularly well because, given a lack of social consensus on how such behavior ought to be regarded and dealt with, labeling processes have become pivotal in shaping outcomes. From this point of view borderline forms of deviance seem to be especially good candidates for labeling analysis and those deviations on which widespread consensus exists (homicide, incest, and so on) less promising candidates.

Recently, Ira Reiss (1970: 78–87) has attempted to apply the labeling orientation (and several other theoretical perspectives) to consideration of premarital sexual behavior as a type of deviance. Noting the low visibility of sexual activities, Reiss has pointed out that public labeling usually occurs only when pregnancy results; even then such labeling can sometimes be avoided through abortion or mobility. Reiss has asserted that this flexibility makes the labeling approach difficult to apply. This conclusion, however, rests partly on a narrow interpretation of labeling, which considers only direct negative labeling, rather than all diverse societal definitions of and responses to the behavior. Partly, too, it rests on an effort (somewhat misguided) to link labeling analysis and quantification. Thus, Reiss has asserted that

The real question is *how much* of the sexual behavior of females can be explained in this fashion? . . . the promiscuous female is statistically very much in the minority. Some of these promiscuous females may have been propelled into their behavior by deviant labeling, but the majority of the experienced females report that it was an intimate love relationship that led to their acceptance of premarital coitus.[4]

Although he has recognized the possibility of subtle effects (guilt feelings and the like) of informal labeling—by adults and even within the peer group at times—Reiss has generally applied only a narrow conception of labeling processes. Of increased peer acceptance of premarital sex he comments, "Such group support also tends to weaken the potential effects of other groups' labels and thereby lessens the relevance of labeling theory."

Actually, under a broader conception of labeling and with recognition that the meaning of behavior is derived from a calculus of negative *and positive* definitions and responses, such "counter-labeling" can be viewed as confirming, rather than challenging, the relevance of labeling theory. Indeed, Reiss' reference to "other groups' labels" shows that he has recognized that what the peer group is doing is also labeling. One problem that Reiss has acknowledged at various points in his paper is just how "deviant" we should consider premarital sex, given current attitudes. Yet his analysis rests largely on the assumption that such behavior is in fact "deviant" (at least as a violation of still dominant adult standards); on that basis he has proceeded to examine the usefulness of various orientations in "explaining" it. This method raises the important issue of whether we can begin from

---

[4] Reiss (1970: 81); italics have been added. For a somewhat similar critique of labeling analysis in the area of mental illness, see Gove (1970).

such an assumption, or whether on the other hand the very degree of labeling must somehow be built into the way we define deviance in the first
place.

Defining Deviance

Very likely a major reason for the confusion and controversy surrounding
labeling is its apparent failure to provide a clear-cut definition of deviance
that can be easily made operational for research purposes. In the absence of
such a definition the critics wonder how the sociologist can make the kinds
of comparisons required as a basis for any valid generalization about deviance. In Becker's remark that "deviant behavior is behavior that people so
label," precisely what does "so label" mean? Without doubt it is this uncertainty that has led Gibbs to ask what kind of reaction, or how much reaction, is necessary before we can say that deviance is present. Clearly,
Becker did not mean that people must literally use the term "deviant" for
the behavior to be so classified; although everyday use of this term is probably growing, it is hardly yet widespread. Nor does it seem that any kind of
negative reaction to any kind of behavior is enough to define such behavior
as deviant. Yet, as Becker has correctly stressed, to define deviance solely
in terms of rule-violation, as many sociologists have been wont to do, is to
risk inadequate attention to the crucial role of the processes of making and
applying rules.

In accordance with the broad interpretation of labeling to be developed
here, a workable definition of deviance must both encompass a wide range
of different types of deviation and control behavior and recognize the contingent, almost fluid, nature of the social processes through which deviant outcomes are "produced." As already mentioned, we should not limit ourselves to instances in which individuals actually feel the weight of formal
control procedures. On the other hand, to include in the definition all instances in which formal control *might* have occurred (that is, all rule violations, whether recognized and reacted to or not) seems a bit unwieldy. For
our purposes, it would also be inadequate to consider only breaches of formal rules as the basis for deviance; a wider range of behavior should be covered by any meaningful definition. Indeed it is questionable that the notion

of rules itself is broad enough to describe deviation. This point is clearest in the instance of physical disability. As we shall see, there are several good reasons for wanting to define deviance to include reactions to certain personal conditions and disabilities, which really involve no rule violation (except perhaps the extremely nebulous "rule" that one should not be disabled). From this point of view, reference to departures from expectations may be more useful than is reference to violations of rules.

We therefore suggest the following working definition of deviance (the most crucial phrases are italicized): Human behavior is deviant *to the extent that* it comes to be viewed as involving a *personally discreditable* departure from a group's normative expectations, *and it elicits* interpersonal or collective reactions that serve to "isolate," "treat," "correct," or "punish" *individuals* engaged in such behavior. This formulation seems to meet most of the requirements that we have just stated. Its scope encompasses quite diverse types of departures from normative expectations, from violations of formal laws to deviations from patterned expectations in extremely informal situations and inter-personal encounters that *may* qualify as deviant, *to the extent that* the specified definitions and reactions occur. Furthermore, it is the degree to which such definitions and responses *are* elicited, rather than the formal possibility that they could be, that determines the "extent of deviantness" (a conception in sharp contrast to that of the "presence or absence of deviance," which underlies much traditional research in this area). A normative breach that could be but is not condemned or punished under existing formal rules is clearly *less deviant* than it would be if negative sanctions were actually applied. The stipulation that the normative departure must be *personally* discreditable reflects the view that "violations" that do not reflect unfavorably on the individual's overall identity (for example, some forms of "approved deviance" in organizational settings) are less deviant than are those that do. Similarly, in the absence of the indicated types of response, mere statistical departures from norms do not reflect substantial degrees of deviantness.

Finally, the kinds of reaction involved in attaching the quality of deviantness to behavior are attempts to "deal with" deviating individuals. Particular individuals who exhibit certain behavior or conditions are those about whom "something should be done" (even if only indirectly, as when "rehabilitation of the community" is favored as a way of dealing with individual criminality). This stipulation allows us to distinguish (at least partly) be-

tween reactions that breed deviantness and the somewhat similar stigmatiz-
ing reactions directed primarily against groups or social categories. The
most obvious example of the latter is "minority groups." Although the line
between individual deviance, on one hand, and collective behavior and
group conflict, on the other, is often extremely hazy (and one may sometimes be the forerunner of the other), for our purposes it hardly seems useful
to consider all minority-group members "deviant."

The difficulties in using this kind of contingent, or qualified, definition
for quantitative purposes are obvious. Rather than providing a means of
neatly separating acts or individuals into two clear-cut categories—deviant
and nondeviant—it highlights the fact that the "deviantness" of an act or an
individual is always relative, changeable, a matter of degree, and that the
degree depends mainly upon the extent to which the behavior is viewed and
responded to in certain ways. It is the perceived methodological limitation of
such shifting formulations (which, whether explicitly admitted or not, is
clearly necessitated by the labeling approach) that seems especially to irk the
most vocal critics of labeling. We shall return to this matter when we consider the relation between labeling and other orientations. Critics may, of
course, claim that the difficulty of labeling analysis in respect to operational
definitions casts doubt on its validity. Alternatively, however, we can stress
the limitations of operational definitions in analysis of deviance and control
processes. (Nevertheless it should be understood that operational and quantified research are not entirely ruled out when deviance is defined in this
way. Rather, classifications must be established on narrower, more specific,
bases. It is thus perfectly legitimate, from a labeling point of view, to establish for some research purposes a category of "persons admitted to mental hospitals" or a category of "youths who have not appeared before the juvenile courts." But these categories clearly are quite different from [and,
labelists would argue, much more likely to be workable than] the categories
"deviants" and "nondeviants" or even "mentally ill" and "nondelinquent.")

It may well be that "deviance" is most usefully viewed as a "sensitizing concept" (to adopt Blumer's phrasing), rather than as a "definitive"
(operational) one. Noting that such sensitizing concepts rest on "a general
sense of what is relevant," Blumer has further remarked:

A definitive concept refers precisely to what is common to a class of objects, by
the aid of a clear definition in terms of attributes or fixed bench marks. This definition, or the bench marks, serve as a means of clearly identifying the individual in-

stance of the class and the make-up of that instance that is covered by the concept. A sensitizing concept lacks such specification of attributes or bench marks and consequently it does not enable the user to move directly to the instance and its relevant content. Instead, it gives the user a general sense of reference and guidance in approaching empirical instances (Blumer, 1969: 147–148).

As Gideon Sjoberg and Roger Nett (1968) have recently pointed out, a preference for sensitizing over operational concepts is consistent with, and in fact rests upon, a view of the social order that emphasizes fluidity and the ability of the actor to reshape his environment. It should be clear from our earlier comments that this view, largely associated with the school of symbolic interactionism, has significantly shaped the labeling approach to deviance. Even if our working definition of deviance goes a bit farther toward specifying "bench marks" than Blumer's comments seem to prescribe, a general characterization of it as sensitizing, rather than as operational, is probably warranted.

References

Becker, Howard S. 1963. *Outsiders*. New York: Free Press; London: Macmillan.

Blumer, Herbert. 1969. *Symbolic Interactionism: Perspective and Method*. Englewood Cliffs, N.J.: Prentice-Hall.

Cohen, Albert K. 1965. "The Sociology of the Deviant Act: Anomie Theory and Beyond," *American Sociological Review* 30 (February):9.

1966. *Deviance and Control*. Englewood Cliffs, N.J.: Prentice-Hall, ch. 4.

Denzin, Norman K. 1969. "Symbolic Interactionism and Ethnomethodology: A Proposed Synthesis," *American Sociological Review* 34 (December).

Erikson, Kai T. 1962. "Notes on the Sociology of Deviance," *Social Problems* 9 (Spring):308.

Garfinkel, Harold. 1956. "Conditions of Successful Degredation Ceremonies," *American Journal of Sociology* 61 (March):420–24.

Gibbs, Jack P. 1966. "Conceptions of Deviant Behavior: The Old and the New," *Pacific Sociological Review* 9 (Spring):9–14.

Gove, Walter R. 1970. "Societal Reaction as an Explanation of Mental Illness: An Evaluation," *American Sociological Review* 35 (October):873–84.

Kitsuse, John I. 1962. "Societal Reaction to Deviant Behavior: Problems of Theory and Method," *Social Problems* 9 (Winter):248.

Lemert, Edwin M. 1951. *Social Pathology*. New York: McGraw-Hill.

1967. *Human Deviance, Social Problems, and Social Control*. Englewood Cliffs, N.J.: Prentice-Hall.

Matza, David. 1964. *Delinquency and Drift*. New York: Wiley, chap. 1.

Reiss, Ira L. 1970. "Premarital Sex as Deviant Behavior: An Application of Current Approaches to Deviance," *American Sociological Review* 35 (February):78–87.

Rubington, Earl and Martin S. Weinberg (eds.). 1968. *Deviance: The Interactionist Perspective*. New York: Macmillan, p. vi.

Schur, Edwin M. 1969. "Reactions to Deviance: A Critical Assessment," *American Journal of Sociology* 75 (November):309–22.

Simmons, J. L. 1965. "Public Stereotypes of Deviants," *Social Problems* 13 (Fall):225.

1969. *Deviants*. Berkeley: Glendessary.

Sjoberg, Gideon and Roger Nett. 1968. *A Methodology for Social Research*. New York: Harper & Row, p. 59.

Strauss, Anselm. 1962. "Transformations of Identity." In Arnold M. Rose (ed.), *Human Behavior and Social Processes*. Boston: Houghton Mifflin, pp. 63–85.

Sutherland, Edwin H. 1939. *Principles of Criminology*. 3d ed. Philadelphia: Lippincott, p. 1.

Tannenbaum, Frank. 1938. *Crime and the Community*. Boston: Ginn, pp. 19–20.

Waller, Willard. 1936. "Social Problems and the Mores," *American Sociological Review* I (December):922, 923.

Weber, Max. 1947. *The Theory of Social and Economic Organization*. A. M. Henderson and Talcott Parsons (trans.). New York: Oxford University Press, ch. 1.

Authors Appearing in This Book

ARGYLE, J. Michael	Reader in Social Psychology The University of Oxford
Assembly Committee on Criminal Procedure	California Legislature Sacramento
BECKER, Howard S.	Department of Sociology Northwestern University
CAMERON, Mary Owen	Department of Education Hunter College City University of New York
CAREY, Sandra H.	Department of Sociology Texas Christian University
CHIRICOS, Theodore G.	Department of Criminology Florida State University
CLARK, John P.	Department of Sociology The University of Minnesota
CLASTER, Daniel S.	Department of Sociology Brooklyn College City University of New York
CRAWFORD, Thomas J.	Department of Psychology The University of California Berkeley
ERIKSON, Kai T.	Department of Sociology Yale University

HAYNER, Norman S.	Department of Sociology The University of Washington, Seattle (Professor Emeritus)
HOGARTH, John	Institute of Public Policy Analysis Simon Fraser University
JENSEN, Gary F.	Department of Sociology The University of North Carolina
LAFAVE, Wayne R.	Department of Law The University of Illinois
LINDESMITH, Alfred	Department of Sociology The University of Indiana
MCINTYRE, Jennie J.	Department of Sociology The University of Maryland
QUINNEY, Richard	Department of Sociology New York University
RIVERA, Ramon	3163 North Pine Grove Chicago, Illinois
ROGERS, Joseph W.	Department of Sociology and Anthropology New Mexico State University
SCHUR, Edwin M.	Department of Sociology New York University
SCHWARTZ, Richard D.	Faculty of Law and Jurisprudence State University of New York Buffalo
SHORT, James F., Jr.	Department of Sociology Washington State University
SIMON, Rita James	Department of Sociology The University of Illinois
SKOLNICK, Jerome H.	Center for the Study of Law and Society The University of California
SUTHERLAND, Edwin H.	deceased (formerly Department of Sociology Indiana University)

TANNENBAUM, Frank   deceased
                          (formerly Department of History
                          Columbia University)

TEEVAN, James J.   Department of Sociology
                          The University of Western Ontario

TENNYSON, Ray A.   Institute of Criminal Justice and
                          Criminology
                          The University of Maryland

TURNER, Ralph H.   Department of Sociology
                          The University of California
                          Los Angeles

WALDO, Gordon P.   Department of Criminology
                          Florida State University

WALKER, Nigel D.   Reader in Criminology
                          The University of Oxford

YOUNG, Jock   Department of Sociology
                          Middlesex Polytechnic
                          (G.B.)

We were unable to locate the current address of J. L. Simmons.

Name Index

Subject Index

Amplification of deviance, *see* Deviancy amplification

Anomie, 106; and perceived opportunity, 35

Anti-marihuana laws, *see* Crimes *mala prohibita;* Marihuana Tax Act

Antipolice hostility, 242, 267-72; *see also* Police

Arrest: of shoplifter, 417-20; warning as an alternative to, 274; *see also* Police discretion

Aspirations, 42; and class, gang/non-gang, and racial differences, 42

Assumption of differentiation, 444

Attribution theory, 11, 171

Availability of illegal means, operational definition of, 43; *see also* Opportunity structure theory

Bandwagon effect, 155

Black box model, and sentencing, 172, 310, 312-19

California Personality Inventory, 92

Capital punishment, 55; deterrent effects of, 121-22

Cattell's Junior Personality Questionnaire, 93

Check forgery, and parole success, 325-26

Civil rights, public's concern with, 198

Collective reaffirmation, 63; and crime rates, 17-18

Conflict subculture, 40, 42; maintenance and emergence of, 46-47; racial differences with respect to, 47

Consensual affirmation, and occupational norms, 9

Correctional decision-making: and perception, 172, 321-41; subjective nature of, 327

Credibility, folk concept of, 210-11

Crime: anxiety about and victimization, 189-90; and class conflict, 380-88; fear of, 191-92; heightened concern with, 187; ideologies of, 386; mass media portrayal of, 177-82; moral seriousness of, 128-43, 148-52; as national problem, 186; as news, 177-78; as objective reality, 2; property crimes, public fear of, 194; public's conceptions of, 169, 175-82, 185-202; public's explanations of, 194; public's failure to report, 199-201; reasons for public's failure to report, 199-200; and related behavior patterns, 384-85; sex offender, fear of, 230-32; significance of fear of, 192-94, 197; social interpretations of, 168; social reactions to, 175-76; social reality of, 2, 175, 380-88; and social types, 179-82; unreported, 104; vicarious nature of concern with, 188-90

Crime problem: criminal perception of, 85; heightened concern with, 187; as national problem, 186; perceived solutions to, 82-84, 85; public's attitude toward, 82-84

Crime rate: deterrence, and studies of, 122-23; deviancy amplification and, 17-18; labeling theory and deviance rates, 446, 449; public's tendency to underestimate, 190-91